COMPETENCY IN GENERALIST PRACTICE

COMPETENCY IN GENERALIST PRACTICE

A GUIDE TO THEORY AND EVIDENCE-BASED DECISION MAKING

ELIZABETH MOORE PLIONIS

OXFORD

UNIVERSITY PRESS

2007

OXFORD

UNIVERSITY PRESS

Oxford University Press, Inc., publishes works that further
Oxford University's objective of excellence
in research, scholarship, and education.

Oxford   New York
Auckland   Cape Town   Dar es Salaam   Hong Kong   Karachi
Kuala Lumpur   Madrid   Melbourne   Mexico City   Nairobi
New Delhi   Shanghai   Taipei   Toronto

With offices in
Argentina   Austria   Brazil   Chile   Czech Republic   France   Greece
Guatemala   Hungary   Italy   Japan   Poland   Portugal   Singapore
South Korea   Switzerland   Thailand   Turkey   Ukraine   Vietnam

Published by Oxford University Press, Inc.
198 Madison Avenue, New York, New York 10016

www.oup.com

Oxford is a registered trademark of Oxford University Press

Library of Congress Cataloging-in-Publication Data
Plionis, Elizabeth Moore.
Competency in generalist practice : a guide to theory and
evidence-based decision making / Elizabeth Moore Plionis.— 1st ed.
    p.   cm.
Includes bibliographical references and index.
ISBN-13 978-0-19-517799-2
ISBN 0-19-517799-1
1. Social service—Decision making.   2. Evidence-based social work.
3. Core competencies.   4. Social work education.   I. Title.
HV41.P56   2007
361.3—dc22   2006007094

1 3 5 7 9 8 6 4 2

Printed in the United States of America
on acid-free paper

I dedicate this book to my husband, Dimitri, and my children, Alex, Dean, Nick, and Elena; and to my mother, Bessie, my father, James, and my brothers, Jim and Terry. I thank you for your constant emotional, intellectual, and creative support. You have sustained and enriched my life beyond belief. I also dedicate this book to Mrs. McCree.

Preface

As an educator with more than 25 years of experience, I have observed two developments that have had a dramatic impact on teaching students how to make competent practice decisions. The first development is generalist practice. Generalist practice requires students to engage in the open assessment of the different-sized systems found in direct and indirect practice. Students must consider multiple theories prior to reaching a decision in a specific case or situation.

The second development is evidence-based practice. Evidence-based practice requires students to additionally evaluate a vast empirical literature when determining which intervention is better than another. Presented with an array of evidence and method and theory choices, students report having considerable difficulty in deciding which intervention is the best under the circumstances of a specific case or situation. Until now, tools for teaching students how to make such a decision did not exist. Students have traditionally been taught to apply a dominant theory (for example, psychodynamic theory) to one system size (for example, the individual).

This process does not lend itself to complex case data requiring the use of more than one method and more than one theory when targeting more than one system size in the same case. For instance, advocacy may be needed to change an organizational policy to ensure that a specific client receives needed treatment. As a consequence, many clients (subpopulation) will benefit from the policy change.

I have written this book to assist teachers, supervisors, and students in navigating existing knowledge and a vast empirical literature when making case-specific decisions in accord with the standard of best practices. Best practice is defined as the conscientious, explicit, and judicious selection of an effective (evidence-based) and appropriate intervention strategy for a specific client or situation (Sackett, Richardson, Rosenberg, & Haynes, 1997). If one is to consider systems in direct and indirect practice in the same case, students need a text that teaches such content side by side. The skills associated with direct and indirect practice are different and cannot be merged or interchanged one for the other. Thus the book presents different skill sets needed for direct and indirect practice in alternating chapters. The framework is integrative without being reductionist.

Several factors have prompted me to write this book. First, I have been influenced by students who observe that there are too many theories and no mechanism to help them know which theory is better than another in a specific case and by those who feel a disconnect between what is being taught in the classroom and what they experience in their field placements. Similarly, students express a disconnect (and polarization) between direct and indirect courses in the curriculum. Students in policy, advocacy, management, and community practice frequently observe that they are being taught content relevant to clinical students at the cost of not getting content they need for their practice area. Clinical students similarly perceive that their policy courses have little relevance to their clinical practice. Generally, students express frustration with first-year descriptive survey courses that rarely lead to reasonable prescriptive interventions for the cases they encounter in the field.

Second, I have been motivated by the dismay instructors and students feel when faced with the large number of required and supplemental texts needed for a course. Books tend either to be specialized or too general. To compensate, instructors prepare reading packets or place readings on electronic reserve. Students complain about difficulties in accessing such materials and the cost of purchasing more than one text per course. They observe that much of what is in their required text either needs to be supplemented or goes unused. This book significantly reduces the number of course-required and supplemental texts and the need for instructor-prepared packets of readings.

Third, I have been influenced by the need for teaching tools. This text combines classic teaching tools with new teaching tools. The decision tree that is a key feature of this book is a teaching innovation that helps instructors, field supervisors, and students manage the multiple variables identified in open assessment. It rank orders the obtained information to create a hierarchy where decisions are prioritized. For instance, the decision tree begins by assigning priority to those facts of the case that have life-threatening and survival relevance. It goes on to consider crisis intervention, urgent concrete services, advocacy, and clinical interventions with individuals, families, and groups. The user applies overarching cultural and ethical principles at the outset and during each step of using the decision tree. Process recordings (beginning, ethnographic, and advanced theory-driven) illustrate work with individuals, families, groups, and agency management, while cases and treatment matrices correspond step by step to the decision hierarchy. Finally, decision schemas summarize the content of each chapter and guide students in using chapter-specific information and evidence to arrive at a competent decision for that step.

Fourth, I have been influenced by the need to differentiate theories appropriate for clinical practice (borrowed from biology, psychology, and social psychology) from those appropriate for nonclinical practice. Students in policy, advocacy, management, and community practice observe that they are taught the skills they need but not the theories from which the skills are derived. These theories are borrowed from sociology (conflict and order, common good versus individual rights), political science, economics, and administration. All students, whether they develop, implement, administer, or offer direct face-to-face services, must be aware that the policies and programs with which they are associated are normative in their end goals. Therefore, all students need to be taught the comparative theories of social justice found in moral philosophy.

The overarching theme laced throughout the book is that of competency. Competency in social work practice requires that students

- acquire and value skill sets for both direct and indirect practice,
- critically assess the available empirical evidence when making decisions,
- realistically appraise a variety of theories, and
- master the art and science of relationship building in direct and indirect practice.

It is my hope that this text presents complex material and a range of skill sets in a substantive and practical way to help students to become competent social workers.

Acknowledgments

I wish to acknowledge my mentors: Dr. Harris Chaiklin, who was the intellectual power behind my doctoral education; Dean Joan Mullaney, who exemplifies ethical and effective social work leadership; and Professor Mary Flynn, who mentored me as a novice educator. I am grateful to Dr. Elizabeth Timberlake, Dr. Sandra Chipungu, and Dr. Mary Jeanne Verdieck for their support. I thank Dean James Zabora, who granted me the sabbatical to write this book. I am grateful to the Catholic University of America, which allowed me to pursue a career in academia and a very active family life at the same time. Finally, I wish to acknowledge the intellectual contributions of all the students whom I've taught and the faculty with whom I've taught over the years. I am grateful for the friendship and advice of Dr. Barbara Bailey Etta and Dr. Patricia Evans.

I wish to identify and thank all the persons who have assisted both directly and indirectly with this project. I am grateful to Dr. Al Roberts, who facilitated the connection with Joan Bossert and Oxford University Press. I am grateful to those who peer-reviewed the manuscript and offered such constructive critiques and suggestions for additional content. I am especially thankful for Maura Roessner, Mallory Jensen, and Stacey Hamilton, who guided both the manuscript and me through production. I cannot praise enough the keen eye and gentle commentary of copyeditor Merryl Sloane.

Contents

COMPETENCY IN GENERALIST PRACTICE

1

Introduction to the Decision Tree and the Text

■ Introduction

Navigating the Complex Knowledge Base of Social Work

Unlike other helping professions, social work is committed to both individual change and social change. Consequently, social work content is complex and the teaching of it difficult (and often polarized). Two recent developments, one conceptual (generalist practice) and the other empirical (evidence-based practice), further complicate the teaching and learning of social work theory and practice. Generalist practice requires the open assessment of all system sizes when ascertaining the facts of the case at hand and the consideration of multiple theories and methods when selecting among available treatment options. Evidence-based practice adds to this the appraisal of the empirical literature that supports one treatment option over another. In an environment of broad and complex knowledge, it is difficult to assure competency in making case-specific treatment decisions consistent with best practices without a tool that can navigate what is known.

The Case Scenario

Traditionally, educators (Dorfman, 1988, 1998; Bisman, 1994) have relied on the case scenario to demonstrate how theory is used in practice to explain (explicate) the facts of the case and to guide intervention. The case scenario has been invaluable in teaching students how to apply a specific theory to limited case facts. In real practice, client data do not conform to the premises and concepts of a single theory. A different tool is needed to illustrate how more than one theory and more than one intervention can be applied to complex client case data. In contrast to the case scenario, which limits focus, the decision tree expands focus.

Decision Tree

The *decision tree* is a tool that uses a systematic and exhaustive process to organize thinking consistent with existing knowledge and empirical evidence in order to reach a treatment decision consistent with best practices. *Best practice* is defined as the conscientious, explicit, and judicious selection of an effective (evidence-based) and appropriate intervention strategy for a specific client or situation (Sackett, Richardson, Rosenberg, & Haynes, 1997). The decision tree helps the practitioner to systematically and logically navigate what is known in order to produce prescriptions that are case-specific. The tree does not produce new knowledge. It cues practitioners to ask all relevant questions, identify all relevant variables, consider all possibilities (theories), and evaluate all evidence (whether positive or negative) in a proper sequence before arriving at a treatment decision.

It is important to note that the decision tree prompts the practitioner to access and evaluate the empirical evidence for or against a particular treatment decision. Although the decision tree in its aggregate, programmatic form has not been empirically assessed, it provides defensible accountability through documentation of process, a process which is systematic, logical, exhaustive, and hierarchically ordered. While the decision tree cannot guarantee treatment success, it does increase the probability of arriving at an intervention plan that has taken all relevant factors into account. The decision tree is compatible with the development of new treatments. If substantiated, a new treatment may replace or join existing treatment options on a relevant branch of the decision tree.

How the Decision Tree Works

The steps on the decision tree prompt practitioners to engage in open assessment, scanning for information that lies along a continuum ranging from personal problems to public issues. Once the facts have been determined, the decision tree helps the practitioner to manage the multiple variables identified in open assessment. Because the decision tree rank orders the obtained information, it is able to create a hierarchy where decisions are prioritized. For instance, the decision tree begins by assigning priority to those facts of the case that have life-threatening and survival relevance. By combining open assessment with the decision tree, the practitioner can choose to intervene with more than one system size, can choose to use more than one method, can choose to apply more than one theory, and can use more than one skill set (Plionis, 2004).

The practitioner is asked to review each step of the hierarchy to determine its relevance to the case at hand. When a step in the hierarchy is deemed to be relevant, the hierarchy identifies criteria to be used in selecting a method and theory appropriate to the treatment goals and objectives at that step. If a step in the hierarchy is not relevant to the case at hand, the practitioner moves on to the next step. In this manner, the practitioner builds a model of practice unique to the situation at hand that is inclusive of all relevant variables. If the practitioner focuses only on one step of the hierarchy, the focus is limited to one system size, one method, one theory, and one skill set. Cultural diversity and ethics are conceptualized as overarching principles. Practitioners are asked to elicit facts relevant to diversity. Theories and evidence are in turn screened for their cultural relevance to the case at hand. Ethical analysis is part of the process of arriving at an appropriate intervention.

■ Overarching Cultural Principles

Overarching cultural and ethical principles, consistent with the Standards of Cultural Competence in Social Work (NASW, 2001), guide practitioners in the use of the decision tree.

Standard 1: Ethics and Values

Consistent with this standard, all actions of social workers must conform to the Code of Ethics of the National Association of Social Workers (in Canada, the Canadian Association of Social Workers–Code of Ethics). Practitioners must be cognizant of the distinction between personal, professional, and client values. Clinicians must be aware of the ideological and value premises of clinical theories. Macro practitioners must be aware of competing ideological and value premises when determining the desired end-goals of policies, programs, and reform efforts. Tactics to achieve such end-goals must be ethical and legal.

By definition, an *ethical dilemma* is the conflict between two goods (community rights versus individual rights) or a conflict over the lesser of two evils (whether to provide services under circumstances of an excessive workload). According to Kirst-Ashman and Hull (2000), ethical dilemmas require analysis. Ethical analysis includes the recognition of value conflicts, skills in teleological and deontological reasoning, data gathering on diverse perspectives and possible resolutions, and the application of ethical and legal screens.

Clinicians must conform to licensing regulations and practice within the law. Macro practitioners must follow standard accounting procedures, recruit, hire, and fire within the laws regulating employment, and refrain from malfeasance while in administrative authority. Community practitioners must practice within a democratic, political process.

Standard 2: Self-Awareness; Standard 8: Professional Education

Consistent with these standards, all social workers must develop an understanding of their own personal and cultural values and beliefs. Each practitioner must recognize the relativity, rather than the universality, of his/her own cultural framework. Controversy exists as to how practitioners gain self-awareness; through didactic lectures or experiential learning. It is important to recognize that everyone (including practitioners and client groups) are exposed to different degrees of privilege and discrimination based on race, diversity, religion, gender, sexual orientation, and health status. Practitioners should regard self and other as communal and linguistic constructions open to exploration within the work-client relationship. Cultural missteps in the helping process need to be recognized and corrected.

Practitioners in policy, advocacy, management, and community practice must be cognizant of the toxic social forces (poverty, marginalization, violence, inequality, political under-representation) that necessitate social policies and programs.

Standard 3: Cross-Cultural Knowledge; Standard 8: Professional Education

Consistent with these standards, practitioners must possess descriptive knowledge (cultural sensitivity) of diverse client populations, especially those client groups with whom they work. Practitioners must assess class, gender, sexual orientation, religious affiliation, degree of skin color, and other physically differentiating features within groups as well as between groups. It is important to resist the tendency to reduce cultural complexity to stereotypes.

Clinical practitioners must take into account how culture shapes family life, individual identity, priorities, and help-seeking behavior. Clinical practitioners must be cognizant of how diverse cultural groups conceptualize or construct health, illness, and help-seeking and help-giving behavior. It is important that practitioners recognize and draw upon the cultural strengths of diverse client groups.

Practitioners must examine theories and empirical evidence for cultural relevance (bias). Desired end-goals must be examined for their value and ideological assumptions. Macro practitioners must be aware of the empirical evidence that supports the continuation or demise of an agency, policy, program, planning, or change effort.

Standard 4: Cross-Cultural Skills; Standard 5: Language Diversity;
Standard 10: Leadership

Consistent with these standards, clinical practitioners must take into account cultural values and preferences when forming a collaborative worker-client partnership and treatment approach. Clinicians should be skilled in the use of ethnographic interviewing techniques. Clients should be used as cultural guides, and practitioners should acquire a client-taught ethnographic mental lexicon. Practitioners should acquire competency in the utilization of appropriate ethno-psychotherapies (cultural responsiveness) or refer clients to clinicians with such competencies. Because not all social work occurs in English, practitioners should refer clients to same-language clinicians or use trained translators.

Practitioners in policy, advocacy, management, and community practice need to be aware that groups differ in their desired normative end-goals. Policies, programs, and fundraising efforts are marked by in-group and between-group competition and conflict. Practitioners need skills in managing in-group and between-group tensions. Macro practitioners must promote tolerance for difference and dissent and engage in effective and ethical leadership.

Standard 5: Service Delivery; Standard 7: Diverse Workforce

Consistent with these standards, clinical practitioners must recognize and take into account issues of racism (and other "isms") that may exist within the agency, and among the agency, worker, and client systems.

Practitioners in policy, advocacy, management, and community practice must take into account social work's equity goal. Are policies, programs, and services reaching highly vulnerable populations in need of services? Who is being served? Which client populations are not being served because they are difficult to work with or to reach? What proportion of rendered services is in-house, home-based, community-centered, or outreached? Are service or practice models culturally responsive or do they need to be modified?

Management practitioners must recruit and hire practitioners who are bilingual, bicultural, and racially diverse. Agency personnel should match the diversity of the client population being served.

Standard 6: Empowerment and Advocacy

Consistent with this standard, practitioners need to assess power. Who is empowered? Who is disfranchised? How does each theory and each practice model construct power? What is the power distribution in the worker-client relationship? Practitioners should be familiar with conflict and empowerment theories. They should possess skills in managing group dynamics and in conflict negotiation. As warranted, practitioners should align with indigenous leadership and with disfranchised clients. Practitioners should possess both case and class advocacy skills.

■ Open Assessment and the Decision Tree: Managing
Multiple Variables

To illustrate the concept of open assessment, several case scenarios are presented.
Each scenario falls along a continuum ranging from personal problems to public
issues. The sociodemographic characteristics of the client (Mr. R) change and the
facts surrounding the theme (smoking) change in each scenario, prompting the
use of different theories and methods in each scenario. This is done to illustrate
how variables found as a result of open assessment correspond to different points
on the decision tree and trigger the selection of different methods, theories, and
skills (see pp. 18–24).

Scenario 1

Case Facts

You are a social worker in private practice, specializing in brief therapy. You have
a contract with a large employer in the area to provide services through their
employee assistance program (EAP). Mr. R is a 45-year-old Caucasian male who
has been referred to you following a recent myocardial infarction because his
physician told him he needed to stop smoking to improve his health and to prevent the occurrence of another heart attack. He has been smoking since the age
of 16 and in the last year has smoked 2 1/2 packs of cigarettes per day. Mr. R has
health insurance through his employer. His EAP offers treatment for smoking
cessation.

Decision Tree

Because Mr. R has been medically treated, he is not in a life-threatening situation (step 1: assure safety). Nor is Mr. R in a state of crisis (step 2) or in need of
immediate or long-term concrete services (step 3). It could be argued that Mr.
R is in the aftermath of a medical crisis. Steps 5, 6, and 7 address methods.
Method choices include work with individuals (step 5), work with families
(step 6), and the use of groups (step 7). Mr. R is an individual adult, which
makes step 5 an appropriate choice. He may also be a candidate for a smoking-
cessation group (step 7). It is less likely that family therapy (step 6) is an appropriate method of choice in this case. Mr. R's sociodemographic characteristics
appear to be consistent with mainstream Western culture (cultural awareness).
As a male (help-seeking behavior), he is probably reluctant to seek therapy but
open to the idea of needing help to eliminate his smoking behavior and to prevent another heart attack (male culture). Because he has health insurance that
will cover treatment, he is not in need of advocacy (step 4). Mr. R is a voluntary
client seeking help for smoking cessation. There are many theory-based therapies

that the worker and client can consider when selecting a treatment option within a method.

In step 5, one selected theory could regard smoking as an addiction to nicotine and use the patch to produce a gradual withdrawal and cessation of smoking (biological). Learning theories offer many options. Biofeedback could be used to control the urge to smoke. Alternatively, Mr. R could be cued (classical conditioning) to avoid smoking stimuli and to respond to cues that signal alternative, non-smoking behavior. Positive and negative reinforcement could be used to punish smoking behavior and reward nonsmoking behavior (operant conditioning). Another option could focus on changing Mr. R's cognitions (show him pictures of black lungs or present him with the evidence related to smoking-related cancers). If Mr. R comes to believe (core cognitions) that smoking is actually life-threatening, he may change his behavior. Alternatively, Mr. R's smoking could be viewed as a symptom of internal unconscious dynamics, i.e., smoking is a symptom and coping mechanism for underlying tensions (psychodynamic theory). After all, something is causing Mr. R's smoking frequency. Here the worker would identify the underlying problem and work on resolving it rather than focus directly on the smoking behavior. Eliminating the symptom of smoking might lead to symptom substitution, i.e., alcoholism if the underlying problem is left unaddressed.

In selecting the most appropriate method (individual or group) in this case, the worker would evaluate each method for its cultural compatibility with the client and the worker's skills. The worker could access the empirical literature to find evidence of the efficacy of one method over the other. As part of contracting, the worker and client could choose to combine methods, using both individual and group treatment.

Similarly, there are several therapy choices. The use of the patch could facilitate withdrawal from nicotine addiction or pose an additional risk to client health, should the client continue to smoke while wearing the patch. One of the talk therapies mentioned above could also be chosen. As with the choice of method, the worker would have to evaluate each therapy option. Each option should be evaluated for evidence of its efficacy *and* for its cultural compatibility with the client. Given Mr. R's sociocultural background (cultural diversity in treatment preference), he is more likely to favor a learning theory–based therapy than a psychodynamic therapeutic approach. The worker and client could choose to combine more than one therapy, e.g., the patch and one of the talk therapies.

Comment

The assumption in this scenario is that the worker possesses a single skill set (clinical), and it is appropriate to the case data presented. What is less sure is whether the social work practitioner would be familiar with and skilled in the use of both individual and group methods or be familiar with and skilled in the use of the multiple therapeutic options that could be applied in this case. The practitioner might assume worker-client cultural compatibility on treatment preference and fail to take into account gender differences in treatment preferences. In this scenario, the practitioner does not take into account the social forces that may have contributed to Mr. R's smoking, e.g., commercial advertising, peer pressure, social stress, tobacco subsidies to growers, health care legislation and laws, and third-party reimbursement for smoking-related illnesses.

Scenario 2

Case Facts

You work in the Department of Social Services at Xavier Hospital doing discharge planning. Mr. R is a 70-year-old African-American male who has been referred to you for discharge planning following hospitalization for second-degree burns to his torso. Mr. R fell asleep while smoking in bed. Because Mr. R lives in an assisted-living facility, his forgetfulness and his smoking endangers others as well as himself. The director of the assisted-living facility has refused to let Mr. R return to Sunrise Assisted Living.

Decision Tree

The worker's context of practice (agency auspices) limits and directs the worker's choice of method (steps 5, 6, and 7) to one method option (step 5: individual). The worker's discharge function further constrains the focus to one aspect of Mr. R's situation: to find Mr. R a place to live once discharged (step 3: concrete services in a timely manner). Mr. R is no longer in immediate danger (step 1: assure safety). His condition has been stabilized by medical treatment, and his burns have been treated (step 1: assure safety).

Comment

The potential for several different interventions with different system sizes is present in this case scenario. All of the clinical options regarding smoking cessation in scenario 1 could equally apply to Mr. R in scenario 2 but are unlikely to be entertained. Advocacy skills could also be invoked to facilitate Mr. R's return to Sunrise but are unlikely to be used if the worker does not have agency sanction, the time, or possess this skill set. The worker is most likely to limit assessment and intervention, using direct practice case management skills to meet Mr. R's immediate discharge need for residential living. Mr. R's status as an African American warrants assessment to assure that he has access to the same treatment options, legal advice, and living arrangement that would be offered if Mr. R were Caucasian (equity goal: cultural responsiveness).

Despite the potential for multiple interventions, only one is likely. However, the following treatment options are consistent with open assessment and generalist practice. First, it could be argued that Mr. R is in the aftermath of a medical crisis caused by his addiction to nicotine and therefore is in need of smoking-cessation therapy to prevent another crisis. All of the clinical options regarding smoking cessation in scenario 1 could equally apply to Mr. R in scenario 2. Second, case management skills are needed to locate residential resources. Mr. R is in need of an assisted-living residential facility. The worker must use skills to network with those controlling admissions to shelters or assisted-living facilities in order to provide Mr. R with a needed concrete service. Third, advocacy could be used as an intervention targeting the administrator of Sunrise to facilitate the return of Mr. R to that facility. Finally, the worker should assess for bias in access to treatment options (nondiscrimination as a component of cultural responsiveness).

Scenario 3

Case Facts

You are a social worker in management practice. As director of the Sunrise Assisted Living facility, you have refused to readmit Mr. R, a former resident who is about to be discharged from Xavier following hospitalization for burns suffered when he fell asleep while smoking. You are dealing with the impact of this event on Sunrise as an organizational entity (step 2: organizational crisis). The facility has a policy of not accepting any resident who is unwilling or incapable of complying with the ban on smoking inside the facility.

Decision Tree

As a social work management practitioner (step 7: method), you have the fiduciary responsibility (step 1: duty to protect) to assure the safety of all residents and staff who work in the facility. You must consider the good of the assisted-living community against the request of one resident (Mr. R) to return (ethical dilemma). The event (Mr. R's injury) precipitated a crisis that threatens the stability of the organization (step 2: organizational crisis). Administratively, maintaining the stability of the organization (in this case, Sunrise Assisted Living) is a primary goal. An investigation has been initiated. Policies, rules, and regulations on smoking are being reviewed and staff questioned. Feedback will be used to take corrective action.

Legal counsel is involved in the anticipation of a potential lawsuit. Licensing regulators have scheduled a visit. They have the authority to suspend the agency's license to operate. Several families have expressed concern about residents' safety and are considering moving their relatives. This poses a potential loss of income to the facility, possibly culminating in a financial crisis. The media has picked up on the incident. You are preparing a press release to manage potential negative publicity. Efforts are being made to assure current residents of their safety. Efforts are under way to assure the community that Sunrise continues to be a valuable resource to the community. The social worker from Xavier Hospital has requested Mr. R's return to Sunrise. Questions of racial bias have been raised regarding your decision to deny Mr. R's request to return to the facility.

Comment

As in previous scenarios, the smoking theme continues, but the needed skill set differs. As in scenario 2, the worker's position focuses the parameters of assessment, this time on maintaining the stability of the Sunrise Assisted Living facility in the face of an organizational crisis precipitated by the behavior of one of its residents. The selection of methods and theories necessary to address an organizational crisis differs from those needed in scenarios 1 and 2. Maintenance of the structure (facility) and its function (providing assisted living for the elderly) is the primary goal of the director of Sunrise.

The residents of Sunrise, including Mr. R, are beneficiaries (or not) of how well the facility is run. Another beneficiary group is those who make a profit (ownership) or who make a living (wages/salary) from Sunrise. A conflict of interest (ethical dilemma) is possible between these beneficiary groups (those who accrue financial gain through the operation of Sunrise and those who are served by it). How resources are budgeted to balance the need for profit and the need for resident safety is a component of management practice.

In this scenario, Mr. R has changed from being a beneficiary of Sunrise to a possible victim of organizational malfeasance. From an organizational perspective, Mr. R has changed from an asset (paying resident) to an organizational liability (potential source of lawsuit). In neither case is Mr. R perceived as an individual client in need of a smoking-cessation program (as in scenario 1) or as a client about to become homeless once discharged (as in scenario 2). From a generalist perspective, Mr. R is in need of a smoking-cessation program, is about to be homeless if discharged without a residential placement, and is a liability to Sunrise. Though the social worker at Xavier and the director of Sunrise Assisted Living are both social workers and probably went to the same school of social work, each is likely to regard the other as the type of social worker s/he does not particularly understand.

Scenario 4

Case Facts

Following the suspension of three students (R, N, and A) who were caught smoking in the school lavatory, Mr. S, the principal of a local high school, has arranged for you to consult with parents, teachers, staff, and students about an educational campaign (step 7: use of groups: educational campaign) directed at teenage smoking, which he wants to initiate in the school.

Decision Tree

As in scenario 3, unauthorized smoking poses a safety hazard, this time to all members of the school community (step 1: duty to protect). It is also a violation of school policies and is therefore a cause for suspension (step 7: management/authority). The administrator, Principal S, has exercised his authority and has suspended the three students for 3 days. He has invited you to consult with the school community (step 7: method) in the hope that the community will become more supportive of maintaining a smoke-free environment. He has asked you to organize a smoking-prevention campaign (step 7: use of groups in educational campaign).

Two skill sets are needed. One set involves the use of group skills to mount an antismoking campaign while the other set involves the use of clinical group work skills. In both instances, the worker needs skills in the use of small groups. Small groups are needed to implement a campaign (step 7: method). Clinical understanding of group dynamics is needed (step 7: method) to bring about attitudinal and behavioral changes in the target group.

From a planning perspective, organizing a smoking-prevention campaign requires the worker to identify relevant constituent groups within the school community (school administrators, parents, teachers, members of the athletic department, staff, and students) who are likely to support the smoking-prevention campaign. Opponent groups must also be identified. Logistical skills are needed. Space has to be obtained for community assemblies and small task-group meetings. Individuals need to be assigned to task groups and materials provided. Small group meetings need to be scheduled and coordinated. Flow charts providing visual oversight of time management and task completion must be maintained. Volunteers from the school community need to be recruited to join the campaign. A critical mass is necessary to create power through numbers. Popular students (strategic role models) need to be enlisted as symbols in the antismoking campaign, i.e., not smoking is cool. Posters, skits, and pep rallies can visually highlight the upside of not smoking while depicting its downside.

It is also important to learn as much as possible about those who are likely to oppose the campaign. Parent meetings reveal concern about the measures taken by the principal to suspend students caught smoking. This parental concern has been identified as an issue that might undermine the success of the campaign. The principal and a few representatives of the parent group are brought together to see if a compromise (conflict negotiation) can be reached, given the seriousness of a suspension for the college application process. Having met with the three boys who were suspended for smoking (subgroup: likely opponents to the campaign), you become concerned about R (step 5: method: individual).

Comment

The theme of smoking continues. In this scenario, the problem is not perceived as any one individual's problem (R, N, or A) as in scenario 1. Nor is it strictly considered a management problem (the integrity of the school as an organizational entity is not threatened) as in scenario 3. The situation does not pose an immediate danger necessitating immediate action to assure safety (step 1: duty to protect). There are however, long-term health consequences to smoking, and suspension from school carries its own consequences. There is no need for concrete services (step 3) as in scenario 2.

In this scenario, the choices are about methods, the theories that inform such methods, and the skill sets required to implement them. As one of three students caught smoking, R is one member among many who make up the target system of those who refuse to comply with the ban on smoking in the high school. The goal of the campaign is to convert smokers to nonsmokers and noncompliers to compliers to benefit the community as a whole. Consistent with symbolic interaction theory, peer pressure and socialization will be used to change smoking attitudes or perceptions of a small-size client population (high school population).

In the above scenario, the clinically trained social worker is likely to possess the knowledge and skills needed to use the dynamics of groups to influence teen attitudes, perceptions, and behaviors. S/he is also more likely to be familiar with the complex causes and treatment options available for treating those who are addicted to nicotine. S/he recognizes that "just say no" is a limited option to those addicted to nicotine. On the other hand, the social worker who is trained in the use of groups to organize an educational campaign (macro practice) is likely to possess the skills needed to strategically plan and implement an antismoking campaign. It is unlikely that one practitioner would possess both skill sets.

Scenario 5

Case Facts

You are a family therapist. R has recently been suspended from school for smoking in the lavatory. The family was referred to you by the social worker involved in the high school's antismoking campaign. This is R's second suspension since school started in September. The family has just moved to the area following the father's mandatory job relocation. R's 14-year-old sister, J, was diagnosed with leukemia in August. R's mother is preoccupied with J's health.

Decision Tree

R's behavior (two suspensions) could be a reflection of normal adolescence or a reflection of situational crisis (adjustment reaction) precipitated by the family's recent move. R does not have a delinquent status nor is he at risk of outplacement (family welfare policy/program). Traditional family therapy is a treatment method (step 6) option in this case. Consistent with traditional family therapy models, R's individual behavior (adolescence, two suspensions, one for smoking) is redefined in terms of family structure and patterns of transaction. When families are stressed, normal structures and patterns change to accommodate the stress. These changes can be both functional and dysfunctional (family systems theory).

R's behavior is perceived as a "healthy" call for help for his family. Several external stressors (father's mandatory job relocation, the family's move to a new state, increased medical expenses, R's loss of friends) and several internal stressors (sister's leukemia, mother's involvement with J) are impacting the stability of the family as a whole. No member of the family is in immediate danger (step 1: duty to protect) nor is the family in need of concrete services (step 3). Advocacy (step 4) may be needed to keep R in school if he continues to engage in behavior that gets him suspended.

According to family systems theory, new structures and patterns of transaction are in operation. Dad is bounded by the new job and is distant from the family. The mother has formed a boundary with the daughter over her leukemia and its treatment. R has become cut off from mother, father, sister, and friends. Given the circumstances and an understanding of family systems theory, the decision to treat R through family therapy has merit.

Comment

Though the skill set is clinical, it represents a clinical specialization in family therapy. Family therapy requires a specific course of study (a concentration) and field training to understand its theory base and to acquire skills in its application. R could easily have remained under the radar as a member of a high school student group targeted in an antismoking campaign (scenario 4). Family therapy allowed R's behavior (suspension for smoking) to be viewed in the context of his family's structure and dynamics. In neither scenario (4 or 5) is R perceived as an individual in need of smoking cessation therapy or supervision for neglect.

Scenario 6

Case Facts

You are a rural social worker. Mr. R went bankrupt and lost his farm due to the elimination of government subsidies to tobacco farmers. Mr. R is one of several small tobacco farmers in the area who have lost their farms. The farms are being auctioned to pay off accrued debts. Mr. R and his wife will soon have no income and no place to live. They have spent all their savings trying to save their farm. They do not want to live with their grown children.

Decision Tree

As a rural social worker, you are aware of the number of small tobacco farmers who are losing their farms. You are also aware of the cultural norm (cultural diversity) that prevents many rural residents from publicly seeking help. Aware of the pending auction, you stop by the R family farm to introduce yourself (community clinical mental health outreach). You learn that they have 1 month following the auction to vacate the premises (step 3: assessment of needs in a timely manner). Though the Rs have grown children, all live out of state. Mr. and Mrs. R seem to be immobilized (evidence of a crisis reaction: step 2) by their current status. Many of their friends are in similar straits (loss of natural helping network, community-based clinical practice).

In talking with them, you learn that the situation poses no immediate danger (step 1: duty to protect) to them. You also know that depression following such a loss is common and can pose a risk of suicide or spouse abuse (step 5: individual need for therapy). The Rs are experiencing concrete losses (step 3: need for concrete services) of income, farm, and home as well as psychological losses of self-worth and independence (step 5: need for therapy). While the cause of the Rs' loss lies in broad-scale social changes in the environment (legislation regulating the growth, sale, and use of tobacco; cutbacks on tobacco subsidies), Mr. and Mrs. R are affected personally. Due to the pending eviction, the Rs' apparent immobilization, their loss of a natural helping network within the community, and the distance of family members, you offer to visit again later in the week (community practice: outreach).

Comment

In this scenario, five distinct types of intervention could be applicable. Crisis intervention is applicable but needs to be modified as outreach given the rural context within which the family lives (cultural responsiveness). The family will need some concrete services in a month or two (step 3). Perhaps either or both Mr. and Mrs. R will need supportive counseling to deal with depression and loss in the near future (step 5). Given the number of tobacco-growing families affected by this turn of events, the worker could turn to community organizing (step 7) to empower affected families and to help the community recover by planning economic alternatives (class advocacy). A different organizing approach leading to political action could be undertaken to try and change the legislation that reduced agricultural subsidies to tobacco growers. However, since you are in favor of a smoke-free environment (normative value), you choose not to become involved in trying to reverse cutbacks to tobacco farmers. You are interested in organizing to find economic alternatives for affected farmers.

■ Aims and Layout of the Text

Aims

Through the use of a decision tree, this text aims (1) to promote critical thinking in making treatment decisions consistent with best practices, and (2) to enhance the teaching, learning, and practice application of complex and often polarizing social work content. The decision tree guides the foundation-year student in open assessment and the selective use of one or more practice theories and methods. It requires students to evaluate treatment options according to existing empirical evidence. Interventions are subjected to ethical analysis and screened for their cultural relevance. The text promotes competency in the use of two skill sets: one for social work clinical practice and another for social work policy, advocacy, administration, and community practice.

Layout

Clinical content and content on policy, advocacy, management, and community practice needed by foundation-year students are presented in alternating chapters. The fiduciary duties of the clinician are presented in chapter 2 while the policy and administrative context of professional practice is presented in chapter 3. Clinical communication skills are presented in chapter 4. Nonclinical communication skills needed by practitioners in policy, advocacy, management, and community practice are presented in chapter 5. The worker's use of self in the art of healing and in the art of leadership are presented in chapters 6 and 7.

Chapters 8–17 provide content for each step (or branch) of the decision tree. Each chapter contains a schema to guide assessment and intervention specific to the chapter. Addressed are clinical crisis intervention and crisis management (8 and 9); case management (10); case and class advocacy (11); clinical psychotherapy (12 and 13); family therapy (14) and family and child welfare (15); and the use of groups in clinical practice (16) and in policy, advocacy, administration, and community practice (17). The book concludes with a chapter on research (18).

EXHIBIT 1.1 *Decision Tree*

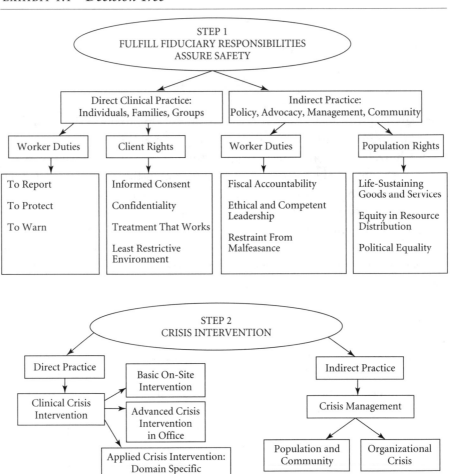

EXHIBIT 1.1 (*continued*)

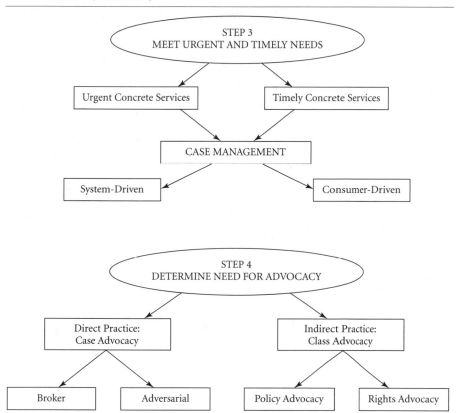

EXHIBIT 1.1 *(continued)*

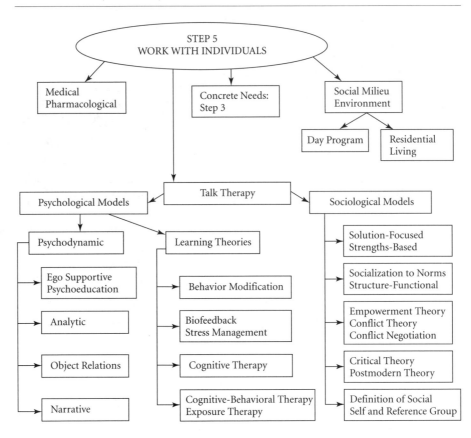

EXHIBIT 1.1   (*continued*)

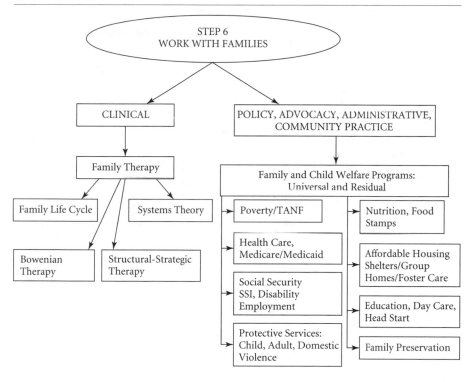

EXHIBIT 1.1 *(continued)*

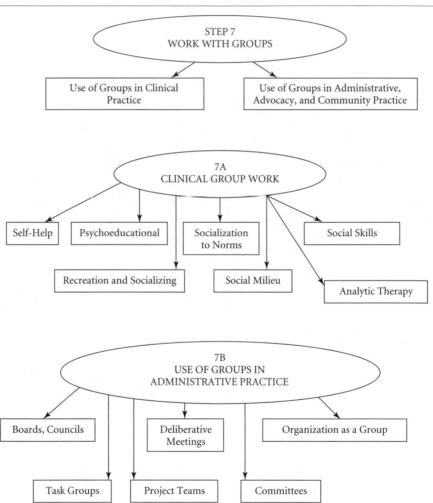

EXHIBIT 1.1 (*continued*)

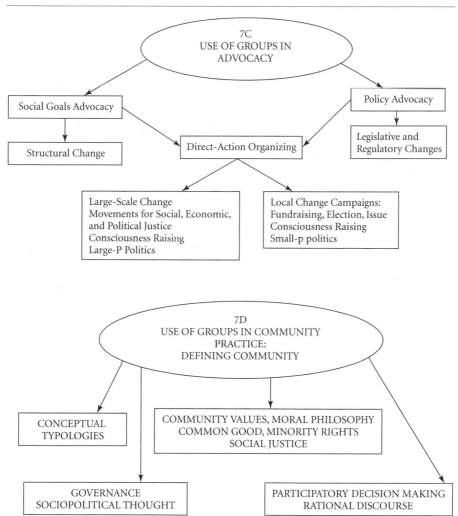

EXHIBIT 1.1   (*continued*)

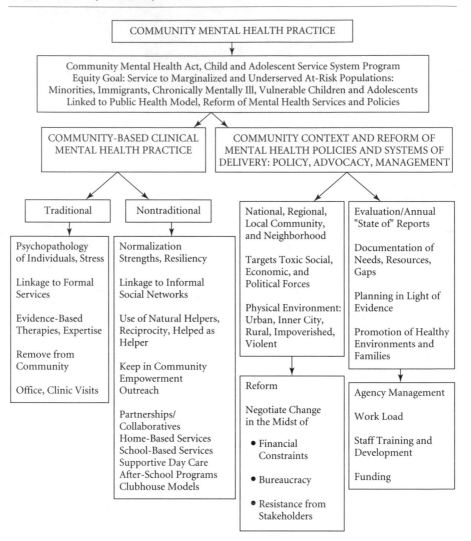

Basic Premises

The text is based on the assumption that competent practice is tied to the concept of best practices. Evidence is critical to establish the effectiveness of one treatment option over another. Therefore, the text accepts science as a way of knowing and subscribes to the premise that we live in a world that is largely measurable. It also accepts linearity and probability as valid premises for making inferences. The book maintains that explanation allows for prediction (cause and effect) and subsequently prescription (prevention or intervention) and that this scientific process is necessary for competent practice. While accepting the link between evidence-based practice and best practices, this text also holds that theory and critical thinking are essential to making treatment decisions consistent with best practices. Empiricism is necessary but not sufficient to build knowledge. Statistical techniques alone cannot produce cumulative knowledge. As knowledge, theory is critical to the enactment of treatment.

The decision tree incorporates value analysis as well as analysis of political and economic factors when arriving at a treatment decision. At each step of the hierarchy, the practitioner is asked to assess cultural diversity and evaluate the cultural relevance of selected treatments and the empirical evidence associated with them. The text values logic and philosophical proof in addition to empirical evidence. In an effort to incorporate the contributions of all social work scholars, models of practice based on postmodern perspectives are included as part of open assessment and treatment choice.

2

Social Work and the Law: Fiduciary Responsibilities

■ Legal Parameters

Step 1 of the decision tree requires practitioners to assure client safety, inform clients of their rights, and comply with the duty to report, to protect, and to warn. These actions are referred to as *fiduciary responsibilities*. Executing one's fiduciary duties requires knowledge of the law as it applies to social work practice. Laws that govern social work practice vary from country to country and often between jurisdictions within the same country. At the federal, state, and jurisdictional levels, legislative acts, statutes (made by administrative or regulatory bodies), and judicial rulings based on common law or case law establish the legal parameters of social work practice. While social workers do not practice law, they must conduct themselves in accordance with the laws that govern social work practice in their country, jurisdiction, and area of expertise. To learn more about the law and social work practice in the United States, see Albert (2000). Canadian students should consult Regehr and Kanani (2006).

In addition to general legal parameters governing professional practice, practitioners must be familiar with legal parameters that are agency- or population-specific. The fiduciary model of practice is based on the sociological (legal) authority given to the profession to act on behalf of individual clients (advocacy) and on behalf of the public interest and common good (social control). It is assumed that social workers have specialized knowledge and skills that their clients do not possess. Therefore when clients consult a social worker, they essentially grant the professional the authority to influence them in unforeseen ways and trust that the professional will act in their best interest. The social work Code of Ethics in Canada (Canadian Association of Social Workers, 2005) and in the United States (National Association of Social Workers, 1999) state that social workers have a fiduciary duty to act in the best interest of the client.

■ Privacy and the Release of Information

Social workers are responsible for the information obtained during their contact with clients. The knowledge obtained must be used for professional purposes and the client's privacy protected to the extent legally possible. Generally, privacy legislation regulates how client information is collected, used, retained, transferred, disclosed, and disposed of. In Canada, two federal laws protect the rights of citizens to privacy: the Personal Information Protection and Electronic Documents Act (2000) and the Privacy Act, R.S. (1985). Additional legislation governs the right to privacy within Canada's provinces and territories (Regehr & Kanani, 2006). The Federal Privacy Act of 1974, P.L. 93-579, governs the right to privacy in the United States. The U.S. Health Insurance Portability and Accountability Act (HIPAA Title II; 1996) requires the adoption of standards that will improve the efficiency and effectiveness of the nation's health care system by encouraging the widespread use of electronic data exchange in health care. Standards must assure the privacy and security of electronic data gathering, usage, transmission, storage, and disposal.

Under the Federal Privacy Act of 1974, a social worker may not release information about a client without a client's written consent. In *MacDonald v. Clinger* (1982), the courts ruled that a client may sue if a professional divulges information learned in therapy without the client's consent. To disclose confidential information outside of mandated grounds is actionable under statute as professional misconduct and is also actionable in Canada under common law and in the United States under civil law (nuisance, trespass, libel, slander, defamation, assault, battery, and breach of contract). On-line counseling, or e-therapy, poses challenges to privacy legislation.

■ Client Access to Records

In both the United States and in Canada, privacy legislation allows clients to access their records. The Supreme Court of Canada (*McInerney v. Macdonald*, 1992) established the right of clients to have access to all mental health and medical records regarding their care. Additional setting-specific legislation, statutes, and judicial rulings govern health records, education records, mental health records, social service records, and records within the criminal justice system (see Regehr & Kanani, 2006).

■ Informed Consent, Permission to Treat

New practitioners commonly think that the client's right to privacy is upheld when they obtain the client's written consent before details about that client are released to another person or agency (informed consent). Though securing the release of confidential information is part of informed consent, informed consent goes much further to include permission to treat.

According to Kutchins (1991), *informed consent* (or the principle of *full disclosure*) is a legal requirement that must be met to conduct treatment. The principle of informed consent aims to enhance the client's control over his/her own health by maximizing his/her knowledge. The right to permit or refuse treatment is a principle that has been enunciated by the Supreme Court of Canada (*Ciarlariello v. Schacter*, 1993, 2, SCR 119 at 135). In the United States, the principle of informed consent originated in *Schloendorff v. Society of New York Hospital* (1914). The judge ruled that every individual has a right to determine what shall be done with his/her own body. In both Canada and the United States, the profession's Code of Ethics endorses this principle under provisions of client self-determination. The Federal Privacy Act of 1974 defined *informed consent* as the "knowing consent of an individual or his legally authorized representative, so situated as to be able to exercise free power of choice without undue inducement of any element of force, fraud, deceit, duress, or other form of constraint or coercion" (*Federal Register*, 1975, p. 579). Kutchins (1991) argues that for consent to be informed, the client must be advised about the decisions and methods that relate to his/her treatment. To be valid, consent must be informed, voluntary, and within the capacity of the individual.

■ Standards of Care and Customary Practices: Malpractice

An aspect of informed consent is the duty of the practitioner to practice within the professional parameters of standards of care and customary practices. Clients have the right to sue practitioners for malpractice. As part of informed consent, clients should be apprised of the effectiveness of proposed treatment options. According to Reamer (1987), clients should be informed of (1) the nature and purpose of the proposed intervention, (2) advantages and disadvantages, (3) potential risks, (4) potential effects on family, job, social activities, and other aspects of the client's life, (5) possible alternative interventions, and (6) the costs of treatment. The criteria for informed consent is similar in Canada. The Supreme Court of Canada in *Reibl v. Hughes* (1980) ruled that practitioners have a duty to disclose all material risks. In addition to the criteria mentioned earlier, some jurisdictions require disclosure similar to Reamer's six points. Some require that clients be informed of an intern's student status. Standards of practice or customary practices provide the context within which expert testimony is solicited when clients sue practitioners for negligence. Both workers and agencies may be sued for malpractice.

Malpractice charges have been filed in the following situations: providing treatment without obtaining proper consent, keeping inaccurate or inadequate records, administering radical or inappropriate treatment, failing to consult with a specialist or seek proper supervision, failure to prevent a client's suicide, failure to warn third parties of potential harm, failure to report child abuse or neglect, breach of confidentiality, abandonment of clients, failure to disclose student status, failure to maintain an appropriate worker-client boundary, failure to practice within one's area of competence, failure to maintain competence, misrepresentation of expertise, and failure to provide service within customary standards of practice. Failure to protect may be tried in both criminal and civil courts. When criminal or civil charges are made, clients are viewed as waiving the right to confidentiality and implicitly consenting to the disclosure of confidential information relevant to the action (P. (L.M.) v. F. (D) 1994).

■ Clinical Record Keeping: Affidavits and Reports

The Clinical Record

Record keeping is an essential component of clinical social work practice. Practitioners have a fiduciary obligation to maintain client records. The contemporary social work record differs from that of the past. According to Regehr and Kanani (2006), clinical record keeping began with registration-type documentation during the period of friendly visiting and the charity organization movement. During the settlement house period, record keeping expanded to include the verified facts of the case, resources provided, and the subjective opinion of the worker. During the psychoanalytic period of clinical social work practice, records included process recordings that were part of supervision intended to review techniques. Process recordings gave way to narrative summaries during the 1940s and 1950s.

Current record keeping is designed to facilitate service delivery rather than to provide a basis for supervision. Brief recording strategies, such as outlines, checklists, forms, log of contact dates, and progress notes, are used to record information. Clinical records are legal documents and are subject to subpoena in legal proceedings. For the most part, clinical records are not privileged. Records may be scrutinized (with identifying client information removed) as part of a third-party accreditation process.

Agencies have the obligation to train students in documentation and record keeping consistent with their policies and procedures. Students have an obligation to learn the policies, procedures, and terminology specific to the agency. In order to advise clients of their rights to privacy and confidentiality, students must know agency-specific policies and procedures and state statutes that do or do not protect communication. Because students practice on the license of their field instructor, field instructors must review and cosign all written documentation. Private notes as well as legal documents may be subpoenaed. Many agencies have separate filing systems, one for official records and another for the practitioner's private notes. Both can be subpoenaed. Regehr and Kanani note that the practice of keeping separate records contravenes the Canadian social work Code of Ethics, which states that only one master file on each client should be maintained.

Court Affidavits and Reports

According to Regehr and Kanani (2006), two types of documents are prepared by social workers in the majority of court situations: an affidavit and an expert report. *Affidavits* are sworn written statements that provide information that would have otherwise been presented in testimony. Reports are not legal documents. A *report* is the end result of a well-planned systematic search for clinical facts collected from a variety of sources augmented with knowledge of the research literature in the field in order to answer a legal question (e.g., to whom should custody be awarded?). Reports assume expertise based on logical and compelling knowledge, not opinion or belief. Criminal and civil proceedings involve factual evidence and expert opinion evidence. In expert opinion testimony, the practitioner is expected to evaluate the facts and to offer an opinion based on knowledge and experience beyond that of the average layperson. Generally, expert opinion is viewed as scientific evidence.

■ Student Status: Field and Classroom

As part of informed consent, clients have the right to be informed of the student's intern status and those with whom the student will share information as part of supervision and education. Students are frequently asked to complete in-class assignments using their agency as a context of practice and their work with clients as clinical case examples. Students should assure clients that all information shared in the classroom will contain no identifying information and will be for educational purposes only (see a process recording illustrative of fiduciary responsibilities in chapter 4). It is possible for lawyers to subpoena student process recordings and in-class papers. Care in the preparation of official records and student assignments must be taken to protect the client's right to privacy to the extent possible under the law.

General guidelines exist as to the content and procedures for keeping good clinical records (Regehr & Kanani, 2006). Entries should be made immediately after an event occurs or as soon as possible thereafter and dated. Once entered, statements may not be altered. Entries should be legible and factual. As legal documents, client records hold practitioners accountable for the results of their decisions.

■ Evidentiary Privilege

It is an inherent power of a court of justice, within the sphere of its jurisdiction, to compel witnesses to appear before it and to testify concerning any relevant facts within their knowledge in a case pending in that court; concurrently, each person has a duty to give testimony before the duly constituted courts. However, by case law or by statute, certain evidentiary privileges have been established wherein communication arising out of certain relationships need not be disclosed, even in judicial proceedings (Barbre, 2006). Usually included are communications between husband and wife, doctor and patient, and lawyer and client.

■ Confidentiality and Privileged Communication

Confidentiality is governed both by law and by the profession's Code of Ethics. Confidentiality is a moral prescription contained within the profession's Code of Ethics. It broadly refers to a practice principle that protects an individual from the unauthorized disclosure or misuse of information provided in the context of a professional relationship.

Privileged communication, though an aspect of confidentiality, is a legal determination. The question of whether privilege extends to social workers involves a threshold problem of defining the term *social worker*. It also involves two basic and sometimes conflicting interests: the interest of society (common good) in having such information disclosed to facilitate justice in the courts and the interest in establishing and maintaining certain desirable relationships between client and worker.

In deciding cases of privilege, the courts have relied on Professor John Wigmore's four conditions for the establishment of privilege: (1) The communications must originate in a confidence that they will not be disclosed; (2) this element of confidentiality must be essential to the full and satisfactory maintenance of the relationship between the parties; (3) the relationship must be one which, in the opinion of the community, ought to be sedulously fostered; and (4) the injury that would inure to the relationship by the disclosure of the communication must be greater than the benefit thereby gained for the correct disposal of litigation (Barbre, 2006).

For social work clinicians, privileged communication, to the extent it exists at all, is a very limited privilege. It is limited both by state statute and by case law. Some jurisdictions grant privileged communication to social workers, others do not. Case law may or may not uphold such statutes even where they exist (Barbre, 2006). Therefore it is the workers' responsibility to know and clarify with their employing agency the nature of the state statutes regulating confidentiality and privileged communication. When obtaining informed consent to treatment, social workers must be up-to-date and clear about the limits of confidentiality and must convey these limits to their clients.

■ Determining the Client's Capacity to Consent to Treatment: Validity

According to Regehr and Kanani (2006), there are two types of consent: express (oral or written) and implied (i.e., implied by action). The capacity to consent to treatment is a legal determination. Most legislation defines the client's capacity to consent in terms of the individual's ability to understand the relevant information presented to him/her when making a decision about treatment and the ability of the client to appreciate the reasonably foreseeable consequences of a decision or lack of decision (Regehr & Kanani, 2006).

Legislation differs on the capacity of a minor to consent to treatment. If an individual meets the standards for an emancipated minor, the child may be able to consent to or refuse treatment (emancipated minor rule). Maturity (assessed intellectual and emotional development) is another criteria whereby an individual may be viewed as having the capacity to consent (mature minor rule). Social work ethical guidelines in Canada and the United States are largely silent regarding the capacity of children to consent to treatment. Where children do not have the legal capacity to consent, social workers have adopted the practice of obtaining assent to treatment. For the most part, clinicians must obtain parental consent or, in the case of guardianship, legal consent to treat minors.

Workers should obtain a general consent to treat at the point of client entry, i.e., the first intake contact. Most agencies include a consent form as part of their intake procedures. Workers assigned to a particular client should include fiduciary matters as part of their first session even if there is a general consent form on file. Clients have the right to withdraw their consent to treatment at any time and have the right to refuse treatment (*Ciarlariello v. Schacter*, 1993). Any treatment provided without consent may result in criminal charges of assault or civil actions of negligence or battery (Regehr & Kanani, 2006). A client must be informed if anything has changed (new knowledge) following his/her original consent to treatment (Kutchins, 1991).

When determining the capacity of a client to consent, different statutes apply depending upon the jurisdiction in which decisions are made and on the nature of the decision. Different statutes apply to health care decisions, financial matters, and testamentary matters (writing a will). The determination of incapacity for an adult (generally defined as someone at least 18 years of age) occurs when the adult, because of mental illness, mental retardation, or any other mental or physical disorder, is unable to communicate or to make an informed decision because of impaired judgment.

■ Health Care Decision Acts

Statutes known as *health care decision acts* allow patients to make advance directives that govern organ donation, end-of-life decisions, and palliative care. Criminal codes prohibit assisted suicide and euthanasia. Two types of advance directives exist. One is an instructional directive enumerating the specific treatments that should or should not be administered should the client become incapacitated. The second, referred to as a proxy directive, designates a substitute decision maker.

Instructional Directives

End-of-life decisions fall into three categories: (1) withholding or withdrawing treatments that will prolong life (including do-not-resuscitate directives), (2) providing potentially life-shortening pain medication under palliative care, and (3) euthanasia, mercy killings, or assisted suicide. The practice of administering palliative interventions that may shorten life is legal in Canada; assisted suicide (the administration of drugs to cause death) is illegal in both Canada and the United States (section 24 of the Criminal Code of Canada; *Vacco v. Quill*, 1997, in the United States).

Deemed Consent to Treat

Deemed consent is assumed when a health care worker, public safety officer, enforcement officer, or other person has been exposed to bodily fluids that may transmit infections, such as HIV or hepatitis B and C. Under circumstances of a public health crisis, legislation authorizes medical officers to enter a place and conduct an examination to determine the existence of a communicable disease. If a serious communicable disease is present, individuals may be apprehended, examined, detained (quarantined), and treated without their consent.

Surrogate Decision Makers

A *surrogate decision maker* could be a court-appointed guardian or conservator, a spouse, an adult child of the client, a parent if the client is a minor, an adult sibling of the client, a religious superior if the client is a member of a religious order, or the nearest living relative of a client. Individuals may grant power of attorney to a designated decision maker (e.g., one for health care decisions and another for financial decisions) prior to becoming incapacitated. Disputes regarding determinations of incapacity are referred to boards, panels, or the courts.

In the United States, surrogate decision makers cannot, according to most state statutes, consent to abortion, sterilization, psychosurgery, convulsive therapy, or behavior modification on behalf of a client. In health care, emergency medical treatment may be given where the patient is unable to consent and no one else is available to consent.

■ Duties

Duty to Report: Abuse and Neglect

Throughout Canada and the United States, legislation imposes the responsibility on all citizens to report suspected child abuse or neglect perpetrated by a parent, caregiver, or guardian. Professionals such as doctors, teachers, psychologists, and social workers have a specific duty to report (only lawyers within the context of privileged communication are exempt from mandatory reporting of child abuse and neglect). In all other instances, the duty to report supersedes the obligation to maintain confidentiality or privilege. Professionals have ongoing duties to report any new concerns that are not discharged by an earlier report to child welfare authorities. Reports are made to the police or to child welfare agencies. The determination of whether or not the suspicion of abuse or neglect is founded is made by a child welfare agency. Reports must be made when there are reasonable and probable grounds to suspect abuse or neglect. All states offer immunity provisions that protect those who are required to report by law. Reports may be anonymous. All reports are kept confidential to the extent legally possible. Failure to report can result in civil penalties. Licenses may be revoked and an injured client may sue for malpractice.

Duty to Protect: Child Abuse

Legislation governing the duty to protect varies between countries and between jurisdictions within the same country. In the United States, every state passed legislation prohibiting child abuse between 1962 and 1967. The Child Abuse Prevention and Treatment Act of 1974 (CAPTA) was recently reauthorized (June 25, 2003) as the Keeping Children and Families Safe Act (P.L. 108-36). The Social Security Act (Title V, 1935) authorized limited funds for child welfare services. In 1967, child welfare funding under Title V of the Social Security Act became Title IV-B, Child Welfare Services. Child welfare agencies administer child abuse and neglect programs consistent with authorizing legislation, statutes, and court rulings. See chapter 15 for social work service provisions to families and children.

According to Regehr and Kanani (2006), child welfare services have historically encompassed mandatory apprenticeships, placement in orphanages and training schools, removal from the parental home, and placement in foster care. Public outrage over physical battering and child sexual abuse led to legislation to protect the child. Subsequent legislation tried to balance the safety of the child with parental or family rights. Inherent conflict exists between the worker's duty to act in the best interest and safety of the child and the duty to preserve families. This often poses an ethical dilemma for practitioners. In order to hold policy makers, administrators, and child protective services workers accountable, coroners hold inquests into the deaths of abused children. Child fatality boards or commissions evaluate the evidence associated with child fatalities and make recommendations to improve service.

Protecting the Unborn

Several controversies exist surrounding child welfare practice. One issue has to do with whether child welfare can extend protection to the unborn child. In Canada, the courts have ruled that social workers may not impose health care on pregnant women who place their unborn child at risk due to the use of drugs or alcohol, exposure to illnesses such as AIDS, or failure to secure adequate prenatal care. Practitioners may alert hospitals to the pending birth of a child whom the worker regards as at-risk. Intervention may occur before the child is released from the hospital. In the United States, 31 states have passed laws within child protection statutes that address the issue of parental drug and alcohol abuse. In a few states, maternal drug use during pregnancy may lead to charges and prosecution. Some states mandate specific reporting procedures at the birth of an infant who shows signs of addiction withdrawal. Under state statutes, parents who make, sell, distribute, or use drugs may be charged with child abuse (National Clearinghouse on Child Abuse and Neglect Information, retrieved January 30, 2006).

Distinguishing Physical Punishment From Physical Abuse

Another controversy involves the distinction between physical punishment and physical abuse. The Supreme Court of Canada recently upheld the constitutionality of the physical punishment of children (Regehr & Kanani, 2006). In the United States, there is no specific legislation permitting or forbidding physical punishment. Severity of the injury determines abuse.

Religious Beliefs

The Supreme Court of Canada has ruled that the state has the right to intervene when parental conduct falls below the standard accepted by the community. When parents engage in physical punishment consistent with their religious beliefs, child welfare has the jurisdiction to intervene when the punishment constitutes assault or results in severe injury. Child welfare also may intervene when parents refuse necessary medical care for their children based on religious grounds. Similar legislation exists in the United States.

Exposure to Domestic Violence, Prostitution, and Sex Trafficking

In addition to verbal threats, social isolation, intimidation, and exploitation, recent legislation has modified the legal definition of *emotional abuse* to include exposure to domestic violence. Since this change in definition, reports of emotional abuse have increased dramatically in Canada (Regehr & Kanani, 2006). In the United States 26 states and Puerto Rico have enacted legislation that extends legal protection to children who witness domestic violence in their homes (National Clearinghouse on Child Abuse and Neglect, retrieved January 30, 2006). The inclusion of exposure to violence under emotional abuse is controversial. The Trafficking Victims Protection Act (TVPA, 2000) made forced prostitution and sex trafficking a federal crime in the United States. Prior to this, no comprehensive law existed to protect children or to prosecute offenders.

Duty to Protect: Child Neglect

Social workers have the duty to protect neglected children. In the United States, authorizing legislation lies in the Social Security Act of 1935. Programs of cash assistance, such as Aid to Dependent Children and Their Families, are administered through child welfare agencies. Subsequent legislation authorized new, more restrictive programs, such as Temporary Assistance to Needy Families (TANF). The Personal Responsibility and Work Opportunity Reconciliation Act (1996) and the Balanced Budget Act (1997) have modified the conditions of benefit. See chapter 15, which details service provisions to families and children in need.

Cases of child neglect are usually triggered by neglect of basic needs (poverty), educational neglect (failure to attend school), health neglect (failure to get immunizations, seek proper medical attention, and/or comply with medical directives; failure to provide proper nutrition), or supervisory neglect (children are left alone unsupervised). Through no fault of their own, neglected children may become temporary wards of the state while their parents receive treatment. Changes in parental conduct lead to reunification.

Older children often defy attempts at parental oversight and are classified as children in need of supervision. Their behavior often results in acts of delinquency that trigger proceedings in the juvenile justice system. When this happens, an adolescent becomes a separate client system in need of intervention. Alternatively, family preservation may be used to avoid outplacement (see chapter 15).

Duty to Protect: Elder Abuse and Neglect

The Older Americans Act was reauthorized in 1992. A new Title VII, Chapter 3, was added for the prevention of abuse, neglect, and exploitation. Amendments in 2000 and 2001 included a provision of a long-term care ombudsman and a provision to develop state legal assistance services. Most state laws require frontline helping professionals (doctors, nurses, home health care providers) to report elder abuse. Mandatory reporting is required when an elder tells a worker or health care professional that abuse has occurred, when the worker witnesses an incident of abuse, or when the worker has reasonable suspicion that abuse has occurred. Some states require all citizens to report suspected elder abuse and neglect.

The duty to protect elders from abuse and neglect involves two types of assessment: (1) an assessment of the elder person's capacity to care for her/himself in an independent living arrangement, and (2) an assessment of the perpetrator engaged in the exploitation, neglect, or abuse of the elder. As with child abuse, action begins with an investigation of an allegation that exploitation, abuse, or neglect is occurring. If so determined, several program options are available. Current policies and programs on elder care are based on a philosophy of aging-in-place. If at all possible, the elderly are supported in maintaining their independent living arrangements. Depending on the capacity of the elderly to care for themselves, there is a continuum of residential programs that range from the least restrictive to the most supportive, from gated communities to assisted-living facilities, to level-three (total incapacity to care for self) nursing care.

Financial independence requires income security (Social Security or pension) and the ability to manage one's money as one ages. The elderly are often at risk of being financially exploited by their adult children or other family members, by their caregivers, by scam artists, or by their own impaired response to appeals from religious or humane organizations. If it is determined that financial exploitation has occurred or that the elder person can no longer manage his/her money, the court appoints an executor to manage the elder's financial affairs. The perpetrator of the exploitation is dealt with in the criminal justice system. Often states have special statutes governing caregiver neglect and abuse.

When the determination of neglect is based on self-neglect, a competency hearing must occur to determine if the elderly person is capable of performing the activities of daily living. A mental health status examination is performed to determine whether or not the elder person's judgment is impaired, creating a risk to self, e.g., does the client wander and not know where s/he is? Does s/he forget to turn off the stove or lock the door? If a determination of self-neglect or impaired judgment is made, the court appoints a guardian to make decisions on behalf of the elder person to assure his/her safety.

Duty to Protect: Mental Illness—Voluntary and Involuntary Admission

The duty to protect extends to those who experience pervasive developmental disorders, including mental retardation, and those who experience serious or chronic mental illness. Mental health legislation in Canada and the United States attempts to balance the civil liberties of individuals with the responsibility of society to care for those with diminished capacity while assuring the safety and security of the general public. Practically, this fiduciary obligation involves the involuntary admission or coerced care of those who pose a danger to self or others because of their condition. In Canada, laws governing admission to asylums or mental health hospitals began to be enacted as early as 1871, with the most recent enacted in 2000 (Regehr & Kanani, 2006). In the United States, no federal law governs involuntary admission to a psychiatric facility. All states have passed legislation under mental hygiene statutes that regulate involuntary admissions. There is variability across states.

Risk Assessment: Admissions and Release

The definition of a mental disorder is both a scientific and legal determination. In both Canada and the United States, its scientific definition has been and remains controversial. Scientifically, mental illness is defined by the *Diagnostic and Statistical Manual* (American Psychiatric Association, 2000). Several scholars challenge the definition of mental illness contained within this manual (Szasz, 1963; Goffman, 1961; Psychiatric Survivor Action Association of Ontario, 2006; Kutchins & Kirk, 1997; Saleebey, 2001).

Historically, mental health legislation authorized the detainment and custodial care of those with mental illness. Subsequent legislation specified the conditions under which institutionalized clients could be released and cared for in the community. Legislative revisions have attempted to limit involuntary admissions by establishing criteria to determine the potential for harm, its imminence, and its seriousness. Current Canadian mental health legislation attempts to provide earlier intervention by removing the term "imminent" from previous legislation and by authorizing the creation of community treatment orders (CTOs; Regehr & Kanani, 2006).

Clients may voluntarily admit themselves to a psychiatric facility. Such clients have the legal right to leave the facility at any time. The criteria for involuntary admission are similar throughout Canada and the United States, though some regional and state differences do exist. Generally, danger is the primary criterion for involuntary admission, although the terminology to define danger also varies. In the United States, the criteria of serious, foreseeable, and imminent danger must be met when making a determination that the individual poses a threat to self or others. Danger to self is based on a determination of whether the individual is at risk for suicide and/or whether the individual is competent to perform the activities of daily living and self-care. An allegation of dangerousness, suicide risk, or incompetence due to mental impairment needs to be investigated and substantiated.

When danger is alleged and the client will not consent to voluntary admission, the law authorizes involuntary admission for a specified number of hours or days for the purpose of a psychiatric assessment. In Canada, when a clinician, family member, or police officer observes an individual behaving in a manner that meets the criteria for involuntary admission, s/he may go before a judge, who may issue an order that instructs the police to assist with transporting the individual to the hospital for assessment. Initial assessment determines whether involuntary admission is warranted. In Canada, physicians complete certificates for involuntary admission. Where there are physician shortages, a nurse or psychologist may perform the task (Regehr & Kanani, 2006).

In the United States, a social worker can petition for an emergency psychiatric evaluation through the police and courts. An emergency evaluation must be signed by two medical doctors, one of whom must be a psychiatrist. Depending upon the outcome, an individual may be involuntarily committed for 72 hours after which a second evaluation and determination of competency or risk must be made. An in-patient psychiatric institution or ward must provide a period of observation and review of status in 10 days on any involuntary admission.

According to Regehr and Kanani, hospital admission does not provide the practitioner with consent to treat. When an involuntary client is admitted and cannot provide valid consent, alternative authority for consent to treat must be sought. When clients with mental illnesses are stabilized and deemed competent, they may write an advance directive governing their care in a mental health emergency.

The client's right to effective and least restrictive treatment often results in a revolving-door policy of mental health treatment. The client enters care voluntarily or involuntarily, receives short-term stabilization, and is released on medications, only to return at a later date because of destabilization (usually related to noncompliance with prescribed medications). Care of the mentally ill in the community is controversial. Legislation in both Canada (Ministry of Health and Long-Term Care, 2000) and the United States (Community Mental Health Centers Act, P.L. 88-164, Title II, 1963) promotes a community-based continuum of care. Outpatient care of the mentally ill is challenged, however, by a client's noncompliance with medication and the lack of funding to implement wrap-around community care.

The Intersection of Mental Health and Criminal Justice

Individuals with mental disorders sometimes come into conflict with the criminal justice system. In such cases, the offender may be diverted to a mental health program for low-risk mentally disordered individuals or be held for trial. Canada has recently established a court for mentally disordered offenders based on the principles of therapeutic jurisprudence (Regehr & Kanani, 2006). This court is based on a model introduced in Dade Country, Florida, in 1989 (Steadman, Davidson, & Brown, 2001).

If an individual with a mental disorder is held for trial, a determination must be made of the offender's fitness to stand trial. In both the United States and Canada, the law requires that an individual be physically present and mentally capable of understanding and participating in the court proceedings. Mental status regarding fitness to stand trial is determined at the time of trial.

The state must prove the offender to be guilty of both a wrongful act and a guilty mind. In the United States, a *guilty mind* refers to knowing the difference between right and wrong (some would add "and the ability to act on that knowl-edge"). In cases involving an allegation of murder, offenders may enter a plea of not guilty by reason of insanity (criminal codes of Canada and the United States). At trial, an offender may be found guilty of the wrongful act and responsible or may be found guilty of the wrongful act but not responsible.

If a client is determined to be unfit to stand trial, the court may order treat-ment until such time as the offender becomes fit. If the client is found guilty but not responsible, there are three discharge possibilities following assessment of re-lease risk. If the client is assessed as posing no threat, the client may be discharged unconditionally. If some threat exists, conditions are imposed to manage the threat once discharged. When serious threat remains, the offender is discharged into cus-todial care, usually a psychiatric facility for the dangerously and criminally insane.

Duty to Warn

Mental Illness

Social workers must also determine if a client poses a danger to others because of his/her mental health status. In *Tarasoff v. Regents of the University of California* (1976, 3d. 177), the California courts ruled that a mental health professional must take action if the professional learns that a client poses a serious, foreseeable, and imminent danger to another. Most social workers therefore use the Tarasoff rul-ing as a guide. The worker has a duty to warn the appropriate law enforcement of-ficials and to warn the person who is the target of the threat so that actions to assure the safety of the potential victim can be taken. The Supreme Court of Canada upheld the practitioner's duty to warn in *Smith v. Jones* (1999).

Domestic Abuse

The determination of risk of harm is also made in domestic abuse cases. Workers in the criminal justice system must be able to assess the forensic risk posed by perpetrators of domestic abuse. Execution of one's fiduciary duty in cases where the client poses a threat to others includes removal of the perpetrator from the home or community, criminal prosecution, and incarceration in a correctional facility or a secured mental health facility.

Forensic social workers also have an obligation to assure the safety of victims of domestic violence to the extent legally possible. Workers should review the le-gal options available to victims of domestic violence, including medical docu-mentation of the abuse, filing charges, getting a restraining order, moving to a domestic abuse shelter, and leaving the relationship. Because many victims of do-mestic abuse return to the abusive relationship, the worker should review with the client the pros and cons of remaining in the relationship. The worker and client should assess where the client falls on the abuse continuum in terms of its duration, frequency, and seriousness. To the extent possible, clients should be taught the warning signs that signal that an episode of abuse is imminent. Clients should prepare a safety kit and take it with them should they have to flee to avoid an abusive episode (Roberts & Roberts, 2005).

■ Client Rights

To summarize, clients have the right to privacy, the right to treatment that works, the right to treatment in the least restrictive environment, and the right to withdraw from or refuse treatment. Clients have a legal right to be advised about the decisions and methods that relate to their treatment and the right to access their records. Often the client's right to self-determination conflicts with the professional's duty to protect. When situations such as this arise (and they often do), it is important to make decisions based on an assessment of the legal and ethical merits of the case at hand. What is in the client's best interest is not always apparent, especially when such a determination runs against the client's perception of his/her best interest and the client's legal rights to consent to, withdraw from, or refuse treatment. Similarly, what the client perceives to be in his or her best interest may not be in the best interest of the public or common good.

Social workers have other fiduciary duties related to specialized areas of practice. Social workers should be familiar with laws pertaining to work with adult and youthful offenders, immigrants and refugees, and minorities who experience discrimination. They must know the laws that govern marriage, divorce, and child custody. Practitioners should be aware of laws relevant to victims of violence (rape, assault, domestic violence). These specialized areas are beyond the scope of this chapter.

■ Authentic Contracts

The most common concern expressed by students is the fear that clients will not trust them if clients are apprised of their rights, the worker's duties, and the worker's status as a student. No sound contract can exist, however, without authenticity as its foundation. The worker-client contract for service must be open, honest, and transparent. There cannot be any hidden agendas. False contracts cannot lead to the establishment of a healthy working relationship. Assigned cases and assigned intake hours provide the context for developing a contract for treatment but do not constitute the contract itself.

According to Seabury (Compton & Galaway, 2004), there are four types of contracting situations: (1) the ideal situation, (2) the impossible situation, (3) the problematic situation, and (4) the contraindicated situation. Contracts are both sociological (court-mandated) and psychological (agreed to by clients).

Contracting with court-mandated or involuntary clients falls under the category of a problematic contracting situation. Clients in these situations are present because others have determined that they should be present. Mandated clients are court ordered while involuntary clients have been pressured by a family member or a service requirement. The sociological authority that provides entry must be converted into psychological authority. A working relationship is based on psychological authority to pursue mutually agreed-upon treatment goals. In such contracting situations, it is possible but difficult to achieve agreed-upon outcomes. Other difficulties arise when the client lacks the capacity for informed consent to treatment. Under such circumstances, the worker must expand the client system to include those who are surrogate decision makers.

There are two conditions that create an impossible contracting situation. The first consists of the situation where the client seeks services that are beyond the resources of the agency or its service network. A worker cannot provide a resource that is not available. Nor can a worker agree to provide services to help a client reach a goal that is beyond the client's physical or mental capacities. A worker cannot promise mobility where there is paralysis or a career as a medical doctor where there are significant intellectual and educational deficits. The first step to authentic contracting in such a situation is to set mutually realistic expectations for service with a clear understanding of the limitations involved.

The second impossible contracting situation occurs when a client seeks an objective that creates a fundamental value clash between the client and the worker or the client and the agency. For instance, abortion counseling may be in value conflict with some agencies/workers and not in conflict with other agencies/workers. In such situations, it is important to acknowledge the value conflict and refer the client to another worker or to another agency.

A contraindicated contracting situation occurs under conditions of corrupt contracting. Corrupt contracting occurs when either the worker or the client or both enter into a contract with a hidden agenda. A contract can be corrupted when others in the client's network or the worker's network engage in deceit or pursue conflicting goals. For instance, in a school setting, the goal of the teacher may be to remove the student from the classroom; the goal of the principal may be to expel the student from the school; the goal of the student may be to get expelled; and the goal of the worker may be to keep the student in school and in the classroom. In such situations, it is important to identify the conflicting agendas, work out the differences, and establish mutually agreed-upon goals. If this cannot be done, it is important to recognize that there is no authentic contract for service.

The ideal contracting situation rarely occurs. When it does, it consists of an explicit, mutual, flexible, and realistic working agreement between the client and the worker based on common values and perceptions of what is the matter and what is the solution. In an ideal contracting situation, resources are available to match the client's expressed needs, and both the client and the worker

EXHIBIT 2.1   *Law and Social Work Practice: Fiduciary Responsibilities and Malpractice*

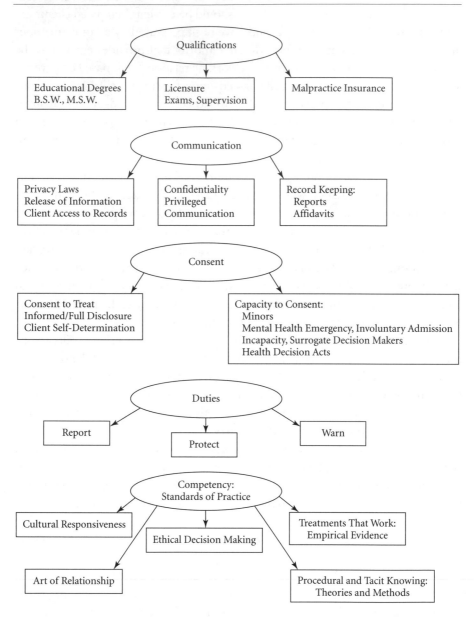

participate in the assessment and treatment process, which is ongoing. Contracting is an important first step in working with clients. Students should be assured that apprising clients of their rights, the worker's duties, and the worker's status as a student will lead to an authentic contract and a positive worker-client relationship.

3

The Policy, Program, and Administrative Context of Direct Practice

■ The Social Policy Context of the Profession of Social Work

The Keynesian Welfare National State

The policies, programs, and administrative structures of indirect practice serve as a context within which a direct service practitioner works. Welfare policies vary around the world and over time (Kennett, 2004). Until the 1980s, a Keynesian model of the welfare national state dominated Northwestern Europe, North America, Australia, and New Zealand. Comparative social policy scholars suggest that globalization is now changing the Keynesian welfare national state (Kennett, 2004). Global social forces are affecting the welfare policies of the national state.

According to Jessop (2004), the Keynesian model of the welfare state reflects two macro institutions: democracy and capitalism. Nations that are neither democratic nor capitalistic (or that meet one but not both conditions) have been traditionally excluded from comparative social policy analysis based on the dominant Keynesian typology. According to comparative policy scholars, this typology represents an ethnocentric bias in that contemporary regimes in the United States, Canada, and the United Kingdom are usually regarded as welfare states despite the fact that they deliver meager benefits on the basis of need as a last resort to those who are unable to support themselves through market activities. To counter this bias, Esping-Andersen (Kennett, 2004) has proposed a typology that allows comparison of the social policies of these nations with those nations that are neither democratic nor capitalistic (or where they meet one criterion but not the other). Readers interested in cross-national comparative social policy analysis should consult Kennett (2004). The social policy context of social work practice in this chapter will be discussed within the Keynesian welfare national state and the Schumpeterian workfare postnational regime.

The Keynesian model holds that the conditions for profitable growth and full employment are possible in a closed national economy where there is demand-side management and a provision for a national infrastructure. According to this model, capitalism involves dependence on the market as the principal method of distributing social and economic resources. The model is designed to rectify market failures but not to eradicate the market system. By providing incentives to work, capitalism ensures a workforce and promotes consumption to drive demand.

According to the Keynesian model, democracy is a social principle that assures equality of political rights among individuals regardless of their status and means. To support democracy as a social principle, some accumulated capital is redistributed to the less well-off (obligation of the state to support its citizenry). The Keynesian model rests on the idea that political citizenship enables individuals to access a range of welfare benefits that are either universal and/or need-based. Under this model, citizens are entitled, as a right, to minimum income support.

The Schumpeterian Workfare Postnational Regime

Since the 1980s, scholars have observed the tendency of governments in various parts of the world to reduce social expenditures and curtail social programs. Neoliberal ideology has prompted governments to reduce public expenditures, curtail social spending, impose more demanding eligibility requirements, and require recipients of income benefits to engage in paid employment. In America, Clinton's Personal Responsibility and Work Opportunity Reconciliation Act (1996) placed a 2-year cap (within a 5-year period) on income benefits, abandoning the universal right to minimum economic support under the Keynesian model.

Though nations vary in their specific social policy provisions (e.g., Canada has universal health care, the United States does not), Western nations have tended to develop welfare provisions within a capitalistic economy and a democratic institutional structure. Whether Keynesian or Schumpeterian, the models assume that an individual can attain a decent standard of living despite the unequal distribution of market-based incomes. To correct market flaws or respond to individual circumstances (case-by-case need), it is the responsibility of the state to provide and administer a range of universal and selective/residual welfare services. In both Keynesian and Schumpeterian models, local and state governments act mainly as relays for policies framed at the national level. State policies and programs are augmented by nonstate, nonprofit organizations (NGOs) and private sector agencies.

Globalization

Scholars speculate about the effects of globalization on the welfare state. According to Kennett (2004), sovereign national states territorialize political power. However, economic development, the job market, and the labor pool are increasingly international. Local social problems are increasingly tied to global social problems such as poverty, mass deprivation, and oppression. The national welfare state may be moving beyond political boundaries as a response to globalization.

■ Context of Practice

Within a national state, specific policies, programs, and administrative structures form a context of practice within which a direct service practitioner works. A context of practice is bounded by goal-directed parameters (contained in an agency's mission statement), a defined field of practice and setting, program-specific regulatory policies and procedures, an organizational entity (agency) with a defined administrative structure, and a client population. What a direct-service social work practitioner can and cannot do to meet client needs is constrained by the agency context within which the practitioner works.

Mission Statements, Policies, Public Laws, and Programs

Mission statements articulate the purpose of an agency. Informed by values, agency mission statements generally seek to adjust public resources to meet the social welfare needs of individuals within identified client populations. Mission statements become agency-specific when objectives are specified according to the type of services and resources offered. The values contained in agency mission statements get institutionalized through policy in the form of public laws.

A social policy is a set of principles (values), usually expressed in laws and governmental regulations, that guides the delivery of specific services. Social policies assign specific benefits and opportunities to eligible client populations. A social program (e.g., Temporary Assistance to Needy Families, TANF) is the means by which agencies (state and local Departments of Human Service) implement a social policy (e.g., Personal Responsibility and Work Opportunity Reconciliation Act, PRWORA, 1996) through service provisions to a client population (e.g., impoverished families). Procedures are the specific written directions to professional staff who implement the program. Procedures are usually contained in an agency's operational manual.

Fields of Practice and Agency Settings

Schools of social work teach a generic curriculum in the foundation year. Generic skills are first refined by a student's field placement setting and later refined by the student's choice of concentration or specialization in the advanced year. A setting belongs to a field of practice which is characterized by the need for some specific knowledge, e.g., knowledge of diseases and medical terminology in medical social work, knowledge of education and educational terminology in school social work, knowledge of child neglect and abuse in protective services, knowledge of spousal abuse and forensic risk assessment in domestic violence, etc. Settings within a field of practice can vary. For instance, in the field of mental health, a practitioner may work in an acute psychiatric ward of a medical hospital, in a school setting (elementary, secondary, or higher education), in a clubhouse setting for the chronically mentally ill, in the workplace (employee assistance program), in a rehabilitation center, or in an assisted-living facility.

Regulatory Oversight: Credentials, Licensing, and Contracts

Credentials and Licensing

Social work is regulated both by the standards of the profession (in the United States, the NASW Code of Ethics, and in Canada, the Canadian Association of Social Workers Code of Ethics) and by state (or province) statutes that govern the licensing of mental health professionals. In Canada, provincial acts regulate social work practice. Such acts identify which professionals can use the designation *social worker* or *social service worker*; define the responsibilities and scope of practice; specify which governing body regulates the profession; and ensure the competence of individual professionals (Regehr & Kanani, 2006). According to the U.S. Constitution, the legal regulation of professions is delegated to the authority of individual states or their equivalent (Association of Social Work Boards, 2006a, b). State legislatures enact enabling legislation that establishes and empowers a board of social work to adopt regulations and carry out the purpose of the law. The practice act sets the minimum requirements for licensure or certifications, including education, experience, supervision, and the necessity for successfully completing a minimum competence examination. Most jurisdictions regulate two or more levels of practice. Typically, the board licenses four categories of practice: bachelor's (baccalaureate degree upon graduation), master's (master's degree in social work [M.S.W.] with no experience), advanced generalist (M.S.W. with 2 years post-master's supervised experience), and clinical (with 2 years post-master's direct clinical social work experience). Some jurisdictions license at the associate level. The Association of Social Work Board offers five exams: associate, bachelor's, master's, advanced generalist, and advanced clinical. Because each jurisdiction in the United States has its own laws and regulations, a social work license is not transferable from jurisdiction to jurisdiction unless there is a special agreement between states to do so.

The ASWB maintains a database that contains the basic elements of social work regulation in the 50 U.S. states, 10 Canadian provinces, the District of Columbia, the U.S. Virgin Islands, and Puerto Rico. Tables include information on board structure, level of practice, minimum requirements for licensure, exemptions, supervisory qualifications, reciprocity/endorsement, continuing education, privileged communication, practice definitions, and other elements (see www.aswbdata.powerlynxhosting).

Social work degrees must be obtained from schools of social work that are accredited by the Council on Social Work Education (CSWE) in the United States and by the Canadian Association of Schools of Social Work (CASSW) in Canada or by other nationally recognized accrediting agencies. Degrees earned outside the United States and Canada must be determined to be equivalent (see International Social Work Degree Recognition and Equivalency Service, ww.aswb.org). Non–social work degrees are accepted in some instances at the basic level in the United States.

All graduate students, regardless of concentration, earn a master's of social work (M.S.W.) degree. Those who concentrate in policy, advocacy, community, or management practice do not need to be licensed. Those who intend to practice clinically either as an advanced generalist or as a clinical or independent practitioner must be licensed. Practitioners in administrative practice may be hired in a management position but are required to hire a clinical director to oversee the agency's clinical programs and staff.

To practice, a clinical social worker must pass an entry-level licensing exam: the AGSW for students with a bachelor's degree in social work and the LCSW for students with a master's degree but no experience. Advanced licensing for bachelor graduates requires a social work master's degree. Advanced licensing for M.S.W. graduates requires an average of 2 full-time years of employment under supervision (approximately 4 hours of individual and/or group supervision a month by a licensed independent clinical social worker). Because states differ on the number of work and supervision hours required and who is eligible to supervise, it is important to refer to the *Social Work Laws and Regulations Online Comparison Guide* (Association of Social Work Boards, 2006b). Once licensed, the clinical practitioner must accrue continuing education credits throughout his/her career. The highest licensing credential is board-certified clinical social worker.

Contracts: Four Types

Between Society and the Profession.   Social work is self-regulating. The Association of Social Work Boards (ASWB) administers registration, sets professional standards of care, and implements discipline. Both federal and state governments have authority to pass legislation governing areas within which social workers practice, such as laws that regulate privacy, duty to report, duty to protect, and duty to warn (see chapter 2). Federal laws tend to lead to consistent practices whereas state (or provincial) laws tend to be more variable (see Regehr & Kanani, 2006).

A legal mandate exists between a society and the professions it sanctions. In the mandate between society and a profession, society agrees to recognize and accept the profession's areas of expertise, to give the profession control over the distribution of certain resources, and to allow the profession to set standards and to judge peers.

The primary purpose of regulatory legislation is the protection of the public. Regulations ensure that professionals have a certain level of competence and that they adhere to certain standards of practice. Following a complaint, social workers may be subject to disciplinary actions by their professional regulatory board or their professional ethics board and may be subject to civil damages and criminal proceedings. Social workers practice within a profession sanctioned by society. Agencies accept this general contract and specify it by subscribing to a circumscribed functional area of expertise. Agencies have control over the distribution of a specific, limited range of resources, such as income, food, housing, or health care, depending upon their field of practice.

Between the Profession and the Professional.   In the contract between the profession and the professional, the profession agrees to uphold standards of care and best practices, educate future members through a standardized and accredited curriculum, protect and maintain the integrity of the profession, and provide a forum for discussion of professional issues. The professional agrees to follow the Code of Ethics, conduct practice in a competent manner, maintain currency through continuing education, and contribute to the knowledge base of the profession.

Between Employer and Employee.   In the contract between a professional employee and an employing agency, the clinician agrees to function in a competent and professional manner, to carry out assigned duties, to follow the agency's policies, to support the agency's mission, and to educate him/herself regarding the agency's client base and issues. The employing agency agrees to pay an employee a salary and benefits and to provide supervision, consultation, evaluation, and other support services. It agrees to make its policies and procedures known to the worker (usually in what is called an agency's *manual of operation*) and to maintain open lines of communication with the worker. The agency agrees to provide a suitable environment for clinical practice and to make known the criteria to be used in evaluating the professional performance of the employee. Job descriptions further clarify the employer-employee contract.

Between the Worker and Client.   The contract between the professional worker and the client is based on the worker's ability to establish a working relationship with the client. Chapter 6 discusses the worker-client relationship in detail.

Auspices: Public, Nonprofit, and For-Profit—Primary and Host Settings

Auspice is a term used to describe the patronage of an agency. Direct-practice social workers are employed in public agencies (departments of health and human services), in community agencies (hospitals, schools, health centers), and with nonprofit social service agencies (e.g., Catholic, Lutheran, or Jewish social services). Social workers may also be employed by for-profit organizations, such as an accounting firm or an auto manufacturing company, through the company's employee assistance program (EAP). When licensed as an independent clinical social worker, a social worker may establish her/his own private practice. Whether the auspice is public, nonprofit, or for-profit, all practitioners are obligated to adhere to federal and state statutes that regulate the fiduciary responsibilities of mental health practitioners.

Organizations designated as primary social work settings have as their primary function the delivery of social services, e.g., public departments of human services, departments of social services, or departments of family and social services. Private nonprofit agencies, such as Catholic, Lutheran, or Jewish social services, are also considered primary social work settings. They embody in their mission statement the goals and objectives of social work practice, and they are run and staffed by social workers.

Social workers also practice in host settings, such as in schools, hospitals, or correctional facilities. The primary function of a host setting is something other than social work. In schools, the primary function is education, in hospitals, health care. Host settings may include in their organizational structure a department of social work. In such instances, the function of social work is to support the mission of the host agency. In a school setting, the function of social work is to support student learning. In a health setting, social workers focus on the psychosocial correlates of illness and health.

Team meetings are particularly common and important in host settings where members of many different disciplines provide services to the same client or the same client group. Team meetings serve both a clinical and an administrative function. Such meetings coordinate the assessment and interventions of professionals from many different disciplines (medical doctors, nurses, psychologists, occupational therapists, social workers, educational specialists, etc.). Often, weekly clinical case conferences are held to focus on a complex case. Social workers need clinical skills, advocacy skills, and management skills as a team participant in a host setting. Issues often arise on multidisciplinary teams between professionals regarding their respective areas of expertise.

Organizational and Administrative Social Work Practice

Agency-based clinical social work practice occurs within an organizational structure. Organizations are dynamic systems that have both formal and informal structures. They are legal entities that have a purpose, a mission, and goals which sanction and dictate the process (procedures) by which policy is implemented through programs in the agency. Every agency has an administrative structure consisting of an appointed executive board, a hired professional administrative staff, a hired professional clinical staff, and a hired support staff. While the informal structure of an agency can be learned only by being on the job for a significant period of time, the formal administrative structure of an agency can easily be viewed by looking at the agency's organizational chart.

Position titles demarcate the administrative chain of command or hierarchy. Depending on the size of the agency, the organizational structure may contain one or more departments, each running its own program. Several theories inform organizational and management practice (bureaucratic, scientific, humanistic). These theories are usually taught as part of a second-year curriculum within identified concentrations. It is important, however, for foundation-year students to understand how the organizational structure and administrative style of an agency affects the conduct of direct practice.

Organizational staffing patterns (professional and support staff) are resources for direct practice. An agency may be rich or poor in its staffing numbers and the assets each staff member does or does not bring to facilitate the work of the agency. A good staffing pattern matches the client population served by the agency in terms of racial composition and language proficiencies. Professional expertise should match the concerns of the client population. Every agency serves a geographical catchment area where a client population resides. Though the geographical area remains static, the population demographics can change over time. Therefore it is important to maintain up-to-date information on the client population served by the agency as well as on the pattern of changing needs. Within every agency, there is a prescribed route to service, which entails a referral source and intake procedures (forms) to determine client eligibility for the services offered by the agency.

■ The Sociology of Social Welfare

Social welfare is the primary policy context of agency-based practice. Social welfare is a concept with ideological roots in philosophy (theories of social justice), political science (theories of government), and economics (theories of capitalism and communism). It is a difficult concept to define because social welfare is the end result of attempts to reform societal institutions (social change) as well as the end result of societal attempts to respond to those in need and to exercise social control over its citizens. It is therefore a complex concept that carries certain tensions and contradictions (Popple & Leighninger, 2002).

As an exercise in social justice and reform, social welfare is regarded positively. Social work advocates (distributors of resources) and social work reformists (agents of social change) seek to build a humane and just social order. They advocate for a universal minimum standard of well-being based on job opportunities, a living wage, health care, and housing for all citizens. Included in the vision of well-being are programs to meet the needs for psychological and social well-being, such as education, counseling, recreation, and socialization. Those who view social welfare as an exercise in social justice value more government intervention, the use of tax dollars to support social programs, and the provision of programs based on universal entitlements.

As an exercise in social control, social welfare embodies two dominant moral values: (1) the norm of reciprocity, which is linked to work, and (2) individualism, which is linked to attributions of personal responsibility. Recipients of welfare are stigmatized when a moral judgment is made that there has been no return (work as reciprocity) for the benefits (welfare) received. The concept of individualism attributes success or failure, whether economic or noneconomic, to the individual. Noneconomic areas of individual responsibility include child rearing, marriage, and mental health.

Those who view social welfare in terms of its social control function express values consistent with political and economic conservatism. They value less government, a free market, lower taxes, family rights, parental authority, and a safety net to make urgent, temporary adjustments to a cyclical, free-market economy. The public good is valued over the good of any one individual. Given divergent ideologies, it is not surprising that the history of social welfare policies and programs lies on a continuum marked by harshness at one end followed by residual, needs-based, means-tested programs in the middle and programs of universal entitlement at the other end.

Political Ideology and Social Welfare

As a social science, political science is an area of scientific study. However, people subscribe to political positions based on ideology (values) and desired end goals. Social welfare policies and programs continue to be central to political debate (conservative and liberal). As a political ideology, conservatism believes in individual and family responsibility and prefers private rather than public action. Individual factors are viewed as the dominant causal source of social problems. Individual strengths and weaknesses are perceived as rooted in family and community. The major function of social work consistent with this ideology is the provision of minimum, means-tested, residual social welfare programs. Conservatives see solutions in informal networks consisting of family, community, and organized religion (faith-based initiatives). Conservatives and liberals often differ on the allocation of resources to fund social welfare programs.

The political ideology of liberalism focuses on the ways in which existing economic and social institutions contribute to poverty and social inequities. Liberals believe in social causality. Liberal ideology supports the redistribution of resources through universal or residual programs. An extension of this ideology (radical ideology) seeks the broad restructuring of existing political, social, and economic institutions. Radical ideology is critical of social work policies and programs that seek simply to adjust or redistribute economic resources to meet needs.

Economics and Social Welfare

As a social science, economics is an area of scientific study. However, like politics, individuals subscribe to economic positions based on desired end goals. The two major economic systems are capitalism and communism. Each economic system embodies different value positions on work, the nature of human behavior, the creation of wealth, and the distribution of income.

Both economic systems produce poverty: capitalism because of the cyclical nature of the free market and its creation of economic inequality; communism because it fails to produce economic growth or tie production (supply) to consumption (demand). The connections among capitalism, poverty, and discrimination are well described by Schiller (2001).

Fiscal conservatives in a capitalist economy hold that poverty should be addressed on a case-by-case basis. Conservatives believe that economic growth, not the redistribution of income, will eliminate poverty. They hold that it is the moral obligation of those who are more fortunate to give (charity) to the less fortunate. Liberals in a capitalist economy believe that individuals, by virtue of their citizenship, are entitled to an adequate standard of living and to other life-sustaining services. Liberals note that the top 1% of the U.S. population owns more wealth than the bottom 90% of the population and that the rate of growth of inequality is faster in the United States than in any other industrialized country (Eitzen & Zinn, 2004, 2003; Popple & Leighninger, 2002). As desired end goals of economic policy, liberals value job opportunities, a living wage, and economic redistribution to offset a flawed market economy.

■ Social Work and Poverty

Social welfare programs designed to address poverty are policy-driven. Competing political and economic ideologies vie to determine the desired end goals of such programs. As social welfare, such programs are defined as economic transfers outside the marketplace. Programs can be universal (institutional), spread across all socioeconomic classes as entitlements, or programs can be selective (residual), assigning benefits solely to designated groups based on a determination of need and eligibility. Social welfare programs are closely related to unemployment, underemployment, unaffordable housing, problems with health and mental health, substance abuse, educational deficits, and domestic and child abuse. Some of the problems result in poverty while others result from poverty. It is the frontline, agency-based social worker in direct practice who links the beneficiary client population to policy initiatives through programs that deliver goods and services.

The Cost of Social Welfare Programs

Society has a stake in solving social problems related to poverty, housing, and health care. Enlightened self-interest dictates that by helping others one ultimately helps oneself by preserving order and stability. Besides being a target of change itself, the economy is also the source of funding for social programs. The United States devotes a portion of its gross national product, through taxation, to the solution of certain social problems without changing the basic nature of the economy. Debates over federal, state, or local funding focus on which level of government (or which tax-payer group) will bear the cost of welfare. Conservatives place the burden on states or local districts. This creates inequalities between localities and between states. Those most in need of welfare services are most likely to reside in localities that are economically depressed and therefore least able to fund services because their tax base is also depressed. For this reason, liberals advocate for federal funding of social welfare programs to assure that needs will be met universally at a satisfactory level.

Universal Entitlement

As a result of the economic depression that began in 1929, society recognized that a conscientious workforce could be plunged into poverty due to the cyclical and flawed nature of a free-market economy. To protect workers and their families against such poverty, the federal government created Social Security. Both employers and employees contribute a portion of their yearly earnings to fund it. As a non-means-tested program, Social Security provides economic support to retirees (old age), widows and their children (survivors), and those who become disabled (disability insurance). Because of the norm of reciprocity (work record), the beneficiaries of such Social Security programs are not stigmatized; rather they are perceived as entitled to the benefits of such programs. Other programs that provide financial support for lost income are unemployment insurance, workers' compensation, and worker and veteran pensions. Nonstigmatized health care is provided by Medicare, which serves disabled workers and those over the age of 65. Veterans are served by veteran health services. Canada offers universal health care while the United States does not.

Residual Programs: Needs-Based and Means-Tested

For those without a work history, a system of means-tested public relief has been established. Two types of programs exist: (1) cash support programs, and (2) in-kind programs. Cash support programs include assistance programs such as Temporary Assistance to Needy Families (TANF), Supplemental Security Income (SSI), and general assistance. In-kind public housing programs provide shelters, subsidized housing, and energy assistance. Nutrition programs consist of food stamps, child nutrition programs, and nutrition for Women, Infants, and Children (WIC). Health care programs consist of Medicaid and community, maternal, and child health care, both of which provide medical care for the poor. Native Americans are served by the Bureau of Indian Affairs' Health Services. For greater elaboration of social welfare policies and programs, readers are referred to materials used in their social policy courses.

It is important that social workers in direct practice understand the policies and programs that inform their practice as well as the public debates that surround such policies and programs. Three negative but prominent public views of residual social welfare are (1) it creates dependency, (2) it is too costly, and (3) taxpayer money is being squandered through inefficiency and fraudulent claims by consumers and providers alike. Currently, universal entitlement programs in the United States, such as Social Security, are under attack as unaffordable. The cost of welfare is perceived to threaten the common good.

Evidence: Are Welfare Programs Working?

Citing recent reports by the Center on Budget and Policy Priorities, Dionne (2005) observes that welfare programs are successful. According to 2002 census data, the earned-income tax credit "lifted 4.9 million working poor out of poverty, including 2.7 million children" (p. 7). He goes on to note that 27 million Americans are lifted from poverty by our system of public benefits every year. More than 80 million receive health insurance through a government program such as Medicaid, Medicare, or the State Children's Health Insurance Program (SCHIP). Federal spending on Medicaid and SCHIP represents 1.5% of gross domestic product (GDP). Federal financing for the rest of the low-income programs consumes just 2.3% of GDP. In comparison, defense spending consumes 4% and interest on the national debt consumes 1.5% (Dionne, 2005).

■ The Function of Social Workers in Direct Practice

Social workers in direct practice are licensed and perform two functions: (1) the provision of concrete services associated with policy-based social welfare programs, and (2) the provision of therapy. To fulfill the first function, social workers in direct practice deliver concrete services to highly vulnerable client populations, usually through a model of practice referred to as case management (see chapter 10). To fulfill the second function, social workers in direct practice deliver therapy to both highly vulnerable populations and traditional client populations (see chapters 12 and 13).

Client Populations

A field of practice contains a client population. Highly vulnerable client populations consist of those who are dependent on the state because of their age; their impoverished status as dependent, neglected, and abused children; or their status as juvenile or adult offenders. Highly vulnerable client populations also include the homeless, those with chronic mental illnesses or mental disabilities, and those who are severely physically disabled. This client group is likely to need long-term concrete services from multiple providers. Services include health care, housing (or assistance with residential living), education, job training, and employment. Step 3 of the decision tree and chapter 10 address the timely provision of concrete services to highly vulnerable client populations. Despite the separation of services from therapy, highly vulnerable client populations often need support to access and conform to service provisions.

Managed Behavioral Health Care

Steps 5, 6, and 7 of the decision tree address methods and therapeutic options. In addition to their concerns about the cost of welfare, economic conservatives have raised concerns about the cost of health and mental health. Managed health and behavioral health care are defined as "a set of health care systems and technologies aimed at organizing and managing both the clinical and financial aspects of service provision to a given population of customers" (Popple & Leighninger, 2002, p. 391). Social workers in direct practice have a stake in the fiscal parameters governing the delivery of behavioral health and mental health care.

Under managed behavioral health care, treatment decisions rest with a third-party insurer, not with the consumer or the provider of such services (Austrian, 1998). Cost has become a variable in treatment decisions, often overriding case-indicated treatment. In order to secure services, acute problems are often classified as medical necessities while chronic problems are classified as acute problems in need of stabilization. The right treatment, by the right provider, for the right duration, at the right cost is offset by fiscal considerations of least intrusive, least extensive, least intensive, and least costly. Social workers, whether working in private or public practice, raise concerns about the compatibility of good social work practice with managed-care policies and procedures. Social workers in direct practice improve their competency to the extent that they possess the knowledge and skills related to indirect practice.

4

Communication Skills for Direct Practice

■ Professional Communication

The communication skills needed by social workers in direct practice differ significantly from the communication skills needed by social workers in policy, advocacy, community, and management practice. This text presents both sets of communication skills in consecutive chapters. Nonclinical communication skills needed for policy, advocacy, community, and management practice are presented in chapter 5. This chapter focuses on the communication skills needed for direct practice. Because communication is first and foremost culturally bound, the chapter begins by examining how culture influences language. Generic interviewing skills are presented, followed by ethnographic interviewing techniques and theory-guided inquiries. Beginning and ethnographic interviewing skills are illustrated in the process recording at the end of the chapter. Advanced theory-guided process recordings are illustrated in chapter 13.

Process Recordings

For purposes of education, students capture worker-client dialogue in process recordings. Process recordings reflect three social work processes: (1) the enactment of relationship, (2) data gathering (interviewing) for purposes of assessment, and (3) the delivery of theory-based interventions (advanced process recordings). Because language is a cultural product, worker-client dialogue also reveals the world views of the participants. Generally, process recordings are grounded on the assumption that the client possesses intact cognition and adult language competency.

The Direct-Practice Social Work Interview

Unlike a casual conversation, the professional social work interview is purposeful. The worker's actions must be planned, deliberate, and consciously selected to further the purpose of the interview. It is the worker's responsibility to assure unity, progression, and thematic continuity so that the interview moves toward its goal. In doing so, the worker must be able to recognize what is extraneous material (diffuse content) and what is pertinent. A professional interview has a formally arranged meeting time, place, and duration. Interview management is the responsibility of the worker. The informational interview begins with the client's point of entry with the agency.

The greatest enemy of communication, says Kadushin (1990), is the illusion of it. In direct practice, the interview is the most important and most frequently employed social work skill. The interview involves three communication processes: transmitting (encoding), receiving (decoding), and processing. Processing a communication relies on the recall of stored information. The worker is required to think about and relate a new message to relevant stored information. In evaluating the message, the worker must refer it to some frame of reference (theory) for its understanding.

Generally, once a message is sent, it is out of the hands of the transmitter. How a communication is received, ignored, misinterpreted, or distorted is beyond the sender's power to change. This is not the case in a professional helping relationship, where communication is the substance of assessment and the interactive dialogue is the form of intervention.

Decoding and Encoding

Every communication, whether professional or personal, consists of a sender, who encodes a message, and a receiver, who decodes it. Both sender and receiver use culturally and personally acquired filters to encode and decode exchanges. As a result, what is sent is often not what is received. Consider, for instance, the following common dating communication: "I'll call you later" can be encoded by the sender to mean "I'll call you tonight" or "I'll call you whenever I don't have anything better to do." It can be decoded by the receiver to mean there is a mutual attraction and a call will be made soon or that it represents a rejection and no call will be made. Both encoding and decoding are selective. Culture influences the selective encoding and decoding of messages.

For instance, in Greek culture, the word *avrio* (maybe tomorrow) is a common response to a request that cannot be immediately fulfilled. If a merchant is out of feta cheese and a customer asks for it, the merchant is likely to reply "maybe tomorrow." This response is based on a world view of expectation and hospitality. A consumer from a Western culture is likely to regard "tomorrow" as a fact-based response having to do with known shipping and arrival times (i.e., the culture of Western business). When the consumer returns the next day for the feta cheese, the merchant again replies *avrio*. Because of the differences in cultural world views, the Westerner is likely to make an attribution of incompetence. In turn, the Greek is likely to make an attribution of impatience or rudeness.

Language is not a neutral medium of communication. Workers and clients express their ethnicity through language. Before the worker can use theory-specific interviewing techniques, such as empathic responding, to explore the subtleties of client communication, the worker needs first to learn the cultural context within which clients express such sensibilities.

Cultural Linguistics and Mental Lexicons

Many factors, such as culture, race, ethnicity, gender, age, and class, affect the use of language and its interpretation. Language is a cultural product. It is a behaviorally active agent and a signifier of an individual's ethnic affiliations. According to the Sapir-Whorf hypothesis (Green, 1995), the real world is constructed according to the received linguistic traditions of a culture. We see, hear, and otherwise experience as we do because the language habits of our community predispose certain choices of interpretation.

Closely associated with the idea that language is culture-bound is Aitchison's (1983) idea of a mental lexicon. In a mental lexicon, words have an identification function. They stand as proxies for specific ideas, relationships, and actions. The human mind organizes information by filtering it through linguistic mazes that constitute a cultural template. Words are organized into semantic networks or fields so that they tend to cluster. For instance, for every individual, the single word "flu" links to different mental lexicons about what causes it, how one knows one has it, how it should be treated, and how benign or dangerous it is. No two people are likely to share the exact same mental lexicon on flu.

Being aware of one's own and another's filters is an intellectually and emotionally intensive activity. This is especially true in the helping professions. The social work profession's curricular emphasis on teaching communication skills is therefore critical to competent direct practice. According to Ivey (1994), 80% of communication is nonverbal. Nonverbal behavior, such as use of space, eye contact, gestures, silence, and orientation to time, are influenced by culture. Cultural filters can and do bias assessments and the choice of interventions. They can interfere with the establishment of a working relationship (Sue & Sue, 2003).

■ Worker-Client Differences

Cross-Cultural Social Work

When practiced in the United States, *cross-cultural* social work refers to a worker-client relationship where the worker is native to the United States and the client is foreign-born and has as his/her first language one other than English. The term also refers to American social workers who engage in international social work practice in foreign countries. Sometimes the term is used to connote worker-client differences based on race, ethnicity, gender, and class though both worker and client were born in America and share English as their first language. Ethnographic interviewing is appropriate in those situations where the client is foreign-born and in those situations where worker-client differences based on diversity impact the establishment of a working relationship, accurate assessment, and appropriate intervention. Studies (e.g., Sue, Zane, & Young, 1994; Vargas & Koss-Chioino, 1992) show that the failure to use culturally appropriate language and techniques when interviewing seriously compromises the worker's ability to engage minority clients in a helping relationship.

Racial and Ethnic Differences Between the Worker and the Client

Words do more than label; they impose an order on perception, create categories of things, and suggest something of what the categories might be worth (values). Words reveal a person's storehouse of information about how the world is organized and how it operates. To assume that race and ethnicity make no difference because we are all human and because one's pain is no less painful than another's is an error. To adopt a stance of sameness or color-blindness is to discount and devalue the individual's heritage. It is also an error to assume that worker-client differences are so great that communicating and establishing a working relationship with each other is impossible.

The worker-client alliance is critically important in cross-cultural social work and in work with diverse clients. The statistically typical social worker in the United States is middle class, college educated, white, young, and female. The statistically typical client in the United States in need of concrete services is an older female with less than a high school education from a lower socioeconomic class who is a member of a minority group. The client often lacks information on what social work is and how the client should behave with the worker. Lacking specific knowledge of the client's culture, the worker also does not know how to engage or treat the client in a manner that is culturally familiar and appropriate.

A number of studies on racial and ethnic matching have been conducted (Atkinson, 1983; Leong, 1986). Such studies report that racial, ethnic, and gender matching, in and of itself, is no guarantee that a working relationship between the worker and client will be formed. There is also ample evidence that working relationships can and have been established in the absence of such matching. Nonetheless, how attitudes and stereotypes about race, color, ethnicity, class, and gender are processed within the therapeutic arena is an important area to be discussed when establishing a competent working relationship. Another error is to assume that similarity and a shared language produce a shared reality. Similar users of the same language create alternative realities as well.

Ethnically Sensitive Practice and Culturally Responsive Practice

A stance of being open to difference is not adequate for developing an understanding of others. Culturally competent practice requires substantive descriptive knowledge specific to different cultural, racial, and ethnic groups. Texts that cover topics on developmental landmarks, beliefs about gender and role, norms about emotional expression, and attitudes about sexuality and identity represent a passive appreciation of difference. Such an approach is referred to as *ethnically sensitive* practice (Devore & Schlesinger, 1998). Adding to this perspective, Vargas and Koss-Chioino (1992) advocate for what they call *culturally responsive* practice. The goal of culturally responsive practice is to integrate the culture of each ethnic minority into the form and process of direct practice, to develop ethno-psychotherapies.

In developing specific ethno-psychotherapy models, Vargas and Koss-Chioino distinguish culture as content and culture as context. *Culture as content* consists of the pattern of religious beliefs, world views, and self-views that can be described in ethnically sensitive texts. *Culture as context* refers to the particular features of a subpopulation's status within a dominant culture. Oppression, prejudice, racism, immigration, resettlement, acculturation, poverty, separation from family of origin, and generational conflicts are subpopulation themes for which individuals who are members of a minority group may need therapy. It is an error to limit social work practice with members of minority groups to the provision of concrete services only. Members of minority groups are entitled to a full range of services, including therapy.

■ Interviewing Skills

The Ethnographic Interview

The interview (worker-client dialogue) is a process through which information is gathered as part of assessment and through which intervention is carried out and a relationship enacted. Ethnographic interviewing is one way to move beyond Western culture when gathering client information.

While there is no single, standardized procedure for ethnographic interviewing, the central idea is to focus on the linguistic features of client dialogue. One

such linguistic feature is the presence of casual phrases and words that are familiar to the client but that stand out to the cultural outsider. The literature in cultural anthropology refers to such words and phrases as *cover terms*. The collection
and annotation of cover terms by the worker is basic to ethnographic interviewing. Exploring such terms structures the narrative flow of the interview. The
worker uses the client in the role of guide to acquire descriptors of a culture that
is unfamiliar to the worker. This differs from and goes beyond such interviewing
techniques as paraphrasing and prompting.

When the client is used as a cultural guide in the exploration of cover terms,
the worker develops a client-taught ethnographic mental lexicon. Communicative competence is to hear and respond appropriately to the language habits that
are familiar to someone else. It does not mean that the worker uses the terminology of the client; it means the worker understands how the terminology reflects
the cultural and personal language habits of the client. This is the beginning of
real communicative cross-cultural competence and must precede any interview
techniques that probe for deep sociological or psychological meaning related to
the client's situation. The purpose of the ethnographic interview is to gather
ethnographic data specific to understanding and defining the needs of the client
and to defining interventions that the client regards as acceptable.

Foreign Language: Using Translators

Not all social work can be done in English. Different languages do create and express different realities. All languages contain an extensive vocabulary descriptive
of physical and mental discomfort. It is important for the worker to understand
the language of illness and pain as well as the language of strengths in the culture
of the client. Nuances of meaning are best conveyed in one's first or native language. Cross-cultural sensitivity is not a matter of grammar or pronunciation. It
is a matter of understanding how vocabulary expresses a client's distress. When
the worker is not fluent in the language of the client and the client speaks little or
no English, it is essential to use a translator.

It is the worker's responsibility to overcome language barriers. Monolingual-
ism is a handicap in cross-cultural social work. One way to overcome this handicap is to learn the language of your client population. When an agency serves a
client population characterized by multiple foreign languages, it is critical that
the agency provide and the worker have access to translators.

Kadushin (1990) provides several guides to using a translator. The first is to use
a trained translator and not a member of the client's family. Using a member of a
client's family can violate the kinship and power structure within a family. This
must also be considered when using an outside translator. It is important to know
where power resides within a specific cultural group and how kinship affiliations
are structured. The assignment of a translator to a client is more complex than
language fluency alone. Many cultural groups have norms against "prying" into

unpleasant matters, and an untrained translator, though fluent in the language, may sanitize or shield the questions and answers. Beyond being fluent, a good translator is one who is practiced in interviewing and who accurately and fairly translates both sides of the dialogue. When using a translator, it is important for the worker to look at and speak to the client, not the translator. Extra time should be allowed, and the agenda should be kept short. There should be frequent summaries to check understanding, and a report should be written immediately after the interview.

■ Generic and Theory-Specific Interviewing Skills

Generic Interviewing Skills

There are some interviewing techniques that are common to all interviews. The two primary techniques are the use of open- or closed-ended questions. An open-ended question is phrased to elicit unrestricted information, e.g., "Tell me about . . ." or "Say more about that." Open-ended questions are phrased in such a way as to preclude a single, one-word response. Closed-ended phrasing such as "Can you tell me what happened?" can cue a one-word response: "No." A closed-ended question is designed to elicit specific and limited information, e.g., "What is your date of birth?" or "Are you employed?" Interviewing techniques such as prompting (nodding, leaning forward, saying "umm" or "go on"), furthering (and that . . . , then . . . , and you . . .), paraphrasing ("you felt her comment was disrespectful"), checking ("do I understand correctly that . . . ?") can be used to facilitate any interview process. Many of the interviewing techniques associated with psychodynamic theory have been used generically to establish a warm, authentic, and genuine helping relationship (Hepworth, Rooney, & Larsen, 2002).

Theory-Based Lines of Inquiry

It is important to recognize that mainstream psychotherapies and their interviewing techniques are historically and culturally situated. Therefore, any theory-based line of inquiry must be critically examined for cultural bias. Like culture, theory-specific lines of inquiry order perception, create categories of things, and suggest something of what the categories might be worth (values). A theory-based line of inquiry directs the worker-client dialogue in a manner consistent with the theory's premises and concepts.

Psychodynamic Interviewing Techniques

Social workers trained in this model observe both verbal and nonverbal communication. They are taught to be aware of content (what is actually said) and process (how it is said, in what sequence). They use a "third ear" to discern metacommunication. The third ear is based on the premise that what is communicated is both manifest (what is actually said) and latent (what is said indirectly or left unsaid). A basic tenet of the model is that encoding and decoding is selective; some information will be ignored and other information rearranged. It holds that information that threatens self-esteem, that is rejecting, or that provokes anxiety will be neither encoded or decoded.

The psychodynamic model refers to this reluctance as resistance reflective of suppression or unconscious repression. It understands such reluctance as the ego's subconscious or unconscious attempt to defend itself. Therefore, in this type of interview, the interviewer employs psychological principles and procedures in an effort to exercise a deliberate, controlled influence on the psychic functioning of the interviewee. Often, the worker will use techniques to make explicit what is often recognized but left unstated in the interview. The interviewer attends to nonverbal communication as an indicator of subconscious or unconscious influences on verbal communication. Vocalizations, pauses, inflections, amplitude, and tone are all considered to be as significant, if not more significant, than what is directly conveyed verbally. According to this theory, individuals employ defense mechanisms in their communication. They often mistake who said what (displacement) or hear the opposite of what was said (reaction formation) or project onto the interviewer their own thoughts or feelings (projection). The worker also uses techniques to eliminate counterproductive communication patterns in the therapeutic interview (Hepworth, Rooney, & Larsen, 2002).

The techniques are such that unpleasant facts and feelings are not to be avoided. Beyond eliciting information for diagnostic purposes, psychodynamic theory directs the worker's use of self in the therapeutic relationship primarily through empathic responding. This will be elaborated upon in chapter 6 (the clinical relationship).

Other Theory-Specific Lines of Inquiry

When the purpose of the interview is to determine a client's eligibility for concrete services (step 3 of the decision tree), such an interview is guided by task-centered lines of inquiry. Closed-ended questions are asked to elicit facts relevant to the determination of client need and eligibility for services. This is likely to involve one to three interviews. The determination of need and eligibility structures the worker-client relationship. The worker possesses the authority to allocate resources based on client need.

When the purpose of the interview is to change client behavior through talk therapy (step 5), the social worker may choose behavioral learning theory. A behavioral line of inquiry elicits information on the frequency (baseline) of the behavior identified as in need of change. It identifies antecedent cues and responses (stimuli-response: classical conditioning) and consequent events (positive and negative reinforcement: operant conditioning). Because behavior modification is often used with those who have impaired cognitive functioning or with those under the care of others, the worker's relationship may be primarily with collateral sources (parents, teachers, guardians). The worker educates those who are in positions of authority to change the contingencies that maintain the behavior targeted for change. Often, there is no direct worker-client relationship. See the process recording in chapter 13 on Kyle for an illustration of behavior modification with a young child.

Given theory choice, the worker may select a line of inquiry consistent with strengths-based social work. This model focuses on discovering strengths that the client already possesses. Inquiries probe for goals rather than past events (DeJong & Miller, 1995). In the interview, the social worker asks questions pertaining to exceptions (when things went well) and identifies past coping skills (skills used previously when the client faced adversity). Inquiries elicit client goals by asking the miracle question, i.e., what would be different if a miracle happened while you were sleeping?

Not exhaustive, these examples demonstrate that gathering information during interviews is more theory-specific than not. Critical thinking skills are needed to take into account information that is discrepant from the line of inquiry that is being pursued. Discrepant information should trigger a reassessment of the worker's choice of theory and line of exploration.

Interviewing Special Populations

Children

Students often complain that texts that illustrate interviewing techniques are based on an assumption of adult language competency. Foundation-year students, particularly, are often assigned clients whose language is compromised by development or by illnesses that affect expression. Interviewing children, adolescents, and less-verbal clients requires a modification of interview technique regardless of one's theory choice. Infants lack language and for toddlers, it is developing. The child's grasp of reality is tied to language (Piaget, 1950). Nonetheless, infants and young children have a great deal of experiential history long before they have the language skills to capture and convey it. Infants communicate through body language. As children acquire a vocabulary, it is important for the interviewer to place the child's verbal communication within an appropriate stage of language development. Interviewing then consists of direct observation. As minors, no child or adolescent may be observed or interviewed without parental or legal custodial consent. In fact, parents or other caretakers are essential collateral sources of information on the behavior and needs of infants and children. Many beginning social work students (because of their own age) express a preference for working with children or adolescents. They fail to realize that they must also acquire skills and competence in working with the adults who care for these children and adolescents. Dealing with dyads (parent/child) requires greater sophistication of knowledge and technique.

With children, it is important to assess language development (expressive, receptive language disorders, speech and hearing, intellectual functioning) as well as fine and gross motor skills and relationship skills. The social worker must consider a child's play as communication (Timberlake & Cutler, 2000). Play is differentially assessed depending on one's theory. The same play content could reflect emotional development through fantasy and magical thinking (Fraiberg, 1959) or the preoperational stage of cognitive development (Piaget, 1950). Alternatively, play could function as a means of indirect communication regarding real events in the child's life (e.g., play could depict abuse). Finally, play (as fantasy) could be perceived as imagination and creativity, leading to a sense of self-esteem and competence, and as a mechanism of socialization and skill training.

Adolescents

Ethnographic techniques can be put to excellent use when interviewing adolescents. Interviewing this client population requires knowledge of the adolescent's capacity to take into account the view of another as well as his/her capacity for formal operational thought (Piaget, 1950). Adolescence is a developmental stage. It is also a culture defined by the historical period within which it occurs. The worker's adolescence is not the client's adolescence, culturally speaking.

When interviewing adolescents, the interviewer should avoid the use of the personal pronoun "you." The adolescent should be used as a cultural guide. Inquiries should be cast in terms of the impersonal generalized other. Phrase an inquiry in terms of "What would make an adolescent do that?" or "What are adolescents thinking when they . . . ?" or "Tell me what some adolescents find so powerful in such music, or such lyrics, or such a movie?" In interviewing adolescents, encourage the narrative. Have them describe the meaning behind tattoos, bands, clothes, shoes, jewelry, concerts. Do not use the language of the adolescent. Explore adolescent terminology to gain an understanding of their world view. By explaining the general adolescent, the individual adolescent will often differentiate him/herself. Avoid power struggles if at all possible. Remember, a student interviewer cannot make an adolescent talk even if a process recording is due.

Chronically Mentally Ill and Delusional Clients

For many students, their first interview is with an individual diagnosed with chronic and persistent mental illness. *Chronic* is a time marker indicating that the mental disorder has developed over a long period of time. *Persistent* refers to the ongoing nature of the disorder. *Mental illness* refers to a particular pattern of abnormal behavior. The *Diagnostic and Statistical Manual* (DSM-IVR) categorizes such disorders by describing observable behaviors, the origin of the disorder, its

EXHIBIT 4.1 *Sample Beginning and Ethnographic Process Recording*

Thinking Declarative Knowledge	Dialogue Theory-Driven Therapeutic Process	Worker Self-Awareness Monitoring Skill and Feeling
Greeting Ethnic difference, names are important	Worker: Hello, Mr. S. My name is Mary Gatto. Did I pronounce your name correctly?	Afraid I'll mispronounce his name
He is willing to be a cultural guide	Mr. S: Well, it is difficult to pronounce. It means son of Stavros. Stavros means "cross" in Greek. Your name is Italian, isn't it?	Worried that I might not understand him if his English is poor
Most people from foreign cultures have multilingual skills Informed consent: student status	Worker: Yes, it is. I am impressed. I am a member of the hospice bereavement team, but actually, I'm a graduate student in social work doing an internship at the hospice.	Relief: his English is very good Afraid he won't want to talk with me because I'm a student
Purpose Closed question	Worker: We usually check in several times in the first year of bereavement to see how people are doing. How are you doing? Mr. S: Fine.	Incompetent: I asked a closed-ended question
Open-ended request	Worker: Tell me more about how it has been for you since your wife died this past summer.	I feel intrusive on his private pain
Nonverbal, not doing so fine, discrepancy between his words and his behavior	Mr. S's eyes fill with tears.	Panic: I've hurt him Sad: my own grandfather died just 6 months ago
Empathic responding, validating both verbal and nonverbal	Worker: Even though people are doing well after they lose someone they love, they can still feel sad.	Competent
	Mr. S: I'm so glad you stopped by. I have wanted to talk to someone.	Relieved
Identifying armband as cultural cue, asking Mr. S to be a cultural guide	Worker: I see you are wearing a black armband. I think it is a sign of mourning. Can you tell me how your culture deals with death?	Curious

(continued)

EXHIBIT 4.1 *Sample Beginning and Ethnographic Process Recording* (*continued*)

Thinking Declarative Knowledge	Dialogue Theory-Driven Therapeutic Process	Worker Self-Awareness Monitoring Skill and Feeling
Cultural norms around grieving, strong ethnic ties	Mr. S: In my culture, we signify that we are in mourning for a year. Most wear armbands or black clothes. We are not like you Americans, acting as if nothing happened in 2 weeks.	Interested
	Worker: I think the way your culture grieves may be better.	Reflective
Contracting for service	Worker: If you like, Mr. S, I could check in with you once a month for the next 6 months to see how things are going and to talk about your plans, your interests.	Concerned that he might not want me to come back
Consent to treatment	Mr. S: I'd like that.	Glad
Limits to confidentiality, informed consent	Worker: Good, so would I. When we talk, I'd like you to know that, for educational purposes, I will share what we discuss with my supervisor, who will know your name. When I am in class, I will never use any identifying information about you when I talk about my placement. With these exceptions, what you say to me will be confidential. If there is a reason to share information with anyone else, I will get your written consent.	Awkward: afraid he'll say no thank you
	Mr. S: OK.	Wow
Duty to protect, duty to report, duty to obey the law	Worker: I have three other obligations. If you tell me that you plan to harm yourself or someone else or break the law, I must report it and take actions to assure your safety and that of others.	Unsure of how he will react
He has strengths	Mr. S: It's always good to have someone looking out for you.	Feel good

Thinking Declarative Knowledge	Dialogue Theory-Driven Therapeutic Process	Worker Self-Awareness Monitoring Skill and Feeling
Availability, access	Worker: Thanks, Mr. S. I will see you next month. Here is my number in case something comes up and you want to talk before then. Nice to meet you. I look forward to our next meeting.	Hopeful

prognosis, and likely course over time. Schizophrenia and other psychotic disorders are prominent among the chronically mentally ill subpopulation. A common feature of these disorders is the presence of delusions. A *delusion* is defined as an inaccurate belief that cannot be changed by rational argument or a demonstration of relevant facts.

Students are unlikely to be prepared for their first interview with a member of this subpopulation. This is especially true where schools have opted to eliminate psychopathology from their curriculum or have pushed it to the second year as part of a clinical concentration. Unprepared students immediately report a disconnect between what is being taught about interviewing in the classroom and what they experience in the field.

Lacking preparation, student and client are endangered. The student may not be aware of the seriousness of the disorder and its potential for flare-up should medication no longer control it. The student may overreact to the florid aspects of delusions and hallucinations. Client delusions may contain primitive expressions of impulses which are often sexual or violent in nature. Student and client safety require that the student have knowledge of psychopathology and knowledge of the procedures and techniques used to deal with symptom manifestation. Students often report that the purpose of the interview is unclear to them when they are sent to interview a nonverbal or low-verbal client or a client whose expressive language is compromised by serious illness. Class and field supervisors must be more directive in educating students to work realistically with such clients.

Clients With Delirium and Dementia

Similarly, students are often assigned to work with elderly clients who suffer from delirium or dementia. Students express confusion and frustration when asked to produce process recordings when assigned such clients. While a student could contact a family member of an elderly client so assessed, the contact would have to have a defined purpose. The purpose of assigning students to clients with dementia may be to acquaint the student with the manifestation of the illness and its progress. When working with such nonverbal clients, activities could be utilized, such as playing music, reading, applying nail polish, brushing hair, going out for a walk, etc. Such activities may be categorized as improving the quality of life of the client. For the purpose of student learning, a student needs to have some clients with intact verbal skills.

5

Communication Skills for Policy, Advocacy, Management, and Community Practice

■ Nonclinical Communication Skills

Most social work foundation-year texts, including social work generalist texts, focus on the communication skills needed for entry-level clinical practice. The frequently offered rationale is that such communication skills are needed for foundation-year field placements (they are) and are transferable and appropriate for use in policy, management, community, and advocacy practice. While such skills may be an asset, they are not sufficient for the tasks performed by social workers in policy, advocacy, community, and management practice (sometimes referred to as *macro* practice). Communication skills different from those used in social work clinical practice are needed.

Macro communication skills support method and theory choice in steps 2 (crisis management), 3 (case management), 4 (advocacy), and 7 (use of groups in policy, advocacy, management, and community practice). Nonclinical communication skills are needed when the case at hand requires assessment of and intervention with social forces. Despite their utilization within second-year specializations, familiarity with such skills is needed by foundation-year and B.S.W. seniors. Entry-level social workers often need to communicate with nonclients (Garvin & Seabury, 1997), know how to negotiate agency bureaucracy, work with colleagues, and advocate for clients.

Communication Formats

In clinical social work practice, communication is condensed into a few common written formats: client records, progress notes, case studies or case presentations, intake forms, transfer or termination summaries, documentation for reimbursement by managed-care or other third-party payers, affidavits, and reports. Oral communication occurs in clinical case conferences and team meetings. The primary form of interactive communication is the worker-client therapeutic session discussed in chapter 6.

In contrast, communication in social work macro practice produces advocacy networks, white papers, policies, and social events (actions). Communication in macro practice occurs in written format as formal narratives, statements, reports, letters, written policies and procedures, memos, regulations, e-mails, agendas, and minutes of meetings. Oral communication occurs as public testimony and public speeches. Communication also occurs as social events and social actions. Communication in social work macro practice is said, written, and acted. It is both formal and static and informal and dynamic.

The Concept of the Nonclient

Kirst-Ashman and Hull (2004) provide language that is helpful in understanding the concept of other client systems. They identify three basic client systems with which the generalist practitioner is likely to work: the target client system, the change agent system, and the beneficiary client system. The *beneficiary client system* is defined as those clients who potentially benefit from a policy, program, project, or organizing initiative. Direct communication between a macro practitioner and this client group is rare unless its members are enlisted (empowered) to become part of the change agent system. The *change agent system* consists of the practitioner who initiates change and those who join with the practitioner as allies in the change effort (activist volunteers, professional or nonprofessional). The third group is referred to as the *target client system*. Members of this group are targeted for change because they support the status quo and block desired reform. On any given day, a macro social work practitioner may communicate with peers, supervisors, subordinates, task groups, boards, committees, those more influential and powerful, those who are disfranchised, those who are targeted for change, and those who are volunteers in the change effort. Communication in social work macro practice often involves the coordination of many individuals working independently of each other. There are four types of communication in macro social work practice: (1) communication that conveys fiduciary responsibilities, (2) communication that facilitates getting the job done (task), (3) communication that deals with public relations, and (4) communication that is motivational, persuasive, and inspirational.

■ Fiduciary Conduct and Misconduct

Policy Practice

The fiduciary context of policy practice lies in policy legislation that gets institutionalized as public law. Court rulings uphold or overturn existing authorizing legislation or public laws. Written regulatory policies are found in governmental organizations with oversight functions while agency-specific policies are contained in agency operations manuals. Fiduciary misconduct in policy practice occurs as false testimony before a legislative body or in a court of law. It occurs as failure to comply with rules and regulations in the determination of eligibility and in the distribution of resources.

Advocacy Practice

In advocacy practice, activists often challenge the status quo through acts of civil disobedience. Nonviolent and peaceful demonstrations require notification of the planned events to authorities and the acquisition of appropriate permits. Participants in acts of civil disobedience must be informed of their legal rights and of the legal consequences that may befall them because of their participation in such events. Fiduciary misconduct in advocacy practice involves acts that fall outside legal parameters. By definition, the tactics of social action involve speech that can be viewed as incendiary and therefore prohibited, despite the legal protection of free speech. The right to assemble can be viewed as trespass, and a march can be seen as a provocation to riot. Written or verbal attacks aimed at individuals targeted for change can result in lawsuits based on claims of libel, slander, or harassment.

Community Practice

Research surveys gather information to ascertain community needs and patterns of resource utilization. The collection and presentation of such data are expected to be valid, reliable, and free from bias (nonfraudulent). Surveys that involve human beings must comply with ethical standards governing human-subject research. Participants in survey research have the right to informed consent. Because community practice deals with incremental change within an ordered, existing system, community planners must comply with the laws and regulations of appropriate state, regional, county, and city/town governing bodies and their designated agencies. A participatory democratic process requires that all citizens be notified of proposed community changes and their input sought at community hearings. There is the fiduciary assumption that a fair and honest democratic process (including voting on a proposal) will be followed to determine community needs, resources, and goals.

Fiduciary misconduct lies in the falsification of data and the failure to comply with regional, state, and local planning regulations and procedures. Failure to follow and abide by established democratic processes or procedures is misconduct. Bribery and the undue use of influence and power can undermine fair proceedings.

Management Practice

In social work management practice, fiduciary communication occurs in several forms. It occurs internally in written format as mission statements, agency operations manuals, and job descriptions. Employee contracts delineate the tasks to be performed and ensure workers of their rights and entitlement to benefits. Fiduciary communication with external bodies involves documentation of compliance with licensing standards and work regulations established by regulatory bodies. Communication involves the preparation of annual fiscal reports to appointed boards and outside funding sources. Official written reports go to regulatory bodies that have oversight functions, be they professional organizations or federal, state, regional, or local bodies of authority. For purposes of planning, agencies must track requests for services and service delivery. Sociodemographic statistics and patterns of service utilization must be kept.

When communicating with those who have oversight authority, managers must communicate in numbers to verify need, progress toward goals, supply fiscal accountability, and evaluate outcome success. Communication with regulatory bodies must contain evidence of compliance with specified standards. Like all other businesses, social work agencies are required to adhere to nondiscrimination laws in hiring, promotion, and firing and must adhere to laws governing sexual harassment in the workplace. All agencies should have a formal grievance procedure for handling conflicts between employees and between employees and their employer. Agencies are also obligated to take all reasonable precautions to assure the safety of employees on the job. Safety plans and procedures must be in place.

Fiduciary failures in management practice usually fall under fiscal irregularities or noncompliance with rules and regulations. Usually, bodies with oversight function ask that financial irregularities be fixed and require agencies to become compliant with rules and regulations. Often, agencies are placed on probation or, in some cases, if public, placed in receivership until they can meet regulatory standards.

Chief executive officers or managers can become involved in fraudulent acts. This often involves falsification of records or documents (including data) or the embezzlement of funds. Embezzlement is a felony offense leading to fines and imprisonment if one is found guilty. Where there is malfeasance in the execution of administrative duties, directors can be charged, fired, or forced to resign.

Finally, agencies are held accountable for the safety of their clients. In cases where resident clients are injured, attack other clients or agency personnel, or hurt themselves, agencies are potentially liable. Usually there will be an investigation to determine culpability. Pending the outcome of such an investigation, penalties will follow. Students who are in an agency at a time when such events occur are cautioned against discussing such events in the classroom because of the legal liabilities involved.

■ Task Communication in Policy, Advocacy, Community, and Management Practice

Communication about getting the job done is referred to as *task communication*. Tasks differ in each of the four areas of macro social work practice.

Policy Practice

Communication in policy practice has three purposes: (1) policy analysis, (2) policy development, and (3) policy implementation. Proposed or existing policies are analyzed for their legislative and judicial history, for their value premises, for their socioeconomic and political impact, and for their feasibility. Once implemented, policies are analyzed for their delivery infrastructure, i.e., authorizing legislation, programmatic components, eligibility rules and regulations, intended recipients, level of funding, and organizational structures to ensure service delivery.

Policy development begins with the articulation of values. Theories of social justice usually inform communication about the desired end goal of a policy or a policy initiative. Because policy groups often differ either in their articulation of desired goals or in the means to those goals, communication must use persuasive speech to inspire support for policy initiatives. The implementation of one value-based policy initiative over another usually requires the tactics (techniques) of power and influence. Such tactics are informed by conflict theory and cognitive political theory.

Policy communication must attend to the audience. Communication with supporters will differ from communication used with opponents, and both types of communication will differ from that used to communicate with the general public. Task communication in social work policy practice targets specific interest groups to gain support and to minimize opposition.

Advocacy Practice

Advocacy practice may occur as part of incremental change or as part of revolutionary large-scale social change. When part of incremental change, advocacy communication relies on leadership, consensus building, and conflict negotiation.

When advocacy involves large-scale or radical structural change, communication involves the logistics of moving small and large groups to engage in actions (civil disobedience, nonviolent protests). Structural change is associated with large-scale social action, such as the civil rights movement, the labor movement, and the feminist movement. Indigenous, charismatic leadership is needed. Social workers often play a supportive role. Social action requires recruitment of both a core group and a larger membership group that can be called upon as needed. This requires motivational speech to recruit and maintain a dedicated corps of activist volunteers. The task of coordinating the movements of small and large groups requires planning and logistical skills.

Primary communication tasks in social work advocacy practice are to raise consciousness among the disfranchised about their oppression and to raise consciousness among the privileged about their lifestyle. Both empowerment theory and the theories of small groups for social action inform this type of communication. Participants in advocacy efforts must be educated as to their rights and potential violations of those rights. Like conflict theory, empowerment theory challenges an ordered (legal) perspective. The purpose of advocacy practice is to remedy a status quo that is perceived to be oppressive and nonresponsive to the needs of some members of the community.

Community Practice

Task communication in community practice involves the assessment of needs and resources. It requires the identification of indigenous leaders and the identification or recruitment of a critical mass of community members who desire change (or who wish to prevent encroachment on their community). This type of communication is informed by rational planning. PERT (Project Evaluation Review Technique) charts or other procedural step models are used to achieve agreed-upon community goals. Communication in social work community practice requires knowledge of local political and social structures. Community practice is informed by order theories that seek incremental change within the status quo.

Management Practice

Task communication in management practice serves three purposes: (1) to ensure the delivery of a quality product or service, (2) to establish a workforce that is competent and cooperative, and (3) to provide corrective feedback. As a tactic aimed toward an outcome, the goal of task communication in management is to get things done effectively by working with and through others. Therefore, it is important that managers have the communication skills to establish and convey tasks that require technical or professional expertise and communication competence in managing human resources. A competent administrator must manage ideas as well as personnel and must assure that tasks and activities are carried out in a timely manner. This requires skill in managing and communicating with individuals and work teams. It requires both internal and external communication and communication with superiors and subordinates. Interagency communication must also occur to avoid duplication of services and to assure a coordinated system of care. Advanced technology makes the coordination of services feasible through the electronic transfer of records and the maintenance of data banks. Technology improves the internal monitoring of service delivery to assure quality.

■ Public Relations Communication

Policy Practice

In social work policy practice, public relations communication humanizes social issues. Profiles of individual social workers or specific social work clients are often used to justify the expenditures associated with service delivery or to illustrate the inadequacy of resources to meet a need. Case scenarios are often presented in testimony before governmental bodies and often appear as features in newspapers or in television reports. Books on homeless women (Elliot Liebow's 1993 *Tell Them Who I Am: The Lives of Homeless Women*), on intimate partner abuse (Roberts and Roberts's 2005 *Ending Intimate Abuse*), and on welfare (Kotlowitz's 1991 *There Are No Children Here*) illustrate the need for social policies through the lives they document. Movies, documentaries, DVDs, and videos visualize social issues. For example, *It's Elementary* (1996) talks about gay issues in schools; *The Milagro Beanfield War* (1988) deals with racism, classism, and poverty; *The Saint of Ft. Washington* (1993) shows homelessness, poverty, and mental illness. On occasion, public relations communication must also troubleshoot negative publicity.

Advocacy Practice

In contrast to the solidarity sought in community planning, public relations in organizing practice accepts polarization as a healthy and inevitable aspect of practice. The aim of a public relations campaign is therefore to get a story (ideology) out. It is a one-sided argument for a particular value-based position in opposition to the views and positions presented by others. In this sense, it is similar to a legal brief that advocates for one outcome over another.

Public relations communication in organizing practice targets three groups: (1) those with similar values to enlist their support in the cause, (2) those who are neutral in the hope of maintaining their neutrality and preventing them from going over to the opposition, and (3) those who are opponents by responding to and countering their talking points in an effort to win public opinion.

Community Practice

In social work community practice, public relations communication is aimed at establishing an appropriate working relationship between community practitioners (external: outsiders) and indigenous members (internal: insiders) of a community. Professional community practitioners must introduce (sell) themselves as resources and facilitators of a community-led initiative. The insider-outsider dynamic requires practitioners to be foot soldiers in promoting and coaching internal leadership. An effective public relations campaign must sell a vision of a valued product (planning outcome), its costs and benefits to the community as a whole, and a timeline within which the envisioned changes are to occur and the outsiders are to depart. Public relations communication must respect local culture and, if possible, minimize the polarization of community subgroups. Change should occur within the nonpolarizing context of building community solidarity. The practitioner's code is, first, do no harm.

Management Practice

In social work management practice, public relations communication occurs with professional constituents, the general population, and the clientele of the agency. Conveying what the agency does and how well it does it requires communication skills in public relations. Recognizing that social work serves the disfranchised and marginalized, public relations campaigns strive to create a receptive (or at least neutral) climate among the general public. Part of public relations in management practice involves fundraising. Cultivating persons with financial resources and/or social influence establishes the agency (whether public or private) as a valued community resource.

An important component of public relations communication in social work management practice consists of advertising the agency's services to potential clients. Such communication must be multilingual to take into account language differences among the client populations targeted for service. The conditions of eligibility, hours of operation, agency location, and types of services provided need to be communicated. This is done in brochures, multilingual automated phone directories, advertising on buses, and in institutions such as churches, health clinics, grocery stores, etc. Agencies also advertise positions for professional and support personnel.

Public relations communication with professional constituents consists of sponsoring or hosting in-service trainings, workshops, symposiums, and conferences. Fundraising social events or galas where awards are presented and speakers address topical issues serve as another format for public relations. Public relations communication is used to recruit volunteers and to develop them as ambassadors for the agency and its mission. Students in field placements are expected to be goodwill ambassadors of the agency in their conversations with their peers, other professionals, the general public, and the clients they serve.

■ Persuasive Communication and Motivational Speech

Persuasive communication differs from public relations communication in that the message advocates for a view or action. According to O'Keefe (2001), persuasive discourse has the capacity to move hearts and minds and to transform people and situations in remarkably powerful ways. It is concerned with directing and shaping belief, achieving consensus, and moving others to action. Successful persuasion requires adapting the discourse to the audience's state of mind.

Source Characteristics

The two most influential characteristics of those who engage in persuasive communication are credibility and liking. A speaker's credibility (believability) is based on audience perception of the speaker's competence (expertise, knowledge). Whether or not audience members find the speaker likable also influences their receptivity to the message. Characteristics such as physical attractiveness, ethnicity, and perceived trustworthiness (honesty, sincerity) influence the determination of likability. How the speaker is received by other members of the audience also influences another member's judgment of the speaker. Some members of an audience are influenced by the quality of the presenter's argument and the evidentiary nature of the facts presented. Others are influenced more by the speaker's likability.

Message Characteristics

Characteristics of the message also influence how it will be received. There are three characteristics: (1) message sidedness, (2) emotional appeals, and (3) conclusion explicitness (O'Keefe, 2001). *Message sidedness* refers to how the speaker handles opposing arguments. A speaker can ignore the opponent's view and present a one-sided argument; the speaker can discuss opposing views in a comparative fashion; or the speaker can refute opposing arguments, point by point. Evidence suggests that one-sided messages are less persuasive than messages that refute an opponent's argument point by point.

Another message characteristic is its appeal to emotion. Fear appeal is a message designed to arouse a sense of threat in the audience in the hope of motivating acceptance of the speaker's recommended course of action. Other appeals target such emotions as pity, guilt, or idealism. An appeal to fear is more powerful than other types of emotional appeal. Messages with explicit conclusions are more persuasive than messages with implicit conclusions.

Changing Attitudes and Mobilizing for Action

Two theories explain attitudes: the expectancy-value model and the functional model. The first model holds that beliefs about something are structured. According to the expectancy-value model, each belief is associated with a valence and an evaluation of the likelihood that belief in the policy, proposal, product, or person will in fact produce what it purports. For instance, public attitudes toward Social Security are subject to current efforts by the two political parties to change the valence associated with "security" from a guaranteed minimum income to a potentially greater amount if invested through personal accounts.

Another technique for changing attitudinal valence is to introduce uncertainty about a policy, product, or person. For instance, claims of impending bankruptcy of the Social Security system introduce uncertainty. Members of an audience are more likely to change their attitude under such circumstances. When uncertainty is inserted about a new initiative (e.g., can it do what it says it can do?), members of the audience are less likely to adopt favorable attitudes toward it.

The functional model of attitude change suggests that a person's self-image is based either on symbolic or instrumental values. To change attitudes, persuasive appeal must match the instrumental or symbolic needs of the audience. For instance, to sell cars, persuasion must resonate either with how good one looks or feels in a specific car (symbolic value) or with its gas mileage and ease of parking (instrumental value).

It is one thing to change another's attitude about a social issue through persuasive speech and quite another to get that person to engage in activist behavior. How difficult it is to perform a desired behavior (personal cost) is likely to influence whether behavior change follows attitudinal change.

■ Application of Persuasive Communication and
   Motivational Speech to Macro Practice

Policy Practice

Persuasive speech can be used as a tool in principled advocacy or as a tool of propaganda. According to Webster (1977, p. 923), *propaganda* is defined as the spreading of ideas, information, or rumor for the purpose of helping or injuring an institution, a cause, or a person. Propaganda is the deliberate and systematic manipulation of public opinion, generally by the use of symbols such as flags, monuments, oratory, and publications. It is used to control group (mass) attitudes. The purpose of propaganda is not to inform but to persuade, to encourage belief or action with the least thought possible (Gambrill, 1997, 2005). Social work macro practitioners must be taught how to distinguish the articulation of values from the oratory of propaganda. Political social work often accompanies social work policy practice (Reisch, 1997; Haynes & Mickelson, 2000). Getting the message out is part of a political campaign. Ethically, messages should be truthful, factual, and informative.

Advocacy Practice

In advocacy practice, persuasive motivational speech consists of raising consciousness among the oppressed and the privileged. A charismatic leader (e.g., Mahatma Gandhi, Martin Luther King, Jr., Desmond Tutu) uses speech to energize an apathetic citizenry and to tap into dormant discontent. The combination of charismatic leadership and motivational speech creates a following often referred to as a movement (civil rights, women's rights, antiwar, prohibition, etc.). Such movements are capable of bringing about large-scale social changes (child labor laws, laws prohibiting racial discrimination, etc.). Inspirational speech conveys optimism for change. Speech turns into activism. Some activists work within the law and some outside the law. Acts of civil disobedience include work stoppages or strikes, slowdowns, marches, demonstrations, protests, sit-ins, blockades, and boycotts. Legitimatization of hard-fought rights usually follows through the passage of legislation and public laws.

Community Practice

In community practice, one's persuasive power lies in creating networks of influence. This is consistent with Homan's social exchange theory (Poloma, 1979). Those who engage in community practice must know of and become known by other members of the community who have power and money. Community practitioners are power brokers who attend or host events within which social exchanges can occur. The theory holds that people enter into social exchanges with the expectation that the exchange will be rewarding to both parties. In social work, the beneficiary of such an exchange is a social work agency or a client population.

Management Practice

Persuasive motivational speech in management practice is linked to leadership. Since leadership is discussed at length in chapter 7, no discussion occurs here.

■ Information and Persuasion in Decision Making in Macro Social Work Practice

Unlike clinical social work practice, persuasive speech and power influence the decision-making process in macro practice. It is important, therefore, that social work macro practitioners distinguish rational argument (discourse) from persuasive speech when making management decisions. Gambrill (1997, 2005) warns against the illusion of discourse. She identifies five common tactics used to create the illusion of discourse. One tactic is to allege certainty in the absence of evidence. A second tactic is to use sweeping generalizations, while a third is to misrepresent an opponent's position or view. Diversion is a fourth tactic, designed to direct attention away from the main point of an opponent's argument. A fifth tactic is to appeal to emotion in the absence of evidence.

Discourse, involving science and values, is predicated on rational argument. Its purpose is to inform. In discourse, the information presented (whether a value argument or a scientific argument) is consistent with the rules of logic. An argument is used to suggest the truth or to demonstrate the falsity of a particular claim. Arguments for or against an action are evaluated as are alternative courses of action. In contrast to the use of discourse in decision making is the use of opinion. At its core, opinion reflects unexamined ideology and personal preferences. Opinions are likely to contain unproven or misrepresented facts. Persuasion in the form of emotional appeal or power (alliances) gives opinions form, as they cannot stand on their own merit. When discourse is excluded from the decision-making process in macro social work process, the decisions are likely to be misguided.

6

Relationship in Clinical Practice:
The Art of Healing

■ The Differential Use of Relationship in Clinical
and Macro Social Work Practice

The differential use of self in social work practice is necessary for competent practice. Unique to this text is the conceptualization and presentation of relationship from two perspectives. The first (this chapter) examines the worker's use of self in a helping or therapeutic alliance. The second (chapter 7) examines the worker's use of self to orchestrate social change and to perform administrative functions through the use of authority and leadership. Both leadership and healing are grounded in science and art.

This chapter captures the differential use of self in direct practice to deliver concrete services and/or to engage in therapy. The question of whether relationship stands apart from theory-based therapies is explored. Meta-analyses are presented both on therapy outcomes and on the therapeutic process itself. The concept and evidence for empirically supported treatments is explored and critiqued. The text accepts the premise that relationship is itself a dynamic for change.

The Clinical Social Work Relationship: Purpose and Belief Bonding

The social work literature has traditionally distinguished a professional relationship from other types of relationships by claiming that a professional relationship is purposeful. A professional relationship reflects the function of the agency (discussed in chapter 3), different stages of worker-client engagement (beginnings, middles, and ends), different levels of relationship intensity or depth of treatment (case management or therapy), and different roles and functions for the worker and the client. The purpose of the relationship is to provide services (chapters 10 and 11) and to heal through a therapeutic alliance (chapters 12 and 13).

A helping relationship is based on an emotional interaction between the help seeker and help giver. It is a connecting bond of feeling that gives a sense of alliance (Perlman, 1979; Kadushin, 1990). The bond mirrors the facilitative conditions of an effective relationship: empathy, warmth, acceptance, and actual interest in the client. Truax and Carkhuff (1967) speak of empathic understanding, unconditional positive regard, nonpossessive warmth, congruence, genuineness, and authenticity. According to Kadushin, these orientations are assumed to be the necessary conditions for effective interviewing and the core conditions for developing a helping relationship. At a minimum, relationship begins with belief bonding. Not all interviews need the same level of relationship intensity.

Relationship as a Dynamic of Change

The social work research literature provides ample support for the importance of relationship as a dynamic of change (Orlinsky & Howard, 1986; Patterson 1984; Maluccio, 1979; Sansbury, 1975; McKay et al., 1973; Jones, Neuman, & Shyne, 1976; Beck & Jones, 1973). According to the Milford conference (American Association of Social Workers, 1929), the dynamic of relationship is the flesh and blood of social work. The evidence for the necessity, if not the sufficiency, of accurate empathy and/or warmth and therapeutic genuineness is incontrovertible. According to Patterson (1984), the effectiveness of all methods of counseling or psychotherapy may be due to the presence of a therapeutic relationship.

Efficacy and Effectiveness of Relationship to Outcome

Historically, the most consistent finding in studies of the effectiveness of casework, counseling, and psychotherapy is the importance of the relationship. In a nationwide study, Beck and Jones (1973) found a highly statistically significant association between therapy outcome and the counselor-client relationship. The counselor-client relationship more than doubled the predictive power of the second highest factor related to outcome. Orlinsky and Howard (1986) in their review of 1,100 research studies concluded that one of the more consistently supported findings was that positive outcome was related to the nature of the bond between worker and client.

Relationship as Researched and as Practiced

Within the helping professions, there has been a waxing and waning of interest in the concept of relationship and its association with best practices (Paul, 2004). The concept of relationship has been researched, validated, and deconstructed (Drisko, 2004). Yet the idea that relationship is a dynamic for change in and of itself has survived. Currently there is renewed interest and controversy over relationship as a therapeutic ingredient in successful psychotherapy outcomes. This controversy concerns relationship as researched and relationship as practiced.

■ Terminology Turmoil: "Therapy" and "Direct Practice"

Attempts to define relationship within clinical social work practice have resulted in terminological disarray. Clinical social workers have been variously described as direct practitioners (Hepworth, Rooney, & Larsen, 2002), case managers (Rothman, 1994), allocators of resources (Cowger, 1994; Tallman & Bohart, 1993), therapists (Barker, 2003), and traitors to the profession (Specht & Courtney, 1994). More than rhetoric, this turmoil over terminology reflects deeply held, often opposing, ideological convictions about the profession of social work and its mission. It also reflects ideological assumptions about the causality of personal problems and public issues.

Historical Perspective: Two Functions

Historically, assumptions of individual causality led clinical social work practitioners to attribute the unmet basic needs of an individual or family to moral failure or flawed character. Concrete services were linked to efforts to bring about changes in the individual. With the advent of Freudian psychology, assumptions of individual causality shifted from moral judgments to attributions of unconscious dynamic forces within the individual. Efforts continued to focus on individual change as concrete needs were met. It was not until after the economic depression that began in 1929 that clinical social workers began to accept social causality as an explanation for the unmet basic needs of individuals and families. As a consequence, licensed clinical social workers in direct practice perform two functions: the delivery of concrete services and therapy.

Berzoff, Flanagan, and Hertz (1996) illustrate the ideological split over the two functions performed by social workers in direct social work practice when they write:

> While the postgraduate student did an excellent job of connecting Martin to legal services, advocating on Martin's behalf educationally, and making sure he was taking his prescribed psychiatric medication, Martin remained emotionally immobilized and in great pain because he was so messed up. . . . the student, in turn, felt he had no vocabulary and no tools to understand the reason for Martin's emotional pain and immobilization. (p. 7)

The degree to which the two functions should or do operate independently of each other is a matter of debate.

Relationship in the Delivery of Concrete Services

Clinical social workers deliver programmatic and policy benefits in the form of concrete social services to individual clients through face-to-face (direct) contact. When performing this function, licensed clinical social workers form a worker-client relationship based on belief bonding. The declarative knowledge needed to deliver concrete services requires knowledge of the law related to the execution of fiduciary responsibilities and knowledge of benefit programs. It requires skill in establishing a worker-client relationship and in determining client eligibility, skill in networking and case advocacy, and skill in matching resources to need. The delivery of concrete services in direct practice is frequently referred to as *case management* (see chapter 11).

Core Values in the Direct-Practice Social Work Relationship

According to Biestek (1957), a professional social work relationship in direct practice is defined by core social work values, such as acceptance, adopting a non-judgmental attitude, and honoring client self-determination. Added to this is the worker's obligation to assure client confidentiality and to view each client as a unique individual. Similarly generic and descriptive, Rogers (1957) defines relationship in terms of the worker's authenticity. If authentic, the worker is able to relate in a natural, sincere, spontaneous, open, and genuine manner. Generally, a professional social work clinical relationship is defined as the observable ability of the worker and the client to work together in a realistic, collaborative manner based on a mutually committed belief in the helping relationship (Bisman, 1994).

Worker and client bond in the belief that mutually agreed-upon activities will bring about changes in the client's circumstances that will both benefit the client and enhance the client's self-worth. The worker believes in the client's worthiness, and the client believes in the worker's competence and trustworthiness. While not all worker-client interactions in direct practice are considered to be therapy, all worker-client interactions are intended to benefit the client and are therefore therapeutic. Some refer to belief bonding as the establishment of rapport or a working relationship. Generic or descriptive definitions of a professional clinical social work relationship are independent of theory.

Relationship as Therapeutic Alliance: Declarative Knowledge

When performing the function of therapy (or counseling), a licensed clinical social worker may be employed in a direct services agency or nonprofit primary or host setting, or s/he may be self-employed in private practice. The declarative knowledge needed for therapy differs from that needed for case management. In therapy, relationship depends on the formation of a therapeutic alliance. Therapeutic alliance requires declarative knowledge of specific theories which, through their prescriptions, direct the enactment of a therapeutic process (see chapters 12 and 13).

Generic descriptions of the social work relationship cannot tell a practitioner how to enact a therapeutic process through relationship. Enactment competency relies on the linkage between congruent theories of human behavior (normal and abnormal) and the treatment process. According to Binder (2004), all other therapeutic competencies are anchored in this connection. One cannot engage in a discussion of how to do therapy in social work direct practice without linking that discussion to how humans behave and change (theory and practice).

The declarative knowledge needed to enact a therapeutic alliance depends on the causal knowledge of individual resilience (normality) and vulnerability (abnormality) taught in the human behavior sequence. Knowing what interferes with the unfolding of resilience leads to practice theories about what needs to change. Declarative knowledge of human behavior (what goes right and what goes wrong) is transformed in the therapeutic alliance through the worker's enactment of a therapeutic process. The worker's use of self in the therapeutic process is the art of healing. Individuals become more resilient and less vulnerable through therapy.

Two Functions: Steps 3 and 5 on the Decision Tree

Clinical social workers in direct practice do not dismiss social causality. Rather, they recognize that social reform, policy, and program initiatives take time and may be won and lost (reversed or cut) over time. They recognize that the day-to-day survival of individuals often cannot wait for social change to occur. They recognize that sometimes more than a timely injection of resources is needed. They recognize that external events and interpersonal relationships can traumatize. What is external (outside) can come inside and threaten the very core of a person's being. Internal events (biology) can create vulnerabilities. In light of this reality, clinical social work practitioners in direct practice deliver concrete services and engage in therapy as warranted. They recognize the value of both types of intervention to help individuals acquire the resiliency needed to survive adverse conditions, whether from within or without, in a timely manner.

Who We Are and What We Do

Other professions, such as psychiatry and psychology, also provide therapy. Federal statistics indicate, however, that social workers provide more mental health services (a large proportion of which is psychotherapy) than do professionals from all other disciplines combined (Drisko, 2004; O'Neill, 1999). Committed to open assessment and multicausality, social work promotes best practices by allowing the practitioner flexibility in theory and method choice. Compared to other professions, the social work clinician in direct practice has access to models that work from the outside in (resource allocation) as well as from the inside out (Reid & Epstein, 1972; Berzoff, Flanagan, & Hertz, 1996).

■ The Science of Relationship

So far, this chapter has explored the terminology issues associated with defining the clinical social work relationship. It has examined the literature on the qualitative attributes (art) of a good helping relationship. Now it is time to examine the science of therapy.

Therapy Outcome and Therapeutic Process

The trend toward evidence-based practice has renewed interest in therapy outcomes and therapeutic processes. This is important for three reasons. Outcome studies (does it work?) benefit clients when clinicians use best practices. Process studies (how does it work?) benefit educators by driving curriculum and optimizing training for practice. Finally, in the era of managed care and diminishing financial support for mental health services, therapies that can demonstrate that they work and that they are cost effective (which therapy works best?) will be funded.

Does Therapy Work?

Early research to investigate whether psychotherapy worked concluded that there was no evidence that psychotherapy was more effective than no treatment at all (Eysenck, 1952). Spontaneous remissions and expectancy (being on a waiting list) appeared to be as effective as therapy. Such research foreshadowed the current evidence-based movement. In his review of the empirical literature, Eysenck noted that most empirical studies were published as narrative formats with little attention paid to the rigor of the research design, the standardization of measurement, or the power of the statistical analyses. Such narrative reviews of empirical studies tended to fall into three categories: one-third of the studies showed therapy had positive outcome effects; one-third showed negative outcome effects; and one-third showed that therapy had no significant effect. In the quest for greater scientific rigor, researchers turned to meta-analytic approaches to determine if therapy worked.

Meta-Analysis and Effect Size

Meta-analysis pools results from multiple studies and calculates an effect size across studies. An effect size is a statistical procedure capable of transforming different measures with differing numerical scores from multiple studies thereby allowing for fair statistical comparison to create a larger standardized statistical measure of change.

$$\text{Effect size} = \frac{\text{Mean of experimental group} - \text{mean of control group}}{\text{Standard deviation of control group}}$$

A focal point around which studies are to be selected (e.g., depression) is determined first. To promote scientific rigor, the researcher must find well-conducted studies and document their inclusion or exclusion for purposes of audit. Some meta-analyses are based solely on efficacy studies while other analyses include both efficacy and effectiveness studies (Drisko, 2004). Cohen (1997) considers an effect size of .8 as large. For instance, if a given meta-analysis yields a psychotherapy effect size of .7–.8, it would mean that the average client completing psychotherapy is better off than 79% of untreated controls (Rosenthal, 1984). The effect size across multiple studies of psychotherapy demonstrates that therapy does work better than no treatment (Smith & Glass, 1977; Glass, McGaw, & Smith, 1981; Hunter & Schmidt, 1990; Lipsey & Wilson, 2001; Wampold, 2001).

Population-Specific Meta-Analyses: Adults, Adolescents, and Children

Meta-analyses of adults in psychotherapy indicate that therapy does work for this population (Ahn & Wampold, 2001; Stevens, Hynan, & Allen, 2000; Wampold et al., 1997; Wampold, 2001). Drisko (2004) concurs with these findings, noting that there is considerable evidence based on empirical meta-analyses that adult psychotherapy for anxiety and depression generally work well. A comparable meta-analytic effect size for children and adolescents in therapy has also been found (Casey & Berman, 1985; Kazdin & Weisz, 2003; Levitt, 1963; Weisz et al., 1995). Psychotherapy works with adults, adolescents, and children (Smith, Glass, & Miller, 1980).

Is One Model of Therapy Better Than Another?

Initially, Luborsky, Singer, and Luborsky (1975); Luborsky, McClellan, Diguer, Woody, and Seligman (1997); and Luborsky, Rosenthal, Diguer, Andrusyna, Berman, Levitt, et al. (2002) found that many treatments work, thus the often-cited quote of the Dodo bird from Lewis Carroll in *Alice in Wonderland*: "Everyone has won and all must have a prize." Several current meta-analytic studies (Jones & Pulos, 1993; Lambert & Hill, 1994; Roth & Fonogy, 1996; Castonguay, Goldfried, Wiser, Raue, & Hayes, 1996; DeRubeis, Hollon, Amsterdam, Shelton, Young, & Salomon, 2005) have begun to find small differences between therapies when compared. The difficulty of detecting differences between therapies on outcome variables led to the search for nonspecific factors to explain how the process of therapy works. According to Kazdin (2001), evidence that theory is an active ingredient in therapy has yet to be proven. Relationship, however, appears to be a common factor across therapies.

Chance, Expectancy, and Placebo

Nonspecific ingredients of therapy that influence outcome are related to chance, expectancy, and the placebo effect. According to Wampold (2001), some of the variance in therapy outcome success can be attributed to chance alone. To chance, Frank and Frank (1991) add the concept of expectancy. Outcome success is related, they claim, to the expectancy (hope) that things will get better as a result of help-seeking behavior. Expectancy includes participation in a ritualized format where hope is instilled that things will get better, i.e., a positive response to a healing process. Expectancy refers to client and worker knowledge that the client is receiving treatment that is believed to have an ameliorating, restorative, healing, or curing power (Drisko, 2004).

A placebo effect is similar to expectancy but differs in that the client is given some form of clinical management plus a pill (where medication is appropriate) with a nonactive ingredient. Placebo studies usually are double-blind studies where neither the researcher nor the client are aware of who is receiving the placebo and who is not.

Relationship as the Active Ingredient in Therapy

Research efforts have also focused on identifying the active ingredients (sometimes referred to as *nonspecific factors*) of the therapeutic process. Several studies have concluded that nonspecific common factors are more important to positive therapy outcome than are specific techniques (Ahn & Wampold, 2001; Hubble, Duncan, & Miller, 1999; Lambert & Bergin, 1994; Luborsky et al., 2002; Wampold, 2001). Orlinsky, Grawe, and Parks (1994) state that relationship is the largest curative factor in therapy.

Generally, outcome variance can be attributed as follows: (1) 30% relationship, (2) 15% technical or specific therapeutic procedures, (3) 15% expectancy and placebo, and (4) 40% to extratherapeutic factors (the context of practice and client factors). Currently, efficacy and effectiveness studies dominate the literature on relationship.

■ Efficacy Studies and Empirically Supported Treatments

Drisko (2004) notes that, despite the extensiveness of meta-analytic studies, few enduring differences in the outcomes of different psychotherapies are reported. Efficacy studies compare therapies with each other and with an untreated control group. Efficacy-based outcome and process studies promote scientific and design rigor. Study participants tend to be homogeneous and have no comorbidity. They are randomly assigned to different treatments and to control groups. Treatment is standardized, and therapists are trained to deliver the intervention according to a manual's protocol. Standardized pre- and posttest measures are administered by blind raters. The measures are specific to the defined treatment goals (i.e., are not generalized measures of overall improvement). Follow-up measures are obtained at several points postintervention. Efficacy-based outcome studies are concerned with process because replication requires standardization of process. When therapist expertise is controlled for by study design (efficacy studies: type 1 designs), greater confidence can be placed in the conclusion that the observed outcome is attributable to a specific theory (cause and effect). An unintended consequence of efficacy studies is the rift between therapy as it is researched and therapy as it is practiced in the real world (Seligman, 1995; Paul, 2004).

Manuals, Handbooks, and Desk References

Proponents of evidence-based practice support treatment protocols to control for therapist variation (expertise) across therapies. Several desk references, handbooks, and treatment manuals have been written to identify empirically supported treatments (Roberts & Yeager, 2004; Kazdin & Weisz, 2003; Gordon & Trafton, 2003; Nathan & Gorman, 1998, 2002; Norcross, 2002; Barlow, 2001; Christopherson & Mortweet, 2001). Empirically supported treatments are supported both by the American Psychological Association task force on the promotion and dissemination of psychological procedures and by the American Psychiatric Association.

Research on the use of treatment manuals (Robinson, Berman, & Neimeyer, 1990; Guthrie, 2000; Mitchell, Reithoffer, & Blythe, 2000; Beutler, Machado, & Neufeldt, 1994) concluded that their use led to more positive outcomes than did therapy without such manuals. However, the researchers noted that not all empirically supported treatments are equally effective under all conditions. Others reference the fact that non–empirically based (pop psychology) therapies also deserve critique (Lilienfeld, Lynn, & Lohr, 2003).

Critique of Empirically Supported Treatments: Impact on Therapeutic Relationship

In his review of handbooks, treatment guidelines, and desk references on empirically supported treatments, Paul (2004) makes the following observations on the impact of such materials on the therapeutic relationship. On the plus side, Paul notes that efficacy-based research and empirically supported treatments allow the results of proven treatment protocols to be replicated at various treatment sites. Empirically supported treatments promote research into efficacy and component analysis of critical procedures and allow for rigorous comparison of diverse treatments.

On the negative side, Paul (2004, p. 398) notes that even where evidence-based practice has shown efficacy, there remains a substantial number (approximately 30%) of individuals who are nonresponders, and of those who do respond, many are still symptomatic. Paul worries that such manuals influence their adoption by third-party payers (health insurance) disproportionate to the evidence they contain. He observes that few empirically supported treatments deal with V codes (conditions not attributable to a mental disorder that are the focus of attention or treatment; included are problems related to abuse or neglect and to relational problems) or personality disorders. By research design, treatments control for both client factors and therapist factors. Such control, he says, may result in the underutilization of therapist skill. Paul also notes that under evidence-based practice, single-subject ABA designs (the mainstay of cognitive-behavioral treatment) are no longer regarded as rigorous research (they do not meet type 1 standards of scientific rigor).

Extraneous Factors That Influence the Process and Outcome of Therapy

Extraneous factors that influence the process and outcome of therapy fall into three categories: (1) client factors, (2) context factors, and (3) factors associated with the problem to be worked. Initially conceptualized as client suitability for therapy, more recently, client factors have been reconceptualized as the therapy's suitability for a given client (Binder, 2004). According to the literature, making predictions about therapy outcome solely on the basis of client characteristics is rarely successful (Garfield, 1994; Lambert & Asay, 1984; Prochaska, 1999).

Contextual factors (familial and cultural) influence therapy outcome (Reid, 1997). Therapy outcome is affected by the degree of support (or nonsupport) a client receives from family and significant others. To be effective, therapy must be culturally responsive (Sue, Zane, & Young, 1994; Vargas & Koss-Chioino, 1992; Gutierrez, Parsons, & Cox, 1998; Pinderhughes, 1983; Comas-Diaz & Greene, 1995; Comas-Diaz & Griffiths, 1988; Jacobs & Bowles, 1988; Chestang, 1976).

According to the literature (Paul, 2004), the number of client-identified problems and symptoms and their severity affect therapy outcome. A recent National Institute of Mental Health (NIMH) study on treating depression found that the severity of the problem at the onset of treatment did affect treatment outcome (Elkin et al., 1995). Paul notes that in outpatient practice (in contrast to the researcher's controlled laboratory), there is comorbidity, greater pathology (the greater the client pathology, the fewer the type 1 studies found in the efficacy literature), more V codes (problems in living that do not reach DSM-IV criteria), and more Axis II (personality) disorders. He observes that personality disorders are often not the focus of efficacy studies or empirically supported treatments. Therapy outcome is improved when the client is able to identify a focal problem to be worked.

Effectiveness Studies: The Practice of Psychotherapy

As an alternative to efficacy-based outcome and process studies, effectiveness studies allow for greater clinician spontaneity and flexibility (less standardization, some would say) in process and a more expansive definition of change and outcome success. Practitioners hold that effectiveness studies are more aligned with the complexities encountered in real-world practice.

According to Maione and Chenail (1999), effectiveness studies are inherently self-correcting. They do not determine the number of sessions in advance; they are applied to clients with multiple problems (comorbidity); and outcome is often evaluated in terms of improvement in overall or global functioning rather than in terms of theory-specified or problem-specific treatment goals. Effectiveness studies allow the clinician to be creative and to improvise by actively "shopping" for what will work in the enactment of therapy in contrast to rigid adherence to the therapeutic process required in an efficacy-based protocol. Competent clinical social work practice requires the practitioner's use of self in a therapeutic process backed by evidence of the therapy's efficacy or effectiveness.

7
Relationship in Policy, Advocacy, Management, and Community Practice: The Art of Leadership

■ The Exercise of Authority, Influence, and Power

The Conceptualization of Indirect Practice

In this text, the term *indirect practice* refers to the use of policy, advocacy, community, and management as methods of social work practice to bring about a more humane and just social order. Indirect practice may benefit all citizens through policies and programs of universal entitlement, or it may benefit individuals who are members of a subpopulation specifically targeted by selective social welfare policies and programs. Social work practitioners in indirect practice believe that individual problems are caused by social forces. Consistent with the acceptance of social causality, the practitioner's use of self in indirect (macro) practice is to exercise leadership, power, and authority to make resources available to those in need through policies, programs, and social reform.

The declarative knowledge needed by the indirect (macro) practitioner focuses on theories of causality associated with functional and dysfunctional social forces and societal structures. This declarative knowledge gets transformed into interventions consistent with the social work methods of policy, advocacy, community, and management practice. By targeting societal dysfunction directly, such methods benefit individual members of population subgroups that are disproportionately affected by dysfunctional social forces. The use of self in macro or indirect practice is based on the practitioner's use of leadership in the exercise of authority and power to bring about social change and reform.

Good and Bad Leadership

The art of relationship required for social workers in policy, advocacy, community, and management practice differs from the art of relationship required in direct practice. The latter is characterized by belief bonding and therapeutic alliance, while the former is characterized by the use of authority, influence, and power. A different skill set is needed. Few textbooks, if any, directly address this differential use of self. However, such a distinction is critical to practice competency. The use of self in the execution of authority, influence, and power supports the methods of policy, advocacy, community, and management practice. Though much is written about the social work relationship as the art of healing in clinical practice, little is written about relationship as the art of leadership in macro social work practice.

The content on leadership as authority, influence, and power presented here also differs from presentations in other texts. Most of the scholarly literature on applied leadership (public and private enterprise) is focused on the personal qualities and attributes of a single individual. At a minimum, leadership is presented as a benign construct. Until recently, only political philosophers and historians have documented bad leadership. From the 1990s to date, however, awareness of the pervasiveness of bad leadership in all domains of public and private endeavor has increased while tolerance for it has decreased (Kellerman, 2005). Defining bad leadership and knowing how it happens (cause and effect) can advance good leadership.

Application to Social Work Practice

Macro social work practitioners act to secure the respect and cooperation of others in order to administer agencies, initiate policies, or bring about change in organizations, communities, and societies. The tool of relationship in social work macro practice is leadership. However, the exercise of leadership as part of student learning goes unmonitored. The consequences of an unexamined and unmonitored use of self (leadership) in social work macro practice are as dangerous as the unexamined use of self in clinical practice. Bad leadership affects many directly and many more indirectly through bad decisions or good decisions left unmade. According to Kellerman, the failure to monitor how individuals exercise authority, influence, and power results in bad leadership and in bad followers.

This chapter presents a checklist (Exhibit 7.1) developed by the author to monitor interpersonal skills in the use of authority, influence, and power. It allows field instructors to provide corrective feedback to students seeking to learn the leadership skills needed for macro practice. Similar to the process-recording format used to teach and monitor clinical skills, a process-recording format is used to teach and monitor leadership. The middle column captures the dialogue between the leader and his/her audience. The left-hand column shows the worker's application of declarative knowledge (procedural knowing) on leadership to the dialogue. The third column monitors the practitioner's reflection on self in action (tacit knowing). The fourth column (far right) reflects supervisory corrective feedback of both the practitioner's declarative knowledge (procedural knowledge) and the practitioner's reflection on his/her use of authority, influence, and power (tacit knowing).

EXHIBIT 7.1   *Leadership Checklist: Interpersonal Skills in the Execution of Authority, Influence, and Power*

Positive Interpersonal Skills	Negative Interpersonal Skills
Shows tolerance for others' point of view	Shows intolerance
Avoids making personal attacks	Engages in personal attacks
Nondefensive acceptance of constructive criticism	Sees constructive criticism as a personal attack
Remains calm under provocation	Explosive displays of anger
Shows patience	Shows frustration
Promotes understanding of another's input	Blocks the input of another
Refutes the argument, not the person	Attacks person rather than the argument
Accurately reflects what another says	Twists what another says
Empowers others	Tries to dominate others
Thinks before speaking	Speaks before thinking
Clarity of presentation	Gives confusing presentation
Listens while others speak	Interrupts while others speak
Stays on topic	Changes the subject as tactic of diversion
Builds on ideas of others	Complains, shoots down ideas of others
Supports expression of all points of view	Intimidates others to limit expression or support for other ideas
Sends clear messages	Sends mixed messages
Respectful of audience and/or speaker	Disrespects audience and/or speaker
Uses humor to relieve tension	Uses humor to ridicule or attack others
Uses time appropriately	Monopolizes, wastes time
Talks within area of expertise	Exaggerates own importance, talks outside area of expertise
Comments are inclusive of others	Comments are dismissive of others
Gives credit where credit is due	Claims credit for work done by others
Keeps discussion focused on common good	Turns discussion into personal rivalry or polarizes discussion: in-group/out-group
Keeps an open mind until all facts are heard	Commits self to point of view without weighing all factors

(continued)

EXHIBIT 7.1 *Leadership Checklist: Interpersonal Skills in the Execution of Authority, Influence, and Power* (continued)

Positive Interpersonal Skills	Negative Interpersonal Skills
Engages in open, transparent, and independent argument	Exerts power to get own way through use of cliques, premeeting scripts
Comments are designed to factually inform	Comments are designed to mislead and misrepresent
Sensitive to emotions of others, promotes cooperation	Stirs up emotions and provokes polarization
Facts are accurate and checked	Presents inaccurate or unchecked facts
Assumes responsibility for own mistakes	Blames others for his/her mistakes
No hidden agenda	Has a hidden agenda
Honest compliments	Insincere flattery
Work load and pace are reasonable	Sets unreasonable pace or work load
Avoids listening to or spreading rumors	Spreads, is receptive to rumors and gossip
Comments encourage and inspire	Comments are patronizing
Tells others of another's accomplishments	Engages in left-handed compliments to put another down
Holds tongue	Makes cutting and snippy remarks
Respects boundaries	Pries into another's business
Judicial use of conversation	Talks incessantly
Actions, comments are for the common good	Actions, comments are self-promoting
Uses timelines appropriately, balances talk with action	Engages in delaying tactics, stalls
Realistic appraisal	Overcommits self, others, and organization
Consistent, can count on person once word is given or decision is made, trustworthy	Waivers, is indecisive, changes mind, lacks courage of convictions
Negotiates and compromises, transparent	Inflexible, won't change course
Shares information and resources	Withholds information needed by another
Body language expresses support and respect	Body language expresses disrespect, distrust, anger
Comments make another feel competent and liked	Comments or behavior designed to make another feel incompetent or disliked
Doesn't jump to conclusions	Blames others without getting the facts
Looks for what works and what goes well	Finds fault, engages in petty bickering
Allows time for discourse	Rushes to action to prevent discourse
Able to enlist commitment of others, is inspirational	Uses coercion or undue influence to get others to go along

■ Leadership

Definition

For the purposes of this chapter, *leadership* is defined as the exercise of authority, influence, and power to accomplish tasks for which there is some degree of consensus (between leaders and followers) as to the desired outcome of organized, structured activities. Conceptualizing the practitioner's use of self as leadership in macro practice is not to say that clinicians are not leaders in their field; they are. Rather, it is an acknowledgment that a primary aspect of the use of self in social work macro practice is leadership. Leadership is a complex concept about which much is written.

According to Bennis and Nanus (1997), decades of academic analysis have provided more than 850 definitions of leadership. They note that more than 1,000 empirical studies were conducted in the 75 years preceding their book. In 1999 alone, more than 2,000 books on leadership were published (Goffee & Jones, 2000). Yet, there is no single definition capable of providing a wholly adequate explanation of leadership. Kellerman (2005, p. 17) asks: "[G]iven the universal need for leadership and the readiness of so many to fill the position of leader, why does so much go wrong?"

Credentials

The use of self in macro practice involves both science and art. For executives who manage organizations, the science of the application of leadership is found in the master of business administration (M.B.A.) degree. For those who enter government or public service, leadership and its application lie in the master of public administration (M.P.A.) degree. In social work, the science of management lies in the master of social work (M.S.W.) degree. Some choose to concentrate in administration in their second year of an M.S.W. program while others enter agencies as M.S.W. clinicians and through seniority and promotion become agency administrators (Patti, 1983). The assumption is that the science of managing organizations, businesses, or governments can be taught. However, the art of leadership is difficult to identify, measure, and develop. It cannot be taught. The scholarly literature on the art of leadership refers to judgment and character.

Inspiration

Some authors (Peters & Waterman, 1982; Bennis & Nanus, 1997) write about the art of leadership as a right-brain function and link it to the ability to inspire others through charisma. Inspirational leadership is an emotional transaction between leader and led. The inspirational leader captures hearts, minds, and souls based on the leader's passionate, uncompromising strength of conviction or particular world view. The downside of such conviction and passion is intolerance. Inspirational leaders are as likely to lead others in the commission of immoral acts (unjust wars, genocide, torture, etc.) as they are to lead them in acts that elevate humankind and the human condition. Hitler, Stalin, and Mao Tse-tung are cases in point of the former while Mahatma Gandhi, Desmond Tutu, Martin Luther King, Jr., Winston Churchill, and Franklin D. Roosevelt make the latter point. Charismatic leadership is known to produce outcomes that are good or evil, principled or petty, or a mixture of both good and bad. Inspiration engages emotions. In the absence of critical thinking, inspiration allows emotions to overrule conscience. Emotionally aroused individuals or groups, under the influence of a charismatic leader, engage in behavior in which they would not otherwise engage under ordinary circumstances.

Rationality

On the other hand, we learn from Weber (1958) that not all rational behavior is moral. While most scholars agree that effective leadership is linked to rational qualities, they also recognize that effective leadership can be linked to unethical conduct (Kellerman, 2005). Where reason is involved, as in the case of Weber's technical bureaucrat, the rationale for the suspension of critical thinking or moral judgment lies in the obligation to follow orders. Milgram's (1974) studies on obedience (the administration of an electric shock by one individual to another because someone in authority ordered it done) led to the conclusion that U.S. culture has failed to inculcate internal controls on actions that have their origin in authority. Similarly, Zimbardo's (Peters & Waterman, 1982) prison experiment documented the swiftness with which abuse of power occurs when there is a strong, closed, internal culture that permits the use of coercive power as an exercise of authority. Bennis and Nanus (1997) note that much of the human element of leadership, whether emotional or rational, is either avoided or shortchanged in most curricula.

Power

Because of its polarizing properties, power is rarely discussed openly. In the absence of such discussion, leaders cannot be held accountable for the power they exercise.

> Curricula on leadership has systematically neglected without exception, POWER, the basic energy to initiate and sustain action translating intention into reality. Power is the quality without which leaders cannot lead. Most current paradigms of organizational life be they "new age" or older have failed to consider power. (Bennis & Nanus, 1997, p. 14)

According to Etzioni (1968, 1993), leadership and power are inevitably linked. Kellerman (2005) observes that bad leadership cannot be stopped or prevented by avoiding its discussion.

Though much is written, little is known about how to stop or prevent bad leadership and bad followers. By extrapolation, little is known about how to promote, with any degree of certitude or predictability, good leadership and good followers. Most of what is known lies at a descriptive level of knowledge, either as case studies (historical books on political figures) or as typologies (Weber, 1958; French & Raven, 1959; Kellerman, 2005). French and Raven describe five sources of power in their typology: legitimate, expert, reward, referent, and coercive. Weber's typology describes leadership in terms of rationality and bureaucracy. Kellerman's typology describes good and bad leadership in terms of effectiveness and ethics.

■ Setting a Standard (Norm) for Good Leadership

The Concept of Transformative Leadership

According to Bennis and Nanus (1997), the process of becoming a leader is much the same as the process of becoming an integrated human being. Leadership, then, is a creative and deeply human process that speaks of moral character not charisma. Peters and Waterman adopt McGregor's (1960) concept of transformative leadership as their standard of good leadership:

> *Transformative leadership* . . . occurs when one or more persons engage with others in such a way that leaders and followers raise one another to higher levels of motivation and morality. Power bases are linked as mutual support for a common purpose. Transforming leadership ultimately becomes *moral* in that it raises the level of human conduct and ethical aspiration of both the leader and the led and thus has a transforming effect on both. (Peters & Waterman, 1982, p. 83)

Moral Demagoguery

However, as Hoffer (1951) notes, some of the most atrocious acts against humankind have been carried out in the name of religion (God) and patriotism. Therefore the determination of "moral" requires critical thinking and the capacity to differentiate the symbols used to portray morality from the actual performance of moral acts themselves. Kellerman offers two dimensions: ineffective leadership and unethical (immoral) leadership to nuance the idea of bad leadership.

■ Theories of Leadership: Historical Perspective

Great Man or Great Event: Crucible Theories

The *great-man* theory holds that leaders are born, not made. Accordingly, the theory holds that power is invested in a very limited number of people who, because of their inheritance or destiny, are called to be leaders. In contrast is the theory of *great events*. It holds that events and the availability of followers combine to make leaders of otherwise ordinary people. The crucible is a contemporary offshoot of these theories (Bennis & Thomas, 2002). A *crucible* is defined as a confluence of powerful intellectual, social, economic, or political forces, which meld character to form a leader. Leaders define a crucible as a turning point in their lives. Having survived a difficult event, such leaders emerge with a distinctive voice.

Rationalism and Enlightenment

According to Goffee and Jones (2000), theories of leadership were initially (18th-century rationalism and enlightenment) based on a belief in reason, progress, and the perfectibility of man. In the 19th century, Freud and Max Weber undermined belief in rationality and progress: Freud through his concept of the unconscious (all behavior is not rational) and Weber through his concept of bureaucracy (all rational behavior is not moral). As a result, skepticism about the power of reason and continuous progress marked the study of leadership in the 20th century.

Personal Traits

For both pragmatic and philosophical reasons, an intense interest in the concept of leadership began to develop in the 20th century. Numerous empirical studies conducted in the 1920s attempted to identify characteristics common to effective leaders. Little was learned from the vast amount of research on leadership traits during this period other than the existence of an association between height (above or below average) and leadership. Despite their dismissal by academics, Kellerman argues that traits do matter. Intelligence, sociability, persistence, verbal facility, level of energy, adaptability, and an even disposition are found more often in leaders than in the general population. Leaders possess skills in communication and collaboration. They are able to mobilize others. Kellerman observes, however, that the leadership trait package is often mixed; negative and positive traits coexist side by side. According to Kellerman, the ordinary trait of greed (craving more money, more power, more whatever) has high explanatory power when investigating bad leadership.

Leadership Style

When writing about leadership, historians and political philosophers focus on leadership style in governance. Governance, it is held, is necessary given human nature. Early writers believed that to ensure self-preservation, individual rights had to be subsumed under the rights of a state charged with keeping order (Hobbes, [1660] 1997). Rousseau ([1750, 1754, 1755, 1762] 1987) agreed that it was in an individual's self-interest to surrender at least some individual rights. Machiavelli ([1513] 1976) held that order, however secured, was a ruler's first and primary task. In contrast to those who focused on the rights of the state, John Locke ([1690] 1994) focused on the rights of the led. The *Federalist Papers* argued for a system of government based on checks and balances (the rights of the state and the rights of the led). Research on leadership in governance examined three styles: autocratic, democratic, and laissez-faire (the invisible hand). A democratic style marked by checks and balances was found to be the only style of governance that made free government possible. Because human beings are irrational (emotional) and unjust (immoral) in addition to being rational and just, a system of checks and balances is needed.

■ Leadership as Management: Theories

From the 1970s to date, leadership has been conceptualized, studied, and written about in terms of administrative and management practice. Turning from leadership as governance, studies in this era focused on management efficiency. Time and motion studies were conducted and books were written on management by objective (MBO). The Hawthorne experiment typified the era of scientific management. It was discovered, however, that the practices associated with efficient management lowered employee morale and decreased work motivation. Efficient management, it was discovered, was not the same thing as effective leadership.

Human Relations Model

In response to the efficiency model of management, the humanist school (Hodgetts, 2001; Mayo, 1977) introduced the human relations model of managing human resources. Typical of this period, employers were encouraged to attend to the emotional needs of their employees. Coworkers and supervisors alike were given sensitivity training and diversity training. Tavistock groups and quality circles were used to improve employee morale and to foster a better, more motivated workforce. Despite this humanizing effort, employer-employee relationships continue to be a source of tension in the workplace.

Humanistic or inspirational models of management practice are critiqued for engaging in feel-good transactions devoid of strategies and tactics capable of getting the job done. Emotional transactions (not rational evidence) influence attitudes and move people to act. Arthur Koestler (1967) warns that management by inspiration can also be used to appeal to the basest of human emotions (greed, revenge, dominance); humans have predilections for war and destruction.

Theory X and Theory Y

McGregor (1960) offers theory X and theory Y in an attempt to reconcile the needs of employers and employees. He explores assumptions about human nature and work. Theory X assumes that the average human being is lazy and has an inherent dislike for work. It holds that workers generally want to avoid responsibility and have little ambition. Therefore, managers must use supervision to motivate employees to put forth effort to meet organizational goals. Management is a top-down operation. Workers conform because they get paid to do so.

Theory Y holds that external control and the threat of punishment are not the only ways to motivate employees to work. It holds that the typical human being does not inherently dislike work and will assume responsibility under the right conditions. Motivation is tied more to positive reinforcement (reward) than to negative reinforcement (punishment). It maintains that employees gain more than a paycheck from a job well done.

Both theories have their critics. Rational models of management have been criticized for failing to recognize that behavior is less rationally motivated than they perceive it to be. Scientific managers are criticized for being out of touch, insensitive, and unresponsive to the needs of workers. Humanistic models have been criticized for failing to produce a quality product or service in a timely manner. Theory Z combines theories X and Y (Ouchi, 1981).

Contingency Theory

Since the 1940s, contingency theory has informed leadership practices. Contingency theory holds that context determines leadership (Bennis & Nanus, 1997). Since there are endless contingencies, there are endless varieties of leadership. According to Bennis and Nanus, three major contexts define leadership in the 21st century: (1) downsizing/diminished commitment, (2) complexity/chaos, and (3) credibility. The downsizing of the 1980s left society with millions of laid-off workers as well as workers who are in part-time or dead-end jobs. Long regarded as expendable by employers, workers are reluctant to invest loyalty in any organization or its leadership.

Complexity refers to the speed with which change occurs. Rapid and spastic changes create chaos or emergent complex messiness. Such messiness falls outside the parameters of known solutions. Derived from the principle of nonlinear dynamics, chaos theory recognizes that strategies used to manage chaos must be spontaneous and based on trial-and-error experimentation. Such experimentation may lead to false starts, temporary failure, and dead ends. It can also lead to learning (the learning organization) based on spontaneous innovation, creativity, improvisation, brainstorming, cooperative enterprise, and other "evolutionary" attempts to respond to the unknown.

The third context is credibility. As scholars (Kellerman, 2005; Bennis & Nanus, 1997) note, there is a growing intolerance for failed or bad leadership. Leaders are scrutinized in their private and public lives. In his reflection on the future of leadership, Bennis et al. (2001) states that one of the major unanswered questions is "how to ensure that strong leadership contributes to the common good, not self-interest; that the leader works toward ethical ends; and that leadership makes the world a better place to live" (p. 253).

The Empirical Evidence on Leadership

When all is said and done, leadership lacks conceptual definition and therefore empirical verification. One cannot measure what eludes definition. The only consensus appears to be that leadership is not a benign concept.

■   What Accounts for Bad Leadership?

According to Kellerman, the source of bad leadership lies in human nature. Human beings (whether leaders or followers) cannot be relied upon to behave well. Kellerman says that we behave badly because of who we are (character) and because of what we want (motivation). She holds that leadership is bad in one of two ways: It is either bad because it is ineffective, or it is bad because it is unethical. Sometimes, it is effectively unethical. She is quick to acknowledge that the lines often blur between these dimensions and that ideal types can only be clearly seen at the extremes.

Human Nature: The Need for Power and Affiliation

When bad leadership is attributed to flaws in human nature, it is most commonly associated with explanations related to unconscious needs. Some (e.g., psychodynamic theorists) hold that exercising power compensates for feelings of inferiority and anxiety (Gummer, 1990). Satisfaction is gained by being able to control, manipulate, and/or hurt others. Bad leadership is also attributed to the need for affiliation. Leaders with affiliative needs are more concerned about being liked than with exercising power, therefore they often fail to appropriately address internal organizational conflict, allowing it to escalate and become more destructive. Kellerman (2005) uses the term *character flaw* to denote the intractability of core dimensions of personality related to one's moral compass (Kellerman, 2005, p. 21).

Human Nature: Why Do Followers Follow Bad Leadership?

Kellerman notes that followers usually follow even when they know that a leader is misguided or malevolent (2005). They follow, she says, because even bad leaders satisfy basic human needs for safety, simplicity, and certainty. Self-preservation (safety) is the strongest motive for following bad leadership. Getting along by going along is one of life's earliest lessons. We learn to follow the leader as well-behaved children who follow directives from parents, teachers, coaches, and ultimately bosses. We toe the line and do what we are told. We follow the rules even when the rules are unfair and when those who set them are badly equipped or badly disposed (in intent). We follow because the cost of not following is too high.

Kellerman goes on to note that the construct of leader per se is a manifestation of our preference for the simple over the complex. Followers obey authority because it is the easiest way to keep things simple, especially in a stressful situation. As the Milgram experiment demonstrated, it is easier to assume that leaders know what they are doing than it is to challenge them.

According to Kellerman, all individuals are vulnerable to existential angst. Individuals fear helplessness and isolation. As a consequence, followers want to transcend the isolation of individualism to become part of a winning team. Organizations are filled with irrational, emotional human beings who thrive on camaraderie. Becker (Peters & Waterman, 1982) sees the situation of the employee as somewhat more complex. He posits that humans are driven by "dualism"—the need to be a part of something and a need to stick out. An individual wants to be a conforming member of a winning team and to be a star in his or her own right (Peters & Waterman, 1982). The desire to be a star is linked to the need for self-determination. If individuals think they have even a modicum of personal control over their destinies, they will persist at tasks. The tension for the individual in the workplace is between the push of self-determination and the pull for security. For many, workplace security is tied to where they live on the organizational chart. Security seekers are willing to yield to authority (e.g., the Milgram and Zimbardo studies) in exchange for financial security and a meaningful definition of self within the world of work.

Dysfunctional Organizational Cultures: Why Followers Behave Badly

Followers also follow bad leadership because of group dynamics. Groups go along with bad leaders because even bad leaders provide benefits to the group in terms of cohesion, identity, and work. To follow a bad leader by going along is one thing, says Kellerman, but to knowingly and deliberately commit oneself to an unethical leader is something else. In the first instance, followers usually conclude that it is in their best interest to go with the flow. To protest against the powers that be takes time, energy, and more often than not courage. Followers put up with bad leadership and dysfunctional organizational cultures because they are inseparable from the needs and goals of followers (Peters & Waterman, 1982). Poorly performing organizations usually have strong dysfunctional cultures.

When followers knowingly commit themselves to unethical leaders, usually they stand to benefit (financially or politically) from the relationship. Such followers are themselves bad (Kellerman, 2005, p. 25). Unethical leadership is usually accompanied by three types of followers: bystanders (those who go along), collaborators (active participants in unethical means), and dedicated believers (co-architects of unethical ends).

Learning From the Mistakes of Leadership in Management

Some hold that it is as instructive to study failed leadership as it is to study good leadership. Bennis and Thomas (2002) identify five fatal mistakes of leadership. Mistake one is to assume that personal integrity is sufficient to the task of leadership. Failure to see or adapt to change or to engage others in envisioning outcomes and processes will lead to failed leadership. Mistake two is to surround oneself with yes men and women to the exclusion of those who speak truth to power. Mistake three recognizes the tendency of some leaders to alienate members of the workforce through an authoritarian leadership style. A fourth mistake is to restructure before the members of the organization get behind the restructuring effort. A fifth mistake is to permit unprofessional conduct (personal attacks) to go unchecked in the workplace. The staff becomes demoralized (even if they initiate or participate in such behavior) if such conduct is left unchecked.

■ Application of Leadership to Policy, Advocacy, Community, and Management Practice in Social Work

Declarative Knowledge: Leadership in Administration and Management

Case studies and typologies on leadership can raise consciousness and suggest directions for change. They are, however, no substitute for monitoring the enactment of leadership in practice. Social workers in macro practice are apt to exercise leadership in administration and management. Therefore the remainder of this chapter focuses on the use of declarative knowledge (procedural knowing) in administrative and management practice. A leadership checklist to monitor the macro practitioner's tacit knowing (reflection of the use of self when exercising authority, influence, and power) may be found in Exhibit 7.1. A process recording of a management meeting is in Exhibit 7.2 and the student's summary is in Exhibit 7.3. For purposes of comparison, unprocessed minutes of the same meeting are shown in Exhibit 7.4.

EXHIBIT 7.2 *Sample Process Recording: Management Meeting*

Thinking Declarative Knowledge	Dialogue Theory-Driven Therapeutic Process	Worker Self-Awareness Monitoring Skill and Feeling	Field Instructor
Tense atmosphere, organizational change is always source of tension	Student: Audience seems upset and anxious	Curious	Why? Relate tension to employee needs for safety, simplicity, and stability
Probably reflects subgroup affiliations	S: Many sidebars going on as group assembles	Left out	In-group/out-group dynamics, watch. *Student feeling indicative of affiliative need?*
Attention to timeline, respect for others' time	Director: Hello, I would like to start the meeting on time.	OK	Rational approach, task orientation
Clear purpose of meeting, recognizes emotional dynamic of audience re: change	I know all of you are anxious to learn more about the organizational changes that are occurring.	Nervous	*Explore student comfort with use of authority.*
Employer-employee relationships, rigid compartmentalization, bureaucratic	I know all of you are anxious to get back to your jobs.	Dismissed	Why is workforce anxious to get back to work? *"Dismissed": good intuition by student. Director comment put staff back in their place rather than empower them to buy into new vision and reorganization. Perhaps director fears there won't be a buy-in.*
Audience is attentive	Individuals stop side conversations.	Anticipation	
Following agenda	D: As you know, the agenda for today is to	Calm	Director shows transactional leadership, day-to-day operations

110

Thinking Declarative Knowledge	Dialogue Theory-Driven Therapeutic Process	Worker Self-Awareness Monitoring Skill and Feeling	Field Instructor
	introduce you to Mr. Jones, who is the new VP of quality control and program operations. He will tell you about himself and the plan to open a new site.		
Legitimate authority by position	VP: Hello, I have recently been hired by United Caring, which runs Jackson Hill, to increase its growth and quality of care.		VP hired to correct a perceived flaw in the organization.
End goal clearly stated; presentation is rather authoritarian		Worried	*Student worry shows concern about end goal.*
Leader polarized self and audience	Whispered sidebars between audience members: What does he mean by increase quality of care? I think we provide quality of care.	Tense	Lack of emotional intellect, statement consistent with rational model of management, sets targets
Establishing expertise as source of authority, power, also length of time in position	VP: For the past 3 years, I worked for Behavioral Health Care. I doubled their productivity in 1 year.	Sorry for staff	*Student connects with audience, not leader.* VP misjudges audience: his expertise may resonate with those who hired him but not with this workforce audience.* (*continued*)

EXHIBIT 7.2 *Sample Process Recording: Management Meeting* (continued)

Thinking Declarative Knowledge	Dialogue Theory-Driven Therapeutic Process	Worker Self-Awareness Monitoring Skill and Feeling	Field Instructor
Lost the audience	Audience body language and facial expressions indicate annoyance.	Uh-oh	Not an inspirational leader. *Student grasps importance of leader-audience connection.*
Challenge to authority	Member: Who is going to decide how staff will be reassigned? Do we have a say in this?	Empathy for staff	Challenge to vision and restructuring, top-down vs. bottom-up management style
Program director attempts to respond, human resources concern	Director: Well I will be . . .		Conflict between upper and middle management
Arrogant, dismissive	VP: Could you hold this question until after I leave? I have another commitment and my time is short.	Dislike tone	Perhaps driven by power motive, self-aggrandizement. *Student does not identify with authoritarian tone.*
Claim of unique skills, power base	VP: United Caring hired me because I have skill in helping organizations grow.		VP sees self as leader, higher up the hierarchy than the director. Senses lost audience, therefore tries to regain
Claim of credentials to establish power base	I have an M.B.A. from X University.		control by exerting power through claims of unique expertise and credentials
Effort to connect on emotional level	VP: I am very excited about being here.		Self-serving?

EXHIBIT 7.3   *Student Summary*

The above meeting was used to hand down a decision (vision and restructuring) made by others to those who have to implement such a decision. This reflects a top-down management style. No effort was made to involve all members of the organization in the vision and restructuring before it occurred. That someone from the outside was brought in (as opposed to internal promotion) speaks to the perception that the agency suffers from a dysfunctional culture. The excerpt shows a classic differentiation of a leadership role (VP) focused on vision and restructuring and a management role (director) focused on tasks and day-to-day operations. The director is more in touch and sensitive to the needs of the workforce than is the VP, who is more removed and higher up the chain of command. Emphasis on improved quality and increased performance is consistent with theory X, which focuses on the bottom line. The tone set by the VP reflects a supervisory model which emphasizes control. His assumption about the nature of the workforce (human resources) appears to be more aligned with negative reinforcement (punishment) rather than with positive incentives. Clearly the VP's message lowered workplace morale. The uncertainty related to the details of the restructuring increased the tension in an already tense atmosphere. His use of time at the meeting was insufficient to meet the needs of the audience given the emotional impact of the announcement.

The leadership style of the VP seems to be autocratic and authoritarian. His use of authority relies on the following types of power: legitimate, expert, and reward. As a new person, he has little referent power (other than that from those who hired him). His lack of emotional intelligence and his self-serving comments indicate that this is a leader who could potentially resort to coercive power to advance an agenda.

I have several areas I need to work on during this internship to improve my leadership skills. In reviewing this recording, I seem to identify with staff rather than with the leadership role. I do recognize emotional intelligence and I do have the capacity for empathy when working with staff as human resources. Less clear is my comfort with authority and my ability to take on a leadership role. I do reject an authoritarian style. My concern about feeling left out may indicate a need for affiliation. I need to balance this need with the capacity to be independent and critical in order to lead. I do show intuitive skills in being able to read the motivations of others and I demonstrate beginning use of theory and knowledge on leadership and management in column one.

If this meeting were not processed as dialogue, the minutes of the above meeting would look as follows:

EXHIBIT 7.4   *Minutes of Jackson Hill Day Program*

September 3, 1995
Attendance: Director (chair of the meeting), social workers, psychologist, art therapist, recreational therapist, job coaches, and psychiatric technicians.
Guest: The new vice president for quality assurance and program operations.
Absent and excused:
Call to order: The meeting was called to order by the director at 9:30 a.m.
Minutes of the previous meeting were read and approved.
The *agenda* for today's meeting was approved.
Minutes:
The director introduced Mr. Jones, the new vice president for quality assurance and program operations.
Mr. Jones provided the following facts about himself. He has an M.B.A. from X University and comes to Jackson Hill after 3 years at Behavioral Health Care, where he improved its quality of service and doubled its service productivity.
After Mr. Jones left, the director engaged in a question-and-answer session with staff regarding changes in work locations and schedules necessitated by the opening of a new site.
The meeting was adjourned at 10:30.

As can be seen, a processed dialogue is a tool that lends itself to increased teaching, learning, and monitoring of the use of self when exercising leadership, authority, and power.

8

Clinical Crisis Intervention

■ Step 2: Crisis Intervention

Two Different Skill Sets: Clinical Crisis Intervention and Crisis Management

Media coverage of recent events, such as the terrorist attacks of September 11, 2001; the December 26, 2004, tsunami; and Hurricane Katrina in 2005, have brought renewed focus to crisis and the response to it. This chapter presents content relevant to step 2 of the decision tree. A crisis may affect individuals (clinical practice) or populations and communities (disasters and public tragedies). Two different crisis intervention skill sets are needed, one for clinical practice (this chapter) and another for crisis management (chapter 9). This chapter summarizes basic, advanced, and applied (domain-specific) crisis intervention skills for clinical practice. Basic and advanced crisis intervention schemas are presented at the end of the chapter. Three cases illustrate the differential use of basic, applied, and domain-specific crisis intervention skills.

Overview of the Clinical Application of Crisis Intervention

By definition, a crisis exceeds the resources and coping mechanisms of an affected individual, population, or community. According to Roberts (2005), a clinical crisis has three phases: pre-crisis, the crisis, and the crisis aftermath (or post-crisis). These phases correspond to three different models of crisis intervention: basic, advanced, and applied. Basic crisis intervention deals with a crisis (emergency) as it is unfolding. Advanced crisis intervention deals with the crisis aftermath (i.e., individuals may experience loss and/or trauma). Applied crisis intervention deals with individuals who live with a condition or in circumstances that occasionally flare up, creating the need for an emergency response (e.g., a medical emergency, a mental health emergency, a situation of domestic violence). In their books, both Roberts (2005) and James and Gilliland (2004) have applied crisis intervention to cases of sexual assault, domestic violence, workplace violence, hostage situations, suicide prevention, addiction, bereavement and grief, medical emergencies, child abuse and neglect, and posttraumatic stress disorder.

By definition, *crisis intervention* is a brief model of talk therapy (action-oriented and directive) used by social workers in mental health direct practice to prevent or reduce psychological harm to individuals in a state of crisis. The pre-crisis phase focuses on prevention. For purposes of this chapter, the term *crisis* is used to denote a sudden, shocking, intense, often catastrophic event perceived by those involved as a situation that overwhelms the coping capacities of individuals and families. The situation calls for an immediate response. A decision schema related to the clinical application of crisis intervention (Exhibit 8.5) is presented at the end of the chapter.

Who Needs Crisis Intervention? Client Population

Those who need help in managing crises are ordinary people who experience extraordinary events, individuals who are sent into harm's way (e.g., members of the military), and individuals with preexisting volatile psychopathology. Those who need help also include individuals who bear witness to the trauma of others, first responders who engage in rescue and recovery, and mental health professionals who serve high-risk clients and respond to critical incidents.

Those in need of crisis intervention are referred to as survivors rather than as victims. The terminology is more than conceptual. Janoff-Bulman (1992) writes that the pathway from victim to survivor lies in the reconstruction of a viable, nonthreatening assumptive world. Being a survivor necessitates the rebuilding of assumptive trust. Such trust incorporates a view of the world as benevolent—but not always. Such trust accepts that what happens makes sense—but not always. Such trust believes that the self can be counted on to be competent and to remain decent, while recognizing that not all things are up to us. The concept of survivor embodies hope and tempers disillusionment.

■ Review of the Literature

Conceptual and Definitional Clarity

There is conceptual and definitional overlap in the literature regarding the terms *crisis*, *trauma*, and *stress*. Sometimes these terms are used interchangeably to refer to the same phenomenon. At other times, a single term, such as crisis, refers to quite disparate phenomena lying at different degrees of abstraction. That is, the term crisis is used to refer to an individual in crisis, to an interpersonal incident of violence, or to a large-scale natural or manmade disaster. The term crisis may also refer to both the event and the reaction to an event by an individual, group, or community. It may refer to different phases of the same event: pre-crisis, crisis, aftermath/post-crisis.

Furthermore, the term crisis may refer to an event source such as a developmental stage of normal growth (Erikson, 1963), a family life-cycle disruption such as marriage or divorce (Carter & McGoldrick, 2004), or moments in life that require adaptation (Caplan, 1964; Parad, 1965). It can refer to mourning in the aftermath of a life-threatening physical event such as the Coconut Grove fire (Lindemann, 1944). A crisis can also refer to life-threatening interpersonal interactions (Roberts, 2005; James & Gilliland, 2004). In terms of duration, a crisis may refer to an acute event, its aftermath, or continuing exposure to ongoing stressors. It has been used to describe the reaction of those directly affected by such events as well as the reactions of those who are secondarily or vicariously affected (i.e., witnesses of or responders to crisis events). It is used to describe interventions applied by first responders to save lives and minimize injury and to interventions by social work mental health professionals to supply concrete social services and to prevent or reduce psychological harm.

For purposes of this chapter, *crisis intervention* is defined as a model of practice that responds to individuals who are exposed to an acute, life-threatening event. A crisis is distinguished from stress by its acute onset and short duration. Conceptually, *stress* refers to continuing exposure to work or life events that keep an individual's autonomic nervous system in arousal (allostatic overload). Conceptually, trauma and crisis are not equivalent terms. Not all those exposed to a crisis experience the event as traumatic. Therefore, the term *trauma* applies only to those individuals who develop one or more persistent symptoms of posttraumatic stress following exposure to an acute, out-of-the-ordinary event.

Scope: Prevalence and Incidence

According to Regehr and Bober (2005), between 1980 and 2002, more than 600,000 people were killed in the United States due to natural disasters. Data from the National Center on Health Statistics, a branch of the Centers for Disease Control, indicate that in 2002 there were 106,742 deaths due to unnatural causes. Of this number, 44,065 died from motor vehicle accidents. There were 17,638 deaths due to assaults and homicides. According to Roberts and Roberts (2005), 1,400 women a year are murdered as a result of domestic violence. In 2002, there were 31,655 suicides, 1,500 of which were in-patient suicides. There were 110.2 million visits to hospital emergency rooms, 2 million of which were related to mental disorders. Of these, 509,000 presented with suicidal ideation or attempts. None of the above figures takes into account those who have been injured or those who have witnessed or responded to such events. Nor do they take into account the loved ones of these individuals.

Given the potentially high number of clients who may present in crisis as well as the increase in violent events and persistent exposure to crisis events through media attention, all practitioners need to possess basic crisis intervention skills as part of their repertoire whether or not they choose crisis intervention as a clinical specialization. In a survey of foundation-year M.S.W. students, it was found that 30% of first-year student interns had a client who presented in crisis (Plionis, Bailey-Etta, & Manning, 2002).

Distinguishing Crisis Events From Individuals in a State of Crisis

It is easier to define a large-scale event as a crisis than it is to determine whether a specific individual is in a state of crisis or trauma. Objective criteria exist by which large-scale events are defined as disasters (i.e., amount of property damage, lives lost, disruption of community infrastructure). In contrast, the criteria for determining whether an individual is in a state of crisis or trauma rely on that individual's report of subjective discomfort or on a practitioner's observation of the individual's behavior. The same event can and does affect people differently. Neither the scale of the event nor its classification in terms of degree of horror accounts for the variance observed among those who react to it. Not all people will have a traumatic stress reaction to a catastrophic or horrifying event (Regehr & Bober, 2005) nor exhibit transient symptoms associated with a crisis.

Typology of Events Classified as Crises

Because the concept of crisis is complex, several typologies have been developed to organize thinking about it. The typology in Exhibit 8.1 categorizes the type of event usually classified as a crisis. Excluded are those crises defined as developmental in nature, i.e., normal individual psychosocial stages of development (Erikson, 1963) or disruptions in family life-cycle stages (Carter & McGoldrick, 2004). Also excluded are those crises deemed to be "unpredictable life events" to which adjustment is required (Caplan, 1964).

■   Theories That Explain Individual Reactions to a Crisis

Biology

In the face of acute threats, biology serves as a protective factor. According to Hans Selye (1936), human beings are biologically wired to respond to a threat. During a crisis, respiration and blood pressure increase. Oxygen and energy shift to large muscles and away from the immune, digestive, and reproductive systems to equip the body for action. Such physiological reactions constitute an automatic, short-term biological response to a crisis.

When the threat is over, the body attempts to return to its normal biological state. Some individuals, however, are unable to do so. Unable to rid themselves of

EXHIBIT 8.1   *Typology of Events Classified as Crises*

Macro Practice	Clinical Practice
Large-Scale Events: Immediate Response *Disasters, Populations*	*Small-Scale Events: Immediate Response* *Interpersonal Critical Incidents*
NATURAL Hurricanes Earthquakes Volcanic eruptions Tornadoes Blizzards Mud slides Drought or famine Forest fires Tidal waves	VIOLENCE Domestic abuse Child abuse Sexual assault, rape Shootings CRIME VICTIM Workplace violence School violence
MEDICAL (BIOLOGICAL) Diseases, Epidemics	PSYCHOPATHOLOGY Psychiatric ER Substance abuse Suicide
MANMADE Bombings	PTSD, trauma OTHER EVENTS
ECOLOGICAL Oil spills Chemical spills	Accidents Life-threatening illness Loss of material goods Reaction to disasters: natural or manmade
POLITICAL War refugees	
ECONOMIC Poverty	

autonomic arousal, such individuals wind up in a state of continuing exhaustion. This is often referred to as stress. A body can physically stay in a state of crisis for a limited time. After that time, an individual is perceived to be in a chronic state of stress. The notion that there is a window of opportunity associated with a crisis when an individual is more amenable to change is based in this theory.

Stress

In addition to being physiological, stress can also be psychosocial in nature. McEwen (2000) and Sterling and Eyer (1988) add to Selye's third stage of crisis reaction (physical exhaustion) the concept of allostatic load (Regehr & Bober, 2005). According to these authors, stress is not only a result of a short-term biological response to physical risk. Stress can be a persistent state of arousal caused by on-going traumatogenic (Bloom, 1998) social forces, such as poverty, discrimination, or societal violence. A preexisting or current stress level may compromise an individual's resiliency when s/he is faced with a new crisis event. Stress then can be an outcome of a crisis or it can play a mediating role in an individual's capacity to deal with a crisis at hand.

Cognitive Appraisal Theory

Lazarus and Folkman (1984) contribute to the understanding of crisis the concepts of primary and secondary cognitive appraisal. They note that individuals are not only on physiological autopilot in a time of crisis. Primary cognitive appraisal refers to whether the individual perceives the event as a threat that poses harm or loss or whether the individual perceives the event as a challenge and opportunity. Secondary cognitive appraisal refers to how the individual assesses his/her ability (or inability) to cope with the event. The meaning that an individual attributes to an event and the impact it has on his/her personal identity and integrity affects the appraisal of the event as a crisis (Bandura, 1997).

Psychodynamic Theory: Resiliency and Vulnerability

Resiliency (psychodynamic theory) holds that most individuals are quick to recover in the face of adversity because of genetic predisposition and an experiential history that has contributed to a strong ego. On the other hand, preexisting *vulnerability* (psychopathology) can precipitate an individual or interpersonal crisis that might turn into an emergency (e.g., suicide attempt, drug overdose, interpersonal assault). Vulnerable individuals (those with preexisting mental illnesses) need help when they experience a flare-up of their condition or life circumstances. In addition, such individuals may find their coping skills compromised or their symptoms exacerbated due to the loss of structure during and following an external crisis event. Vulnerable individuals are likely to need advanced crisis intervention to stabilize their condition or circumstances of living.

■ Clinical Practice Theories

Prevention Theory: Pre-Crisis

Psychoeducation and Skill Acquisition

No single theory or school of thought informs the application of social work crisis intervention with individuals. Individuals in a crisis may present on a continuum ranging from resilient to traumatized. Primary prevention relies on education to prepare individuals for predictable crises. Psychoeducation teaches individuals to problem solve possible events and to develop skills that promote coping. Primary prevention promotes a sense of self-efficacy and competency in the face of adversity. For example, citizens are prepared for disasters by their participation in civil defense and fire drills. Individuals are prepared for a variety of life events (birth, hospitalization, marriage) through psychoeducational groups and may even prepare for violence through self-defense classes. Training and skill acquisition make an individual more self-reliant and therefore more resilient.

Debriefing

Psychological group debriefing originated as an intervention to support emergency personnel (first responders) following their exposure to critical events (Dryegrov, 2003; Everly, 1995). The therapeutic process in debriefing is based on the premise that continuing exposure to life-threatening, violent, and traumatizing events places individuals at mental health risk. The theory holds that affect, accompanied by physiological and cognitive components, is inevitably triggered by life-threatening or horrifying events. If feelings associated with an event are left unprocessed, they are likely to turn into ruminations, preoccupations, dreams, and other forms of intrusion that interfere with thought and social functioning.

In the case of first responders, repeated exposure to horrifying events in combination with unprocessed feelings may pose an occupational health risk. Psychodynamic theory holds that verbalizing emotions can bring them under control. Debriefing is thought to promote mental health because it processes feelings. *Debriefing* is a one-time intervention that occurs within 3–4 days of an event and lasts between 2 and 3 hours. *Defusing* uses the same process but occurs on the same day as the event. The term *critical incident stress debriefing* (CISD) is used in the United States. Psychological debriefing parallels operational debriefing. Operational debriefings are commonly used to review the technical aspects of a rescue-and-recovery mission to improve subsequent missions.

No Treatment and Spontaneous Remission

Because individuals are more or less resilient, it is important for practitioners to recognize that many individuals will not need mental health treatment after exposure to a crisis event. They will not need debriefing, short-term therapy, or long-term therapy. Even when serious symptoms of posttraumatic stress exist, Regehr and Sussman (2004) note that between the crisis event and a 3-month post-crisis marker, many initially assessed as having posttraumatic stress disorder will experience spontaneous remission or significant reduction in the severity and number of symptoms.

Practice Theories and Basic Skills During the Crisis Phase

Mental Health Triage

Initial mental health crisis intervention consists of removing individuals from the scene to reduce their exposure to the imagery of the crisis. As part of crisis management, basic concrete needs are met through the provision of safety, shelter, water, food, and clothing. The focus of mental health counseling during this phase is to assess an individual's risk of danger to self or others (including lethality of means) due to disorientation, grief, or trauma. Efforts are made to normalize reactions to the event and to provide psychoeducation about the potential for symptom development in the crisis aftermath. Mandating mental health counseling (especially debriefing) in the immediate aftermath of a crisis is controversial though all agree that mental health counseling should be available.

Triage is an important tool in the rapid assessment of individuals in crisis. In basic crisis intervention, assessment usually occurs on-site. First responders (medics) use triage to assess injuries to determine their severity and to prioritize medical intervention. *Mental health triage* begins with an initial assessment of whether an individual is in a crisis state and therefore poses a risk of harm to self or others. If warranted, a contract for safety is initiated. Risk assessment is followed by an assessment of an individual's cognitive, affective, and behavioral state to determine his/her capacity to function on a day-to-day basis.

Transient Symptoms

Individuals in a crisis state are likely to exhibit temporary physical reactions, such as a pounding heart, crying, a startle reflex, fainting, moaning, shouting, screaming, and hyperventilation. Cognitively, they may appear to be disoriented and experience a loss of memory and concentration. Their ability to think clearly, plan effectively, and make decisions may be compromised. Affectively, individuals in a state of crisis may feel irritable, insecure, inadequate, helpless, and out of control. They may experience temporary feelings of anxiety, fear, anger, sadness, depression, despair, grief, guilt, outrage, and frustration. Behaviorally, they may be temporarily immobilized and find it difficult to return to the normal activities of daily living. They may seek to avoid reminders of the event.

Practice Theories and Skills in the Crisis Aftermath (Tertiary Intervention)

Resource Loss

Tertiary intervention implies a broad array of traditional social services involving the delivery of both ongoing concrete services and ongoing mental health counseling. Resource loss is an outcome in many crises. Individuals may be faced with a loss of housing, livelihood, or community. Children, adolescents, and young adults experience stress when their education is significantly disrupted. An injection of resources through social work case management or through social work advocacy can reduce the stress of those who suffer concrete losses.

Treating Bereavement in the Crisis Aftermath

According to Regehr and Sussman (2004), theories designed to treat bereavement have their foundation in psychodynamic theory, particularly in relational theories. Despite resiliency, some individuals may develop complicated mourning. Bereavement or grief therapy focuses on detaching from the deceased, working through feelings, and incorporating the loss into a new definition of self without the other. According to the theory, loss-related anxiety is linked to fear of separation. A normal grieving period is thought to last between 1 and 2 years. Resolution of grief is conceptualized as movement through the stages or phases of mourning (Kubler-Ross, 1969).

The acute stage is marked by numbness, frequent yearning for the deceased, and denial of the permanence or reality of the loss (this lasts up to 8 weeks). The second phase consists of an extended period of disorganization and despair (lasting several months). The third phase is one of reorganization. Treatment is largely based on reminiscence and the need to confront grief-related emotions and develop a balanced and realistic memory of the deceased, neither completely negative nor completely idealized. Lost roles and self-concept are reformed by engaging in activities and new relationships. Unresolved grief is thought to lead to depression.

Treating Trauma in the Crisis Aftermath

Trauma theory focuses on exposure to horrifying and life-threatening events (Van der Kolk, McFarlane, & Weisaeth, 1996, 1997). From the earliest of times, trauma was thought to leave indelible and distressing memories from which the sufferer could not escape. In addition, it is now known that autonomic hyperarousal mechanisms related to the event (Regehr & Sussman, 2004) continually recur and are exacerbated by traumatic memories and images. Sensory images of the event are stored in active memory, where they are repeatedly experienced. Therefore, to cope with trauma, individuals often avoid stimuli reminiscent of the event and/or shut out memories of the event. Trauma-related anxiety is related to threat and fear. It is hypothesized that unresolved trauma leads to posttraumatic stress.

Secondary or Vicarious Traumatization

According to Regehr and Bober (2005), the determination of whether an event is traumatizing or not is related more to an individual's capacity for empathy than it is related to the characteristics of the event itself. The capacity for empathy, though a prosocial attribute, may place an individual at risk of taking on the trauma and suffering of others. This helps to explain secondary or vicarious traumatization.

Direct exposure to potentially traumatizing events places individuals at risk of developing symptoms of posttraumatic stress. *Secondary trauma* refers to the effects of loving or feeling responsible for someone who is directly traumatized and consequently experiencing their symptoms. *Vicarious traumatization* refers to the transformation of a worker's inner self as a result of empathic engagement with a traumatized client (Regehr & Bober, 2005, p. 34). Similarly, the concept of *compassion fatigue* describes the results of caring for traumatized individuals over a period of time (Figley, 1995). The conceptualization of secondary or vicarious trauma is particularly relevant for social workers who are continually exposed to stressful work conditions and to high-risk clients who frequently present in crisis.

The Use of Brief Cognitive Therapy in the Crisis Aftermath

Short-term cognitive therapy (based on cognitive attribution) is brief (12 weeks) and conscious. It explores an individual's core beliefs and world views, recognizing that such beliefs have developmental, historical, and cultural components. The goal of the therapy is to help the individual become aware of and change the meanings they have attached to the event. Healing occurs when the individual is able to redefine the meaning of an event and integrate its occurrence into his/her definition of self. People gain control of crises by changing the meaning they attach to things and self. Many experience cognitive disruption on a moral or spiritual dimension (Linley, 2003). The event causes them to question their personal integrity, identity, values, and core beliefs. In facing up to the effects of violence in any form (natural or manmade), human beings attempt to reckon with the violence done to them or by them (Bloom, 1998). According to Linley, wisdom can be both a process and an outcome of trauma.

Stress Management in the Crisis Aftermath

Behavioral and cognitive models of stress management are useful to help individuals reduce and manage their stress levels. Biofeedback or cognitive restructuring are techniques that help individuals to manage traumatogenic social forces and life events.

■ The Use of Self (Relationship) in Crisis Intervention

Any social worker could find him/herself involved in a critical incident. For this reason, all social workers in direct practice need to possess basic crisis intervention skills. It is a practitioner's duty to protect when a crisis poses a danger. Not all practitioners will choose nor are they all suited to crisis intervention as a specialized field of practice. In basic crisis intervention, the social worker must be able to quickly establish rapport and to engage in rapid assessment of risk. The worker must be directive and active in helping the client to secure the resources needed for safety, food, water, and shelter. Ego-supportive techniques are used to help the client recover and return to the normal activities of daily living.

In a crisis, it is important that the social worker remain calm under duress, poised, and in control. Where the unexpected is the norm, the ability to follow systematic actions must be tempered by creativity and flexibility. The social worker must possess energy, tenacity, courage, and belief that the crisis can be favorably resolved. In a crisis, a practitioner must be more active and directive than in other models. Social workers who engage in crisis intervention as a specialization are repeatedly exposed to life-threatening episodes and hear trauma-related material on a continuing basis. Such practitioners need to be resilient and to consider care for themselves. Those who work in crisis intervention come from multiple disciplines. They are medics, nurses, firefighters, police, social workers, and psychologists. Professionals and volunteers work side by side.

■ Evidence: Treating Crisis-Related Loss (Bereavement) and Trauma

According to Regehr and Sussman (2004), trauma has psychodynamic, biological, and cognitive formulations. Some individuals suffer both loss and trauma from the same event. However, the theoretical approach to bereavement and the theoretical approach to trauma are divergent and at times antithetical. Which model is a social worker to choose? According to Regehr and Bober (2005) and Regehr and Sussman (2004), what may look favorable at the lowest level of evidence (i.e., anecdotal or satisfaction survey) may not hold up when a more rigorous design (cross-sectional or randomized control trial) is employed. Higher-order designs may result in findings that are disparate from lower-level findings. Therefore, the literature often recommends and cautions against the same intervention.

Bereavement

According to Regehr and Sussman (2004), the empirical basis for theoretical constructs and resulting treatment approaches in the area of grief work are weak. Based on their review of the empirical literature on bereavement and grief, they come to the following four conclusions: (1) Limited evidence supports the view that expression of grief leads to resolution; (2) those with normal grieving patterns do not seem to benefit from intervention, while those with complex grief seem to benefit from individual treatment; (3) those with an ambivalent relationship with the deceased may benefit from relationally focused treatment; and (4) those with lower relational capacity may benefit from therapy aimed at providing immediate support and problem solving rather than interpretation and conflict exploration.

Trauma

In the area of trauma, Regehr and Sussman (2004, pp. 300–302) come to the following three conclusions: (1) Good evidence exists that individual cognitive-behavioral treatment reduces trauma symptoms; CBT aimed at cognitive restructuring and symptom management appears to be effective; (2) single-session groups may exacerbate symptoms; (3) exposure treatment, while effective with treatment completers, may require the screening out of individuals with high anxiety, suicidal ideation, or other concurrent life crises. Those with traumatic loss may experience increased distress in exposure therapy.

Exposure Therapy

Exposure therapy (Friedman, 2001) addresses the conditioned emotional response experienced by those who suffer from posttraumatic stress disorder (PTSD). Exposure therapy attempts to separate traumatic memory from the conditioned emotional response so that memory no longer has the power to dominate thoughts, feelings, and behavior. Exposure therapy reexposes the client to the traumatic event. It uses imaginal exposure or in vivo exposure (going to the site). Clients are asked to narrate the events associated with the trauma while confronting its imagery, repeating the story several times in a given session. It is thought that exposure abolishes the first stage of the conditioned emotional response. Exposed to traumatic stimuli, the client experiences traumatic memories as memories, and this severs the link between recollection of the event and intrusive hyperarousal. If conditioned emotional responses can be abolished, avoidant symptoms are no longer necessary. Some (Friedman, 2001; Forbes et al., 2003) hold that exposure therapy is effective. Exploration of feelings (traumatic bereavement) or cognitions (the meaning ascribed to events) can trigger hyperarousal and retraumatization if exposure therapy has not been utilized or has not led to a successful outcome. Regehr and Bober (2005) caution against exposing a client with PTSD to any therapy without examining the indications for and against the therapy for the particular client at hand.

Evidence: Debriefing

In the area of debriefing, discrepancies exist between the findings of lower-level research designs (anecdotal reports and satisfaction surveys), which tend to be positive, and those that use higher-order designs (cross-sectional or randomized control trials), which tend to be contradictory or cautionary. Overall, the comparative research evidence supports the efficacy of brief models of therapy, including crisis intervention, over long-term models of therapy (Roberts, 1990, p. 303).

Empirical Evidence on Crisis Intervention

Roberts and Everly (2006) have recently completed a meta-analysis of 36 crisis intervention studies. According to the authors, adults in acute crisis or with trauma symptoms can be helped with intensive crisis intervention programs or multi-component critical incident stress management. Single crisis intervention sessions are not effective. Though they report high average effect sizes, they note that 26 of the 36 studies were not experimental studies. Included were studies on in-home intensive crisis intervention with families. The authors conclude that research on crisis intervention is in an early stage of development.

■ Case Illustrations

Three case scenarios illustrate basic, advanced, and domain-specific clinical crisis intervention. Basic and advanced treatment schemas are presented at the conclusion.

Case Scenario 1: Basic Crisis Intervention

You are a social worker with the Department of Social Services in a large midwestern city. Following days of torrential downpours, the Mississippi River has overflowed. First responders are rescuing families whose homes are flooding along the river bank. You are assigned to Margaret playground (one of several sites) where first responders are transporting evacuees. Quonsets huts (left over from World War II) are being set up as temporary housing. It is hot and humid following the summer storms. You are on-site at the playground to provide basic mental health crisis intervention. Consistent with the basic crisis intervention schema, you are conducting a rapid assessment interview with Carolyn and Richard Meyer and their three children: Stacy, age 10, John, age 8, and Mike, age 6. You offer the family water and crackers and tell them that lunch will be served between noon and 2:00 p.m. As you introduce yourself, you assure the family that their immediate needs for safety, shelter, food, and clothing will be met on-site. You tell them that you are there to help them develop a recovery plan for the near future.

Case Explication: On-Site Basic Crisis Intervention

Basic crisis intervention meets urgent need. Relationship in basic crisis intervention is directive, systematic, and active and leads to rapid engagement. The worker uses triage to meet the immediate needs of the Meyer family for physical safety, shelter, food, clothing, health, and mental stability. The interview occurs on-site, i.e., the playground where the family has been relocated for safety along with other flood victims. The family has on-site access to temporary shelter (Quonset huts), food (snack and lunch), and additional clothing. Having met the family's immediate concrete needs, the worker begins rapid assessment of the family's mental health status. She begins with an assessment of transient symptoms. She observes that Mrs. Meyer is crying, Mr. Meyer appears stunned, and the children are uncharacteristically silent and immobile for their ages. The youngest seems to be in need of reassurance and climbs into his mother's lap during the interview. (Mrs. Meyer holds him tightly.) These symptoms are likely to be transient, but the worker keeps them in mind as the interview continues.

To assure safety, the worker seeks additional information as to the physical health status of the family members, checking for minor injuries and the need for any continuing care. She learns that Mike needs to continue on an antibiotic for an ear infection and the father needs to continue on blood pressure medication. There is an interactive effect between stress and blood pressure that increases Mr. Meyer's health risk. The worker refers the family to the medical tent, where they can get the medications they need to continue the health care already in place.

The worker moves to rapid assessment of mental health risk. No member appears to pose a danger to self or others, and there is no indication that a lethality of means is present. The worker educates the family that symptoms of depression or trauma could occur later and asks the family to make a verbal contract for safety. If any family member feels that s/he is not OK or observes that another member is acting in a way that is of concern, each commits to letting the worker know or to calling the hotline on the card given to them. All agree. All members express concern for the family dog, which was lost during the chaos.

The worker continues to explore the family's coping capacity. She assesses each member's cognitive appraisal of the event and the members' perception of their ability to cope with it. The parents express distress (normal) over their losses (all their material possessions, including their house and car) but take comfort in the fact that the family was rescued and everyone is safe. The parents say they have made it before and they will make it again. They begin to identify the resources they have to work with: Mr. Meyer has a job and therefore income; Mrs. Meyer begins to identify family and friends who may be able to help with temporary living accommodations while the family relocates or rebuilds. The children ask about the dog, their friends, and school. Responses indicate that the family is looking toward the future and actively beginning to plan for their recovery. The worker provides Mrs. Meyer with a phone card so she can contact extended family and friends after the interview.

The worker begins to assess the family's needs for concrete services in the near future, e.g., transportation so Mr. Meyer can get to work, return to school for the children, and location of alternate housing as the family recovers. The worker informs the family about formal programs specifically established for flood victims and other programs for which they may be eligible. She talks to them about the potential need for counseling. She educates them about the fact that the same event can affect people differently (even those within the same family) and the same person can be affected differently over time. She provides them with a card that lists behaviors or symptoms that bear watching. She encourages them to contact a counselor to have such behaviors or symptoms evaluated should they occur.

The worker concludes that the family appears to be resilient and already shows signs of actively planning for their recovery. They have assets in that their health is stable, Mr. Meyer has a job and therefore income, and they have a social network (family, friends, church group) which can supply them with resources as they recover. The worker alerts them that any long-term recovery is likely to put stress on the family and may cause family tensions. Changes in family relationships are likely as members try to cope during the recovery phase. She tells them that this is normal and that it is sometimes helpful to talk about family stress with a professional counselor. Recognizing the importance of pets to mental health and recovery, the worker gives the Meyers a list of veterinary clinics and pounds to help them find their missing dog. She tells them about the board on-site where families can post descriptions of lost pets.

Case Scenario 2: Off-Site Advanced Clinical Crisis Intervention

You are a school social worker. Several children who were displaced by recent flooding have entered the school system where you work. Stacy Meyer, age 10, is in the fifth grade. The teacher has referred her to you because Stacy is having academic and social problems in school. She has missed several days of school and often does not turn in homework. She has not made any friends and seems to be a target of a girl's clique. You contact Mrs. Meyer to request her permission to talk with Stacy. She gives her consent. When talking with Mrs. Meyer, you learn that Stacy has always had a positive attitude toward school and received mostly B's, some A's, and some C's in her previous school. Stacy had one good friend, Mary, in that school.

Case Explication: Advanced Clinical Crisis Intervention—School Setting

According to the advanced crisis intervention schema, advanced crisis intervention occurs in the crisis aftermath in a setting unrelated to the site of the original crisis. Despite knowledge of the distal crisis event, the worker perceives the proximate problem to be worked as setting-specific (i.e., school social work). The worker chooses theory- and evidence-based approaches consistent with the setting (school) and the population (school-age students). The worker may or may not consider that she is engaged in advanced clinical crisis intervention.

As Stacy enters the school counseling office, the worker greets her and introduces herself. The worker assures Stacy that the meeting has been approved by

EXHIBIT 8.2   *On-Site Rapid Crisis Intervention Schema Treatment Matrix for the Meyer Family: Flood Crisis*

Procedural Knowing	Worker Action	Desired Goal/Outcome
Rapid engagement	Worker is directive, systematic, active	Rapport, working relationship
Triage	Meet immediate basic needs for safety, shelter, food, clothing	Relocate to playground as safe haven, Quonset hut as shelter, snack, lunch, clothes
Transient symptoms assessment	Determine anxiety, stress level, capacity to plan and make decisions	Identification of transient symptoms, normalization, treatment
Risk assessment: health	Meet medical needs	Supply medications to continue health care
Risk assessment: mental health	Danger to self or others, lethality of means	Contract for safety
Cognitive assessment	Appraisal of event and ability to cope	Support or change appraisal as indicated
Strengths assessment	Determine assets, determine resiliency, social network	Work with strengths Consider no further action
Material resources assessment	Plan for recovery	Link to formal programs for flood victims and with existing welfare programs
Promote mental health	Locate pet	Contact local veterinary clinics, dog pounds; post lost-dog sign on site
Aftermath mental health	Counseling: treat possible depression or trauma in aftermath, treat stress of recovery in crisis aftermath	Normalize possibility of counseling need and provide referral resource
Follow up	Give card, ask family to call in 2 weeks	Maintain outreach, resource connection

both her mother and her teacher (fiduciary responsibility). The worker identifies the purpose of the meeting, saying that it is the worker's job to be sure that the school is a comfortable place for students to learn. You ask her if it is all right with her if you talk with her about how the new school is going for her (fiduciary responsibility, informed consent, and initial contracting). Stacy nods in assent. Unlike basic on-site crisis intervention, the school social worker has time to develop a working relationship with Stacy and time within the interview and over a series of interviews to assess risk (danger to self and others).

You support Stacy's strengths by saying that her mother told you that Stacy is a good student and misses her old school and best friend, Mary. Based on this information, you rule out a history of academic and social problems. You observe that Stacy looks down and sighs. You normalize how difficult it is for anyone to attend a new school, especially after such an event as a flood (distal crisis event). You ask Stacy how her brothers are doing. She says that they both have made friends and don't seem to mind the new school.

Stacy tells you that she hasn't made any friends and in fact there is one group of girls who say mean things about her to others and exclude her on the playground. No one wants to play with her or be her partner in school projects (proximate problem to be worked). She wipes away the silent tears that are dripping down her face. The worker offers her a tissue and acknowledges how painful it is to feel excluded. As the interview progresses, the worker learns that being in the new school and not having any friends makes Stacy not want to come to school. Stacy says she doesn't sleep well at night and reports feeling sick in the morning. She says she doesn't always complete her homework because her father is working overtime and her mother is taking in laundry and baking to earn extra money. She has to watch her brothers when she gets home. Stacy says that she just wants to go back home and attend her old school and be near her friend Mary. She wishes things could be the way they were before the flood (stress associated with coping in the crisis aftermath).

You ask Stacy what she does or how she feels when she thinks about how things are now and how they were before the flood (assess risk-danger to self or others). Stacy says sometimes she cries. She doesn't feel like eating, and she tosses and turns at night worrying about things. She wishes things would get better but doesn't know how to make them better.

The worker concludes that Stacy is not in immediate danger to self or others but that she is at risk for depression related to coping with a new school and new family responsibilities in the crisis aftermath. She exhibits symptoms of autonomic arousal. The worker recognizes that fifth grade is a particularly difficult social environment, under any circumstance. Stacy's experience as a new fifth-grade girl is very different from the transition of her two brothers, ages 8 and 6. In the fifth grade, girl cliques are dominant and create unhealthy in-group/out-group dynamics. A fifth-grade girl's self-esteem is particularly at risk due to the social definition of self made by others (setting-specific knowledge). The worker concludes that Stacy is not experiencing posttraumatic stress. Rather, she is experiencing ongoing stress (in the crisis aftermath) related to role loss, role strain, role conflict, and role disruption both at home and at school.

The worker chooses to intervene using several different theories. She uses ego-supportive one-on-one intervention to provide Stacy with support, emotional containment, and encouragement (they agree to meet for 6 weeks; talk within activity). Consistent with an ego-supportive model, the worker helps Stacy to find activities that will increase her potential to meet others, have fun, and do things that will give her pleasure (promote coping). The worker explores clubs (chorus, band, sports, chess, etc.), youth groups, and church groups. Consistent with interactive theory, the worker identifies a student in the seventh grade who will act as a big sister. She identifies someone in second grade to whom Stacy can be a mentor through art. She works with Stacy's teacher to assign and rotate partners on class projects (milieu change). The worker arranges an after-school homework buddy. She sets up an appointment with Stacy's mother to explore alternative ways of providing after-school care for the boys (concrete service) to lessen Stacy's caregiver role. When they meet, the school social worker will refer Mrs. Meyer to a social services worker to see if the family is eligible for programs that might reduce their financial stress and/or provide them with some respite.

Case Scenario 3: Domain-Specific Crisis Intervention

You are a social worker who has specialized in forensic social work. You are currently working at a domestic violence clinic in an urban area. You are called by a nurse in the emergency room who asks that you come to the hospital to talk with Gloria, who has been assaulted by her live-in boyfriend of 5 years. Gloria's injuries are severe enough to require hospitalization. Current X rays reveal that Gloria has been beaten before. Following her discharge from the hospital, Gloria accepts housing in a shelter as she considers her options.

Explication of Scenario 3

Basic crisis intervention is needed initially to deescalate and to stabilize the crisis situation (medical emergency caused by domestic assault). To assure safety, the worker is active, directive, and systematic in assuring that the client's basic needs for concrete services are met (medical attention, filing of assault charges, and shelter). Once the crisis is stabilized, the worker enters a different phase of treatment, which requires domain-specific knowledge. During this phase, the worker and client often experience difficulty in contracting for service. According to the literature and empirical evidence, victims of domestic violence often choose to return to their abusing partners. Though no level of violence is ever safe, abused partners often attempt to manage their domestic situation rather than leave it. It is important therefore for a forensic social worker to engage the client in risk assessment of her situation and to provide her with survival strategies. Risk assessment requires evaluation of the perpetrator's characteristics as well as the severity, duration, and continuum (trajectory) of the assaults. The fact that Gloria has suffered previous abuse and injuries is indicative that the decision to leave is a difficult one for her. The worker helps Gloria to identify triggers or cues that may allow her to predict that an episode is about to occur. With this skill, she can plan for her safety accordingly and hopefully avoid the occurrence of another assault. The worker has Gloria develop a safety plan and survival kit (see Roberts &

EXHIBIT 8.3 *Treatment Matrix for Stacy Meyer: School Setting*

Procedural Knowing	Worker Action	Desired Goal/Outcome
Interview	Determine the problem to be worked	Improve Stacy's school experience, performance
Belief bonding	Time to develop relationship with Stacy, her mother, and the teacher	Establish working relationship
Risk assessment: monitor for depression	Assure safety	Change sense of hopelessness and increase coping skills
Assess autonomic system arousal	Increase positive activity, involve in sports, music, church group, etc.	Improve sleep and appetite, consider medication if needed
Assess academic behavior in school setting	Find academic after-school support for homework, i.e., a study buddy	Maintenance of academic success in new school, decrease school absences, improve homework
Assess role loss, disruption, strain, or conflict	Locate 7th-grader to be a big sister, locate 2nd-grader to be Stacy's little sister, find way to relieve Stacy from some at-home childcare responsibilities	Establish and expand healthy interactions
Assess environmental hazards and risks	Have teacher assign and rotate partners when assigning group projects	Eliminate project partners as risk source
	Group work with cliques, dynamics of in-group/out-group, scapegoating	Change negative group dynamics of girl groups though group work, do not connect directly to Stacy's situation
Provide brief counseling, use activity-based approach to build on client strengths	Meet with Stacy once a week for the next 6 weeks, talk while being active, e.g., going for a walk, using a computer, playing a game	Ego supportive: improve Stacy's capacity to problem solve and cope, promote Stacy's definition of self as competent and liked

EXHIBIT 8.4   *Domain-Specific Crisis Intervention Treatment Matrix for Gloria: Domestic Abuse*

Procedural Knowing	Worker Action	Desired Goal/Outcome
Basic crisis intervention	Treat emergency	Deescalate and stabilize crisis situation
Assure physical health	Medical treatment for injuries, hospitalization	Restore physical health
Assure legal recourse	Documentation of injuries for use in legal proceedings	Ensure legal protection and client rights, file assault charges, seek restraining order
Fiduciary responsibility	Obligation to report abuse to social services	Provide protective services
Domain-specific knowledge: forensic social work	Use medical, legal, social milieu (shelter, concrete services), and counseling support	Recovery and prevention of recurrence
Social milieu: use of resources: shelters, hotlines	Provide shelter for safety, meet concrete needs, e.g., food, clothing	Eliminate dependency on perpetrator for concrete needs
No level of violence is safe Risk assessment: assess characteristics of perpetrators	Use warning checklist (Roberts & Roberts, 2005, pp. 19–21)	Help Gloria recognize perpetrator triggers or cues that predict episode is about to occur Help her avoid partners likely to abuse
Assess protective factors	Provide Gloria with coping strategies (e.g., Safety Plan Checklist and Survival Kit in Roberts & Roberts, 2005)	Prevent abusive episodes from recurring
Counseling	Empowerment theory, survivor not victim, no one deserves to be beaten	Enable client to leave abusive partner

Roberts, 2005, pp. 114–118). Gloria has dropped the assault charges and refuses to consider a restraining order. She has declined empowerment-based counseling to help her explore leaving the abusive situation. She plans on leaving the shelter tomorrow.

Other examples of domain-specific crisis intervention involve such domains as mental health (suicide attempt or danger to others), drug addiction/overdose, health/medical crisis, etc. In each domain, the worker must first use basic crisis

EXHIBIT 8.5   *Crisis Assessment in Clinical Social Work*

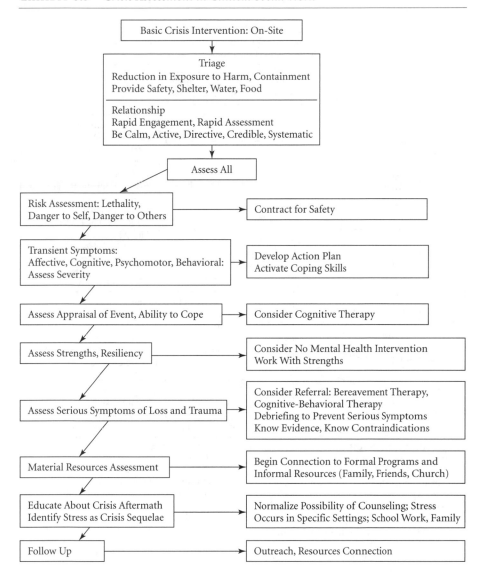

intervention to deescalate and stabilize the crisis situation and then use domain-specific knowledge to continue treatment and prevent the occurrence of another crisis.

■ Basic and Advanced Crisis Intervention Decision Schemas

The schemas for advanced and applied crisis intervention are the same in that each begins with basic crisis intervention to deescalate and stabilize the current crisis or emergency. They differ in that advanced crisis intervention deals with

EXHIBIT 8.6   *Advanced and Applied Clinical Crisis Intervention: The Crisis Aftermath*

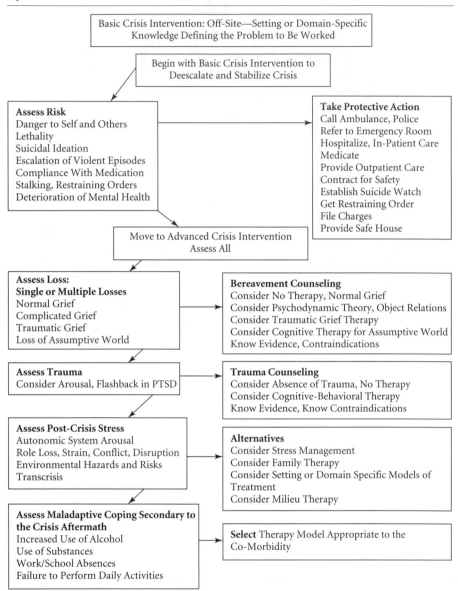

problems in the crisis aftermath (proximal problem) that are linked to the original crisis event (distal problem). Domain-specific crisis intervention deals with flare-ups or emergencies associated with an ongoing pathological situation, e.g., a history of domestic abuse, a history of mental illness with suicide attempts, a physical condition with medical flare-ups, or a substance abuse history with overdose.

9
Crisis Management

■ Public Tragedies, Relief, and Humanitarian Aid

This chapter continues to elaborate step 2: crisis intervention. Here, however, the response is crisis management directed at populations and communities in urgent need of resources due to a disaster or public tragedy (Regehr & Bober, 2005; Lattanzi-Licht & Doka, 2003). Organizations charged with responding to large-scale disasters or public tragedies have two functions. Performed by first responders (firefighters, police/military, and medics), the first function is to secure the scene and to engage in rescue and recovery operations. The second function, performed by planners, policy makers, and administrators, is disaster relief. Here, the mission is to provide relief programs to populations in urgent need and to reconstruct communities in the aftermath of a disaster. Social work practitioners use macro methods of crisis management to respond to disasters and public tragedies.

Policy, Advocacy, Community, and Management Methods

Relief operations require the development of policy-based social programs. The delivery of relief programs by emergency services organizations requires planning, coordination, and management. Emergency services organizations activate warnings and supervise disaster response plans. Such organizations supply and deploy both material goods and human resources. Logistical deployment of resources must occur in a timely manner and oversight must be provided to sustain and maintain resources over time. New plans have to be developed to match unfolding events. In the aftermath of the disaster, communities need to be rebuilt and the populace supported with concrete services.

Elaboration of the Decision Tree: Crisis Intervention
for Populations and Communities

To respond to a disaster or public tragedy, then, a social work practitioner needs
to consider a variety of interventions that lie along the macro-micro continuum.
Two decision schemas are presented at the end of this chapter. Exhibit 9.5 dia-
grams assessment and intervention options consistent with prevention, early intervention, and tertiary intervention. Exhibit 9.6 applies crisis intervention to
international disasters.

■ Social Problems, Social Forces, and Social Dynamics

Definition: Disasters and Public Tragedies

According to the definition of the Federal Emergency Management Agency
(FEMA), a *disaster* is an unforeseen and often sudden event that causes great destruction and human suffering. Though often caused by nature, disasters can
have human origins. Wars, civil disturbances, and acts of terrorism are included
among the causes of disasters. They often destroy homelands and displace people.
Other causes can be attributed to the collapse of a building, a blizzard, drought,
epidemic, earthquake, explosion, fire, flood, hazardous material (toxic chemicals)
leak, transportation incident (air, sea, rail, auto), hurricane, nuclear incident, tornado, or volcano. Disasters lead to significant harm to people and their sustainable environment. A disaster has the potential of permanently damaging the total
ecological system.

A disaster becomes a public tragedy when it focuses national or international
attention and mourning. A public tragedy elicits a societal response and collective
action. Disasters reflect the qualities of adaptability and resiliency between people
and their communities. By definition, large-scale disasters have municipal, regional, national, and international levels of emergency response and law enforcement. Immediate response and long-term recovery require the utilization of all
social work macro methods in crisis management.

What Social Workers Do

Macro social work practitioners work in governmental organizations and non-
governmental agencies in the delivery of mental health services to survivors of
disasters. They work with displaced persons and political refugees. They provide
services to refugees forced to flee their countries because of famine or political turmoil. As community practitioners, social workers rebuild communities impacted
by disasters and public tragedies. Many social work practitioners work with international organizations or ministries to provide disaster and humanitarian relief.

Direct social work practitioners deliver concrete services to individuals as part of humanitarian relief programs developed and managed by social work macro practitioners. Social work practitioners work at both ends of the macro-micro continuum of crisis intervention.

Disaster Typology

There are two types of disasters: One is unexpected and acute, and the other is known and expected because it is gradual and prolonged.

Scale and Scope of the Event

Disasters by definition are measured on a scale calibrated to register massive destruction, multiple casualties, mutilated bodies, and life-threatening situations. The location of a disaster (urban or rural; local, national, or international) affects the timeliness and sustainability of resources and support.

According to Regehr and Bober (2005, p. 50), since the mid-1990s, 2 billion people, one-third of the earth's population, were affected by disasters. Between 1992 and 2000, the United Nations reported 4,989 disasters throughout the world, approximately 500 disasters each year (most not reported in North America). According to reports, on average, 60,000 people are killed each year by natural disasters. When armed conflict, genocide, and terrorism are added to the

EXHIBIT 9.1   *Disaster Typology*

Acute: Disaster Relief	Gradual and Prolonged: Humanitarian Relief
Natural or manmade disasters, intended or unintended	*Known and expected, preventive action possible*
Hurricane	Ecological: drought, famine
Earthquake	Biological: disease, epidemic
Volcanic eruption	Political: war, civil disturbance
Tornado	(destroys homeland and displaces people)
Blizzard	Economic depression
Mud slide	
Tidal wave	
Forest fire	
Oil spill	
Building collapse	
Explosion	
Hazardous material	
Transportation incident	
Nuclear incident	

disaster nomenclature, the death toll mounts. In their review of the 25 largest violent events of the twentieth century, Reza et al. (2001) estimate that 191 million people have lost their lives.

■ Major Theories of Disaster Management

Historical Perspective

Initially, disasters were regarded as rare events of nature (outside forces). They were perceived fatalistically, neither predictable nor preventable. Recovery served as a means for a community to rebalance itself. Over time, it was recognized that human actions also contributed to the occurrence of disasters, either through preventable causes (poor building construction, poor farming techniques) or through deliberate acts of intentional harm and destruction, such as terrorism, genocide, or toxic waste. Following this recognition came the recognition that human action might also be able to prevent or mitigate the effects of disasters.

Prevention Model: Preparedness

Preparedness is based on a model of prevention. The concept of prevention has its origins in public health and community psychiatry. Prevention is conceptualized in terms of primary, secondary, and tertiary interventions. In the case of disaster and public tragedy, primary, secondary, and tertiary interventions require macro methods. Policies and advocacy raise funds and establish relief programs. Relief programs are housed within administrative structures which plan, organize, and distribute material and human resources where needed. Devastated communities are reconstructed. Disaster response has two phases: immediate crisis relief (secondary intervention) and long-term repair of the physical, built, and human community (tertiary intervention). Through preparedness, primary prevention attempts to prevent disasters from occurring.

Primary prevention identifies risks and hazards in an effort to eradicate them and prevent disaster. When events occur unexpectedly or unfold rapidly, comprehensive disaster preparedness plans help to mitigate the effects of the disaster. Early warning systems (communication) are activated; evacuation orders are given; and shelters are opened to receive those fleeing from or removed from the impact area.

Disaster preparedness plans include an operational command structure to deploy emergency personnel and to coordinate involvement of multilevel crisis and relief organizations. Both public education and the training of response teams are aspects of primary prevention. Response team members need to be selected and hired on the basis of needed competencies. Ongoing training to develop and maintain readiness is necessary. The needs of first responders and their families must be considered.

Secondary prevention or early intervention consists of the rescue-and-recovery mission/operation. First responders (firefighters, police, paramedics) are deployed to the scene before other resources are put in place. Their tasks are to gain control of the event or scene, preserve life, treat the wounded (rescue), and locate the dead (recovery). Mental health personnel (including social workers) provide acute crisis intervention on-site. Social workers in community practice help to reconstruct communities and to make repairs to the land, infrastructure, and populace.

The Problem-Solving or Task Model

The problem-solving or task model of disaster management is a practical model. First responders perform the first three tasks: gain control of the event or scene, preserve life and treat the wounded (rescue), and locate and recover the dead (recovery). Secondary responders are involved in all subsequent tasks. The fourth task involves management of the risks on the scene and the establishment of safe zones where victims can be relocated away from the horror of the immediate impact area. The fifth task is to deploy and manage resources needed by survivors, such as water, food, shelter, sanitation, and clothing. The sixth task is to provide security: protect persons and property and prevent looting. The seventh task is to restore communication between survivors and their loved ones and to provide official information on the disaster and the course of recovery. The eighth task is to control rumors to maintain calm and cooperation. The final task is to assess social problems secondary to the disaster, such as health epidemics or displaced persons.

When the problem-solving/task model is applied in the long-term aftermath of a disaster, it involves actions designed to rebuild community infrastructure. When applied to individuals, the problem-solving or task model consists of engaging survivors in their own active coping plans. It is thought that task management requires the mastery of feelings in order to solve problems. Actions substitute for feelings in the management of grief and trauma.

Conservation of Resources Model

A third theory of disaster management is Hobfoll's (1989) theory of conservation of resources (COR). Hobfoll states that material and social resources are key determinants in communal efficacy in responding to disasters. In a disaster, communities attempt to obtain, retain, protect, and foster resources. Where resources are scarce, a police or military presence is needed to regulate access to needed resources and to deter looting.

Hobfoll's theory of COR represents a new attempt to conceptualize resources in terms of stress. This theory recognizes that local communities or governments may not be able to absorb the impact of a disaster with their own resources.

When this occurs, there is a need for directed invitations for outside support. Whether material or human, all resources need to be coordinated when they arrive. Human resources, once there, need to be housed and fed. Like the disaster itself, the arrival of resources can overtax a community. Both resource overload and lack of resources add to the level of stress experienced by a community.

In a disaster, a loss of one resource can quickly cascade into a series of losses. The actual loss of a resource or the failure to regain resources after a disaster are significant predictors of community and individual distress. On the other hand, the timely injection of resources can promote individual and community recovery.

Community Infrastructure

As Eyerdam (2003, pp. 28–29) details in his account of Hurricane Andrew, local structures are often incapacitated or destroyed by the disaster:

> The first structure to be affected was the communication system. Several emergency functions on the same rotary phone switches were compromised: the notification system for special needs citizens, communications and dispatch for police, fire rescue, the National Guard, rumor control, and 911.

Infrastructure services such as power/electricity, sanitation, communication (phone, radio, television), and transportation (road, rail, air, sea) contribute to a community's ability or inability to respond to a crisis in process and to its aftermath. Institutions such as government, law enforcement, health and mental health, social services, and fire departments may become incapacitated. The financial stability of individual families and the community are threatened as businesses go under.

Resource Depletion

The depletion of material resources is a major organizational concern. Eyerdam reports that, in Hurricane Andrew, 92% of the power grid in southern Florida needed reconstruction. An estimated 1.4 million, or 84% of the Florida power and light customers, were without power. It took 34 days to restore power to all customers. More than 7,300 street lights were down, and 21,000 wooden power poles were snapped and needed replacement.

Depletion of human resources is also a concern. Eyerdam notes that in the aftermath of Hurricane Andrew, significant outmigration occurred. A total of 40,000 families, or 83,000 people, moved out of Miami-Dade. Homestead saw the disappearance of much of its middle class. Some refer to this as white flight. Insurance money helped those who had financed homes and cars. The poor, who had no insurance, got poorer. Having fewer options, they remained. According to Florida International University, the median household income declined by 15–41% in some of the areas hit by Hurricane Andrew (Eyerdam, 2003, p. 35).

Other locations, like Fort Lauderdale's western counties, saw a migratory increase of 80% over the previous year.

Organizational Readiness

Structure-functional theory informs organizational practice during a disaster. Two layers of organizations are affected. Each organization has a specialized function. *Local organizations* in the area of impact respond first. A local office of emergency preparedness is responsible for preparing emergency plans, initiating early warning systems, and activating emergency services. First responders are alerted and activated by the nearest office of emergency preparedness.

As part of the operational command structure, experts in communications and transportation supervise evacuation and deploy resources to meet identified needs. Eyerdam's account of Hurricane Andrew portrays the importance of organizational readiness. According to Eyerdam, 79 movable bridges, the responsibility of the state Department of Transportation, waited for lock-down orders that were late in being issued. Evacuation was compromised by the opening and closing of these bridges to accommodate boat owners. Coin-operated tollbooths created bottlenecks and further compromised the flow of the evacuation. When the (hurricane-proof) broadcast tower fell, at least a dozen telephone and radio relay stations used for law enforcement and emergency services went dead. Disaster response plans must be inclusive of those with special needs. Eyerdam (2003) reports that, during Hurricane Andrew, life-sustaining medications for the physically ill were part of comprehensive disaster planning but medications to stabilize the mentally ill were not.

A *second organizational layer* consists of external emergency services organizations invited to assist local communities. Depending on the location of the disaster, getting resources to it may be very difficult. In the case of Dade County, Florida, the landscape had been unrecognizably altered. Many roads had been destroyed, and all signage had disappeared. Even those geographically familiar with the area had difficulty navigating from here to there. Though tons of supplies and hundreds of volunteers awaited deployment, getting them to where they were needed proved difficult. Finding safe structures to house volunteers and safe escorts to protect them was almost impossible. Eventually, the 18th Airborne Division with 20,000 troops was activated. Rangers in Humvees were dispatched to restore order and set up kitchens. Within 24 hours of their activation, there were a million rolls of toilet paper and 4,000 portable toilets distributed.

Traumatogenic Forces

The concept of traumatogenic forces refers to societal conditions that support traumatizing behaviors (Bloom, 1998, p. 27). Though disasters may initially appear as isolated and unpredictable events, closer analysis may reveal societal patterns that support the conditions that lead to disasters. According to Bloom, *traumatogenic forces* are those social practices and trends that cause, encourage, or contribute to the generation of traumatic acts. Capitalism (profit motive) may be a traumatogenic force that can lead to poor construction, soil erosion, lax standards and enforcement, and cost-saving compromises. Political policies that fail to respond to the plight of others (as in Rwanda, Darfur, Germany under Hitler) are also traumatogenic in nature. Immigration policies that deny asylum or resettlement contribute to traumatic conditions. In a very compelling way, says Bloom, being against violence means that we must be for the humane treatment of all other human beings.

■ Policy and Organizational Context of Disaster Relief

Policies Related to Disaster Response and Relief

Several key policies direct national and worldwide emergency response and disaster relief. These policies are identified in Exhibit 9.2.

EXHIBIT 9.2   *Policies Related to Emergency Response and Disaster Relief*

Robert T. Stafford Disaster Relief and Emergency Assistance Act, P.L. 93-288
Congressional Disaster Relief Acts, 1803, 1970, 1974
Congressional Charter, 1905: designated the American Red Cross to provide
    disaster relief services around the world
Aviation Disaster Family Assistance Act, 1996
United Nations Resolution 46/182, 1991: created the Office for the Coordination of Humanitarian Affairs

---

United States

When a community cannot support its citizens, other organizations respond to provide humanitarian relief. There are more than 100 national organizations, including government, business, labor union, religious, community, and other voluntary organizations involved in disaster relief. The Robert T. Stafford Disaster Relief and Emergency Assistance Act (P.L. 93-288) authorized the creation of the Federal Emergency Management Agency. FEMA became the lead federal disaster coordinating agency by an act of Congress in 1803. President Jimmy Carter issued an executive order in 1979 to merge all disaster-related agencies under FEMA. FEMA became part of Homeland Security on March 1, 2003. FEMA's response to Hurricane Katrina (2005) has come under great scrutiny, many attributing its failures to the merger.

Governmental Organizations

Federal Emergency Management Agency (FEMA): congressional acts 1803, 1974

President Carter Executive Order of 1979 merged separate federal disaster-related agencies into FEMA; agency reported to the president now to homeland security

FEMA Program: Disaster Housing Assistance Program

FEMA Program: Individual and Family Grant (IFG) Program

American Red Cross: semigovernmental; congressional charter; governmental appointment and disbursement of funds under federal audit

Stafford Act: Center for Mental Health Services (CMHS), part of Substance Abuse and Mental Health Services Administration (SAMHSA); has responsibility to meet the mental health needs of disaster survivors and responders

Stafford Act: Emergency Services and Disaster Relief Branch (ESDRB) of CMHS in SAMHSA; provides crisis counseling assistance and training; offers grants to states that apply; funds immediate services for 60 days, long-term services for 9 months

Small Business Administration: provides loans to homeowners, renters, and businesses to restore or rebuild; loans must be paid back with interest

Disaster Unemployment Assistance: provided to those whose employment was lost or interrupted as a result of presidential declaration of a disaster; state administered; benefits up to 26 weeks

Internal Revenue Service (IRS): some casualty losses can be deducted from federal income tax

Department of Agriculture: numerous programs that assist farmers in disaster recovery

Executive Orders

A governor can declare a state emergency and call out the National Guard to restore order

Only the president can declare a national disaster and activate FEMA

Nongovernmental Organizations

National Voluntary Organizations Active in Disaster (1970): partnership of organizations; 1997 memorandum of understanding between FEMA and NVOAD

American Red Cross: quasi-governmental and quasi-independent, not-for-profit volunteer organization; administers Aviation Disaster Family Assistance Act of 1996; administers Disaster Physical Health Services and Disaster Mental Health Services

(*continued*)

EXHIBIT 9.3   *Organizations Providing Emergency Response and Disaster Relief* (*continued*)

National Organization for Victim Assistance (NOVA): information about disaster response; telephone consultation to localities; on-site consultation, leadership, and training of local crisis response teams; crisis response team activation within 24 hours of invitation

Religious Organizations
Ministries

Professional Organizations
NASW and APA have formal collaborative agreements with the American Red Cross

Hospice
1990s involvement in disaster relief

Grassroots
Volunteer organizations

International Organizations

The Office for the Coordination of Humanitarian Affairs (OCHA) is a department of the United Nations' Secretariat. It is headed by the undersecretary general for humanitarian affairs. The undersecretary also functions as the emergency relief coordinator (ERC). Resolution 46/182, passed in 1991, is designed to strengthen the UN response to both complex emergencies and natural disasters. Offices are located in both New York and Geneva. The resolution created the Inter-Agency Standing Committee (IASC), the Consolidated Appeals Process (CAP), and the Central Emergency Revolving Fund (CERF).

The core functions of OCHA are supported by 860 staff members located in New York, Geneva, and in the field. OCHA's budget for 2005 was $110.5 million. Only 10% of that budget comes from the regular UN budget. All other monies come from member states and donor organizations. The mission of OCHA is to mobilize and coordinate effective and principled humanitarian action in partnership with national and international actors in order to (1) alleviate human suffering caused by disaster, (2) advocate for the rights of people in need, (3) promote preparedness and prevention, and (4) facilitate sustainable solutions (www.ochaonline.un.org).

The functions of the ERC are (a) policy development and coordination, especially to assure protection and assistance to displaced persons, (b) advocacy of humanitarian issues with political organizations, notably the UN's Security Council, and (c) coordination through the IASC to assure on-the-ground resources.

■ Ideology: Ethical, Sociopolitical, Cultural, and Economic

Competitive ideologies and values influence the decision to offer relief or humanitarian aid. Historically, disaster relief began as humanitarian assistance during times of war.

Humanitarianism

Humanitarianism (Webster, 1977, p. 691) refers to principles and practices based on the doctrine that a person's ethical obligations are bound to the welfare of the human race. Ethical and spiritual in nature, disaster relief and humanitarian aid are expressions of concern for human dignity and welfare. Three of social work's six core values support humanitarian principles. The first is service to others. This consists of providing assistance and resources to help people in need. The second core value is social justice. This value commits social work practitioners to work toward a just society in which all people have the same rights, opportunities, and benefits. The third value is the dignity and worth of each individual regardless of color, language, or geographic location. In addition to these values, social work includes among its cardinal values: (1) resource development and utilization, (2) affirmation of the client's problem-solving capacities and his/her right to self-determination, and (3) protection of client confidentiality.

As absolutists, deontologists argue that providing humanitarian aid is inherently the right thing to do. Teleologists argue that every action requires evaluation based on its potential consequences. Theories of social justice weigh in on the debate over alternative courses of action. Utilitarianism seeks a response that will result in the greatest good for the greatest number. Theories of egalitarianism (equality) and contractarianism (equity) seek fairness in the distribution of goods and services to nations and populations that have great need from nations and populations that have much to give.

Sociopolitical Ideology

Sociopolitical ideologies, domestic and international, complicate decisions to engage in disaster relief and humanitarian aid. Decisions involving the allocation of resources are often associated with ethnic, racial, religious, or socioeconomic class bias. Exchanges between populations with perceived similarities are more readily achieved than exchanges between populations which are dissimilar. Bias, in addition to need, shapes who gets help and how much.

Within nations, conflicts of interest between opposing groups (e.g., management and labor) are common. Political best interest often aligns with the interest of the powerful. In the domestic and international sphere, there are many different publics, each with its own sociopolitical reality. Social exchange theory would argue that relief and aid are proportionate to the cost-benefit exchange ratio between giving and receiving nations.

War and genocide are particularly sociopolitical in nature. Among other outcomes, both result in forced migration, displaced persons, and resettlement. In both situations, an individual's homeland becomes an unsustainable environment. War, whether between tribes, civil factions, or nations, involves combat. Violence and death are actively present in the everyday lives of the civilian population. Homes are destroyed and land confiscated. People are conscripted, detained, beaten, violated, and killed. Resources are restricted. Military occupation replaces civilian government. Even when social justice is the desired end goal, the effects of war on the civilian population are sweeping.

Punamaki (2004) investigated the relationship between a just war and mental health. She argues that fighting against injustice is crucial to preserving a sense of individual and national humanity and is, in that context, healthy. Nonetheless, she notes that even a just war produces suffering. Accepting suffering as an inevitable aspect of a worthy cause can promote endurance in the face of adversity. Nonetheless, many experience poor mental health outcomes.

International organizations are often reluctant to interfere in the affairs of other nations. The decision to send peace-keeping forces into countries often depends on political in addition to humanitarian appraisal. Immigration policies in receiving nations are often discriminatory even though there is a need to resettle refugee populations. Refugees are frequently denied admission because the populace in receiving nations fails to perceive the refugees as similar to themselves. Once admitted, tension may develop between relocated refugee groups and local citizens.

■ Conditions Under Which Emergency Services and Disaster Relief Are Delivered

On-Site Settings

Hardship is incurred for those who deliver humanitarian relief in a disaster. The settings can be cramped, crowded, and extremely hot, cold, or wet. Tents, temporary shelters, and refugee camps are common treatment settings. Practitioners work with little to no sleep. There is no sharp demarcation between being on or off duty. The work is there until it is done. Privacy, the structure of routine, and the comforts of home are distant memories. The food, though nourishing, may be unappetizing. Often, it is culturally unfamiliar. Hazardous conditions continue, and depending on the situation, threat to life remains a reality.

Access to Technology

Technology helps communities to predict, warn of, and respond to disasters. Satellite imagery can monitor conditions on land, sea, and air. Doppler systems can track wind, rain, snow, and other weather fronts. Meteorologists issue weather-related watches (36 hours) and warnings (24 hours). Computers generate models of unfolding events based on data input. Surveillance planes can fly into the eye of a storm. Seismographs measure movement beneath the earth and sea and within volcanoes. Helicopters rescue persons and provide aerial surveys of the damage. Better materials and better construction codes prevent structural collapses in earthquake-prone zones. Building flood dams and dikes in flood-prone areas preserves life, land, and property and minimizes damage. Better farming techniques and improved irrigation systems can combat drought and soil erosion. Forestry policies can reduce potential fire damage to land and property. Wealthier nations have greater access to technological resources to prevent or warn of disasters than do poorer nations.

Media Coverage

The media shape public sympathy by how much time and space they give to covering a disaster. Whom they choose to interview is often related to sociopolitical factors. Mainstream broadcasting networks in the United States devote little sustained attention to ongoing disasters outside of North America. In reporting domestic events, reporters provide factual accounts of what happened, describe its significance, and suggest social action. In the aftermath of a disaster, the media become part of the public inquiry, investigating why it happened and how it could have been avoided. In the process of inquiry, the media often turn heroes into villains.

■ The Economics of Emergency Response and Disaster Relief

Cost

According to Regehr and Bober (2005), between 1980 and 2002, the United States experienced more than 54 weather-related disasters. Each event cost more than $1 billion with a total cost of more than $300 billion. Though monies are budgeted at several governmental and organizational levels to assist communities in crisis, a large-scale event or a series of events may deplete budgeted resources. Fundraising is, therefore, an important aspect of providing disaster relief and humanitarian aid.

Accountability

There are six types of accountability. The first, operational debriefing, reviews the actions taken in order to learn from the experience and to improve performance in subsequent missions (Dryegrov, 2003). In the second, retrospective analysis seeks to identify causality (blame) and performance errors. Risks and hazards are identified and protective factors assessed for what worked. The third form is concerned with fiscal accountability. Managers are held accountable for all expenditures. In the fourth instance, public officials are held accountable for acts of commission and omission related to the cause of and recovery from the disaster. The fifth form of accountability is ethical accountability. Here, actions taken and not taken are evaluated against ethical screens of value hierarchies. In the sixth form, managers are held accountable for the treatment of personnel deployed to deliver services.

■ Case Scenario: Crisis Management at the Local Level

This scenario continues the flood crisis presented in chapter 8 but explicates the crisis event in terms of local crisis management.

Facts of the Case

You are a public welfare social work administrator. Because of your position, you have been appointed to serve on the state's emergency preparedness and response board (authority to respond). You have coordinated the emergency mental health response of one region's agencies (public and private) for the past 5 years (experience). As part of this responsibility, you have maintained a list of agencies (public and private) that have agreed to free a portion of their staffs as emergency mental health responders (organizational preparedness). Over the past 5 years, you have responded to a train derailment, a fire in an apartment complex, and a tornado. Now you have been activated to coordinate (oversee) the mental health response to the flood victims.

Explication of the Case

As part of preparedness, you have maintained a list of agencies with a designated contact person (preparedness communication). You have maintained a list of those personnel who have been additionally certified as crisis counselors. You recognize that there is a turf issue among mental health professionals regarding who is qualified to respond to a crisis. You send out an e-mail (communication) to agency heads alerting them to the fact that emergency mental health personnel have been activated. You pull in your designated emergency staff (use of small

EXHIBIT 9.4   *Matrix for Crisis Management*

Procedural Knowing	Worker Action	Desired Goal/Outcome
Prevention	Authority via position on emergency response board Experience coordinating Regional mental health response List of emergency mental health responders	Crisis preparedness Organizational readiness
Early Intervention: needs assessment	Assess area of impact Number of people in need Type of needs for which resources are needed	Determine need
Early Intervention: activate command structure	Activate response command Use of task groups	Communicate: e-mail, phone contacts, public relations, control rumors
Early Intervention: resources assessment	Ascertain which agencies have which resources Determine availability of mental health responders	Determine resources availability
Early Intervention: deploy resources	Deploy resources, arrange transportation, distribution of resources to site locations	Provide shelter, food, clothing, mental health counselors
Early Intervention	Monitor resources	Assess on-site needs, resources
Early Intervention	Manage resources	Task group to manage volunteers
Early Intervention	Develop resources Fundraisers	Task groups to apply for disaster relief funds
Tertiary Intervention: assess resources losses	Assess property damage, displaced families	Relocate displaced families
Tertiary Intervention: infrastructure damage	Assess schools, jobs, public services	Link evacuees to necessary infrastructures, relocation
Tertiary Intervention: assess environmental risks and hazards	Support efforts to prohibit building on flood plain Support reasonable insurance plans	Safe environment

task group) to begin to assess the availability of material and human resources, knowing that there is likely to have been some turnover in personnel (determination of available resources). Staff follow up on your e-mails and make phone calls (communication). You make coordinating calls to the local chapter of NASW and

EXHIBIT 9.5   *Domestic Disasters and Public Tragedies*

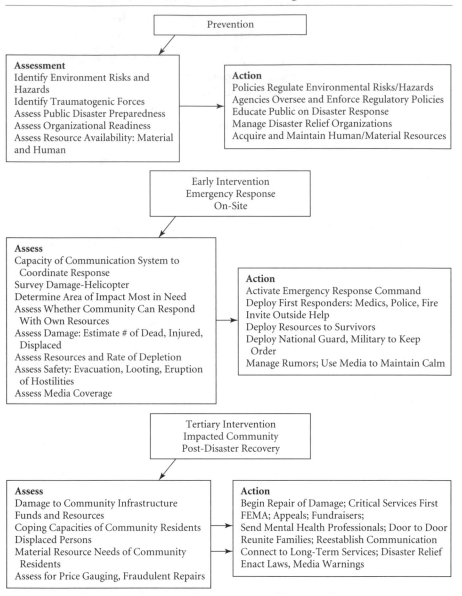

local schools of social work (public relations). You contact the regional heads of other professions (psychology, psychiatry, ministries) to assure response coordination and avoidance of duplication (good public relations). You and your staff determine who can offer shelter, beds, hygiene products, meals, clothing, transportation, toys, and on-site child care (resource availability). You deploy certified crisis counselors to designated sites. You have on-site staff determine what resources are lacking or in short supply at each site (resource monitoring). You then match resource needs with resource availability.

EXHIBIT 9.6   *Two Types of Disasters: Rapid Onset or Looming*

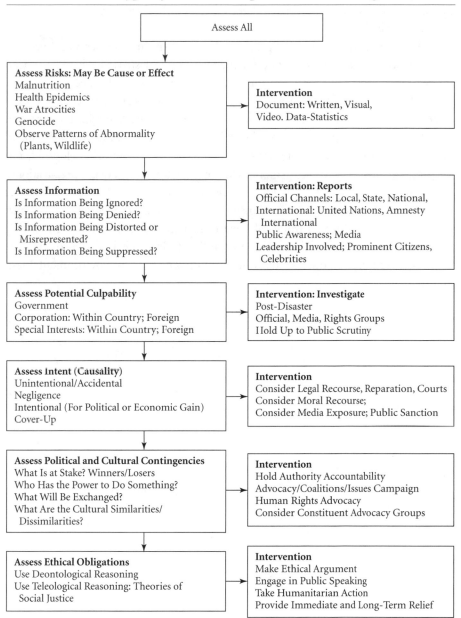

It is your assessment that the mental health community can respond with its own resources to meet the immediate need, but that need will exceed resources in the recovery phase. It is likely that the governor will ask the president to declare the affected area to be a disaster zone, which will make federal disaster relief funds and programs available. You assign some of your staff to begin preparing the paperwork to apply for such funds (task group: secure program funding). Agencies may make appeals and conduct fundraisers to assist flood victims. You assign a staff member to coordinate the calls and activities of volunteers (management of resources, public relations).

The major loss appears to be property damage to homes and schools. Community infrastructures seem to be flood damaged but not destroyed. There have been no deaths, but there are some injuries. Most families had jobs located in areas not affected by the flooding; however, many families have been displaced. It is estimated that displaced families will not be able to return, repair, or rebuild for several months. It is likely that many families will live with relatives during this phase. School systems will have a response role as children are temporarily relocated. You assign a staff member to alert regional schools so that they can begin preparations.

This is the third time this area has flooded in the past 25 years. Insurance companies no longer provide flood insurance. In the past, the regional emergency response board has urged the local government to pass regulations prohibiting residential and commercial building in the flood plain. This crisis provides another opportunity to address this issue. Flood plains pose an environmental risk and hazard.

10

Social Work Case Management: Serving Highly Vulnerable Client Populations

■ The Urgent and Timely Provision of Concrete Services

Step 3 of the decision hierarchy addresses the provision of urgent (within hours or days) or timely (within a week or a month) concrete services to highly vulnerable client populations through case management. Incorporated within case management are day programs and residential living programs to meet the long-term needs of chronically vulnerable populations. Some scholars include advocacy practice as part of comprehensive case management practice. Others address it separately. In this text, advocacy practice is addressed separately as step 4 of the decision tree, and content on case and class advocacy is presented in chapter 11. Case management (this chapter) may be compared to the talk therapy models presented in chapter 12 (step 5 of the decision tree: work with individuals). This comparative presentation allows the reader to contrast the two models of direct social work practice (concrete services and therapy) and to develop the skills needed for each.

Client Population: Who Needs Case Management?

According to Rothman (1994), client populations that benefit from case management are characterized as highly vulnerable people who require a complex array of services and multiple helpers on an ongoing basis. Specifically, these populations consist of the deinstitutionalized chronically mentally ill, developmentally disabled children and adults, clients with disabilities who need medical rehabilitation, those who are HIV-positive or who have AIDS, children and adults in need of protective services, and the homeless. Case management serves all populations that may need assistance in gaining access to a confusing array of services. The goal of case management is to provide services that enhance and optimize a client's ability to remain in the community under the least restrictive circumstances. Services commonly include residential care and skills training.

Rothman notes that these populations have always existed. What is new is the significant expansion of their numbers. Several social factors have contributed to this expansion. Medical advances have contributed to longevity, technological advances have promoted independent living, deinstitutionalization has followed psychotropic medications, and social legislation has shifted treatment from the institution to the community. The extended family has contracted. The adults in extended families are working and/or are geographically scattered. There is a demand for social workers to meet the service needs of this population.

Help-Seeking Behavior: Point of Entry to Service

Clients served by case management are largely involuntary (through child and adult protective services or referred by others in authority) or mandated (wards of the state such as the chronically mentally ill or court-ordered drug-addicted clients, those in delinquent diversion programs). Some, such as the homeless, often refuse formalized care altogether. Many homeless individuals prefer to remain on the street rather than accept services. They will visit soup kitchens, accept sandwiches from a mobile food distribution center, accept blankets in cold weather, and on occasion accept overnight shelter. The homeless require outreach as their point of entry to service. Some will seek medical help in street-front walk-in clinics. It is extremely challenging to establish a working relationship with homeless individuals. Psychological trust is developed over time in relation to repeated nonintrusive contact where concrete goods (blankets, clothes, meals, bed, health care) are provided with no strings attached.

The Case Management Context of Relationship

In many cases, the state has assumed guardianship over clients served by case management. In such instances, the state acts as the client's *in loco parentis*. Clients who need lifelong services experience a series of social work case managers over time. The worker-client relationship consists of multiple, multidisciplinary, and ever-changing helping relationships. For some clients, this experiential history equips them with the skills needed to orient newly assigned workers (and student interns) to the day-to-day operations of their setting and their course of treatment. Usually, such clients have an agency-assigned primary worker who remains relatively stable (employed status) as student interns come and go. Clients who fall into this category readily form temporary relationships with student interns, knowing that they will leave at the end of the year and will be followed by yet another interesting intern as a new school year starts.

Other clients who are served by a case management model react negatively to the high turnover of helping professionals in their lives. It is far more difficult to establish a working rapport with such clients as they view their experiential history of help givers as one of loss or abandonment. Still others resent having to tell their story yet another time to another person who will likely leave at some point, necessitating another retelling. More effort is required to establish, maintain, and terminate relationships with the latter group of clients. It is important therefore that the termination process set the stage for a new relationship.

Contracting

In case management, treatment plans or contracts are to be collaborative. Respect for a client's self-determination is a value in case management as it is in all social work practice models. However, with case management clients, contracting is constrained both by the type and degree of the impairing condition and by the mandated parameters within which treatment occurs. Consistent with authentic contracting, case managers cannot promise resources they do not have nor can they provide resources to which clients are not entitled. In delivering services, workers cannot violate the law or the Code of Ethics.

Social work case managers are often faced with an ethical dilemma when serving vulnerable client populations. Client self-determination and the worker's fiduciary responsibility to act in the best interest of the client often conflict with each other. Case managers walk a fiduciary tightrope, trying to balance their legal authority with the client's rights.

In the process of mutual goal setting, workers must set goals that are reasonable. There must be a match between what it takes to achieve the desired goal and the potential the client has to offer, e.g., a worker cannot promise admission to Harvard Medical School to a client who is severely brain injured. Case plans tend to be individualized and reviewed quarterly, semiannually, or annually. Case reviews determine what is working, what is not working, and what needs to be changed.

Goal/Desired Outcome: Social Functioning, Building on Strengths

The needs and impairments of this client population are often outside the person's volition for cause or solution. Frequently, the individual is thrust into a position of forced dependency. Many conditions are permanent and irreversible. Other conditions are progressive. The impediments to social functioning are by nature long term. Case management clients often receive services in the absence of available family support.

It is especially important to document strengths when working with individuals who have primary conditions that are long term, permanent, or progressive. A strengths-based assessment focuses on helping clients to retain basic strengths so that they can function in a manner that allows them to maintain a reasonable quality of life in a community setting. Environmental accommodations such as foster and kinship care, supervised independent living, halfway or quarter houses, group homes, assisted-living facilities, residential or nursing home care optimize a client's way of life. Structured day programs, recreational activities, and sheltered workshops can add to a client's quality of life. A supportive external environment (social milieu) can compensate for individual impairments and can provide a context for recovery.

■ Definition of Case Management

Case management is a model of practice that denotes the timely provision of resources to meet the basic needs of highly vulnerable populations (Harris & Bergman, 1995; Linz, McAnally, & Wieck, 1989). Highly vulnerable client populations often require multiple services involving professionals from several different disciplines. Case management therefore coordinates a fragmented service-delivery system to those in need. Case managers locate, refer, broker, coordinate, monitor, and expedite care offered by others. Case management is a clinical method of social work practice that works with individuals (one worker to one client) or with families (one worker to one family; see chapter 15).

Case management has both a humanitarian goal and a social control function. As a system-driven practice model, case management is concerned with the determination of eligibility, referral to services, and avoidance of duplication of services. Consistent with a humanitarian perspective and empowerment theory, case managers seek to maintain clients in the least restrictive community environments. Through service provision and counseling support, case managers help highly vulnerable clients to lead lives of freedom and dignity in the community.

■ Types of Case Management

System-Driven Case Management

There are two basic types of case management models, system-driven case management and consumer-driven case management. System-driven case management is concerned with maintaining the agency (organization) as a human services system. As such, system-driven case management relies on programs that have predetermined client needs for which clients must establish their eligibility. System-driven case management creates procedures and routines requiring client conformity. According to organizational theory, the human services agency is a system that has a stake in maintaining its own integrity. Therefore, it operates in a manner that meets the needs of funding sources and the professionals who work within it, sometimes at the expense of meeting client needs.

System-driven case management, then, has roots in organizational and management theory, especially bureaucracy. Moxley (1989) identifies five different types of case management but categorizes the first four types under system-driven case management. *Type one* refers to case management agencies that offer a single service provided one time only (e.g., help with paying an energy bill). *Type two* refers to a bureaucratic task-specific division of labor related to a complex service, such as child welfare (see chapter 15 on child protective services). In type two case management, workers perform a single task or function. Some will do investigative work and risk assessment following a report of child neglect or abuse. Others will remove a child from a harmful environment and place that child in foster or kinship care. Still others will recruit, hire, and train foster parents. Some workers will monitor out-of-home placements while others work with the parent (or parental unit) to reunify parent(s) and child. Alternatively, some will engage in family preservation (see chapter 15) to prevent an out-of-home placement. *Type three* refers to comprehensive case management, which includes day programs, residential services, and advocacy (Rothman, 1994).

Type four, street-level case management, refers to a middle ground between a top-down organizational bureaucracy and a consumer-driven (bottom-up) model of case management. Street-level case management refers to the discretionary power held by individual case managers. Moxley identifies the powerlessness of the frontline service worker to truly meet the needs of the clients s/he is supposed to serve unless the worker challenges (conflict theory) the dysfunctional and inadequate delivery system of which s/he is a part. The street-level model holds that case managers have the power to make structural changes and to obtain resources for clients while being part of a bureaucracy (organizational change from within).

Highly vulnerable clients in need of long-term support are often viewed as the least desirable clients for agencies to serve because agencies are unable to reflect a high rate of success (cure, no need for service). A results-oriented funding philosophy is incompatible with a client population that will continue to need multiple services over time. Success (or the lack thereof) affects funding and public perception of agency efficacy and service outcome. Managed-care entities regard such clients as liabilities because their ongoing need for care requires a disproportionate use of (drain on) resources. Advocacy is needed to change public perception and the perception of managed-care entities as to what constitutes a successful outcome for this client population.

Consumer-Driven Case Management: Empowerment

Type five refers to consumer-driven case management. According to Moxley (1989), consumer-driven case management is based on critical theory. Critical theory challenges the legitimacy of system-driven models of case management. In doing so, it legitimizes client and frontline social worker dissent. It provides clients with an active voice in asserting their needs and in determining how their needs will be met. It places control and self-advocacy in the hands of clients, thus empowering them. The practitioner becomes an ally of the client, who sets his/her own goals. Clients interview potential employees (and student interns) and provide feedback on staff performance. They have input into configuring the supports and services offered and have the opportunity to make meaningful choices among substantive service options. Skills training and vocational rehabilitation further empower client independence.

■ Declarative Knowledge: What Case Managers Need to Know

Knowledge of the Client's Primary Condition or Circumstance

Each client has a primary condition that causes a secondary problem(s) in social functioning. Social work case managers need to be knowledgeable about a client's primary condition or circumstance. For every primary condition or circumstance, there is a body of hypotheses related to causality, prevention, early intervention, and tertiary (remedial) intervention. With the exception of care given to abused, neglected, or delinquent children, most conditions cannot be cured (e.g., spinal cord injury, brain injury, chronic mental illness, mental retardation, autism, Alzheimer's disease, HIV/AIDS, etc.). Long-term care, not cure, informs intervention. The case manager needs to become familiar with the scholarly literature related to the specific primary problem of the case management population with whom s/he works.

Knowledge of Resource Availability to Support Social Functioning

Case managers also need to be cognizant of a client's resources. Resource data are frequently represented in an ecomap, which visualizes a client's personal environment, including familial and social networks, as well as the type of formal agencies, individuals, and disciplines with which the client is involved (social worker, occupational therapist, medical doctor, psychiatrist, psychologist, visiting nurse, clubs, church, mosque, synagogue, workplace, etc.). Some social workers have clients draw or describe their circles of support. These consist of those persons in the client's life who are important to the client and who can come together to support the client.

Knowledge of Needs Secondary to the Primary Condition or Circumstance

Clients may have biological/medical, psychological, social, or spiritual needs related to their primary condition. Needs may be normative, perceived, expressed, or relative. Regardless, all domains require assessment. Nine needs frequently occur within a case management population in addition to those necessitated by a client's primary condition or circumstance. While a social worker may not encounter all nine in the same client case, s/he is likely to encounter all nine over the course of his/her career as a case manager. The first common problem is that of resource allocation.

Need for Resources

The first task of case management is to locate and allocate needed resources in a time-sensitive manner. To accomplish this, the case manager uses interpersonal skills appropriate for networking with peers or superiors to secure needed resources. On the surface, the task of matching a resource to a client need appears to be straightforward. However, one must understand that in the human services delivery system, there are more than 140,000 community-based organizations, 28,000 local governments, and 52 state governments (Rothman, 1994). Rothman observes that, in one particular case, the case manager contacted 42 agencies and took 35 hours to obtain service for a client (1994, p. 15). Social workers in direct practice need to know what resources are available, where they are located, who has control over them, and how to access them to benefit the client at hand. The social worker must be tenacious in meeting clients' needs for limited resources under time pressure.

To locate, manage, and access resources, case managers engage in indexing resources (providing the vital statistics of a program and its service characteristics); storing such information (in a resource manual or computerized data entry); retrieving the data and information when needed; and monitoring the number of clients served and the type of services rendered for quality assurance and funding accountability.

Need for Skills Training

Clients may lack skills because of their primary condition or as a result of the circumstances of their care. Failure to develop the skills needed for independent living or the loss of such skills is secondary to the primary condition and/or the care arrangement.

Informational Needs: The Distinction Between Being Informed and Being Labeled

A third common need is related to information. Clients often lack comprehensive information on their primary condition, the resources available to treat it, alternative treatment options, and their entitlement to a range of services. Clients are often missing necessary information to make informed treatment decisions. Lack of information compromises a client's coping skills. According to empowerment theory, clients benefit from knowing what is the matter, what is available, and how to access it. While clients do not like to be diagnostically labeled, being informed about their condition and available treatment options empowers them.

Sexual Needs

Another common need is related to sexual expression. Despite their primary condition, most clients are or wish to be sexually active. For many clients, finding suitable partners or appropriate outlets to meet their sexual needs is problematic (societal taboo).

Need to Manage Flare-ups: The Revolving Door

A fifth problem is related to the cumulative stress of daily living, which may cause a flare-up of the client's primary condition, thereby precipitating a crisis. Deinstitutionalization has made managing a client's primary condition more difficult. Clients who live with chronic mental illness frequently forget or go off their prescribed medications. This produces a crisis which necessitates short-term hospitalization where the client is restabilized on medication. The client is then discharged, and the pattern of noncompliance with medication, flare-up, rehospitalization, and restabilization repeats itself. This pattern is frequently referred to as the *revolving door policy* of mental health care. Outcome success is defined as community maintenance and the prevention of rehospitalization.

Need to Feel Good: Self-Medicating Behavior

A sixth common problem is a client's attempt to ameliorate his/her primary condition and to feel better through the use of alcohol and drugs (self-medicate). Dually diagnosed clients (those with substance abuse problems and another primary condition) often fall through the cracks of services delivery. Those who work in health, mental health, or addictions are reluctant to accept clients with dual diagnoses. Often, the treatment protocols of one system are contraindicated in the other system.

Need for Compliance

A seventh problem is noncompliance with medications and/or with setting and program rules and regulations. Many clients are "dismissed" from care for noncompliance.

Need for Continuity and Stability of Care: Destabilization of the Care System

Changes in the care system itself trigger client crises. System changes encompass (1) changes in eligibility requirements, (2) changes in personnel, (3) changes in policies related to daily operations, and (4) termination of a program or service due to lack of funding.

Need for Safety: Preventing Violence

A ninth problem is that of violence. Within human services organizations and settings, violent behavior does occur. Though rare, violence is often unpredictable. It can be directed toward staff by clients, or it can be directed by staff (excessive use of force) toward clients. It can occur between staff and between clients. Violence in a human services setting poses a legal liability especially if the institution or a staff member are found to be culpable. Violence poses a threat to the personal safety of those residing in the setting and to personnel working there.

As part of their orientation to field placement, student interns must be educated in agency-specific safety protocols. Prevention begins with education. Students (and staff) need to be taught how to avoid or how to deflect conflict. Students need to be familiar with the safety risks unique to each setting. They need to know how to signal for help and how to position themselves for safety. Where warranted by the setting, the student needs to become familiar with the use of time-outs, restraints, sedation, seclusion, and shows of force. Students need to be able to recognize physiological or motoric cues that signal loss of control or rising anger. Students must be given explicit permission and must be prepared to take action to protect themselves. Some students, especially undergraduates, will not assume permission.

■ Theories That Inform the Helping Relationship in Case Management

At a minimum, rapport begins with belief in the helping relationship. Worker and client bond in the belief that mutually agreed-upon activities will bring about changes in the client's circumstances that will both benefit the client and enhance the client's self-worth. The worker believes in the client's worthiness, and the client believes in the worker's competence and trustworthiness. While not all worker-client interactions in direct practice are considered to be therapy, all worker-client interactions are intended to benefit the client and are therefore therapeutic.

The goal of a case management relationship is service, not therapy. What then guides the direct face-to-face contact between the provider and the recipient of service? Two conflicting theories elaborate this relationship. The first reflects the service-driven model characterized by the worker's duty to protect and to exercise authority. The second reflects a consumer-driven model characterized by an emphasis on client strengths and empowerment. The consumer-driven model has roots in structure-functional theory, and the consumer-driven model has roots in critical theory, postmodernism, and empowerment theory. Postmodernism (like critical theory) is sensitive to the marginalization of disempowered and at-risk populations.

Postmodernism

Ungar (2004) writes that practitioners work on the frontlines of services delivery within the mandate of the profession and the employing agency (system-driven case management). Such mandates, however, conflict with postmodern philosophy and values, which task the worker with the deconstruction of his/her privileged status and position (consumer-driven case management). The worker is perceived as an advocate for and ally of the client. Ungar (2004) writes, "[S]ocial workers interested in postmodernism have been provided an abundance of *principles* but little to guide them in [the] day to day activities" (p. 488).

To rectify this, Ungar offers the two P's (position and power) and the three R's (resources, resistance, reflection) of postmodernism. The first P stands for power, and it refers to the language used to construct the delivery of services. Ungar notes that often the language of services delivery reflects the program, policy, and administrative agenda of those in power but rarely the agenda of those at risk. He observes that the worker-client dialogue is social discourse that privileges (assigns more power to) the worker's discourse over that of the client. Diagnoses, written records, and conversations with clients construct client realities and assign status identities to them (e.g., delinquent, impoverished, perpetrator). Identity is constructed through power-laden language.

Ungar holds that a case manager can equalize the power differential between service organizations and the marginalized populations they serve by using his/her position inside the organization to broker a partnership between the agency and its client population. Ungar views resource sharing as an initiative that combines the resources of formal organizations with the informal resources of the community to deconstruct the myth of scarcity. He notes that a case conference can become an opportunity for communities to support individuals and families (Pennell & Buford, 1997). Wraparound processes can encourage community ownership of troubled youth, for example (VandenBerg & Grealish, 1996).

Ungar defines *resistance* as the worker's obligation to resist decisions and processes that are not in the best interest of those being served. The determination of "best interest" can be made, he says, through mediation and ethnography, which lead to the co-construction of reality. The purpose of *reflection* on practice (third column in process recordings), he says, is to create deliberate awareness of the worker's privileged location in structure (organization or community) and function. Such reflection is not a substitute for action (praxis).

Ungar critiques his thinking by asking, what happens when there is no co-construction of reality? In a case of child abuse, what happens when the worker's narrative says that the situation is not safe for the child, but the parents' narrative says that it is safe?

Strengths-Based Perspectives

Both traditional models of talk therapy and strengths-based perspectives attempt to reduce the problems for which the client seeks or is mandated for help. Critics charge that traditional models of social work practice have led to a "deficit" literature that has overemphasized individual and family pathology. This literature, they argue, has disproportionately disadvantaged marginalized populations (e.g., the language of pathology). To counter this, advocates of the strengths-based perspective focus on how individuals and families cope in the face of adversity. They seek to identify individual and/or family strengths in order to build on these strengths as a way to reduce problems. Here, the emphasis is on resilience rather than deficits. Advocates of the strengths perspective have two agendas: (1) to develop an empirical literature on resilience and strengths to counter the literature on vulnerability and deficits, and (2) to develop an applied model of practice based on individual and family strengths (Saleebey, 1997). Saleeby (2001) offers his own version of the DSM-IV, which he calls the *Diagnostic Strengths Manual*.

Critics charge that a strengths-based perspective, like more traditional perspectives, sustains the social order and the status quo. Second, it gives a pass to "formal services" when such services are inadequate or fail to meet demand by encouraging individuals and families to rely on their own resources. Critics state that scarcity is an objective reality (not a myth) and a root cause of help-seeking behavior among impoverished individuals and families.

■ Theories That Guide Intervention

Task and Role Performance: Duty to Protect

Individuals are expected to perform certain roles in society. When individuals are unable to perform the tasks of daily or independent living, social work exercises its fiduciary and humanitarian responsibility to care for them. The worker's use of self is authoritarian (coercive) in that the worker can mandate compliance by withholding, withdrawing, or providing needed resources based on the client's task completion. Actions in the form of task completion are the mechanism of change.

Social Treatment: Environmental Modification

Many of the primary conditions of vulnerable clients are covered under the Americans with Disabilities Act (1990). Such clients are entitled to an array of services designed to modify their environments (social treatment). Disability is life-long and cyclical in nature (with remissions and flare-ups). Chronic mental illness is included under the Americans with Disabilities Act. It is viewed as a persistent condition with a physiological and probably chemical base that is constitutional.

It can be controlled through a continuing course of medication, but periods of relative remission are interspersed with episodes of flare-up. In chronic mental illness, there is variability in severity, duration, and scope.

Traditional Talk Therapies

Though therapy will not "cure" the client's primary condition nor provide the care (concrete resources) needed, therapy may be able to ameliorate problems secondary to the primary condition. For instance, behavior modification can teach those who are intellectually or developmentally challenged (e.g., autistic) to acquire self-care skills, such as hygiene, feeding themselves, dressing themselves, and interacting appropriately. Numerous therapies are available to help those with HIV/AIDS cope with their diagnosis, live with the disease in an optimal manner, modify their sexual practices to prevent the spread of the disease, face declining health, and confront dying and death. All models of talk therapy are potential sources of intervention when treating problems in living secondary to the client's primary condition. Factors related to the client, the primary condition, the setting, and the clinician's skill influence therapy choice when working with secondary problems in mental health and social functioning. Theory-based therapies, such as pharmacological intervention and psychodynamic, behavioral/learning, or cognitive-behavioral interventions, can modify biology, feelings, cognitions, and behaviors even though they cannot cure the primary condition. See the case management process recording at the end of this chapter.

■ Empirical Evidence

Shera (2001, 2002) states that although, in principle, there is acceptance and support for case management services, we are only beginning to move toward determining its efficacy. Reviews of research on case management have been done by Chamberlain and Rapp (1991); Korr and Cloninger (1991); and Rubin (1992). In 1990, the NIMH funded a number of case management research projects. Three contemporary models of case management are the strengths model (Rapp, 1998), the advocacy-empowerment model (Foster-Fishman et al., 1998), and the partnership model (Shera, 2002). The efficacy of the partnership model was studied in a randomized clinical trial to compare the effectiveness of the broker (traditional) and partnership (innovative) models of case management with severely mentally ill adults. The broker model emphasized system-driven case management services. The experimental condition was the partnership model, which emphasized client-driven case management. The study used a two-group pre/posttest design based on random sample selection and random assignment to the two conditions (treatment/control). Though 219 subjects took the pretest, only 148 subjects completed both the pretest and the posttest. Thus the actual sample

, there is no need for advocacy. Case advocacy may be needed de-
on the availability of an appropriate group home. The ideal group
uld be with some of those with whom she works in the sheltered
p. Generally, class advocacy is needed to develop and maintain group
n the community and to combat discrimination faced by those with dis-
es.

p 4: Need for Therapeutic Intervention

In addition to her employment as a member of a sheltered workshop, Linda's placement in a residential group home is considered to be a social work intervention that modifies the client's personal environment. It is likely that some form of supportive counseling will be needed to help Linda transition from her familial home of 39 years to life in a group home. Group intervention with members already residing in the home will facilitate their acceptance of Linda and a good transition for all.

Step 5: Method Choices

Four methods of intervention are required to handle the complex data of this case. One-on-one case management is needed to ensure that Linda's needs continue to be met over her lifetime. Modification of her environment in the form of sheltered workshop employment and placement in a residential-living group home are needed. Supportive counseling with Linda and her mother (dyad) will be necessary to help Linda make this transition. Mrs. Garrity has been a therapeutic ally to case managers over the years and will play a key role in helping Linda to accept and adapt to her new living arrangement. Group counseling with residents in the home will help to facilitate Linda's transition and their acceptance of her. Having such a placement will help Linda to cope with the eventual loss of her mother.

Step 6: Culturally Responsive Practice

As a population subgroup, those diagnosed with mental retardation are a cultural minority. Some have visible characteristics that distinguish them from the general population, while others do not. Many have distinctive speech or behavioral patterns. Their cognitive, emotional, and moral development does not match their chronological age or their physical and sexual maturity. If not supervised, they are at risk of being harmed by others who will take advantage of them. Those with moderate to mild mental retardation often feel stigmatized by others. They experience discrimination because of their difference.

(pre- and posttest completers) fell short '
cally required 80 subjects per conditi'
tect differences between the two g'
treatment-effect differences we'
erment included the Index
Efficacy (Tipton & Worthin,
Meaghan, Lieberman, & Mullin,
by the Role Functioning Scale (McP.

Competency in G
Step 3: Advoca
168
At this poin
pending u
home w
worksh
homes
abilit
St

■ Case Management in the Field of De
   Scenario 1

Facts of the Case

Linda is a 39-year-old African-American female living wit.
mother, Mrs. Garrity. Linda's primary condition is classified in th.
moderate mental retardation. Linda was diagnosed at birth with L.
drome. Mental retardation is a condition characterized by significantly .
age intellectual functioning and is accompanied by concurrent impairmen.
adaptive functioning. Linda has lived in her parents' home since birth and has r.
ceived concrete services consistent with the Americans with Disabilities Act
throughout her life. Linda works in a sheltered workshop in landscaping. Because
of her failing health, Mrs. Garrity is requesting that Linda become a ward of the
state and be placed in a residential group home. Mr. Garrity has been deceased for
10 years. Mrs. Garrity wants Linda to be able to continue her landscaping job
with her current sheltered workshop group.

Step 1: Assure Client Safety

Linda does not pose a danger to self or others. Because of her irreversible primary
condition (moderate retardation), Linda is in need of supervised care (problem
secondary to her primary condition). This is currently being provided by her
mother, and supervisory responsibility will be transferred to the group home
upon Linda's placement.

Step 2: Determine Urgency of Client Need

Linda is not currently in a crisis situation or a state of crisis. She is facing an expected transition of having to move from one supervised living arrangement (her
parents' home) to another (a residential group home). Linda is not in need of urgent (this day or this week) concrete services. Residential placement in a group
home can be accomplished in a timely manner.

EXHIBIT 10.1   *Process Recording: Case Management with Linda*

Thinking Declarative Knowledge	Dialogue Theory-Driven Therapeutic Process	Worker Self-Awareness Monitoring Skill and Feeling
Primary case manager, co-ordinates fragmented services, work with collateral source, and/or join with mother as therapeutic ally	W: Hello, Linda. It is good to see you and your mother again. Mrs. Garrity, it is good to see you. You are looking well.	Concerned about how Linda will take to the idea of living in a group home
Common behavior among those with Down's syndrome: very trusting and loving, evidence of working relationship	L hugs the worker and smiles.	
	Mrs. G: Hello, Ms. Krista. I am so glad that we can work together on this.	Feel fortunate to have Mrs. Garrity as a thera-peutic ally over the years
Focus on strengths; her work skills indicate that she has skills she can ap-ply to residential living	W: Linda, I hear that you are doing very well as a gardener. You are a good worker.	Happy for her success
	L: Yes, I like it. We have fun together when we work.	
Supporting task perfor-mance	W: I am very proud of you. I know your mother is too.	Comfortable with Mom as part of the therapeutic process; allies
Mom is therapeutic ally Begins to introduce pur-pose of this session	Mrs. G: Yes, I am. It shows me that Linda can do many things without me.	
Linda is picking some-thing up, nonverbal com-munication	L looks at mother.	
Watching the level of my language, use of words that Linda will easily un-derstand, awareness of primary condition	W: Linda, we are all meet-ing today to talk about maybe living with some of your work friends in a group home. What do you think of the idea?	Worried about her response
This reflects some anxiety about the idea of	L: I want to stay with my mama. Who will take care	I anticipated this theme

(continued)

169

EXHIBIT 10.1 *Process Recording: Case Management with Linda*
(*continued*)

Thinking Declarative Knowledge	Dialogue Theory-Driven Therapeutic Process	Worker Self-Awareness Monitoring Skill and Feeling
separation: Linda may need some counseling to deal with this separation and transition	of her if I am not there? She needs me.	
Plays to strengths, growth toward independent living	Mrs. G: You are great company for me, Linda, but I want you to be able to be near people your own age and be more on your own. Like you are in the sheltered workshop. We will still visit each other and do things together.	
Straight to the point Normal to worry	L: Why? Are you going to die? Worried.	Sad
Problem secondary to primary condition	Mrs. G: Well, someday we will all die, but it is not my time yet. I am getting old though, and I want to be sure that things are in place for you.	Glad that Mrs. Garrity knows the right thing to say
Purpose of the session	Mrs. G: How about letting Ms. Krista find some group homes for us to visit?	Model is on target
Task allocation: Who will do what when? Worker will locate possible homes; Linda and her mother will visit; Linda will make list of those homes she thinks will be good for her	W: Yes, Linda. We will begin by looking. You do not have to make a decision right away.	
Contracting, making choices	L: I guess I can look. Can I visit where Jane lives?	Hopeful
Resource location, networking with others to set up visits	W: Yes. Next week, we will meet at the same time and I will have a list of homes and a visiting schedule.	Skilled as locator of resources, good at networking and organizing

Step 7: Ethical Dilemma

There is no ethical dilemma noted at this time. A common ethical dilemma faced by workers in the field of mental retardation is how to help those who live with mental retardation to express their sexuality.

■ Case Scenario 2: Case Management in the Field of Juvenile Justice

Facts of the Case

You are a social worker assigned to the Offender Rehabilitation Division of the public defender's office. J is an indigent 17-year-old, who was referred to public defender services following his arrest for murder during an armed robbery. It is unclear whether J was an accomplice or the perpetrator. As he awaits trial, J is currently being held in a local jail on a wing that holds 30 juveniles pending transfer to an adult facility.

Case Explication

The delivery of direct-practice social work services in this case requires setting-specific and field-of-practice-specific knowledge. Juvenile and adult criminal justice is a field of social work practice. Practitioners must be cognizant of the legislative acts and state statutes that govern the delivery of services to youth offenders. As a field of practice, criminal justice is influenced by both deterrence (custody and punishment) and restorative justice models of practice. Arrest is often considered to be a crisis event (step 2). The rights of the client for safety and judicial due process must be weighed against the right of society for protection and the right of victims and their families for justice (step 1). The law requires assurance that J will be available to stand trial and will not pose a threat (step 1) to the community if released on bail or on his own recognizance. J is currently being held in a local jail on a wing designated for juvenile offenders. The task of the Offender Rehabilitation Department is to coordinate psychosocial evaluations (step 5) that may be used during pretrial, trial, and sentencing and to search for possible juvenile residential facilities (step 3: concrete service), where J can be detained while he awaits trial.

Social work is a host discipline within the correctional system. The charges against J are serious. The social worker's role is secondary to the primary proceedings of arrest, trial, and incarceration. Nonetheless, the steps of the decision tree apply. The social worker's fiduciary responsibility is (to the degree possible) to assure J's safety while being held for trial or when incarcerated if found guilty (step 1). It is a principle of juvenile justice to separate juvenile offenders from adult offenders, but J's age, his previous record, and the seriousness of the crime with which he is charged place him at risk for being tried and sentenced as an adult. Therefore, case advocacy (step 4) may be needed to assure that J remains within the juvenile justice system. Though the crisis of arrest (step 2) has passed, the worker must attend to the crisis aftermath.

Secondary to the legal proceedings, it is important to consider rehabilitation for juvenile offenders whether in or out of prison (step 5). To do so, it is important to base treatment on a comprehensive psychosocial assessment. By reviewing J's previous records (J consented to release of this confidential information), you learn the following: (1) J has a prior history of psychotic depression with suicidal ideation. According to the record, J has experienced both auditory and visual hallucinations. His condition responded well to medication in the past. (2) J has past diagnoses of attention deficit hyperactivity disorder (ADHD), a learning disorder (LD), and borderline intellectual functioning. (3) He has a long history of academic and social problems in school. J was in a residential placement at some point because his aggressive behavior posed a danger to other students and teachers. (4) It is reported that J is a regular cannabis user, and that (5) he was physically and emotionally abused by his father. His mother is seriously ill with a progressive illness. J has a child with a girlfriend (who is now seeing someone else). Though there seems to be an overload of bleak facts within a bleak circumstance, such case scenarios are not uncommon. Social work's moral values compel a practitioner to help J make the most of his life whether in or out of jail. Rehabilitative treatment plans are based on the hope that J will come to understand himself better, experience remorse for his actions, and acquire skills that will enable him to reach his highest potential whether in or out of jail. The worker-client relationship is based on the belief that there is room for hope and improvement despite the system failures and bleak circumstances.

EXHIBIT 10.2   *Treatment Matrix for J*

Procedural Knowing	Worker Action	Desired Goal/Outcome
Duty to protect	Separate facility for juvenile, adult offenders Assess and treat suicidal ideation Assess and treat presence of auditory and visual hallucinations, if any	Assure J's safety, keep J in juvenile detention Prevent suicide Treat psychosis Teach J skills for surviving in adult setting
Crisis intervention (arrest is crisis event)	Crisis aftermath: keep J connected to family	Prevent social isolation of J Keep J informed of the process
Case management skills	Locate youth facility where J can be detained and/or incarcerated	Assure placement in youth facility pending transfer from the jail
Case advocacy: age and criminal record put J at risk for being treated as an adult	Advocate for treatment of J as youth offender rather than as adult offender	Rehabilitation and reintegration as part of sentencing outcome
Class advocacy	Address policies that hold juveniles in adult facilities pretrial and that allow juveniles to be tried and sentenced as adults	Maintenance of juvenile justice system Correct flaws in systems that failed J
Work with individual assessment	Review J's criminal and psychological records Request current evaluation	Prepare report for use in legal proceeding Mitigation of sentence
Work with individual treatment	Assure J is receiving needed mental health treatment and skills for future living	Medication, therapy, education, job skills

EXHIBIT 10.3a *Decision Schema: Case Management*

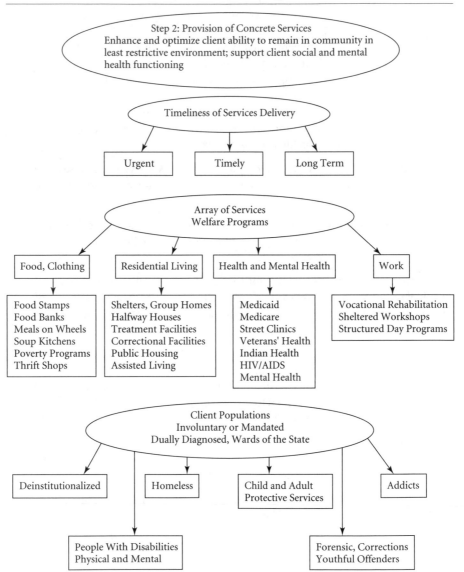

EXHIBIT 10.3b

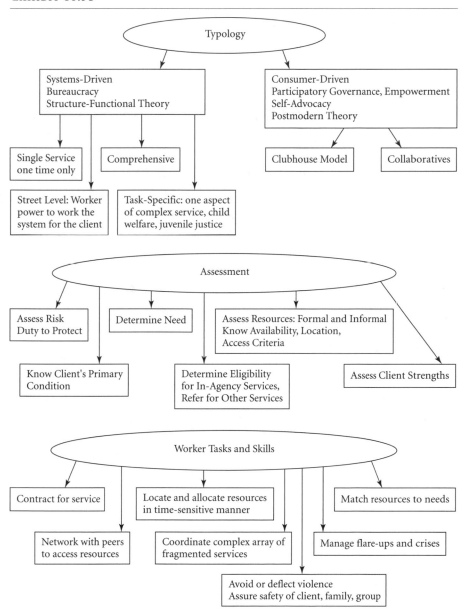

11
Case and Class Advocacy

■ Overview of Social Work Advocacy

Step 4 of the decision tree guides the direct-practice worker in case advocacy and the social work activist (macro social work practice) in class advocacy. When case management fails to secure needed resources (step 3), case advocacy (step 4) is required. Case advocacy can take the form of advocacy on behalf of a client (when services are denied or withdrawn) or it can take the form of a power alliance to increase client autonomy. By comparing case management in chapter 10 with advocacy in this chapter, the reader is able to differentiate the two models and learn the different skill sets. By presenting case advocacy and class advocacy in the same chapter, the reader is able to see the similarities and differences between these two approaches and acquire familiarity with both skill sets.

In contrast to case advocacy (a single client), class advocacy involves an aggregate client population. It is concerned with the redistribution of resources through social policies and programs. Class advocacy seeks a just and humane society. Values (ideology) determine the desired end goals of class advocacy. Social work activists seek reform through political action and civil disobedience. Whether case or class, advocacy has its roots in power.

■ Definition

Advocacy is a term for which there is no universal agreement. It is associated both with a controversial history and with different disciplines, each claiming it as their own. For some disciplines, advocacy is a main task (legal advocacy), while in other disciplines, advocacy is marginal to the main task (medical advocacy, school advocacy). Regardless, there is a common theme of power. To *advocate* is to engage in reasoned argument (Bateman, 1995, p. 2) on behalf of another; to give voice (to the voiceless); to intercede, defend, or plead the cause of another. There are three major styles of advocacy: broker, collaborative, and adversarial (argument and action). Advocacy with and on behalf of individual clients will be discussed first. Advocacy for a just society will be discussed later in the chapter.

■ Advocacy With Individual Clients

Broker Advocacy

On a case level, broker advocacy consists of securing concrete resources or services for clients who have been denied them or who have had such services or resources withdrawn. In addition, advocacy refers to the desired outcome of such services. In broker advocacy, the desired outcome is community inclusion and participation, economic sufficiency, institutional support, social affirmation, and access to needed resources. The quality of the client's participation in accessing and controlling needed resources is a key to power. Advocacy adds to case management (chapter 10) client participation in agency governance. Clients have input into policy and program initiatives and are politically active.

As a client advocate, the worker must also be able to identify and "work" the formal systems that constrain client access to services. Work with family, schools (accommodations), law enforcement (court diversion programs, probation, parole), and health and mental health care systems to broker client services requires that the practitioner have knowledge of the language and power structures of specific institutional systems.

Self and Collective Advocacy

Workers empower clients when they teach (coach) clients the skills of self-advocacy. *Self-advocacy* is a process in which individuals or a group (collective advocacy) speak and act on their own behalf in pursuit of their own needs and interests. The features of such advocacy are (1) the integration of legal action with group dissent, (2) collective organizing, (3) membership consisting of those likely to gain directly from the advocacy effort, (4) partnership with professionals, and (5) collective governance of the advocacy group through participatory democracy (Bateman, 1995, p. 7).

The use of a worker's power and expertise as a client ally is consistent with the definition of a collaborative relationship. A collaborative relationship is based on interdependency and belief in client strengths. The worker acts as an ally to help clients acquire internal and external resources. Techniques to increase client self-esteem and competency include assertiveness training, skills training, solution-focused and problem-solving strategies, and social construction (validation of the client's experiential history). Both worker and client are perceived to have power, which they use in alliance to achieve desired goals.

Advocacy on Behalf of Marginalized Clients

Marginalized clients are served by case advocacy. Social workers possess an eth-class perspective which allows them to understand how race and class play a role in the lives of marginalized clients. They act to empower clients who have been marginalized due to race, gender, sexual orientation, age, or handicapping condition. They advocate for client rights and human dignity in the delivery of social services. As an employee within a human service organization, the social worker can use his/her position as a sociopolitical source of power to partner with clients to bring about desired social changes. The social worker can use his/her position to examine and challenge the organization (where employed) for bias and discriminatory practices.

Social work advocates can use their skills in organizational development, political activism (Hasenfeld, 1987; Haynes & Mickelson, 2000; Fisher, 1995), and action research to effect changes in resource allocation at the agency, state, and national policy levels (DePoy, Hartman, & Haslett, 1999; O'Melia & Miley, 2000). Use of an individual worker's power extends beyond worker-client to include professional collaborative teaming at other levels. This type of advocacy holds that power is generated through a number of collaborative alliances or partnerships.

Healing Therapies for the Experience of Prejudice and Institutional Discrimination

Advocacy practice requires that the worker cast his/her practice with individual clients in accordance with empowerment concepts and principles and a strengths perspective. Assessment consists of identifying client strengths (what is working, past successes, desired goals). It also consists of developing a sociocultural-political client profile. Determining a client's past and current experiential history of oppression, i.e., gender, social inequality, level of poverty, or handicapping condition, is deemed as relevant as (if not more relevant than) assessing a client's personality, emotions, cognitions, and behaviors as discussed in the next chapter.

Using narrative (White, 2000) to elicit a client's story and dialogue to challenge the meaning of events, the worker helps the client to reframe her/his story to gain new understanding and meaning. Power to define what is the matter and its cause is healing. This model is frequently used with survivors of violence and with victims of oppression. *Social constructivism*, or narrative therapy (Eron & Lund, 1996), is a therapeutic approach that takes into account client experiences with profound alienation, institutional discrimination, and violence. The goal of such work is to raise client consciousness of self, to reduce shame and self-blame, and to use client anger as a catalyst toward self and social change.

Constructivism empowers clients by focusing on how individuals make meaning in their lives through their perceptions, the operation of cognitive and affective processes, and the mechanics of memory storage and retrieval (Brower, 1998, p. 205). Social constructivism prompts a client to examine his/her social and cultural milieu to gain understanding rooted in language, cultural beliefs, social interaction, and institutional behavior (Gergen, 1999). Client and worker dialogue focuses on client narration and the construction of meaning.

■ Adversarial Advocacy on Behalf of Clients

Broker advocacy consists of worker activities directed at locating and linking the client to formal organizational or environmental supports, using techniques associated with case management. *Adversarial advocacy* goes beyond broker advocacy in that it relies on skills to secure resources and/or services that have been denied or withdrawn. In adversarial advocacy, there are three parties: the client, the advocate, and the other side. Interaction is marked by tension and resistance. When resources are denied, withdrawn, or nonexistent, worker and client may have to engage in adversarial actions.

Generally speaking, advocacy problems can be bounded (a client-specific denial of benefits) or unbounded (a social problem involving populations). When the problem is bounded, there are usually clear priorities based on knowing what the problem is, its range of possible solutions, and the process by which it can be resolved. The time frame is limited.

Core Skills of Adversarial Advocacy

Adversarial advocacy is indicated when services or benefits to which people are entitled are not given or are provided in a dehumanizing, confrontational, or coercive manner. It is indicated when discriminatory practices occur, when gaps in services cause undue hardships, or when people lack representation or participation in decisions that affect their lives. Advocacy is warranted when government or agency policies and procedures or community and workplace practices adversely affect client groups or when clients are denied legal rights. The need for advocacy cuts across different client populations and service settings.

Adversarial advocacy requires assertiveness. Assertiveness is distinguished from aggressiveness in that assertiveness does not violate the rights of those whom advocacy targets (the other side). An advocate must be prepared, however, to confront those in authority and to invoke sanctions to secure a client's right to service.

Effective advocates possess the following characteristics: natural leadership, strong personalities, expertise in their subject, knowledge about the issue being contested, factual accuracy, political adeptness, reputation of professional integrity, and skills in case presentation. Often a client's right is pitted against an organization's effort to protect resources or to defend its position. The outcome of adversarial advocacy is usually a win-lose situation. Either side may experience serious consequences. Advocacy takes place within a context of tension and resistance. Advocacy can lead to revenge directed at either the client or the worker or both (Bateman, 1995). The proportion of social work practitioners who engage in adversarial advocacy is relatively small. In 1969, NASW made advocacy part of its Code of Ethics and established an ad hoc committee on advocacy.

The Six Stages of Adversarial Advocacy

According to Bateman (1995), effective advocacy requires structure. He identifies six stages. At each stage, a different level and type of skill is needed. Though there is no timetable for the completion of a step, one stage must be completed before the next is undertaken. Stage 1 is marked by awareness of the need for advocacy. Where there is a clear denial of rights or a dispute involving regulations, the problem is clear (bounded). More often, the worker must discover the problem hidden among other issues the client presents. The most common case advocacy needs are related to obtaining money, housing, services, and treatment (medical and psychosocial).

In stage 2, the worker gathers relevant information and obtains instructions from the client. Formal, signed client consent for the release of information relevant to the issue being contested is necessary. Information gathering must include the facts of the situation as perceived by each side. In conversations with the other side, notation of prejudicial comments and bad practices should be made. The worker should keep track of the chronology of the events. If, at this stage, the request for information is obstructed, a more assertive approach to gain access to needed information may have to be used.

Throughout the advocacy process, it is important to put things in writing. Keep a written record of who said what and what was agreed to by those involved at each step. Legal recourse requires written requests. State the legal authority for the request being made. Bounded problems always have legal and procedural issues that can be used to good effect. Do not negotiate verbally or over the phone. Written communication is more likely to get a response. All correspondence should be on letterhead and formal. When sent, get a signed receipt of delivery. Keep a copy of all communications sent and received. If unsure of any facts, begin the sentence with "I understand that . . ." Have the client sign letters written on his/her behalf. Any threatened actions (threat to sue) should be in writing. In advocacy practice, a threat is a clear statement that, unless a particular course of action is taken, there will be certain consequences such as adverse publicity, a formal complaint, or legal action. Such statements should be made in writing without emotive language. The other side is likely to perceive such statements as aggression.

The third step is to engage in legal research. Research should identify the legal and factual issues involved, any gaps in the information, the most effective remedy to solve the problem, and the probability of success for the client. It should also identify who has the power or authority to make the desired outcome a reality. Legal research is used to get the law right. To get the facts right, an advocate needs good interviewing skills, which include checking and validating obtained information. Phone conversations and personal communications should be backed by follow-up letters.

Stage 4 involves interpretation and feedback to the client about possible courses of action and the risks involved. For instance, when the issue is the non-provision of suitable care by a provider, the following actions could be considered: (1) a request can be made that care be provided, (2) a formal complaint can be filed, (3) negotiations to achieve the required type and level of care can be entered, (4) negotiations with the threat to take legal action can be initiated, (5) court proceedings to force the provision of care can be undertaken, and (6) the issue can be made public.

Stage 5 consists of active negotiation and advocacy. If the result of the first five stages is not sufficient, advocacy proceeds to the last stage, litigation. Litigation is not confined to courts and tribunals. It can be brought to arbitration through the use of an ombudsman, a grievance committee, a panel, or a case conference. Litigation is the process that enforces rights.

Three Styles of Negotiation

Bateman notes that there are three styles of negotiation. The first is *competitive* negotiation where threats, intimidation, superiority, and blame characterize the dialogue. Such a style minimizes the risk of exploitation but makes it harder to reach an agreement. *Cooperative* negotiation is based on establishing common ground and emphasizing shared values. Such a style invites manipulation and exploitation. Bateman recommends a third style, referred to as *principled* or *problem-solving* negotiation. This style has six elements: (1) negotiate on the merits of the case rather than bargain, (2) focus on interests rather than positions, (3) find solutions which will produce mutual gain, (4) avoid tricks and posturing, (5) insist that the end result be fair and based on an objective standard, and (6) don't let the negotiations get personal.

Applying the Principles of Least Contest and Controlled Escalation

There are times when a rational argument presented in a highly civil manner does no good. It is then that power is imperative. Generally, it is a wise approach to use the principles of least contest and controlled escalation when applying power. *Least contest* refers to applying the minimum degree of conflict that will bring about the desired result, while *controlled escalation* refers to arriving at an optimal outcome with a minimal expenditure of strategic resources. Based on these principles, there are three levels of intensity: (1) low conflict marked by discussion and persuasion, (2) moderate conflict where prodding occurs, and (3) high conflict where there is some form of coercion. A low-conflict scenario entails speaking, informing, and exploring the facts of the case with a decision maker. Argument is used to persuade the decision maker that the decision should be reconsidered. A moderate-conflict scenario involves prodding. Prodding includes negotiating and bargaining with organizational actors, appealing to higher authorities, and using legal mandates. A high-conflict scenario consists of the use of some form of coercion. Coercion may include going to an agency's funding source, involving a licensing or regulatory organization with oversight, getting media exposure, involving political leaders, and using the courts. Additionally, one can use psychological pressure by making the other side feel insecure, unsure, and vulnerable by keeping the pressure on it.

Summary of Case Advocacy Techniques

Case advocacy skills include conferring with other agencies, initiating legal action, providing expert testimony, educating relevant segments of the community, contacting public officials and legislators, making appeals to review boards, forming interagency committees or coalitions, gathering information through studies and surveys, organizing client groups, and making persistent demands. Case advocacy involves working with and on behalf of individuals and families to ensure that they receive the benefits and services to which they are entitled and that they are delivered in ways that safeguard their dignity. See the case scenario and Exhibit 11.1 at the end of the chapter.

■ Advocacy for a Just and Humane Society

Definitions

There are two types of social work class advocacy: (1) public policy advocacy (Janson, 1999), and (2) rights advocacy, reform through social activism (Alinsky, 1946; Gil, 1998). *Public policy advocacy* is concerned with the just distribution of society's benefits and burdens, including the resources of wealth, power, health, knowledge, and services. Fairness and equity demand that the distribution of goods and services *not* be left to (a) random selection, (b) those in power, and (c) flawed economic systems. Social work public policy is a goal-driven, collective strategy to address inequalities in the distribution of goods and services. *Rights advocacy* addresses discriminatory and oppressive social environments through social activism with the intent to reform structural barriers. In policy and rights advocacy, the problems are unbounded. There is less clarity as to the source of the problem, its solution, or the processes needed to resolve it. The time frame for resolution is also uncertain.

Knowledge Needed for Policy Advocacy

Declarative knowledge for policy practice consists of (1) descriptive content on social welfare policies and programs, past and current, (2) content on the political and organizational processes that influence policy development and implementation, (3) analytical frameworks for evaluating policies for their structure and function (Chambers, 2000), (4) content on theories of social and economic justice, and (5) content that includes selecting and implementing appropriate courses of action for class advocacy. Class advocacy skills are important to competent social work practice.

Historical Perspective: Welfare Policies and Programs

It is important to know the history of social welfare policies and programs. Such content goes beyond the scope of this chapter. The reader is referred to the following authors: Day (2000); DiNitto (1991); Gilbert and Terrell (1998); Karger and Stoesz (1998); Netting, Kettner, and McMurtry (1997); Popple and Leighninger (2002); Segal and Brzuzy (1998).

Descriptive Content on Social Welfare Policies and Programs

Policy advocacy requires knowledge of the legislative history of major social welfare programs, such as income maintenance, health care, housing, health and mental health, and child and family welfare. This content is a necessary part of consciousness raising and socialization to the profession. Such material goes beyond the scope of this chapter. The reader is referred to social policy course syllabi for elaboration of this content.

The Sociology of Social Problems

Historical and descriptive content on social welfare policies and programs are predicated on the documentation of social problems. Texts on social problems (e.g., Eitzen & Zinn, 2003) usually provide quantitative data documenting the prevalence and incidence of large-scale social problems, such as poverty, crime, illness, aging, urban blight, racism, gender discrimination, etc. Such data are usually accompanied by an argument of social causality.

The argument goes as follows. Social problems result from oppressive and discriminatory practices associated with existing societal structures and their functions. Flawed structures (especially capitalism) cause social problems, i.e., capitalism causes unemployment and poverty. Institutional racism results in unequal access to employment, housing, health and mental health services, and education. Content on dysfunctional societal institutions and the societal forces that contribute to their dysfunction is usually taught in sociology or in the human behavior sequence in schools of social work.

■ The Normative Foundation of Policy Advocacy

Values are based on what we find desirable. They are stated in terms of right or wrong, good or evil, beautiful or ugly, appropriate or inappropriate, pleasant or unpleasant. According to Popple and Leighninger (2002, p. 17), two dominant value streams have influenced American policies: (1) capitalist-puritan, and (2) humanist-positivist-utopian.

The capitalist-puritan tradition is consistent with residual, needs-based, and means-tested social welfare. This value stream holds that human nature is basically evil and that people are responsible for their own success or failure. It holds that the acquisition of material prosperity is achieved through hard work. The primary purpose of society is to maintain law and order to protect the acquisition of wealth and property. Those who are unsuccessful or deviant are provided limited assistance. The primary incentives to change lie in economic or physical rewards and punishments.

The humanist positivist utopian perspective is more in line with policies and programs that promote universal entitlements. This value stream holds that the primary purpose of society is to fulfill people's material and emotional needs. It holds that structural barriers limit individual opportunities. Scientific knowledge can understand and help to correct these barriers. Consequently, individuals and society are ultimately perfectible.

Social Work's Grand Narratives

Historically, social work has stood squarely on the side of the economically disadvantaged. Concerns about impoverished individuals and families led to policy and program initiatives to end poverty (see chapter 15). The narrative of economic victimization has accounted for many of the clients served by direct social work practice through the delivery of concrete social services (chapters 10 and 15).

Theories of Redistributive Social Justice

Policy advocacy is based on norms of redistributive social justice. As a grand abstraction, *social justice* refers to an ideal system of government, economic production and distribution, and freedom from structural and institutional discrimination and oppression. Ideas (ideologies) about just social goals are derived from philosophy, theology, and political science. Norms (desired end goals) are driven by competing values-based definitions of the "good" society.

Competing theories of social justice direct the redistribution of wealth in a society. A philosophy of egalitarianism is based on a desire for equal distribution and/or equity in the distribution of a society's goods. Utilitarianism seeks distribution according to the greatest good for the greatest number. Contractarianism justifies some inequality as long as the redistribution doesn't widen the gap between the rich and the poor. The libertarian holds that individual rights supersede group rights.

Social welfare policies and programs are ideologies that vie for support in the arena of public opinion and political referendum. Competition over scarce resources leads to conflict and negotiated trade-offs. Accordingly, some groups are advantaged while other groups are disadvantaged. In the competition for resources, issues of race, gender, sexual orientation, or type of handicapping condition surface. Who, among equally deserving and needy subgroups, will benefit from a policy or program? No scientific, cause-and-effect knowledge can make such a determination. Values-based determinations of resource allocations are just that, values-based. Power, not evidence, aligns with the desired end goals of policy advocacy.

■ Rights Advocacy

Rights advocacy holds that both oppressor and oppressed, as well as those who seemingly stand by or pass by on the other side, are damaged by oppression and are in need of liberation. Rights advocacy is associated with movements such as the civil rights movement, the labor movement, liberation theology, Afrocentrism, the women's liberation movement, gay rights, welfare rights, and the rights of the disabled. Rights advocacy works for a just society based on gender and racial equality, multicultural acceptance, celebration of alternative lifestyles, and appreciation for all age groups and the differently abled. Two activities are fundamental to rights advocacy: (1) critical consciousness (or consciousness raising) or concentiatization (Freire, 1970, 1973, 1990), and (2) social action (Alinsky, 1946; Gil, 1998).

Consciousness Raising and the Political Process

Groups are used to raise consciousness. Empowerment results from the validation of shared experiential histories and views. Such validation is essential to sustain an experience of power. The ability to join with others (alliance) as participants in a political or reform process is empowering. The ability to confront oppression and exert influence over others through social activism enhances personal power and a person's sense of well-being.

During consciousness raising, people are brought together to dialogue, reflect, and act (praxis). Dialectic dialogue (1) challenges the images of social reality, (2) examines ideas, beliefs, and assumptions that people take for granted, (3) examines individual and collective motives, interests, and needs that lead people to behave in the manner they do, and (4) identifies values and ideologies that guide dominant and dominated group relations. Through consciousness raising and the formation of power alliances, the goal of activists is to transform the politics of conventional interest groups into the politics of common human needs. It seeks to evolve new patterns of actions and social relations through collective action.

Political Social Work

Social policy practice is linked with political social work. Policy advocates are taught to provide expert testimony and to influence legislation through lobbying activities. Social work political activists write, issue, and/or respond to legislative alerts. Some work as legislative aides or gain political office themselves. Those who work as case managers in direct practice are in the best position to connect the personal issues of clients with organizational and political policies (Schneider & Netting, 1999). They can make the connection between social and economic justice and individual pain and suffering. Political action is a distinguishing feature of social work advocacy practice (Hasenfeld, 1987). Gil holds that conventional politics pursues short-term goals while rights activists pursue the root causes of oppression and injustice by seeking fundamental transformation in the key institutions of society and in the ideological beliefs of people.

■ Reform Advocacy: Social Action as Adversarial Advocacy

Gil (2000) locates oppression in the social structures and relations of a society. According to Gil, the domination of exploited groups has been institutionalized in the form of economic, social, psychological, and cultural systems that establish privileged conditions of living for certain social classes and peoples and not others. Key institutions that have stewardship over life-sustaining natural and human-created resources shape the circumstances of living and the relative power of individuals and social classes. Institutions organize work and production, oversee the exchange and distribution of concrete and symbolic goods and services, regulate civil and political rights and responsibilities, and govern and set norms for reproduction, socialization, and social control.

Gil observes that oppressive and exploitative institutional practices have social, psychological, and ideological (secular and religious) dimensions that sustain them. Perceptions of relative status and prestige become internalized through socialization and indoctrination. These perceptions are the core of discriminatory ideologies and practices concerning different social groups, classes, and people (i.e., racism, sexism, classism). Values grounded in the notion of inequality, such as competition and self-interest, create occupationally, spatially, and socially segmented and stratified societies.

Those who are privileged possess greater shares of available goods and services and enjoy different levels of rights, responsibilities, and liberty. Legal and political institutions tend to reflect established inequalities and power relations among competing interest groups and classes. Gil maintains that once minor, initial inequalities in exchanges occur, there is a tendency to legitimize, institutionalize, and increase them.

Rights advocacy depends on social activists who pursue fundamental social transformations (Thurz, 1976). Gil cautions that social activists need to differentiate short-range from long-range goals. He sees policy advocacy and the activities of the United Nations as necessary and ethically valid efforts to reduce the intensity of injustice and oppression. Short-range objectives, he says, are not impediments to long-range goals that strategically seek fundamental social changes (the root causes of oppression and injustice). The latter requires lengthy, persistent processes such as (1) countercultural education, (2) the development of critical consciousness, and (3) social movements (praxis).

■ Evidence: Does Advocacy Work?

Armed Conflict

Citing several studies (Bruyn & Rayman, 1979; Lakey, 1987; Sharp 1973, 1979), Gil (2000) observes that armed liberation struggles, whatever their apparent achievements, may have to be followed by long-term, unarmed, active, nonviolent liberation struggles aimed at overcoming the root causes of injustice and oppression (Gil, 2000, p. 52). In armed conflict, the agents and victims of oppression change, but not the root causes that produce oppression.

Public Policies and Programs

Evidence of the success of public policies and programs comes from program evaluation research. See chapter 15, which contains evaluation studies of Temporary Assistance to Needy Families (TANF) and family preservation programs. Such research is based on criteria for judging the merit of specific "real-life" service delivery systems in organizations. Successful program implementation is not proof that the features of the program "caused" the outcome. The claim is only that the policy/program created the necessary but not sufficient conditions for success.

Activist Research

Activist research (Reitsma-Street & Brown, 2002) is another form of adversarial advocacy that occurs on the neighborhood or community level. Research can be used to oppress or liberate. Therefore, activist researchers must attend to how the research will be used and who will benefit or lose from the collected information. Politically savvy, activist researchers focus on whose voice is emphasized, what research strategies are selected, and on whose behalf the research is conducted.

■ Scenario: Case Advocacy: Medical Setting

Facts of the Case

You are a newly employed social worker in a large research and teaching hospital in the South. The hospital serves children and adults who come from all over the United States and the world for cutting-edge and last-resort experimental medical treatment. You are assigned to the pediatric unit. You have brief contact with family members to orient them to the hospital and its procedures. You assist them by locating translators (as needed), temporary housing while their child undergoes treatment, transportation, and limited financial support. You attempt to meet with your clients and their families on the days the client is scheduled for medical appointments.

K, a child from El Salvador, recently underwent life-prolonging (step 1: duty to protect) surgery. Consistent with the existing research protocol, she received procedure A. The surgery was not successful (step 2: crisis). The family is devastated. You are working with the family as part of discharge planning. You learn that there is another procedure (procedure B) that might work, but the hospital policy (position of other side: distribution limited by scarce resources) allows only one treatment per family. You begin broker case advocacy (step 4) by trying to locate (step 3: concrete resources) another hospital that will perform the alternative procedure.

Case Explication

You begin by fact gathering (first stage). As part of your fact-gathering activities, you learn that procedure B is state of the art, and most other hospitals use it over procedure A. It is widely known within the medical community that procedure A has a lower success rate. You also learn (exploration of alternatives) that no other teaching hospital will accept the referral because the child has already had access to a procedure (position of the other side). In your medical fact gathering, you become fairly confident that if the other procedure is performed, the outcome will be successful (your position). You then begin to gather information on the process that led to the decision to perform procedure A rather than procedure B (assessment of the decision-making process). You learn that procedure A is the existing research protocol at your hospital. You evaluate the status and power of those involved in the situation (power analysis). You and your client have the least power in terms of position, reference, and leverage. You do have the power of knowledge. You explore your options with your supervisor (chain of command within the system).

You explore and weigh the pros and cons of available options. Social work is a department in a host setting. There is a professional status differential between

EXHIBIT 11.1   *Treatment Matrix for K: Case Advocacy*

Procedural Knowing	Worker Action	Desired Goal/Outcome
Duty to protect	Facilitate life-prolonging medical treatment	Life
Identify need for advocacy (failed surgery: crisis)	Gather facts about the illness and its treatment	Knowledge, best practices
Broker advocacy	Locate alternative resources Refer to another hospital	Secure needed medical treatment
Adversarial advocacy Know positions	Learn the position of the other side	Establish own position
Know how the system works	Learn why procedure A was used over procedure B	Become knowledgeable about the hospital's decision-making process
Know how reviews and exceptions are granted	Make appointment to appear before ethics board	Reconsideration
Align with power, consult with others, follow chain of command	Form collective action Get support of supervisor	Increase power
Weigh pros and cons, engage in ethical decision making	Factual, scientific, rational, and ethical decision making	Decision to move to adversarial advocacy (moderate level)
Active negotiation Present request to ethics board	Testimony	Agreement to offer procedure B
Management of conflict Principle of least contest	Stance of advocate rather than whistle-blower	Win-win outcome
Successful operation	Discharge planning	Case closed

medical doctors and social workers. You identify an in-house mechanism (ethics board) through which it might be possible to advocate (principled negotiation) on behalf of this particular client and her family. You move from broker to adversarial advocacy. You decide to present (testimony) the information you've gathered to this board and ask (request for service) that the board consider making an exception to allow the hospital to perform the second procedure. You know that an ombudsman sits on the ethics board (litigation stage). You wish to present the information as a client advocate, not as a whistle-blower (least contest, moderate use of power).

You discuss possible repercussions to the social work department (will such an action place the department and/or your supervisor at risk?). Your supervisor has a stake in maintaining the department and her position within it. You explore the possible repercussions to yourself (marginalization, failure to progress, job loss). You juxtapose these possible outcomes against the possibility that your advocacy might result in a life-changing procedure for this child and her family. You check the NASW Code of Ethics. It seems to support several different actions.

Having weighed the options and having consulted with others, you decide to embark on moderate adversarial advocacy. Your supervisor agrees to go with you (alliance of power) to the next scheduled ethics board meeting. On the day of the meeting, your supervisor calls in sick. You go anyway. You present the facts that you have learned and request that an exception be granted to allow the child to receive procedure B. After you present your case, you leave the room. You later learn that the ombudsman argues in favor of the exception and the doctor supports the exception. In fact, the doctor has been intending to change the protocol and uses this opportunity to begin the process (win-win outcome).

Though you, the worker, began with broker case advocacy, your moderate adversarial advocacy resulted in organizational change that impacted a subpopulation of children in need of the same life-prolonging medical procedure.

■   Case and Class Advocacy Decision Schemas

EXHIBIT 11.2   *Clinical Case Advocacy*

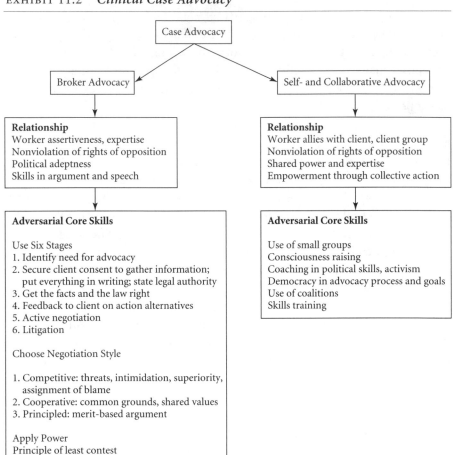

Case Advocacy

Broker Advocacy

Self- and Collaborative Advocacy

Relationship
Worker assertiveness, expertise
Nonviolation of rights of opposition
Political adeptness
Skills in argument and speech

Relationship
Worker allies with client, client group
Nonviolation of rights of opposition
Shared power and expertise
Empowerment through collective action

Adversarial Core Skills

Use Six Stages
1. Identify need for advocacy
2. Secure client consent to gather information;
   put everything in writing; state legal authority
3. Get the facts and the law right
4. Feedback to client on action alternatives
5. Active negotiation
6. Litigation

Choose Negotiation Style

1. Competitive: threats, intimidation, superiority,
   assignment of blame
2. Cooperative: common grounds, shared values
3. Principled: merit-based argument

Apply Power
Principle of least contest
Controlled escalation

Levels of Intensity
High
Moderate
Low

Adversarial Core Skills

Use of small groups
Consciousness raising
Coaching in political skills, activism
Democracy in advocacy process and goals
Use of coalitions
Skills training

EXHIBIT 11.3   *Advocacy for a Just and Humane Society*

Class Advocacy

Public Policy Advocacy

Rights Advocacy

Declarative Knowledge
• Know that problems have social causality
• Know social welfare history
• Know major social welfare policies and programs
• Know legislative and political processes
• Be able to analyze a policy's structure and function
• Know the role economics plays in policy making, cost
• Be able to assess public sentiment: for-against
• Know the normative (ideological) foundation of policy
• Know competing theories of social justice

Declarative Knowledge
• Oppressors (dominating, privileged)
• Oppressed (dominated, marginalized)
• Discriminatory practices, structures
• Documentation of rights violations

Action: Redistribution of Resources
• Advocate for a policy change or policy initiative
• Document the scope of the social problem (data)
• Make a rational argument that there is a problem
• Educate the public, raise awareness of social issue
• Use legislative process expertise (testimony, contacts)
• Use political expertise (form alliances, coalitions, PACs)
• Know opponents and their position
• Know who will benefit and who will lose

Action: Reform
• Use of small and large groups, social action
• Consciousness raising, dialectic dialogue
• Validation of experiences, narration
• Appeals: public speech, video, pictures
• Formation of coalitions for collective action
• Movements: marches, demonstrations, protests
• Application of power
    • Legal recourse
    • Use of court decisions
    • Civil disobedience
    • Coercion: armed conflict
• Use of activist research

193

12

Social Work With Individuals

■ Case-Indicated Need for Therapy

When the facts of the case at hand indicate that therapy is the intervention of choice, the social work clinician must still decide which theory and which method of therapy, individual (step 5), family (step 6), or group (step 7), is the most appropriate. This chapter focuses on work with individuals (step 5). It provides content that guides the practitioner in choosing a theory-guided therapeutic process (e.g., biological, psychological, or sociological) appropriate for work with individuals. The determination of best practices in a given case requires that the clinician evaluate potential theory-based therapies and the evidence for or against them when deciding upon a specific treatment.

Shared Similarities

This chapter shares similarities with other texts on clinical social work practice. It (1) builds on previous conceptualizations of clinical social work, beginning with casework and ending with generalist practice, (2) incorporates the concept of planned-change processes (Compton & Galaway, 2004), (3) builds upon the literature of relationship and therapeutic alliance (chapter 6), and (4) places the practice of therapy by clinical social workers within the context of direct practice. To augment this chapter, chapter 13 presents a case illustration involving complex data and case-specific model building. A chart of the assumptive premises of some of the major theories of human behavior (Exhibit 12.1) and a schema to help select the correct theory (Exhibit 12.2) are presented later in the chapter. A direct-practice decision schema (Exhibit 12.3) concludes the chapter.

EXHIBIT 12.1 *Comparative Cause-and-Effect Premises of Theories of Human Behavior*

Theories	Cause-Effect Premises
Biological framework: nature	This framework holds that individual behavior has biological determinants. Change occurs through genetic, chemical, or biophysiological interventions.
Psychodynamic framework: nurture	This framework maintains that nurture influences biological growth and development. Nurture is interactive (self-other) and is both past (there and then) and current (here and now). Personality (id, ego, and superego) develops from both nature and nurture. What goes right (normal development) is attached to a theory of pathology (what goes wrong). What goes wrong has been linked to mental health disorders classified in the *Diagnostic and Statistical Manual* (DSM-IVR). What goes right is linked to maturity, defined as rational-emotive balance and interpersonal skills that allow an individual to love and to work. Consistent with this framework, individual change occurs by (1) strengthening an individual's personality (ego) and coping capacities, (2) acquiring problem-solving techniques consistent with the executive function of the ego, (3) bringing difficult material (unconscious) into conscious awareness, (4) providing insight through interpretation, (5) mobilizing and/or containing affect (emotions) by providing a holding environment, (6) providing a corrective self-other emotional experience through experiential learning within sessions.
Behavioral learning theory	This theory states that all behavior is neutral and can be learned or unlearned by manipulating antecedent and consequent events. Classical conditioning shapes (stimulates or cues) behavior while operant conditioning maintains (reinforces) it. Imitation (social learning and vicarious learning) is a form of learned behavior. Change occurs when antecedent and consequent contingencies are changed or the conditions of imitation are changed.
Cognitive learning	This theory holds that feelings and behaviors are influenced by learned cultural and familial meanings that individuals attach to core thoughts or beliefs. Change occurs when one changes the meaning of an individual's core cognitions and beliefs (cognitive determinism).
Socialization theory	This theory claims that the individual is civilized by membership in a social group. Social norms determine individual behavior. Individuals change based on the contexts of their socialization (cultural or socioeconomic determinism); the individual is acted upon. Individual change

Theories	Cause-Effect Premises
	occurs within group socialization. Change occurs when the laws, rules, and norms governing socialized behavior change.
Symbolic interaction Reference groups	Individuals shape and are shaped by their environments. As an actor, an individual may accept, reject, or modify the definitions of self provided by others in his/her environment. An individual can redefine an environment rather than submit to it.
Power Critical theory Group theory Structure-functionalism Empowerment	Inequality (inequity) privileges some at the expense of others (oppression). Discrimination reflects bias or prejudice associated with race, gender, age, ethnicity, sexual orientation, or handicapping condition. In-group and out-group dynamics maintain structural conditions that sustain inequality. Change occurs through nonviolent confrontation (consciousness raising) and through the use of legal (legislation, courts) means or coercive tactics (social action) that change social structures.
Environments Social treatment Social milieu	Environments can be pathogenic or therapeutic. Individuals benefit (recover) when environments are therapeutic. Some environments are custodial (jails, institutions) while others are therapeutic (foster care, group homes, halfway houses, in-patient hospitalization, rehabilitation, day programs).

Differences

Compared to other presentations of clinical social work practice, this chapter conditions the selection of therapy on four criteria: (1) the step format of the decision tree allows for clear delineation and accountability when therapy is selected as the most appropriate intervention for the case at hand, (2) biological, psychological, cognitive, and social processes are presented as separate and distinct foci linked to therapy choice, (3) a commitment to open assessment allows the clinician to take into account complex client data permitting, thereby, (4) the conscientious selection of more than one model of intervention as the case warrants. Competent practice is tied to open assessment and case-specific model building based on evidence and theory selection.

EXHIBIT 12.2   *Schema: Individual Therapy Choices*

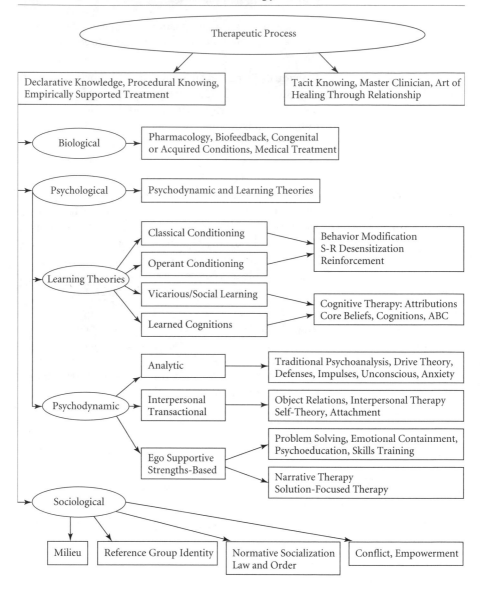

Point of Entry

Point of entry refers to the intersection of help seeking and help giving. A client's point of entry with a help giver begins with an interview. Clients in need of therapy may be voluntary, involuntary, or mandated. Practitioners who give help are, in turn, defined by their field of practice (area of expertise) and agency setting (see chapter 3).

The interview is used for four purposes: (1) to establish rapport or a working relationship with the client, (2) to gather information (facts) relevant to the request for service or therapy, (3) to explore the problem as to possible causality for purposes of diagnosis, problem definition, and prognosis, and (4) to deliver a therapeutic process designed to change feelings, cognitions, attitudes, beliefs, or personal or interpersonal functioning (behavior). How the client enters service is pivotal in the conceptualization of the profession and its planned change process.

■ Conceptualization of Clinical Social Work: The Five W's

The parameters of who receives help, for what, where, when, and why has driven the conceptualization of social work since its inception (Commission on Social Work Practice, 1958).

Who Is the Client?

Who has referred to either the person (Richmond, 1899, 1917, 1922; Hollis, 1964), the environment (Robinson, V., 1930; Reynolds, 1951; Smalley, 1967), or the person in the environment (Karls & Wandrie, 1994; Germain & Gitterman, 1980). It has referred to the highly vulnerable and poverty-stricken individual or to the "traditional" therapy client (Rothman, 1994). It includes all population age groups: the elderly, individual adults, adolescents, and children.

What Is the Matter?

What has referred to those living with primary conditions (Rothman, 1994; Rapp & Chamberlain, 1985) that lead to secondary problems in social functioning and to those who experience acute problems in living. It refers to those who deviate from the norm in role performance (welfare; Commission on Social Work Practice, 1958; Geismar, 1980; Biddle & Thomas, 1966) and to those who fall within the criminal justice system (Becker, 1967; Cloward & Ohlin, 1960). It refers to those with chronic conditions (Rothman, 1994; Sullivan, 2000; Robinson, 1993) and to those exposed to extraordinary circumstances (Roberts, 1991; James & Gilliland, 2004). It refers to developmental conditions (Erikson, 1963; Levinson, 1978; Sheehy, 1977) and to temporary situations (Lindemann, 1944).

Where Is Social Work Practiced?

Where has referred to public welfare agencies, not-for-profit agencies, for-profit agencies, managed-care agencies, faith-based agencies, and private practice, all of which come in a variety of specialized settings. It has referred to comprehensive community mental health centers, wraparound services, and highly fragmented services related to social welfare policies and programs.

When?

Clients enter a help-giving relationship voluntarily when they need concrete services (income, work, housing, health care, mental health care, or education) or when they feel subjective discomfort. Clients enter services when they are encouraged to do so by someone in authority (parent, teacher, spouse) or when they are mandated for services by the courts. It is important for clinicians to understand why a client is seeking help now (proximate time causality). This is separate from understanding distal causality, which refers to the identification of the dynamic forces that created the situation (there and then, past) or that sustain or maintain it (here and now, current).

Why: For What Purpose?

Why has referred to nominal definitions associated with the type of problem to be worked, e.g., "because of " truancy, eviction, suicidal ideation, school failure, job loss, domestic violence, mental illness, or parenting problems (Turner, 1978, 1983); it has referred to single problems or multiple problems (Reid & Epstein, 1972). Why also refers to problem exploration in terms of possible causality: social or individual. Why refers to prevention, early intervention, and tertiary (remedial) intervention (Parad, 1965; Caplan, 1964).

■ Conceptualizations of the Change Process in Social Work

Direct- and Indirect-Practice Methods

A parallel line of conceptualization based on change methods has also defined social work practice. It has referred to the individual served by casework (Richmond, 1899, 1917; Perlman, 1957; Hollis & Woods, 1981), to the individual served by therapy (Strean, 1978, 1985), to the family (Hartman, 1981; Hartman & Laird, 1983; Bowen, 1978; Haley, 1971; Minuchin, 1974; Carter & McGoldrick, 1989; Satir, 1964; Saleebey, 2002; Wells & Biegel, 1991), and to the group (Coyle, 1935; Shulman, 1999; Toseland & Rivas, 2001; Yalom, 1995). It refers to direct methods, such as case management (Davis & Meier, 2001; Moxley, 1989; Vourlekis & Greene, 1992), and to generalist practice (Kirst-Ashman & Hull, 2000). It refers to brief and task-centered approaches (Epstein, 1980; Reid & Epstein, 1972; Reid & Shyne, 1968).

   It refers to indirect social work methods, such as policy practice (Chambers, 2000), to management practice (Daft & Marcic, 2001; Ginsberg & Keys, 1995), and to community practice (Pincus & Minahan, 1973; Braeger & Specht, 1973; Gilbert & Specht, 1987; Rothman, 1994; Etzioni, 1968, 1993; Cox, Erlich, Rothman, & Tropman, 1984). It refers to case (Bateman, 1995) and class advocacy practice (Freire, 1990, 1973, 1970; Galper, 1980; Gil, 1998; Thurz, 1976).

Talk Therapies

Social work has also been conceptualized by the therapeutic processes it uses within talk therapies. These therapeutic processes include specific theory-guided interventions, such as pharmacological interventions, crisis interventions (James & Gilliland, 2004; Roberts, 2005), psychodynamic interventions (Freud, 1969), behavioral-learning interventions (Thomlinson & Thomlinson, 1996; Sundel & Sundel, 1982), and cognitive-behavioral interventions (Lantz, 1996; A. Beck, 1976; J. Beck, 1995; Bandura, 1977), to name some. Change has been variously conceptualized as internal (personality change), interpersonal, and/or transactional (environmental).

In contemporary therapies, change has been conceptualized as solution focused (Miller, Hubble, & Duncan, 1996; de Shazer, 1985; de Shazer, O'Hanlon, & Werner Davis, 1989) and strengths based (Saleebey, 2001, 2002; Cowger, 1994; DeJong & Miller, 1995), as empowerment (Pinderhughes, 1983; Gutierrez, Parsons, & Cox, 1998; Lee, 2001; O'Melia & Miley, 2000), as socialization to law and order (structure-functional; Parsons, 1970, 1977; Merton, 1975; Geismar, 1980), and as postmodern (Ungar, 2004).

Planned-Change Processes

As a profession, social work uses a planned-change process (Compton & Galaway, (2004). This planned-change process consists of five major activities: (1) establishment of rapport, (2) assessment, (3) contracting and goal setting, (4) intervention, and (5) evaluation. The first element of the planned-change process is the establishment of rapport. The establishment of rapport and a professional worker-client relationship has beginnings, middles, and endings. The planned-changed process is dependent on relationship from its inception to its end (termination). Assessment is the second element of the planned-change process. It consists of gathering information (facts of the case) and problem exploration (determining causality). It ends with a definition of the problem to be worked.

Contracting is the third component of the planned-change process. It establishes the treatment goals (outcome) of therapeutic intervention. Orlinsky, Grawe, and Parks (1994) identify the following elements of a contract as being pivotal to outcome success: (1) client preparation for therapy, (2) clarification of expectations about the helping process, (3) agreement on goals, (4) client's active participation in therapy, and (5) the clinician's adherence to a treatment model. To the discussion on contracting, Seabury (Compton & Galaway, 2004) adds the important concept of authentic and false contracting previously discussed in chapter 2.

Intervention, the fourth element of the planned-change process, consists of the application of a theory-based, empirically supported therapeutic process selected on the basis of the best fit between the therapy and the problem as assessed. Finally, the planned-change process evaluates (research as a method) the outcome of the intervention in light of its process (Did the intervention work as intended? Did it produce the intended outcome?).

■ The Values Base of Clinical Social Work Practice

Core Values: Acceptance, Self-Determination, Nonjudgmental Attitude, and Confidentiality

The social work clinical relationship has been defined by core values (Biestek, 1957) that have withstood the test of time. These values are as relevant today as when they were first articulated. *Acceptance* refers to the profession's commitment to serve all clients regardless of their marginalization or the focal problem to be worked. In this sense, social work serves a broad range of clientele. Individualization refers to the practitioner's commitment to view each client holistically, as more than the sum of identified needs, diagnostic labels, assessed problems in social functioning, or maladaptive interpersonal relationships. Each client is unique with a past and present unlike any other, with strengths, solutions, and spontaneities that sustain hope. Acceptance reflects the profession's commitment to avoid bias, stereotypes, and generalizations in its vigilance to be culturally responsive.

    Self-determination refers to the profession's commitment to ensure client rights in the face of the profession's social control function. It includes the client's right to active participation in his/her own treatment (empowerment). The principle of self-determination presumes the client's capacity for reasonable decision making (an aspect of assessment). It is linked to the practitioner's fiduciary obligations (chapter 2) to act in the client's best interest. It includes obtaining the client's informed consent for treatment. A *nonjudgmental attitude* refers to accepting the client as s/he is, not as we wish her/him to be or think s/he should be. By definition, the profession is not moralistic, cold, aloof, derogatory, or disapproving. *Confidentiality* is based on the premise that social work communication is purposeful and privileged (see chapter 2). The client must consent to the release of information. Information is sought not out of curiosity but on the basis of need to know. For further articulation of values and values exploration, see Reamer (1995), Rokeach (1973), and the NASW Code of Ethics (1999).

Declarative Knowledge: What Therapists Need to Know
About Human Behavior

Therapy requires knowledge about human behavior. Content in the human behavior sequence on individual normal and abnormal growth and development is
critical to knowing how to enact a therapeutic process to bring about desired
change. Each theory of human behavior contains assumptive premises of cause
and effect.

■ Enactment of a Therapeutic Process

Worker's Use of Declarative Knowledge

The declarative knowledge needed to enact a therapeutic process depends on
causal knowledge of individual resilience (normality) and vulnerability (abnormality) taught in the human behavior sequence. Knowing what interferes with
the unfolding of resilience leads to practice theories about how to correct what
went wrong. Declarative knowledge of human behavior (what goes right and
what goes wrong) is transformed into a therapeutic process through the worker's
use of procedural and tacit knowing.

Procedural and Tacit Knowing

Novices begin with declarative knowledge. Their mental functioning as clinicians
begins with a cognitive map of learned (taught) theoretical concepts. This knowledge structure is stored in memory as schemas. When faced with fresh client data,
the novice tries to match the facts of the client's case with the stored knowledge
s/he has learned. The novice is proficient when thinking about the procedures of
therapy. The novice reflects on action (process recordings) to advance his/her expertise (see chapter 13).

In contrast, tacit knowing is automatic and identifies the master clinician.
The master clinician is free to improvise. Improvisation is the capacity to reshape
understanding of the situation by departing from established procedures in response to novel or unexpected conditions. The master clinician readjusts her/his
definition of the problem and adjusts strategies and tactics accordingly. Improvisation relies on highly disciplined and automatic procedural knowledge and on a
highly refined self-regulated ability to allow for reflection and adjustment of performance in the therapeutic moment: reflection in action.

Common Factors

According to Binder (2004), every therapy has the following six factors (competencies) in common. Every therapy has some view of personality and interpersonal functioning. Every therapy possesses a theory about cognitive, affective, and
behavioral processes that are activated (or not) during the process of therapy.
Every therapy provides specific guidance on how to formulate the problem to be
worked. Every therapy possesses knowledge of salient maladaptive patterns of behavior and a theory of how change occurs and how problems are solved. Every
therapy defines criteria (goals) to track the course of therapy and measure its outcome success. Every therapy provides strategies for managing the therapeutic relationship. All therapies teach skills. See Exhibit 12.1.

The Therapeutic Alliance and Theory-Bound Therapeutic Processes

At a minimum, a therapeutic alliance begins with belief in the helping relationship. The capacity for empathy (as defined by psychodynamic theory) appears to
be a common factor in establishing belief bonding or rapport with a client. Beyond this, the therapeutic process of relationship is theory-bound. Like scripted
interviewing, the use of self in a therapeutic alliance depends on one's theory of
therapy. Models of talk therapy are based on different theories of how change
(therapeutic process) occurs. Not all theories of change require the same level of
relationship intensity.

The Therapeutic Process of Behavioral-Learning Theory

The worker's use of self in therapeutic alliance may be informed by behavioral-
learning theory. When behavioral-learning theory guides the therapeutic process,
the worker models appropriate behavior during the sessions. Often, clients are
coached (cognitive rehearsal) on how to behave. For example, a worker can coach
a client on how to handle a job interview or to solve a problem on the job; how to
behave on a date; or how to parent a child. The client learns through imitation
(social learning theory) and practice (in vivo exposure). The clinician can use
him/herself as an antecedent (stimulus cue) or consequent (reinforcement) event
during sessions. This theory holds that behavior (ABC paradigm; see below) is
cued by an antecedent stimulus (i.e., classical conditioning) and/or is maintained
by a consequent event (operant conditioning, rewards).

The *ABC paradigm* describes a present-focused, temporal (stimulus-
response; S-R) sequence. In order to change client behavior (B), the practitioner
either changes (unpairs or desensitizes) the antecedent stimulus (A) or punishes,
extinguishes, or positively/negatively reinforces the consequent event (C). Determining a behavioral baseline (frequency of behavior, where and when it occurs),
determining what is rewarding, and determining an appropriate reinforcement

schedule are components of the therapeutic process (Sundel & Sundel, 1982; Thomlinson & Thomlinson, 1996). Changes may be small (shaping) and through chaining lead to larger behavioral changes (e.g., dressing self). Biofeedback, guided imagery, and relaxation skills help clients to manage the biology of physiological tension. As part of the therapeutic process, the client becomes competent in the use of the model and is able to maintain the changes that have occurred and extend his/her learning to new situations.

The model can be used with severely cognitively impaired clients. In such cases, the therapeutic alliance is with others (parents, teachers, guardians, institutional staff), who act as antecedent or consequent events in a client's life. It can also be used with cognitively intact individuals to change a variety of behaviors (e.g., weight, smoking) or to acquire new skills (e.g., parenting, computer literacy). See the process-recording excerpt on Kyle in chapter 13.

The Therapeutic Process of Cognitive-Behavioral Therapy

In contrast to the time sequence (S-R) of behavior modification, cognitive-behavioral therapy is perceptual and mediational. In other words, attributions made about an event, not the event itself, are thought to explain dysfunctional emotions (anxiety, depression, anger) or behavior. An individual's cultural and familial world views (attributions) are learned and can be unlearned. Often, one set of environmental cues is perceived to the exclusion of all others. An activating event (A) is interpreted by core beliefs (and distorted cognitions; B) and results in behavioral or emotional consequences (C). In this model, thinking is regarded as the principal determinant of emotions and behavior. Behaviorists identify several types of distorted thinking styles (e.g., filtering, polarized thinking, overgeneralization, mind reading, catastrophizing, personalization, blaming, "shoulds and musts," and being right).

The therapeutic process in cognitive-behavioral therapy focuses on identifying (automatic thought record), challenging (Socratic questioning), and changing (adaptive cognitions replace) dysfunctional thought patterns. Techniques such as distancing, use of the downward arrow, and asking for evidence initiate changes as part of the therapeutic alliance (Bandura, 1977, 1997; J. Beck, 1995).

The Therapeutic Process of Psychodynamic Theories

Traditional Psychoanalytic (Freudian) Therapy

According to Freudian psychoanalytic theory: (1) mental activities are conscious, preconscious, and unconscious (typographical model), (2) personality is composed of id, ego, and superego (structural model), and (3) energy is finite and affects development and functioning (drive or dynamic model). Development is epigenetic (Freudian and Eriksonian psychosocial stages). Energy can be encumbered by impulses (drives) and internal conflicts, making it unavailable for other uses (rational problem solving).

Psychoanalytic Freudian theory focuses primarily on personality development and social functioning. When nature and nurture are "good enough," individuals are resilient and act in ways that benefit society. Unencumbered energy (libido) promotes growth and development and sustains mature social functioning. *Maturity* is defined as the ability to love and to work. Both nature and nurture contribute to personality development. Experiences in childhood influence psychosocial development and current functioning.

Sometimes, abnormal growth (biology) or development (nurture) interfere with the unfolding of resilience. Behavior may be driven by unconscious forces and may be symptomatic. This is represented in the *triangle of conflict*, which consists of an impulse which triggers both anxiety and a defense (Davanloo, 1980). Discovering (through free association, dream analysis) the underlying causality of what has gone wrong (interpretation) leads to understanding (insight). Insight allows clients to gain conscious control over their feelings and behaviors. Techniques are nondirective, reflective, interpretive (weakening of inappropriate defenses), and confrontational.

Length of treatment (long-term versus brief) is a factor that influences the selection of this model. Prior to managed care, long-term treatment (psychoanalysis) was commonly used by psychiatrists. Social workers have traditionally focused on moderate to brief models of ego-supportive treatment to treat children and adolescents with developmental issues. When working with adults, ego-supportive treatment focuses on the here and now. Within psychodynamic theory, there are different schools of thought, each of which requires different levels of relationship intensity or depth. Social work clinicians (unless they receive additional education and training post graduate school) tend to adopt an ego-supportive, problem-solving practice model (Perlman, 1957; Goldstein, 1996).

Ego-Supportive Model

When ego-supportive theory informs a therapeutic alliance, the clinician acts as a holding environment and engages the client in problem-solving activities (autonomous ego functions). Through empathic responding, the worker becomes a powerful significant other to the client in therapy (attachment theory). Clients who have suffered emotional trauma require emotional containment and support to enable them to reassert emotional control for themselves. The therapist uses him/herself as an emotional bridge to prevent clients from harming themselves or others.

A good psychodynamic alliance acts as an anodyne, an anesthetic to the sharing of painful material. It makes the clinical interview a collaborative endeavor rather than a competitive struggle. It frees the client to reveal him/herself without defensiveness or distortion. It fosters revelation over concealment, recognizing that the protective functions of the client's ego (resistance) are in conflict with its adaptive functions (change). Encoding and decoding communication (see chapter 4) is more accurate when there is a therapeutic alliance.

Problem-solving capacity is part of a healthy ego. There are six problem-solving steps, beginning with acknowledgment of a problem as early as possible. This is followed by problem analysis, which consists of pinpointing a problematic behavior, determining who owns what part of the problem, and specifying the needs of those involved in the problem (Hepworth, Rooney, & Larsen, 2002). Brainstorming to generate solutions is step 3. In step 4, each solution is evaluated. An option is then selected and implemented in step 5, followed by step 6, which evaluates the outcome. Techniques are directive, sustaining, educative, and structured.

When used as part of ego-supportive treatment, such activities presuppose the ego's capacity to problem solve. Not all clients possess the capacity to problem solve. Age (developmental stage), intelligence (e.g., developmental disorders, brain injuries, dementia), and mental health (e.g., psychoses, hallucinations, delusions) can interfere with problem-solving activities.

The capacity to engage in reality-based problem-solving activities also presupposes a capacity for secondary process thinking. In contrast to cognitive-behavioral theory, which focuses on the content of cognitions and core beliefs, psychodynamic theory views thinking in terms of primary process thinking (primitive, prelanguage, magical, developmental) and secondary process thinking (rational). The developmental distinction between fantasy (preoperational, egocentric thought) during infancy and childhood and reality (concrete and formal operational thought) in adolescence and adulthood is important to problem solving.

Intrapsychic (id/ego/superego) conflict (tension) can also interfere with rational problem-solving activities. Impulses and emotional conflict (developmental, situational, or traumatic event) can distort thinking (defense mechanisms). Within an ego-supportive therapeutic alliance, the clinician may offer limited, here-and-now interpretations to provide the client with insight. This frees energy (used in intrapsychic conflict) for problem solving. Sometimes, the clinician loans (supervises, acts *in loco parentis*) the executive function of her/his ego to the client.

A healthy ego uses energy to control and govern the id. It engages in cognitive activities that promote social functioning. The ego relies on secondary process thinking (planning and problem solving) and acts in accordance with the reality principle to postpone or delay gratification. The ego also mediates demands from the superego (performance standards and conscience). Clients benefit from psychoeducation (learning) as a mechanism of resilience. Added to ego-supportive treatment is the concept of mastery and competence. Through successful interactions with the environment, individuals are able to develop a sense of mastery and competency.

Skills training (because it leads to mastery) is an important element of the therapeutic process in ego-supportive treatment. The ego is strengths based and reality oriented. It engages in coping strategies when faced with the normal crises and stresses of development and life transitions. Self encompasses ego (personality development) plus social self (social identity).

The Therapeutic Process of Relational Paradigms
(Object-Relations Theory)

According to Borden (2000), the relational paradigm has replaced drive psychology as the central paradigm in contemporary psychodynamic thought. Three relational schools of thought inform this perspective: (1) object-relations psychology, (2) interpersonal psychoanalysis, and (3) self-psychology. Fairbairn's (1952) developmental psychology serves as the foundation for contemporary object-relations thought.

As an alternative to drive theory, the therapeutic alliance may be informed by object-relations theory (Fairbairn, 1952; Mahler, Pine, & Bergman, 1975). Personality is viewed as an outcome of a series of chronologically ordered phases (autistic, symbiotic, separation-individuation, and object constancy), each of which leads to major achievements in the areas of separation, individuation, and internalized object relations. During separation and individuation, the child internalizes and integrates self-object representations to form a self (object constancy) separate from the mother.

Personality development is mediated by the internalization of interpersonal experience. The personality consists of core representations of self, others (objects), and modes of relating (self in relation to others). Representations are not memories of events but rather schematic structures that arise from the cumulative experience of interpersonal interaction over the course of development. There is an emphasis on the need for attachment (attachment styles) and connection with others throughout life. Early caregiving is important to internalized objects. According to theory, infants are able, once they achieve object permanence, to internalize images of their caregivers as objects. Attached to such internalized objects are feelings (positive or negative) of how well the caregiver has met the infant's/child's needs.

The theory holds that previous relational conflicts play out in current relationships through repetition compulsion. Current maladaptive interpersonal functioning is related to earlier emotionally traumatizing or inadequate relationships. Within the therapeutic alliance, a triangle forms among the client, another (a person in the client's past or present life), and the clinician. The clinician is able to work with transference to correct past failures in relationship in the here-and-now interactive moment. Clients can experience new ways of being related to and new ways of relating to others in the safety of a therapeutic alliance.

Self-psychology (Kohut, 1977; Kernberg, 1984) accepts that personality develops because of a primary need for connection but emphasizes a fundamental thrust to establish and maintain a unitary, integrated sense of self. The diagnostic focus is on empathic provisions of primary figures, or "self-objects," that are (or are not) attuned to another's subjective state. Disorders of the self are characterized by difficulties in negotiating need, regulating emotion, maintaining self-esteem, and pursuing meaningful goals (Borden, 2000). Therapeutic actions are based in a "responsive self-object milieu," i.e., corrective emotional experience.

Interpersonal psychoanalysis (Sullivan, 1954; Binder, 2004; Messer & Warren, 1995) holds that personality develops as a consequence of interactive experience in relational fields throughout life. The motivation to interact is based in the need for satisfaction and security. According to Sullivan, the clinician is a participant observer in the interactive field of the client, both subject and object in the therapeutic process. Therapeutic action focuses on problematic aspects of interactions with others. This includes problematic aspects of interaction with the clinician during sessions.

Diagnostic factors in the relational paradigm focus on early care taking, trauma, and the enactment of maladaptive interactive behaviors in session. Curative factors in the relational paradigm include acting as a holding environment, empathic responsiveness, mirroring, transmuting internalizations, learning through interpersonal interaction, and experiencing corrective emotional attunement.

Narrative Therapy

This theory holds that social contexts influence the processing of interpersonal interactions (experience). The therapeutic process used to address current problems in interpersonal relationships begins with the recounting (narration) of events. The telling of one's story (narration) reviews experiential history in an attempt to make sense of it. The therapeutic alliance is used to facilitate the telling of the story. The clinician acts as a coparticipant in the client's effort to review experiences, consider alternative views of his/her life, reconstruct meaning, and elaborate adaptive life stories (Greene, Lee, Trask, & Rheinscheld, 2000; White, 2000; Eron & Lund, 1996). In contrast to other theories, narrative therapy allows the worker and client to take into account political, economic, and cultural factors that have impacted interpersonal interactions. What is political is personal. The social constructions of others (about one's story) are challenged. New meanings are co-constructed within the therapeutic alliance.

■ Managing the Therapeutic Alliance

Transference and Countertransference

Through vicarious response (empathy), the professional clinician can experience feelings that correspond to the feelings being experienced by the client while retaining the orientation of an objective observer. However, because relationship is an interactional event, it is subject to transference. To manage potential ruptures and missteps in the therapeutic alliance, the clinician must monitor his/her use of self (countertransference) during the therapeutic process. From a psychodynamic perspective, relationship is created and recreated by the behaviors engaged in by the participants in interactive dialogue. While it is important that the client's earlier relationships replay themselves (transference) through the therapeutic alliance, the practitioner must not let his/her own countertransferences interfere with the helping process. Therefore, the clinician's monitoring of self (through supervision, consultation, and his/her own therapy if warranted) is critical to competent practice with this model (Turner, 1996; Bisman, 1994; Binder, 2004).

Errors and Missteps in the Therapeutic Alliance

According to Binder (2004, p. 219), errors in therapist technique include the following: (1) misunderstanding of the meanings of the client's communication or intention, (2) vague communication by the therapist to the client, (3) mistimed interventions, (4) failure to recognize the implications of client communication, (5) awkward use of transference interpretations, (6) sending mixed messages with implicit hostile meanings, (7) not being able to identify salient interpersonal themes that should be the focus of work, (8) failure to recognize disguised allusions, and (9) failure to track a central issue consistently.

Hepworth, Rooney, and Larsen (2002) offer the following list of missteps: (1) failing to sense important feelings experienced by the client, (2) sending messages that clients interpret as criticisms or put-downs, (3) being inattentive or "tuning out" clients, (4) failing to acknowledge incremental successes achieved by clients, (5) employing inept or poorly timed interpretations or confrontations, (6) manifesting lapses of memory about important information previously revealed by clients, (7) being tardy or canceling appointments, (8) appearing fidgety or drowsy, (9) disagreeing, arguing, or giving excessive advice, (10) appearing to or actually taking sides against a client, (11) not allowing the client to be an active participant in planning his/her treatment, (12) dominating discussions or frequently interrupting clients, (13) failing to recognize clients' limitations by giving assignments and advice that they cannot carry out, and (14) using power to interfere with client lifestyles beyond the range of legal mandates.

Client Cues That the Therapeutic Process Is Not Going Well

The same authors (Hepworth, Rooney, & Larsen, 2002) identify client behaviors that indicate that the therapeutic process is not going well: (1) mental blocking, (2) lengthy periods of silence, (3) inattention or mind wandering, (4) rambling at length or dwelling on unimportant details, (5) restlessness or fidgeting, (6) discussing superficialities or irrelevant matters, (7) lying or deliberately misrepresenting facts, (8) avoiding feelings and problems by focusing on abstract ideas, (9) changing the subject, (10) forgetting details of distressing events or the content of previous sessions, (11) being tardy, forgetting, changing, or canceling appointments, (12) minimizing problems or claiming miraculous improvement, (13) bringing up important material at the end of the session, (14) not paying fees, (15) not applying skills or insight gained to daily life, (16) assuming a stance of helplessness, and (17) using verbal ploys to justify not taking corrective action.

■ Counseling Versus Therapy: Is There a Difference?

In social work practice, the distinction between counseling (B.S.W.) and therapy (M.S.W.) is often a matter of degree. There is no clear-cut distinction between therapy and counseling per se. It can be argued that therapy is more advanced (sophisticated) than counseling because it requires a therapeutic alliance and the enactment of a therapeutic process. If one accepts this premise, then both the B.S.W. and the M.S.W. first-year student are likely to be educational and experiential novices in the art of therapy. They may or may not choose an educational or practice trajectory that moves them from novice practitioner to master clinician. Nonetheless, the foundation for the B.S.W. graduate and the M.S.W. graduate must be the same.

Barker (2003) offers the following differential definitions in the *Social Work Dictionary*. *Counseling* is a procedure often used in clinical social work and other professions to guide individuals, families, groups, and communities by activities such as giving advice, delineating alternatives, helping to articulate goals, and providing needed information (p. 100). In contrast, *therapy* is defined as a systematic process and activity designed to remedy, cure, or abate some disease, disability, or problem. Social workers often use this term as a synonym for psychotherapy, psychosocial therapy, or group therapy. When social workers discuss other types of therapy, such as occupational therapy, physical therapy, recreational therapy, medication therapy, or chemotherapy, they use these more-specific terms (p. 434).

■ Guidelines for Selecting a Theory-Based Talk Therapy

Choose *pharmacological or medical interventions* if your assessment has led you to conclude that "nature" explains in part or in full what is the matter in the case at hand and/or that biological techniques can ameliorate some or all of the situation. Biological change techniques include biofeedback, pharmacological interventions, and needed medical treatment. You may choose biological intervention only, or you may use it in conjunction with a selected talk therapy model. Social workers must collaborate with medical doctors who prescribe and provide necessary pharmacological or medical interventions.

If you are choosing a talk therapy model of change, choose *ego-supportive therapy* when your intent is to change the capacity of the client to cope with life events through the worker's active support of the client's conscious problem-solving skills and coping capacities. This change theory's roots lie in psychodynamic explanatory theory. Awareness of past developmental history is helpful in terms of working with client ego weaknesses and strengths. Clients must have the capacity for formal operational thought and reflection when using this theory and be oriented to person, time, and place. While the theory accepts the unconscious, it does not focus on it.

Choose *object-relations theory* when your intent is to focus on changing interpersonal interactions through insight. This theory holds that current patterns of interaction are unconsciously influenced by past patterns of interaction. This change theory has roots in psychodynamic theory generally but in attachment theory specifically. Past developmental history in terms of interpersonal relationships is important. Transference is an important dynamic. The worker provides experiential, corrective emotional attunement and acts as a holding environment for client emotions and impulses.

Choose *behavioral-learning theory* (classical or operant conditioning) when your intent is to change behavior regardless of insight. According to this model, all behavior is learned and can therefore be unlearned, modified, or shaped. Immediate history in the form of antecedent and consequent events is more important than distant history. Assessment is concerned with determining what is maintaining the behavior in contrast to lengthy exploration of the client's developmental past. This model works well with those who have cognitive impairments or who live or work in settings where others can control the contingencies. This model is often used in behavioral health care with adults where the focus is on changing risk factors, e.g., smoking or overeating, or on pain management. It also frequently is used in school settings.

Choose *cognitive-behavioral* (cognitive awareness) theory when your intent is to change negative behaviors and feelings by changing the cognitions that influence them. Its intent is to manage feelings by putting them under the control of rational cognitions. The explanatory roots of this change model lie in two theories: symbolic interaction (core beliefs, world views, meaning) and social learning theory (socialization and conditioning). This model requires the capacity for self-reflection but holds that cognitions are consciously accessible.

Choose *solution-focused theory* when your intent is to promote coping by building on strengths. When choosing this model, know that explanatory theory is descriptive of and limited to the client's presentation of current needs or wants with a focus on identifying past and current strengths. It does not assess developmental history nor is it problem-focused. The goal of the model is for the worker to help the client identify and link to familial and institutional resources. Techniques

EXHIBIT 12.3   *Schema: Direct Practice*

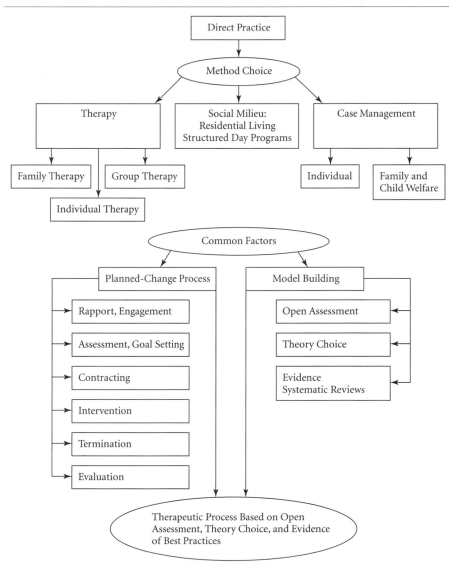

include identification of past coping skills, exceptions, and desired goals (miracle question). Beyond resource linkage and strengths identification, this model often additionally relies on cognitive-behavioral and ego-supportive therapy as complementary models of practice.

■ Other Methods of Therapy

When individual counseling appears to be contraindicated or insufficient, explore other methods of treatment, such as family models of treatment or models of group treatment. Specify the theory base that guides your use of family method (Minuchin, 1974; Haley, 1971; Bowen, 1978; Satir, 1964) or group method (Yalom, 1995).

13
Case-Specific Model Building: Case Presentation

■ The Mentoring Relationship: Procedural and Tacit Knowing

This chapter illustrates how declarative knowledge (of what is the matter) is transformed into practice theory (therapeutic change process) through procedural (therapeutic enactment) and tacit (art and intuition) knowing. The novice's reflection on action is mentored by the master clinician through field supervision (Munson, 2002; Binder, 2004). The student is helped to move from novice to master through (1) open assessment (levels of assessment: intake, current, comprehensive), (2) theory selection based on the use of the decision tree to build a case-specific model of practice, and (3) the enactment of a theory-specific therapeutic process. Excerpts from advanced process recordings provide samples of different, theory-driven therapeutic processes at the end of the chapter.

Complex Data and Model Building

Most client cases are complex. Therefore, building a case-specific model of practice for a given client requires the use of multiple theories and methods. When case-specific model building is combined with the decision tree, social workers in direct practice are better equipped to deal with complex client data and select more than one intervention appropriate to the case (Plionis, 2004). The case of Mr. R illustrates the process of case-specific model building.

Agency Assessment Formats

Two factors impact student learning regarding assessment. One is related to the type of assessment format used by an agency. Agencies vary in what they require. Some agencies require only basic registration information (name, address, phone number, etc.) elicited at intake. Other agencies use intake information plus assessment of current functioning. Others include information on current mental health. Very few agencies require a comprehensive developmental or psychosocial history. Nonetheless, it is educationally important to teach students the full range of assessment frameworks. The second factor impacting student learning is the amount (or lack thereof) of information related to the case at hand. Usually, there is too little or too much information. When there is too much information, students need frameworks to sort it out. When there is too little information, students need guidance as to what information is needed in order to be effective.

Open assessment presupposes a comprehensive level of assessment. Case-specific model building is contingent on the type and quantity of information

EXHIBIT 13.1   *Levels of Clinical Case Assessment*

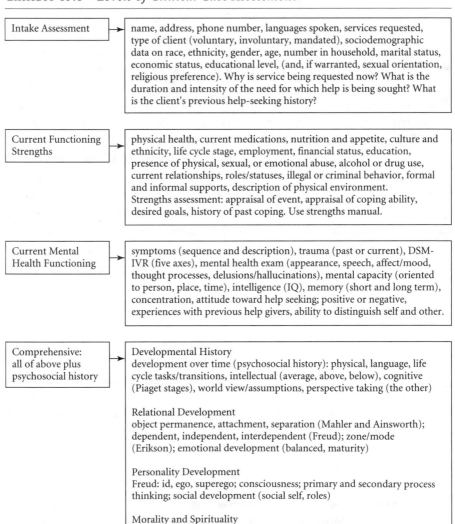

Intake Assessment	name, address, phone number, languages spoken, services requested, type of client (voluntary, involuntary, mandated), sociodemographic data on race, ethnicity, gender, age, number in household, marital status, economic status, educational level, (and, if warranted, sexual orientation, religious preference). Why is service being requested now? What is the duration and intensity of the need for which help is being sought? What is the client's previous help-seeking history?
Current Functioning Strengths	physical health, current medications, nutrition and appetite, culture and ethnicity, life cycle stage, employment, financial status, education, presence of physical, sexual, or emotional abuse, alcohol or drug use, current relationships, roles/statuses, illegal or criminal behavior, formal and informal supports, description of physical environment. Strengths assessment: appraisal of event, appraisal of coping ability, desired goals, history of past coping. Use strengths manual.
Current Mental Health Functioning	symptoms (sequence and description), trauma (past or current), DSM-IVR (five axes), mental health exam (appearance, speech, affect/mood, thought processes, delusions/hallucinations), mental capacity (oriented to person, place, time), intelligence (IQ), memory (short and long term), concentration, attitude toward help seeking; positive or negative, experiences with previous help givers, ability to distinguish self and other.
Comprehensive: all of above plus psychosocial history	Developmental History development over time (psychosocial history): physical, language, life cycle tasks/transitions, intellectual (average, above, below), cognitive (Piaget stages), world view/assumptions, perspective taking (the other) Relational Development object permanence, attachment, separation (Mahler and Ainsworth); dependent, independent, interdependent (Freud); zone/mode (Erikson); emotional development (balanced, maturity) Personality Development Freud: id, ego, superego; consciousness; primary and secondary process thinking; social development (social self, roles) Morality and Spirituality moral development, faith development (Gilligan, Kohlberg, Fowler)

sought. The decision tree helps students to prioritize the information they obtain and to select more than one intervention as the data warrants. Exhibit 13.1 provides a general framework within which information can be understood. Poulin (2000, 2005) provides a series of assessment formats in two texts. Information gathered on Mr. R will be sorted according to the first three levels of assessments in Exhibit 13.1. This allows students to compare the levels of information with which agencies work. Because of length, a complete psychosocial history is not included. The decision tree prioritizes the factual, descriptive information sorted by level of assessment and turns it into a case-specific model of practice that prescribes interventions.

■ Assessment Level 1: Intake Registration of Mr. R

Mr. R is a retired, married, African-American, 65-year-old male who was in a motor vehicle accident a year ago. Mr. R is a cooperative, involuntary client (services were necessitated by the accident). There are no language barriers as Mr. R's primary language is English. Mr. R states that he is a religious man and relies on God for encouragement. Mr. R has a supportive wife and a daughter. He receives a pension of $1,500 per month from the U.S. Postal Service. A motor vehicle accident left Mr. R completely dependent on others. Mr. R has been struggling to regain mobility. He is accruing out-of-pocket medical bills associated with his care. Mr. R was the only occupant of a car that ran off the road and plunged down a gully.

Mr. R's point of entry with the rehabilitation facility occurred almost a year ago. He has had multiple surgeries necessitated by the accident. He has been discharged and readmitted several times over the course of the year. Mr. R was recently readmitted to the facility following hip replacement surgery. He has not been able to stand on two feet since the accident. Mr. R's point of entry with the social worker occurred 3 weeks ago. The worker is currently working with him on a discharge plan.

■ Assessment Level 2: Current Functioning

Risk Assessment

Mr. R does not pose an immediate threat to self or others. However, he is not capable of independently performing the basic activities of daily living on his own. In this sense, it is important that Mr. R's discharge plan contain provisions for his daily care (duty to protect those who cannot care for themselves). Mr. R is at risk of falling down. Mr. R's home poses some safety risks and/or health hazards in that it is not equipped with devices (ramp, grab rails, etc.) that can assist Mr. R, given his physical condition.

Physical Health

Mr. R has extensive medical problems. He has a history of asthma, diabetes, hypertension, and prostate cancer. The accident resulted in a severe head injury, limited mobility, brief memory loss, and loss of vision in the left eye. Mr. R has developed heterotopic ossification (HO), which caused the abnormal formation of bone over six major joints, leaving Mr. R physically immobile and completely dependent on others for feeding, dressing, bathing, and all forms of movement. He has had two successful surgeries on his elbows. He has recently had hip replacement surgery. He is in physical pain. Mr. R is currently diagnosed with HO, diabetes mellitus, and asthma.

Current Medications

Mr. R takes the following medications for these conditions: Norbasc (5 mg), Lanoxin (125 mg), Furosemide (20 mg), aspirin enteric (81 mg), Nexium capsule (40 mg), Docusate Sodium (100 mg), Oxycontin (10 mg), and Calmoseptine ointment. There is no indication of any prior or current use of alcohol or nonprescription drugs.

Nutrition and Appetite

Mr. R has lost weight since the accident. He dislikes hospital food. He is a diabetic and therefore does watch what he eats.

Culture and Ethnicity

As an African-American male, Mr. R comes from a culture with strong beliefs in taking care of the elderly. He is within a generational cohort where extended family members, including grandparents, siblings, friends, and grown children, take care of their own. Mr. R relies on Mrs. R for his primary care with some assistance from formal caregivers, i.e., visiting health professionals. Mr. R does not believe that things come easy, but he believes that hard work and loyal citizenship should bring him justice in the end. He is disappointed in his benefits, saying that "the government has pushed [him] to the side of the road to die." He feels that he has gotten nothing out of the system though he fulfilled his duty as a good citizen and paid into the system as a postal service employee.

Current Life Cycle Stage

At age 65 and with declining health, Mr. R is currently experiencing a life cycle crisis of integrity versus despair. Like others in this age group, Mr. R is experiencing losses. Mr. R has suffered a loss of health and physical mobility. Both of his parents have recently passed. As a consequence of his injuries, Mr. R lost his hobby of pigeon racing. As a retiree, Mr. R has also experienced job loss and reduced income. Like others in this age cohort, Mr. R finds balancing his fixed income (postal pension) against the cost of living to be a challenge. This is especially so given Mr. R's out-of-pocket health care bills. Prior to the accident, Mr. R was very active and enjoyed retirement. During the past year, Mr. R has been in and out of hospitals, rehabilitation centers, and nursing homes. He is struggling to develop a sense of integrity, which includes regaining some physical mobility as part of body integrity. He is also trying to reconcile his beliefs about hard work and good citizenship with the benefits and health care he is receiving. It is common at this stage of life to reflect on the meaning of things.

Current Employment and Financial Status

Mr. R is retired from the postal service and receives a monthly pension of $1,500. Mr. and Mrs. R express frustration with the size of this pension. Mrs. R has been and continues to be a housewife and has no source of income. The R's have Medicare as their primary insurance and Blue Cross/Blue Shield as their secondary carrier.

Education, History of Abuse, History of Illegal or Criminal Behavior

Mr. R completed high school. There is no indication of current or past physical, sexual, or emotional abuse. There is no indication of current or past illegal or criminal behavior.

Current Relationships

Mr. R and his wife have been married 41 years and have a strong, loving, and compassionate relationship. Mrs. R has come to the hospital, rehabilitation facility, or nursing home every day since her husband's accident. They both say that their will to go on is in each other. They have a 25-year-old daughter who lives near them. The daughter helps with transportation and grocery shopping. Mr. R has two sisters in the area. Though they keep in touch with Mr. R by phone several times a week, they too are senior citizens with their own health problems. Mr. R has two male friends who keep in touch regularly and who help out with occasional needs.

The social worker's relationship with Mr. R is professional and formal. They come from different racial and ethnic backgrounds and are in different gender and age groups. They have formed a bond within the helping relationship that is consistent with discharge planning. Their contact with each other is purposeful but limited.

Current Role Assessment

Mr. R is a male, husband, father, friend, brother, church member, senior citizen, postal service retiree, and member of a racial minority group. Until the accident, Mr. R was the head of the household and caretaker for the entire family, including his sisters and his elderly parents before they passed. In his retirement, Mr. R worked as a telemarketer for local newspapers. He loved to garden and race pigeons. Since the accident, Mr. R has experienced several status changes and role losses. He went from healthy to injured, independent to dependent, mobile to immobile, financially stable to financially stressed. He is no longer able to perform the duties consistent with being head of the household. He is now a member of a differently abled, physically challenged population. Role reversal has occurred in that Mrs. R now assumes primary responsibilities for Mr. R. She is Mr. R's primary caregiver. Mr. R's large physical size compromises her ability to physically care for all of his needs.

Physical Environment

Mr. and Mrs. R live in their own one-story home in Jackson County. There are five steps to the entrance and then another small step into the house. The R's have been living in this home for 33 years. They are attached to the house and the neighborhood. They regard the neighborhood as stable and relatively safe. Technically, Mr. R has transportation available, but in reality he cannot access it. Mr. R stated his predicament in the following way: "Unexpected experiences bring many difficult barriers. You would be surprised by the challenge that five steps can have on your life." Mr. R's immobility creates a barrier to transportation services, buses, and cabs that are available but not accessible. The R's have no driveway or ramp to get Mr. R to the curb.

Informal Networks

Mr. R's family network consists of his wife, daughter, and two sisters. Mrs. R has a sister who lives in Kansas, and they speak regularly with each other. Mrs. R visits her husband daily whenever he is hospitalized. The R's daughter takes her mother to and from the hospital as needed and does the grocery shopping. Mr. R has two male friends. One has cared for Mr. R's pigeons until they were recently sold, and another visits him occasionally in the hospital. Both are long-term friends. The R's have attended the same church for years. They both express a deep faith and close relationship with God.

Formal Services and Programs

Mr. R receives Medicare and a retirement pension. Mr. R has received home health care assistance three times a week through Medicare. The nurse assisted with bathing and other basic necessities. Medicare also provided physical and occupational therapy in the home for a few weeks following previous surgeries. The therapy consisted of 45-minute sessions two to three times a week. Mr. R will be eligible for such services again following his current discharge. Mr. R prefers to remain in a rehabilitation facility to receive physical therapy. He thinks that home-based physical therapy is not as effective.

■ Assessment Level 3: Current Mental Health Functioning

Trauma

Mr. R suffered physical trauma as a consequence of a motor vehicle accident. He has spent the majority of the past year hospitalized, on many medications, and in a great deal of pain. The accident left Mr. R with multiple rib fractures, a head injury, and loss of consciousness. He spent 7 weeks in the intensive care unit and was not expected to live. Mr. R does not recall the circumstances of the accident. He wonders how something like this could happen to a law-abiding citizen who has never had any traffic violations. Mr. R reports that some days his mood is up and other days down. He is always dealing with pain.

DSM-IV Assessment

According to the DSM-IV (1994) classification system, Mr. R's five-axis assessment would look as follows:

Axis I: Major Syndrome. None indicated. Though changes in personality can result from a general medical condition, such as brain injury, Mr. R does not appear to exhibit any of the symptoms (Code 310.1). Personality changes due to a general medical condition are coded on Axis I.

Axis II: Personality. None indicated.

Axis III: General Medical Conditions. Brain injury, heterotopic ossification, loss of vision in left eye, hip replacement, numerous surgeries following motor vehicle accident, impaired mobility, pain. History of prostate cancer, asthma, and diabetes. Pain disorder associated with a general medical condition is coded on Axis III. It is further coded either by the anatomical location of the pain (see p. 459 of DSM-IV) or by the disease causing the pain; see appendix G of DSM-IV, 1994).

Axis IV: Psychosocial and Environmental Problems/Stress. Moderate. Mr. R's home is handicapped inaccessible. Though transportation is available to him, it too is inaccessible. Mr. R is experiencing financial stress in relation to mounting out-of-pocket health care bills.

Axis V: Global Assessment of Function (GAF). 61–70. Frequently, psychosocial factors, medical conditions, and the medications used to treat medical conditions interact to cause physical and emotional pain. Mr. R should be monitored.

Mental Health Status Exam

Mr. R usually wears sweatpants, sneakers, and a T-shirt. This is the most appropriate and comfortable attire for his physical therapy sessions. Mr. R's speech is normal in volume, pattern, tone, and speed. Though initially reticent to express affect, Mr. R has begun to express frustration, anger, and sadness related to his condition. He acknowledges that he has experienced depressive moods since the accident. He says that some days are good, other days bad. His affect appears to be normal, considering his circumstances, but this needs to be monitored given his brain injury and the number of medications he is taking. Mr. R has expressed some concerns about his mounting medical bills and his inability to access needed transportation. He feels the government has pushed him to the side to let him die.

Mr. R's thought process is clear and logical. He does not exhibit any hallucinations or delusions. Though Mr. R suffered a minimal loss of memory immediately after the accident, he has experienced no other form of memory loss. He appears to be alert; oriented to person, time, and place; and able to concentrate. He works hard in rehabilitation with the hope of recovery. Mr. R is able to engage in rational problem solving and is an active participant in planning his discharge.

Attitude Toward Help Seeking

With the assistance of his wife, Mr. R has applied for many forms of financial assistance. They are actively seeking additional concrete resources. They are particularly concerned about transportation issues. Though Medicare recipients qualify for transportation subsidies that will assist with transfer from the house into a van, the R's do not meet eligibility standards. Out-of-pocket costs for such assistance run $90 per time. The R's have investigated the possibility of building a ramp. State and jurisdictional building codes regulate the building of a ramp. A ramp averages between $4,000 and $6,000 to build and is not covered by Medicare. The R's property footprint does not meet codes for the construction of a ramp.

Strengths Assessment

The R's own their own home. They have a monthly income of more than $1,500. Mr. R has Medicare, which provides hospitalization, prescription drugs, in-home nursing, and physical therapy. Mrs. R acts as Mr. R's primary caregiver, performing the activities of daily living. The R's daughter does the grocery shopping and helps with transportation. The R's receive emotional support from family and friends. The R's also find strength in their faith. Mr. R works hard at rehabilitation and is showing improvement. Mr. R's past history is one of resilience and success. He grew up in a close-knit family and has created his own close-knit family. Mr. R has a history of working hard and being a good provider.

A more comprehensive (level 4) assessment is beyond the scope of this chapter. The descriptive factual information contained in assessment levels 1, 2, and 3 above is turned into a prescription for action through use of the decision tree to build a case-specific model of practice.

■ Case-Specific Model of Practice for Mr. R

Point of Entry

Mr. R's point of entry with the rehabilitation facility occurred more than a year ago. He was admitted for physical therapy and rehabilitation following a car accident in which he sustained multiple injuries. Mr. R's point of entry with the social worker occurred 3 weeks ago as part of the discharge planning process.

Step 1: Duty to Protect—Assure Safety

Mr. R is dealing with pain from injuries and physical disability associated with a motor vehicle accident. As a senior citizen (age 65), Mr. R has entered a new stage of the life cycle. Mr. R does not pose a current danger to self or others though his physical environment poses some health risks to him. His home is not equipped with devices to assist the handicapped, such as grab bars or rails. Mr. R is at risk of being injured from a fall. His home is not handicapped accessible as it lacks a ramp that would allow Mr. R mobility from the house to needed transportation. Mr. R's physical condition is such that he can no longer independently care for his needs. He is dependent on others, primarily his wife, for activities of daily living. To assure Mr. R's safety, a discharge plan must contain provisions for his daily care.

According to the DSM-IV, Mr. R could experience personality changes due to his brain injury though no symptoms have appeared as yet. He should be monitored for personality changes. Frequently, psychosocial factors, medical conditions, and the medications to treat such conditions interact to cause negative changes in affect. Mr. R should be monitored for harmful affective changes, such as depression.

As part of a contract for safety, Mrs. R has agreed to notify the worker if she observes changes in Mr. R's personality or affect. Should Mr. R become sad and depressed beyond the normal ups and downs of recovery, she will tell a health professional or the social worker. Mr. R agrees to let his wife know if he is feeling excessively sad or depressed. The worker will attempt to find the resources needed to make the R's home safer and more handicapped accessible.

Step 2: Crisis Intervention

Mr. R's crisis event (auto accident) happened more than a year ago. First responders (police, ambulance) got him to emergency medical care where doctors saved his life. It could be argued that Mr. R is now in the crisis aftermath where health care professionals (physical therapists, nurses) are working with him on rehabilitation and recovery from his injuries.

Step 3: Delivery of Concrete Services in a Timely Manner

The R's are seeking help with locating additional financial support, given their mounting out-of-pocket medical bills. They wish to make renovations to their home to make it more handicapped friendly. They want to build a ramp so Mr. R can access available transportation. The R's receive the following concrete services: a monthly pension and Medicare. They are eligible for limited in-home nursing care and physical therapy under Medicare. The treatment goal is to maintain existing resources and to locate additional resources.

Step 4: Need for Case and Class Advocacy

The R's may need advocacy in securing additional financial support and in making their home more handicapped friendly and accessible. Advocacy may be needed to negotiate the building of a ramp that will meet code but that will fit within the R's property footprint. The R's wish to remain in their home and their geographical location. Class advocacy (elderly and disabled) may be needed in relation to accessibility issues. Most buildings and transportation systems have flawed accessibility for the physically disabled.

Step 5: Work With Individuals: Method and Theory Choices

The method of choice in this case is one-to-one work with Mr. R. Mrs. R is viewed as a collateral source of information and as a therapeutic ally. Family therapy is not an appropriate method of choice in this case. Mr. R might be able to benefit from participation in a group for people with disabilities at a later date. The worker's discharge function limits the scope of his/her activities. In working with Mr. R on a discharge plan, the worker may consider what kind of therapy, if any, might be beneficial to Mr. R and make a referral accordingly. Several therapeutic options may be considered.

On a biological and medical level, Mr. R will have to continue his physical rehabilitation and continue with his medications. Medicare will continue to provide health insurance. It is not known how Mr. R will fare under the new federal changes to regulate the cost of Medicare drug prescriptions. Mr. R's access to the drugs he needs will have to be monitored closely. His mood will also have to be monitored for possible interactive effects caused by his physical conditions and the medications used to treat them. If Mr. R should become depressed, he may need antidepressant medication and/or counseling. Mr. R's behavior will have to be monitored for signs of personality changes caused by brain injury.

On a psychological level, Mr. R's near-death experience, his declining health, and the role losses have made Mr. R aware of his own mortality. As part of integrity versus despair (the crisis associated with this stage of the life cycle), Mr. R may benefit from psychodynamic talk therapy using an ego-supportive approach.

Mr. R may be experiencing feelings associated with a stigmatized identity. Mr. R is a large man who was accustomed to using his physical strength to help others. He took pride in his ability to work hard, be strong, and care for others. His identity and body image have been impacted by the accident. He is dealing with a stigmatized self and may benefit from a therapeutic approach which focuses on a redefinition of self.

Mr. R may also be a candidate for a cognitive therapy approach. Mr. R's accident and his care in the year following the accident have led him to question his assumptive world and core beliefs. Mr. R cannot believe that a hard-working law-abiding citizen should lack the resources necessitated by his medical condition.

On a sociological level, Mr. R is experiencing major access issues common to disabled populations. The additional resources he needs (out-of-pocket medical expenses, transportation, ramp to access transportation) are not covered by health insurance. Building codes, his property's footprint, the cost of a ramp, and Mr. R's fixed income create social barriers to Mr. R's quality of life. Whether or not Mr. R can continue to live at home depends on the success of his rehabilitation and/or the degree to which his home can be made handicapped friendly and accessible. Mr. R is in need of advocacy for concrete resources to make his home handicapped accessible. Public funds are not available for building a ramp. Advocacy will have to explore the private sector.

Mr. R's preference is for problem-solving advocacy efforts to help him acquire a ramp so he can get in and out of his house. This is consistent with empowerment theory.

Overarching Cultural Principles

Mr. R and the worker are from different racial, gender, and age groups. Mr. R's membership as a senior citizen (ageism) and as a physically disabled person may affect Mr. R's rehabilitation and recovery. Much of the physical environment is inaccessible for those who are differently abled. Policies and programs for the disabled are often lacking or are not enforced. Being a member of a group that is a racial minority does not appear to play a direct role in this case. Race has likely played a role in Mr. R's educational opportunities and consequently in his socioeconomic class. It is likely, therefore, to be an indirect factor in the size of Mr. R's pension. The worker is attentive to Mr. R's preference about help giving. Mr. R is accepting of problem-solving interventions and concrete resources. He does not wish to participate in individual or group talk therapy.

EXHIBIT 13.2   *Treatment Matrix: Mr. R*

Procedural Knowing	Worker Action	Desired Goal/Outcome
Duty to protect	Contract for safety with Mr. and Mrs. R Mrs. R performs activities of daily living for Mr. R Monitor Mr. R for mood changes, physical conditions, medications. Monitor Mr. R for personality changes, brain injury Make home handicapped friendly and accessible	Assure safety
Crisis intervention	Mr. R is in a post-crisis phase	Stabilization
Concrete services	Monitor access to medications, new Medicare drug prescription laws Continue existing rehabilitation services	Meet needs in timely manner
Advocacy	Look for additional sources of income to cover out-of-pocket health care expenses Look for private sector resources to build ramp	Fill resources gap
Therapy: methods and theories	Pain management Empowerment, advocacy	Reduce suffering Build a ramp

He prefers care by his informal social network but accepts care from visiting health care professionals.

Overarching Ethical Principles

A potential ethical dilemma may arise. Mr. R's desire to remain in his own home (client self-determination) may conflict with the worker's duty to protect. If Mr. R's wife should no longer be able to care for him, or if Mr. R's house cannot be modified to reduce the risk of falls, or if the house cannot be modified to become handicapped accessible, the worker may have to consider alternative living arrangements as part of a future discharge plan.

Summary

All steps of the decision tree have been applied to Mr. R. In building a case-specific model of practice, the worker has put into place a contract for safety, has determined that there is no immediate crisis, and has used case management to continue and to increase concrete resources. Consistent with Mr. R's preferences, the worker has decided to use empowerment theory and engage in advocacy to help Mr. R acquire a ramp.

Organizationally (management theory), the worker has been informed that his/her advocacy goals go beyond the scope of his/her function at the rehabilitation facility and beyond the facility's resources (legitimate contracting). If s/he wishes to pursue these goals, s/he must explore options in the private sector on his/her own time or link Mr. R to an advocate in a different agency. As can be seen, the decision tree converts descriptive information gathered through open assessment into prioritized prescriptive actions. Case-specific model building requires competency with more than one therapy approach and skill set. This chapter concludes by providing samples of theory-driven therapeutic processes captured in process recordings.

■ Samples of Different Theory-Driven Process Recordings

To illustrate different theory-driven therapies, the following excerpts from process recordings are presented.

Psychodynamic Theory: Mrs. Jones

Mrs. Jones is a college-educated, 30-year-old, married, African-American female with two children, Ebony, age 3, and Dewan, age 5. Mr. Jones manages a fast food store. They live in their own house in suburbia and socioeconomically fall into the category of those earning $70,000 a year. This year, she was diagnosed with

EXHIBIT 13.3   *Process Recording: Mrs. Jones*

Thinking Declarative Knowledge	Dialogue Theory-Driven Therapeutic Process	Worker Self-Awareness Monitoring Skill and Feeling
Greeting, probing	W: Hello, Mrs. Jones. How did your week go?	Anxious: Can I keep my own fears in check?
Indirect communication	Mrs. J: Well, I lost it.	Afraid: What does that mean?
Paraphrasing, probing for underlying meaning Following	W: Lost it?	Confident
Is this normal grieving? Is this clinical depression? Words and affect match. Is this anticipatory grief? Is this inability to regulate affect?	Mrs. J: I found myself looking at Ebony and thinking that I would never live to see her get married. I began to cry and couldn't stop myself.	Sad: overwhelmed by her comment
Additive empathy, acknowledgment of here and now, reflection of Erikson age/stage, reflection of life-and-death issues, validation of feelings	W: I see that as you tell me this, there are tears in your eyes. Having cancer at such a young age and knowing that others in your family have struggled with this disease must be very frightening.	Where am I on handling issues of life and death in my own life?
Successful psychosocial development. Because of these successes, she probably possesses many personality (ego) traits that will help her cope with this situation. Also reflects healthy object relations	Mrs. J: My life was going so well. I graduated college, had a job I loved, married a man I love, and have two wonderful children [pause] and then this [looking downcast].	This could happen to me
Checking for suicidal thoughts and intent Support of ego, hope	W: You still have so much to live for. You are not giving up on the hope that your treatment will provide you with a long life?	

Thinking Declarative Knowledge	Dialogue Theory-Driven Therapeutic Process	Worker Self-Awareness Monitoring Skill and Feeling
My wish to make it go away reflects magical thinking and primary process thinking	Mrs. J: Of course I have hope and I'm going to fight this disease every way possible. Yet I also think I have to prepare for the unthinkable.	Relieved: she is not suicidal That she might die and not see her children grow up is unthinkable to me too I wish I could make it go away
Application of transpersonal theory, need to go beyond ego and rationality to another dimension: transcendence or spirituality	W: Sometimes things happen to us, like cancer, and it is difficult for us to come to terms with it. It seems so senseless.	I feel helpless in trying to make a difference

breast cancer and recently underwent surgery to remove one breast. She decided to have radiation treatment post-op. Mrs. Jones has several risk factors for cancer in that her mother, one of her aunts, and an older sister have also had breast cancer. Her mother died of cancer at age 55. As a result of her cancer and its treatment, Mrs. Jones gave up her job as an elementary school teacher. Mrs. Jones is in a support group for cancer survivors. She is also seeing a clinician for individual counseling. The family insurance offers limited benefits for counseling. This is the third session.

Behavior Modification: Kyle

Kyle is an active, 6-year-old, Caucasian male who attends Flint Rock public school as a first-grader. Last year, he attended kindergarten at Brookland school. Nothing unusual was noted in his school record. Kyle is the eldest of two children. He has a sister, Brittany, age 2. Kyle's parents divorced over the summer. Because of the divorce, Kyle's mother moved, which placed Kyle into a new school district. Both of Kyle's parents work, Scott as an electrician and Lily as an office manager. They share custody of the two children.

The family is in a period of adjustment post-separation and -divorce. This is Ms. Hauer's first year of teaching. In her referral, Ms. Hauer states, "Kyle is inattentive. He is unable to complete a task and has difficulty transitioning from one task to another. He does not sit in his seat and he bothers the other children. He appears to be very bright and quick in his work. He finishes before all others but refuses to check over his work." Kyle is in the process of full assessment to rule

EXHIBIT 13.4 *Process Recording: Kyle*

Thinking Declarative Knowledge	Dialogue Theory-Driven Therapeutic Process	Worker Self-Awareness Monitoring Skill and Feeling
Greeting, informed consent School permission, parental permission, contracting with Kyle Many clients here	W: Hi, Kyle, my name is Beth. Your mom and your teacher, Ms. Hauer, said I could talk with you today. I hope it's OK with you?	Uncertain: I've never interviewed a 6-year-old before
I see what the teacher sees in terms of his activity level	Kyle is running here and there, checking out the room.	Exhausted: his energy is wearing me down already
	Kyle: OK [pulling down all the game boxes and knocking counting cubes off the shelf].	
Shaping his behavior, reducing visual stimulation to get attentive response	W sits on the floor with Kyle, putting her body between the games shelf and the counting cubes on the floor.	Comfortable: I like sitting on the floor with kids
Behavioral request	W: Kyle, come here and let's see what we can do with these cubes.	Fearful: what if he doesn't comply?
This is not usual behavior for a 6-year-old	K comes and kicks the cubes all around and laughs.	Surprised
Use of laughter to establish rapport	W laughs too and begins to pretend that cubes are a train.	A part of me wants to shout at him to stop it
Honoring his energy by talking while allowing him to be active but constructively engaged	W: Kyle, bring the chair here. Let's pretend the chair is a tunnel and help me make the train go under.	
I think this is Kyle's way of consenting to be with me today	K brings the chair and begins to join in.	Thankful
Use of praise as reinforcement for following directions and being cooperative	W: Thanks, Kyle. You carried that chair so well. You must be very strong.	Somewhat confident: I know what I did and why

230

Thinking Declarative Knowledge	Dialogue Theory-Driven Therapeutic Process	Worker Self-Awareness Monitoring Skill and Feeling
Informed consent, disclosure of student status	W: Kyle, I'm a student just like you, but I go to a different school.	Second thoughts: Is this what I want to be doing?
This shows some ability to attend and focus	K: Umm [keeps gathering the cubes and making a train that is getting longer and longer].	Anxious: How long have I been in here? How much longer before time is up?
Purpose of the meeting, problem definition, contracting	W: Your mom and your teacher tell me that it is very hard for you to sit still in first grade.	
Ignore this, technique of extinguishing the behavior	K gets up and starts running in circles.	Frustrated: Did I say the wrong thing? Did I trigger this?
Requesting behavior incompatible with running around, use of reinforcement if client complies	W: Kyle, I brought something special with me today just for you. Come sit down on the floor.	Skeptical: hope this reward theory works
	K: What is it?	
Determining what items can be used as rewards to reinforce appropriate behavior	W: Well, I asked your mom what she thought you would like, and she told me a good treat to bring to you as a get-acquainted gift.	Uncomfortable: this model is contrary to my beliefs on child rearing. This seems more like a bribe than a reinforcement
Immediate reinforcement for compliance with request, awareness of importance of reinforcement schedule	As Kyle sits, worker pulls out Pokemon card and gives it to Kyle.	
Grabbing is an impulse-control issue (oops, impulse is a concept from a different theory)	K grabs the card and dances with joy.	Joyful at his happiness, feeling better about myself as a novice clinician
Setting up a token reinforcement schedule for sitting in class	W: Kyle, would you like to have more Pokemon cards?	
	K: Yes, yes, do you have more?	

(continued)

EXHIBIT 13.4   *Process Recording: Kyle* (*continued*)

Thinking Declarative Knowledge	Dialogue Theory-Driven Therapeutic Process	Worker Self-Awareness Monitoring Skill and Feeling
Generalizing reward from specific Pokemon card to token, redeemable later	W: Well, Kyle, your mom and your teacher and I have a plan about how you could earn more Pokemon cards. Are you interested? K: Yes.	

out any developmental disorder. In order to maintain Kyle in the classroom while testing is under way, Kyle has been referred to a student social work intern for behavioral therapy. The M.S.W. student is working with the school social worker and the teacher to manage Kyle's classroom behavior. The current working hypothesis is that Kyle's behavior is a consequence of disrupted parenting and new expectations.

Intervention can continue with a plan to visit "worst" and "best" classes and get a baseline of how many times Kyle gets out of his seat or is off-task. Then, an interval schedule of reinforcement can be established to reward compliance with targeted behaviors (sitting and on-task). Subsequent sessions between Kyle and the worker would focus on the same behaviors as in the recorded session and would apply behavioral techniques. Target behaviors could change over time as behavioral goals are met. The worker will ensure successful implementation by visiting the classroom and checking on Ms. Hauer's implementation of the plan. New rewards will have to be found. Antecedent and consequent events will have to be monitored. Biological determinants (ADD, ADHD, or learning disabilities) are being explored through testing.

Cognitive-Behavioral: Lily

Lily, Kyle's mother, is considered to be the client. According to cognitive-behavioral theory, Lily's problem is redefined as an inability to control Kyle's behavior due to dysfunctional cognitions following her divorce. The ABC paradigm looks as follows:

A: Activating Event. Separation and divorce
B: Belief/Brain. I can't manage anything
C: Consequence/Behavior. Lack of discipline and Kyle's out-of-control behavior

EXHIBIT 13.5   *Process Recording: Lily*

Thinking Declarative Knowledge	Dialogue Theory-Driven Therapeutic Process	Worker Self-Awareness Monitoring Skill and Feeling
Use of homework between sessions: *thought record* is a cognitive technique for having client record situations that occur between sessions.	W: Hello, Lily, I am very glad you were able to come today. Did you bring your thought record today?	Happy that Lily came today
Three columns: situation, automatic thought, mood/emotion	L: Yes, I'm good at identifying the situations but not so good at controlling my reactions.	Impressed: this model is working
Reinforcing awareness of cues, activating events	W: Being able to recognize and identify the situations that make you upset is a very big step in being able to control how you react.	Confident
Probing for activating event Use of present to work on problem	W. From your record, what situation would you like to explore here and now?	
This is the activating event of the previous week Her mother's belief system is a stressor to Lily	L: Well, I received a phone call from my mother. She said she wouldn't send any money to help with rent. She said I should have toughed it out and stayed with Scott. He was a good provider.	I don't like my mother telling me what I "should" do
Technique: check on client view of self following an activating event	W: How did you view yourself when your mother said that?	Worried: this sounds familiar
This is automatic thinking	L: Well, before, I would have seen myself as my mother saw me, as someone who doesn't measure up.	Excited: she said "before"; this is progress

(continued)

EXHIBIT 13.5 *Process Recording: Lily* (*continued*)

Thinking Declarative Knowledge	Dialogue Theory-Driven Therapeutic Process	Worker Self-Awareness Monitoring Skill and Feeling
Reinforcing client's success in identifying automatic pattern	W: Wow, and this time you didn't automatically think that?	
She substituted a functional cognition for a self-defeating one	L: I said to myself, "my mother is wrong in believing that I should have toughed it out."	Happy: this seems to be working
Verbal praise to reward client for using the technique, teaching client to become own therapist	W: I am so proud of you. You really are showing that you understand this model and can use it successfully.	Proud of Lily's achievement
Connecting thinking to feeling	W: Did this make you feel differently?	Hopeful
A: Mom's "should" B: Lily's different thought C: Different emotional outcome	L: Yes, I felt more in control of myself. I even felt a bit sorry for my mother.	Yes!!
Paraphrasing, prompting, open-ended probe	W: Sorry for your mother?	
Exploring learned behavior patterns	L: Yes, I realized that she had toughed it out with my dad all these years.	
Going for intermediate attitudes, rules, and assumptions	W: Have you ever thought about what made your mother tough it out?	Feel lucky that my mom didn't have to tough it out, glad that my mom raised me to be independent
	L: I always assumed it was part of her faith, that a wife is to be obedient to her husband. It's in the Bible.	My belief system is very feminist. I must be careful not to impose this on Lily
Moving toward the exploration of core beliefs	W: What is your belief about the relationship between husband and wife?	

EXHIBIT 13.6   *Schema: Complex Data and Model Building*

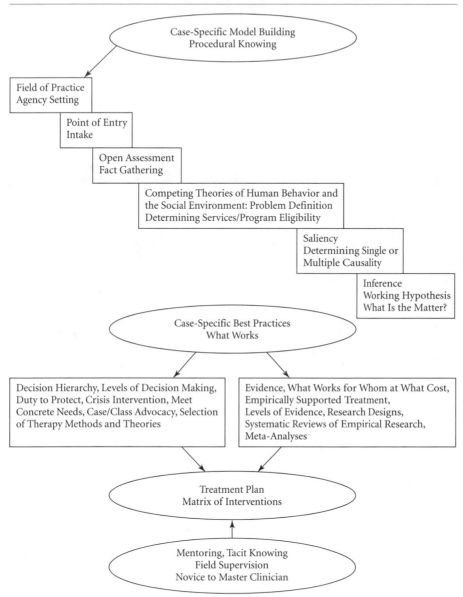

This is the third session. When the social worker first interviewed Lily to obtain her informed consent to meet with Kyle during the school year, the worker was able to contract with Lily to meet for six sessions regarding the impact of the divorce on her ability to parent Kyle and his sister.

14
Clinical Social Work With Families: Family Therapy

■ Distinguishing Family Methods From Individual Methods

Two Different Functions: Welfare Service and Therapy

Steps 5, 6, and 7 of the decision tree guide method choice. When the family is the method of choice (step 6), two different practice models are used, one focused on therapy (this chapter) and the other (chapter 15) focused on service delivery, e.g., financial assistance and protective services. Students are more likely to be placed in and find entry-level employment in family and child welfare settings than in family therapy settings. In many schools of social work, practice content on the family (whether therapy or welfare) is placed in the second-year curriculum, usually as an option. Placing practice content on family and child welfare in a foundation-year practice text better prepares B.S.W. students for entry-level work in departments of human services, and it promotes family and child welfare as a second-year specialization for M.S.W. students. Competent practice requires differentiation of these two models of family practice; each has a different skill set and different conceptualizations of the worker-family relationship.

Point of Entry: Criteria for Choosing Family Therapy as a Method

When therapy is the treatment decision, clinical social workers can choose to do individual therapy, family therapy, or group therapy. Each type of therapy requires specialized knowledge that differentiates one therapy method from the others. The point of entry to family therapy is usually through an identified client who has been referred for individual therapy. Alternatively, the point of entry can be through an adult (usually the wife/mother) who is the designated help seeker for a family that has identified a member (index person; IP) as in need of help.

Family therapy is the method of choice when families deal with the ordinary problems of family life (family life cycle). It is the method of choice when families encounter predictable and unpredictable life stressors. It is the method of choice when improvement in an individual family member will not occur or be sustained without changes in family structures and patterns of interaction.

What Makes Family Therapy Different From Individual Therapy?

The use of therapy with families represents a paradigm change from earlier models of individual therapy based on linear causality. The shift from linear causality to mutual causality brought about shifts in defining the client (from the individual to the family) and in method (from an individual method to a family method). The social work family therapist maintains focus on the family as a whole and focus on each individual member of the family in interaction with all other family members. As a method, it is more complex than work with a single individual.

■ Declarative Knowledge: What Family Therapists Need to Know

There are many different theory-based models of family therapy (Jones, 1980). For the purposes of this chapter, four models have been chosen to illustrate the concepts that differentiate family therapy as a method of practice from individual therapy as a method of practice. These models are (1) family systems theory, (2) family life cycle theory, (3) Bowen's theory (1978) of transgenerational emotional transmission, and (4) Minuchin's structural-strategic theory (1974).

General Systems Theory: Overview

General systems theory (of which family systems theory is a subcategory) focuses on the transactional patterns between components of a system and on the transactions between one system and another. The theory accepts that each component of a system impacts another component and the system as a whole (mutual causality). Every model of family therapy adopts systems concepts shared by every other model; each model is, however, conceptually unique in some way.

Systems

General systems theory (Bertanlaffy, 1968) is a theory found in many disciplines. Systems thinking can be applied to living systems, which extend from viruses through societies. A *living system* is defined as a complex of elements with interactions that are ordered (nonrandom). The term *system* is used to differentiate it from a collection, where the parts remain individually unchanged whether isolated or together. The major explanatory premises derived from general systems theory are (1) the whole is greater than the sum of its parts; (2) a change in one part of the system will lead to changes in other parts of the system; (3) systems are dynamic not static, therefore systems are in a constant state of flux; (4) causality is complex; (5) feedback is a method of controlling how systems function by inserting performance results that allow for correction and change; and (6) all systems must remain stable and change.

Adaptability is essential if a system is to avoid the forces of entropy (decay and dissolution). *Morphostasis* (structural constancy) refers to the system's ability to remain stable in the context of change. *Morphogenesis* refers to the ability to change within the context of stability. Feedback that leads to positive deviation encourages growth, innovation, and adaptive change. *Homeostasis* refers to the maintenance of behavioral constancy in a system. *Tension* refers to the pull between maintaining the status quo and change.

Boundaries, Negative Entropy, and Feedback

Each system has boundaries that identify it as a system. A *boundary* is an invisible demarcation that separates one system from another. *Negative entropy* is a concept that refers to the exchange of energy associated with open systems and semi-permeable boundaries. *Entropy* is a concept that refers to the decline of energy and the decay of a system associated with a closed system and impermeable boundaries. In systems theory, *feedback* (information) corrects the course of the system. Negative feedback brings a deviating system back on course while positive feedback exaggerates the deviation.

Linear Causality and Mutual Causality

Prior to general systems theory, the major focus in the behavioral sciences was on individual functioning as reflected in psychoanalytic theory, classical behaviorism, neobehaviorism, and learning theory. The behavioral sciences operate on linear causality. *Linear causality* holds that behavior is biologically determined (genetics) or reactive based on early childhood experiences, on antecedent (stimulus-response; S-R) events, or on reinforcement schedules. The goal of intervention in linear models is to establish or restore normal functioning through interventions that are biological, cognitive (learning theories), or psychological (e.g., psychodynamic therapies that reduce needs, drives, and tensions).

In contrast, family systems theory is based on a premise of mutual causality. Consistent with this premise, family members are observed in terms of their patterns of interaction with each other rather than on intrinsic personal characteristics. The family's established behavioral sequences and patterns of interaction are the subject of assessment and intervention. *Mutual causality* maintains that every event in a family system is multiply determined, therefore individual symptoms/dysfunctions are redefined as flawed familial structures and patterns of interaction.

When applied to families, the following concepts are borrowed from general systems theory: (1) systems: suprasystem, subsystem, and focal system, (2) equilibrium or homeostasis, (3) structure (hierarchy of subsystems), (4) boundaries (degree of permeability), and (5) function and dysfunction.

Psychodynamic Theory: Family Life Cycle Development

Declarative knowledge also comes from psychodynamic theory, especially life cycle developmental theory and object-relations theory. Life cycle development holds that families seek therapy when stage-specific family or individual tasks get derailed. Progress to the next stage is blocked. Derailment may be caused by predictable, normative, individual, and family developmental stages or may be caused by unpredictable life events.

Assessment Concepts

The theory holds that all families have current family stage-specific tasks that they must master. Symptoms and dysfunctions are viewed in relation to normal functioning. Family dysfunction (symptoms) occurs when there is an interruption or dislocation in the unfolding of the family life cycle as it responds to the developmental needs of its members or to the demands of outside forces. The goal of family therapy is viewed as reestablishing the family's developmental momentum by focusing on stage-specific tasks. Typically, families seek help when they have trouble negotiating developmental transitions.

Family Life Cycle Stages

Carter and McGoldrick (2004) identify six family developmental stages: (1) launching the young adult, (2) the couple, (3) families with children, (4) families with adolescents, (5) launching children and moving on, and (6) families in later life. It should be noted that often a family is in more than one family life cycle stage at a time, depending upon the ages of the children.

The primary task of stage 1 is for the single young adult to separate from his/her family of origin without cutting off or fleeing. Derailment at this stage occurs when families don't let go of their adult children or the adult children remain dependent or rebel. In stage 2, the major task is to form a new family system separate and distinct from the couple's families of origin. Derailment at this stage consists of enmeshment (failure to separate from one's family of origin) or distancing (failure to stay connected). Couples can experience difficulties in intimacy and commitment. In stage 3, the new family is tasked with becoming caretakers to the next generation. Derailment at this stage concerns couple issues and parenting issues. The primary task of stage 4 is to establish qualitatively different boundaries for adolescents than for younger children: more permeability. Derailment at this stage is related to adolescent exploration, friendships, substance use, sexual activity, and school. The primary task of stage 5 is to adapt to the numerous exits from and entries to the family system. At this stage, derailment occurs when families hold on to the last child, when parents become depressed at the empty nest, when the marriage ends in divorce, or when adult children return home. In stage 6, the primary task is adjustment to aging. Derailment occurs related to difficulties with retirement, financial insecurity, declining health and illness, dependence on adult children, and loss of a spouse or other family members and friends.

Predictable and Unpredictable Life Crises

In addition to family life cycle theory, the notion of predictable (normative developmental crises) and unpredictable life events is contained in several practice theories: Erikson's (1963) stages of individual growth and development, crisis intervention theory (Parad, 1965), Bowen's (1978) horizontal and vertical stressors in family therapy, and stress theory (Selye, 1936). Family life cycle theory holds that stress (internal or external) derails a family's stages of development. According to mutual causality, disruption in a family life cycle stage can disrupt individual development. Likewise, disruption in an individual's stage of development can interfere with mastery of a family life cycle stage.

Therapeutic Processes

Therapy is seen as helping families get back on the developmental life cycle track after being stuck or derailed at a particular stage. The therapeutic process is goal oriented (seeking progress from one developmental stage to another). The family therapist helps the family (usually the mother) to understand the developmental needs of an individual member (usually the child/adolescent referred for therapy). For elaboration on individual developmental stages within the family life cycle, see the works of Erikson (1963); Levinson (1978); Sheehy (1977); and Gilligan (1982/1993). For elaboration on the stages of couple developmental issues over the life cycle, see the works of Campbell (1975); Gould (1972); Harry (1976); Schram (1979); and Nadelson and Polonsky (1984). Therapeutic efforts are directed toward helping family members to recognize (insight) their derailments so that they can proceed developmentally. Sometimes, this perspective is used to work with a parent-child or parent-adolescent dyad and is therefore more aligned with a one-on-one method than with a family method. Whether or not one can do "family" therapy with an individual or a dyad is controversial.

Bowenian Theory: Assessment Concepts

Bowen (1978) borrows from psychodynamic theory the concepts of developmental stages, stress, and the importance of familial relationships. Bowen accepts that family stress is often greatest at the point of transition from one developmental stage to another. According to Bowen, relationship patterns established in one's family of origin are predictive of relationship patterns in one's family of formation.

Bowen adds to the previous models of family therapy the concept of *differentiation*. Problems occur when individuals fail to differentiate themselves from their family of origin and recreate flawed *emotional transaction* patterns in their family of formation. He maintains that a family is an emotionally interdependent system. Emotional fields are transmitted from one generation to the next through established patterns of dealing with stress. A three-generational *genogram* is used to visually depict this transmission. Family members replicate the learned emotions and behaviors outside the family setting.

Intergenerational Connectedness: Emotional Transmission

There is intergenerational connectedness within families. The family is an operative emotional field that exists from cradle to grave. Emotional difficulties and individual emotional health are tied to this generational emotional field. Bowen observes that no family relationships are entered into by choice except marriage. No one leaves the family except through death. Pressures placed on members of some families can be so great that in extreme circumstances psychosis may result. Individual dysfunction often reflects an active familial emotional system in need of correction.

Vertical and Horizontal Stressors: Intersection

The theory holds that families are influenced by vertical stressors (emotional norms and rules transmitted across generations) and by horizontal stressors (predictable and unpredictable current events). Families may become dysfunctional (experience stress and anxiety) when they encounter vertical and horizontal stressors. A family is most at risk when vertical and horizontal stressors intersect.

A *vertical stressor* is defined as a pattern of relating and functioning that is transmitted from one generation to the next primarily through the mechanism of emotional triangling. Indicators of the transmission of a problematic or dysfunctional emotional system are family secrets, attitudes, taboos, expectations, labels, legacies, myths, patterns, and loaded issues. Vertical stressors can come from individuals, from the nuclear or extended family, from the community (work and friends), and from one's social, cultural, political, religious, and economic environment. Sources also include place (geographical location) and time (historical period/cohort). Vertical stressors are values-laden norms and rules imposed by others to govern behavior.

A *horizontal stressor* is defined as a stress on the family as it moves through time. Families must cope with familial changes and transitions. Horizontal stressors consist of predictable familial and individual developmental crises (as described in the section on the family life cycle, above) and of unpredictable life events (e.g., a life-threatening illness of a family member). Divorce, remarriage, and chronic illness are horizontal stressors that are viewed in terms of their impact on family emotional transactions and individual symptom formation. When vertical and horizontal stressors converge or intersect, there is a greater flow of anxiety, a greater disruption to the family life cycle, and more individual symptom formation. Family dysfunction is viewed as a maladaptive emotional response to stress.

Bowenian Theory: Therapeutic Processes

Genogram: Work With One's Family of Origin

Therapy is indicated when one member of the family unit cuts him- or herself off from other members, flees, or is in conflict. Family therapy is needed to preserve irreplaceable family relationships that are at risk. Bowen holds that when family members act as though family relationships are optional, they do so to the detriment of their own sense of identity and the richness of their emotional and social life.

A major goal of this perspective is to help individual young adults emotionally differentiate themselves from their respective families of origin so dysfunctional emotional transactions do not get replicated in their family of formation. According to Bowen, young adults who cut off their parents do so reactively and are in fact still emotionally bound to the "family program." Cut-offs never resolve emotional relationships.

The therapeutic process most often involves coaching young adults to reengage with their parents in a new healthy way of relating. *Health* is defined in terms of a mutually respectful and personal form of relating where young adults can appreciate their parents as they are. Emotionally healthy young adults neither need to make their parents into what they are not nor blame them for what they could not be or do.

Boundary Adjustments: Family of Formation and Family of Origin

Another therapeutic process includes boundary adjustments. Young adult couples who are in the beginning phase of family formation have to be able to negotiate their status as a couple separate from but connected to their families of origin (neither enmeshed nor rigid, cut-off). Frequently, this model is used with one member of a family or the spousal couple. Rarely are all members of the family seen at the same time as a group as is true of Minuchin's model of family therapy (1974).

Structural-Strategic Family Therapy: Assessment Concepts

Point of Entry

Consistent with other models of family therapy, structural-strategic family therapy assumes that the family comes to therapy because of a symptom of one member of the family. This member is referred to as the *index person*, or identified patient (IP). The theory assumes that the IP's symptom is a system-maintaining or a system-maintained device. Structural-strategic therapy is consistent with concepts from the sociological theory of structure-functionalism. A family is regarded as dysfunctional when it responds to internal or external demands in a way that reflects a flawed family structure or a dysfunctional pattern of interaction. Families may not be explicitly aware of these arrangements. Dysfunctional patterns block alternative, healthy ways of relating.

Systems and Power Hierarchies

Structurally, a family is a system. When it is the focus of attention, it is referred to as the *focal system*. As a focal system, the family is part of a larger *suprasystem* (extended family, neighborhood, community). The family as a whole and each family member must coexist with external environments, including work, school, religious organizations, and government institutions. An *ecomap* is a pictorial representation of a family's (or individual's) external environment (formal institutions and informal social networks). Internally, families develop a *role structure* that is hierarchical in organization. All families differentiate and carry out their functions through structural subsystems. Families have four major subsystems: (a) spousal, (b) parent-child, (c) sibling, and (d) individual. Other subsystems can form around gender, interests, generation, or functions. Each subsystem can be thought of as a natural coalition or alliance usually situation related and temporary.

Every family has a *power hierarchy* where parents and children have different levels of authority. Every family develops *complementary functions* where interdependency leads to family cooperation. Roles change over time as the family develops or encounters situational demands and as individual members grow and develop. For healthy family functioning, the *boundaries* of subsystems must be clear. Every family system is idiosyncratic. A family may be both functional and dysfunctional at the same time, depending upon the area under question. Individual health is predicated on familial health, which is predicated on the open flow of information (feedback) within the system and between the system and its environment. Semipermeable boundaries allow feedback to flow across boundaries, thereby allowing for correction and adaptation to change.

Functional and Dysfunctional Family Structures

Minuchin identifies several problematic family structures. One is the parental-child structure. In this structure, parental power is allocated to a child. Another problematic structure is that of parental flux. This structure is characterized by a pattern of leaving (military deployment, job-related travel, or incarceration) and returning. A third problematic structure involves families that have difficulty handling stress. This type of family negotiates stress in one subsystem through other subsystems, either by becoming enmeshed or by distancing themselves from each other. Finally, some families have problems with negotiating boundaries between the family and outside systems. Diffuse boundaries can lead to confusion over who is in charge. Rigid boundaries can prevent the healthy exchange of energy between families and outside systems.

Functional Family Transactions: Norms, Routines, and Rules

Families develop *norms* and *rules* that govern how members interact with each other and that influence behavioral sequences and patterns. Repeated transactions establish internal patterns of how, when, and to whom to relate. A system is maintained to the extent that all members of the family adhere to a limited number of rules or implicit agreements that prescribe the rights, duties, and range of appropriate behaviors within the family. Family routines, the flow of information across boundaries, and the performance of family functions (support, regulation, nurturance, and socialization) through tasks (getting up, dinner time, chores) reflect preferred patterns of family transactions.

Families have both explicit and implicit rules. Examples of *explicit rules* are "Be in at 11 p.m." or "No swearing in this house." An *implicit (unwritten) rule* must be inferred by members of the family and by the clinician observing the family's interactions and communications. An example of an implicit rule is "Don't say what you really feel" or "Dad is always right." Though it is common for family members to engage in preferred patterns of interaction, such patterns may not be helpful to the situation at hand. Patterns that were functional at one time or in another situation may not be functional in the current situation. Even though families have alternative interaction patterns available, they are resistant to change their preferred patterns.

Structural-Strategic Family Therapy: Therapeutic Processes

Joining: Therapist Use of Self

Unlike other models of family therapy, the worker actually joins the family as a participant observer to collect assessment data. By *joining* the family, the therapist is able to identify and probe dysfunctional structures (i.e., subsystems, coalitions, hierarchies, and triads). The clinician joins the family in a position of leadership. It is the therapist's job to create circumstances that will allow family transactions that are either diagnostic or corrective. Having joined the family, the clinician not only hears what family members tell him about the way they experience reality, the therapist actually experiences the way the family members relate to her/him and to each other. The clinician accepts responsibility for the success of his/her interventions.

The family therapist recognizes that his/her effort to bring about therapeutic change is accompanied by stress. Consequently, s/he possesses the skills to contain and manage the emotional pain of the family and its members as change occurs. The worker's use of self requires that s/he join the family in a way that is comfortable (syntonic) for the family. The family therapist works to actively transform the family within each session. The therapist uses space (proximity, distance) to mark, create, strengthen, or weaken boundaries. Tasks are assigned to establish new structures and/or to promote interaction and communication between some family members while decreasing contact between others. The therapist can create stress (tension needed for change) by giving a *directive* (e.g., "Ask your parents whether you can have the car tonight" or "Tell Ben that he cannot have the car tonight") or by unbalancing a family structure. *Unbalancing* is accomplished by therapist alignment with one subsystem against another. The clinician's use of self involves support, education, and guidance.

The Use of Probes

The following is an example of a *probe*. The family presents with an adolescent who refuses to do homework. As a consequence, the adolescent is at risk of failing 10th grade. Through inquiries (probes), the clinician learns that Mom and Dad argue over Dad's work and finances. The therapist observes that when spousal conflict arises, it gets detoured to the children, especially to the index adolescent. The clinician forms a diagnostic hypothesis that the mother and IP adolescent have formed an unwitting alliance that diverts conflict between the mother and the father. A probe leads to a *diagnostic map*.

Mapping: Goal-Directed Interventions

A family map is a powerful simplification device. It allows the clinician to manipulate data to arrive at a definition of the problem (diagnostic hypothesis) and its solution (treatment goal). Mapping suggests specific treatment techniques. A *family map* is a contract that defines both what is the matter and the desired outcome of treatment efforts. For example, in the case above, the therapist maps a boundary around the spousal subsystem that will increase the distance between

Mom and the IP adolescent and that will draw the mother and father closer. A directive is given. When Mom and Dad argue over finances and Dad's job, the children will stay out of it. The therapist has the family enact this strategy in session by having the spousal system argue. The children are directed to move away from the parents and to sit with their backs to them as the couple argues.

Blocking

The clinician uses *blocking* as a technique to restructure flawed subsystems. The therapist's use of self can block faulty transactions between family subsystems and the identified patient. For example, in a block, the therapist takes responsibility for the symptomatic behavior of the identified patient (e.g., the clinician takes responsibility for the adolescent's refusal to do homework). By doing so, the clinician acts as a barrier to the usual transaction between the parental subsystem and the IP. According to this theory, the "symptom" of the identified patient is hypothesized to be a transactional pattern that deflects or avoids conflict in other parts of the family system.

Unbalancing

Family therapists use unbalancing techniques to strengthen or weaken subsystems. For instance, the therapist can unbalance an enmeshed subsystem by exaggerating the overinvolvement between the pair to the point that it creates a crisis, necessitating a new family response. Another unbalancing technique is to move another member of the family into the role of the IP. This focuses attention on family patterns rather than on a given individual's "symptoms." The therapist can also unbalance the system by joining one subsystem against another. When a clinician unbalances a family system, the other members experience stress. When unbalancing a system, the therapist must support each member of the family, confirming some aspect of her/his personality even when s/he is disqualifying them in other areas.

Paradoxical Interpretations and Directives: Reframing

The therapist can strengthen subsystem boundaries by labeling (reframing) the relationship in the subsystem in positive terms. This allows members of the subsystem to negotiate their own issues without drawing in a third member of the family. The therapist can offer a *paradoxical interpretation* (e.g., viewing symptomatic behavior as healthy behavior used to benefit the family), offer a directive (no one can speak for another family member), or offer a paradoxical directive (treat an irresponsible member as responsible). These techniques change how members interact with each other.

■ Critique: Cultural Differences and Bias

Cultural Differences

Clinicians recognize the extent of variations between cultures and within cultures in the norms governing family structures. The American family has changed radically in its structure, stages, and forms. Rules governing family processes differ drastically from one culture to another. Western cultures tend to adopt rules that stress competitiveness, assertiveness, and individualism. Other cultures emphasize bringing honor to the family, respect for elders, and sharing what you have with relatives. In some cultures, children are expected to show unquestioning obedience to their parents and wives are expected to submit to their husbands. Self-seeking behavior and individualism are discouraged. Individual problems are perceived as bringing shame on the family. Help-seeking behavior is discouraged. In such contexts, family and group therapy may be contraindicated.

Bias

Like other models that rely on definitions of normal and abnormal, functional and dysfunctional, healthy and unhealthy, concerns are raised as to who determines the criteria for a healthy family. What distinguishes healthy and unhealthy families from one another? Critics charge that dominant group power and bias account for such differentiations. Models of family therapy have also been criticized for their focus on "deficits" or "symptoms" (medical model). The method is viewed as maintaining the status quo, instead of challenging discriminatory norms and practices that affect the family negatively and harm individual members.

Critics note that there are many competing and conflicting ideologically based definitions of the family. Who is and who is not "family" is cultural and political. It is charged that family therapy models are normed on Eurocentric, white, middle-class American families at the end of the 20th century (even within American culture, the norms are not universal).

McGoldrick, Giordano, and Pearce (1996) have attempted to take into account ethnic patterns and cultural variability in life cycle definitions of normal stages of individual and family development. Ultimately, they say, it is the clinician who is responsible for responding to changing norms and sociopolitical realities. Feminists challenge patriarchal norms that maintain the male as the head of the household and assign to women the major responsibility for child rearing.

Critics particularly challenge romanticized versions of the family. They note that the concept of family often masks psychological and physical violence toward women and children while it protects men. Postmodernists critique traditional models of family therapy on the basis that such models maintain discriminatory power differentials and do not adequately address alternative family forms. Models of family therapy do not address the objective realities of racism, discrimination, oppression, and poverty.

■ Family Process Recording

The R family consists of Mrs. R, age 55; Sherry, age 21; Ann, age 24 (married); and Billy, age 17. Mr. and Mrs. R have been divorced for 11 years. Mrs. R has a GS12 federal job and receives no child support. Mrs. R called the clinic (point of entry) about her son, Billy, who is skipping school. Billy claims that he can't wake up in the morning. He forgets to set his alarm. Billy is overweight. The father lives in New Mexico. Mr. R is frequently disparaged by the mother and Sherry as "crude" and not having much job success since Mrs. R divorced him. Billy blames his mother for driving Mr. R away. Ann, married, is reported as "sweet" and as having been able to get along quite well with her father. Present at this meeting are Mrs. R, Billy, and Sherry.

EXHIBIT 14.1 *Process Recording: R. Family*

Thinking Declarative Knowledge	Dialogue Theory-Driven Therapeutic Process	Worker Self-Awareness Monitoring Skill and Feeling
Billy is IP Family tasks: going to school, getting up, grooming, shopping Emotional themes: disappointment, shame, disgust, appearance	Mrs. R [to Billy]: You're such a disappointment to me. I bought you these clothes and you don't like them. You look terrible but you won't go shopping. I'm ashamed to admit you're my son. You make me sick. How can you hurt me like this? You're so fat you disgust me.	Uh-oh
Dysfunctional structures: Mrs. R favors son-in-law over son	B: Get off my back. I don't want those cheap clothes. You gave Tom [son-in-law] expensive clothes at Christmas. You think of me as bargain stuff!	I know jealousy

(continued)

249

EXHIBIT 14.1 *Process Recording: R. Family* (*continued*)

Thinking Declarative Knowledge	Dialogue Theory-Driven Therapeutic Process	Worker Self-Awareness Monitoring Skill and Feeling
Generational transmission: worthy/unworthy, tied to being responsible	Mrs. R: You don't take care of anything. Tom deserves better because he takes care of what he gets.	
Developmental age: separation, cut-off, rebellion, repeat of father's solution: leaving	B: When I'm 18, I'm leaving; that's 7 months away.	I'm too slow in responding
Response escalates deviation, expelling B from family system	Mrs. R: Good. And it will be sooner if you fail out of school.	Don't like threats
B has need not being met (symbolic)	B fumbles in his pockets, looks around the room.	
Attunement	Mrs. R gets her handbag, hands him a cigarette and lighter.	
Attempt at connection	B sticks his legs out straight, touches his mother's chair with his feet and stays in that position.	
Attempt to join the family	Worker: Where would you go, Billy, if you left home?	Want to get control
No contract with B yet	B: That is none of your business! [glares]	Attacked
Transactional pattern: physically and verbally aggressive	Mrs. R furiously kicks Billy in the leg. Mrs. R: You're being very disrespectful and I won't put up with it.	
S aligns with B and then with Mom, forms coalitions	Sherry: Mom, you're too hard on him. He's just nervous being here. Billy, you are immature.	Have a lot to learn

EXHIBIT 14.2 *Decision Schema on Family Therapy*

Is Family Therapy Warranted?

The family has identified a member (IP) as in need of therapy.
The family is experiencing difficulty with a family life cycle stage.
The family is experiencing a predictable life crisis.
The family is experiencing an unpredictable crisis event.
The identified person cannot change unless family transactions change.

Is Family Therapy Culturally Appropriate?

Does the client's culture support help-seeking behavior?
What are the cultural norms governing male-female relationships?
What are the cultural norms governing parent-child relationships?
What are the cultural norms governing definitions of the family?
What are the cultural norms governing definitions of life cycle stages?
What is the cultural definition of the problem for which help is being sought?
How does the client's religious affiliation affect family dynamics?

Is family therapy contraindicated? If so, stop. If indicated, proceed.

Structural-Strategic Family Therapy
Who is the family help seeker?
Redefine IP as family problem
Define family participants (boundary)
Therapist joins the family

Assessment: Probes
        Life Cycle
• Who is the identified (index) person?
• What has been named as the problem?
• In what developmental stage(s) is the family?
• In what developmental stage is each member of
  the family?
• Is there an unpredictable crisis affecting the family?
• Where is the point of greatest reverberation?
  (intersection of developmental stage and unpredictable
  crisis)
        Emotional Transmission
• Consider drawing a three-generational genogram
• Vertical stressors: secrets, taboos, labels, loaded issues,
  legacies, myths, attitudes, expectations
• Patterns of relating: rules, implicit-explicit norms
        Structures
• Boundaries: permeable, semipermeable, rigid; open-
  closed; enmeshed-disengaged
• Subsystems: alliances, coalitions, triads

Interventions

• Get family and individual members
  back on life cycle track
• Provide psychoeducation, insight,
  support
• Revisit family of origin, work on
  separation, remaining connected
• Map (structures): what is the matter?
• Map (structures): what is the desired
  goal?
• Use directives, paradoxical directives
• Use space, sculpting, in session
• Blocking
• Unbalancing

15

Welfare Policies and Programs for Families and Children

■ Family Methods: Welfare and Protective Services

Steps 5, 6, and 7 of the decision tree guide method choice. When family welfare or protective services are indicated (step 6), competent practice requires familiarity with both services. There are two major desired end goals of family and child welfare policies and programs: (1) to prevent or mediate poverty, and (2) to protect children from abuse and neglect (Hartman, 1981).

The NASW Code of Ethics asserts that the profession's

> social change efforts [should be] focused primarily on issues of poverty, unemployment [and] discrimination. Social work is distinguished by its history of service to people who are poor. In the context of family and child welfare, the family is a sociological construct. For purposes of determining eligibility, a family is legally referred to as a household. A household is defined as a group of people living together who are legally responsible for one another. (Anderson, Sundet, & Harrington, 2000, p. 130)

The helping relationship between worker and family is circumscribed by the worker's fiduciary responsibilities and by postmodern principles of worker-family collaboration. A strengths perspective and family preservation programs support services delivery. The two approaches to work with families (chapter 14 and the present chapter) are very different and require different skill sets.

■ The Family as a Sociological Concept

From a sociological perspective, the family is a societal institution. As such, it has a structure and function. According to Parsons (1970, 1977), *societal institutions* are systems responsible for instrumental and expressive functions related to the care of the citizenry on behalf of society. The family, as an institution, is responsible for the procreation, protection, and socialization of its members. Families must provide basic resources (custodial care) and nurturance (psychological care) to its members. The family performs such essential functions as meeting the social, educational, and health care needs of its constituent members. It is largely through the family that character is formed, vital roles are learned, and members are socialized for participation in the larger society. Society has a stake in the family as an institution (Brace, 1973).

■ Structure-Functional Theory: Parsons's Law and Order

The application of general systems theory to society and its institutions is referred to as structure-functional theory. In broad strokes, Parsons argues that families must function in a manner that sustains the integrity of the societal system. Proponents of this perspective hold that what's wrong with society is rooted in the breakdown of the family. The argument goes that because families are not fulfilling their duties as expected, the family poses a danger to self (its members) and others (the community). This school of thought is consistent with social conservatism and the social control function of social work.

As a profession, social work is charged with working with such families to bring their functioning back on course. During the late 1960s and early 1970s, families that received welfare or that were referred for protective services were identified as not fulfilling expected, normative roles and functions. Family-centered casework accompanied financial aid (Geismar, 1980). When the area of identified dysfunction was child maltreatment, social workers traditionally removed children from the household (to protect them) and placed them in foster or adoptive homes (to care for them). One family structure was substituted for another. Preventing out-of-home placements was not a priority until a decade later. Consistent with the philosophy of the times, parents were provided with casework services to facilitate changes needed prior to the child's return from temporary foster care to the family.

■ Merton's Challenge to the Status Quo

Merton (1975) challenged Parsons's assumptions about the causal direction of dysfunction and the value of maintaining the status quo. Again in broad strokes, Merton argued that societal forces and structures could cause family dysfunction. In addition, he observed that some societal institutions benefit at the expense of other systems, such as the family. Furthermore, he observed that the same system could be both functional and dysfunctional at the same time, depending on the area of focus. This school of thought is consistent with social work activism and reform. Social workers target the environment for social change and its institutions for reform (including those institutions that deliver family and child welfare services). According to this line of reasoning, society creates conditions that lead to dysfunctional family arrangements. These conditions are capitalism (labor based on slavery, migrant workers, immigrant workers), power relationships (class, race, and gender dominance), competition, and a philosophy of government that values minimal interference in family matters.

■ The Family as an Economic Unit

In contrast to the psychological depiction of family dynamics in chapter 14, sociologists hold that socioeconomic factors dictate how members of a family relate to one another. From this perspective, the family is perceived to be closely related to the economic structure of a society. Economics (not transactional patterns) either helps or disrupts family structure. Due to *social stratification*, families are embedded in racial and class hierarchies. Consequently, families have different access to resources that support families. Middle- and upper-middle-class families are privileged through access to medical coverage, expense accounts, and credit lines. Their occupational roles tend to be highly valued. In contrast, working-class households lack such supports but increase their access to resources (strengths perspective) by pooling with others in the larger family network. America's economic system is not always congruent with values that support the family. Businesses with generous parental-leave policies are in the minority. The Family and Medical Leave Act of 1993 applies only to companies with 50 or more employees. The United States does not have a comprehensive child and family support policy.

Family and Child Welfare

Poverty Statistics

According to the Child Welfare League of America's National Fact Sheet of 2004 (retrieved July 2005), 16% (12 million) of the children in the United States live in poverty ($14,600 annual income for a family of three). The U.S. child poverty rate is as much as two to three times higher than that of most other major Western industrialized nations. Seven percent of all children (5 million) live in extreme poverty (families with annual incomes of $8,980 for a family of four, which is 50% below the poverty line). Another 37% (27 million) of American children live in near-poor, low-income families. In 1998, 42% of poor children had a working parent.

Causal Hypotheses of Poverty

Sociologically, the family is regarded as a primary economic unit. As such, the family is charged with the responsibility of meeting the basic needs of its members for security, food, shelter, and clothing. Poverty is an outcome of personal tragedy (death, disability) and old age. Poverty is also an outcome of social factors, such as discrimination and oppression that lead to unequal access to opportunities and to workplace exploitation. Poverty is due to flawed economic systems. Both capitalism and communism produce poverty: capitalism because it leads to the unequal distribution of resources and communism because it leads to economic stagnation.

Solutions

Social Security Insurance Programs

Social programs designed to assure the economic stability of families fall into two categories: (1) those designed to prevent poverty through the provision of Social Security insurance to workers and their dependents, and (2) Social Security public assistance to those who lack a work history or who do not earn a living wage. Social welfare policies and programs are methods of responding to poverty. The purpose of social insurance is to help all workers insure themselves and their dependents against the loss of income (resulting in poverty) which may be caused by the death of the primary wage earner or the disability, old age, or unemployment of the primary worker (DiNitto, 1991).

Social Security insurance programs are financed through premiums paid by both workers and employers and are administered by the federal government. Passed in 1935, the Social Security Act has been amended numerous times. Today, it includes a number of insurance programs, including Old Age, Survivors, and Disability Insurance and Medicare (1965). Such benefits are universal (all workers) and have no stigma attached to their receipt. Currently, there are efforts by the George W. Bush administration to privatize Social Security insurance programs. According to some, universal entitlement programs and private company retirement plans are becoming fiscally insolvent as the baby boom generation reaches old age.

In contrast, Social Security public assistance programs are designed to mediate poverty among those who have no work history or who do not earn a living wage (working poor). Public assistance is funded by general tax revenues. It includes several programs, including Temporary Assistance to Needy Families (TANF), Title I of the PRWORA Act (1996; P.L. 104-193), Supplemental Security Income (Social Security amendments of 1972, P.L. 92-603, amended several times), and Medicaid (Social Security amendments of 1965, amended numerous times since). Public assistance is financed conjointly by federal and state funds and is administered at the state level by departments of health and human services. Public assistance programs are needs-based, means-tested programs. The Personal Responsibility and Work Opportunity Reconciliation Act of 1996 and the Balanced Budget Act of 1997 have modified the conditions of receipt. The intent of both Social Security insurance and public assistance is to assure (through the provision of economic resources) that the primary caretaker of children is available for the task of child rearing.

Public Assistance to Welfare Reform

Children are served when they do not live in poverty. Aid for Dependent Children (ADC) and Aid to Families With Dependent Children (AFDC) are part of the Social Security Act of 1935 and were created to provide assistance to children by providing cash aid to their mothers (on behalf of the child). AFDC was funded using a joint federal-state formula. In the 1950s, the program expanded (more cash assistance) to include eligibility for the caretaker (mother) in addition to the child. However, only households without a father were eligible. (This led to the policing period of social work practice.) Legislation providing medical care for poor families with children was included in the 1960s and ultimately became part of the Medicaid program. Between 1956 and 1967, the federal government funded social services to rehabilitate those who were receiving public assistance in an effort to eliminate the need for public assistance. In 1967, Congress officially severed social services from cash assistance programs.

The PRWORA (otherwise known as welfare reform) brought sweeping changes to AFDC. Welfare reform eliminated poor families' federal entitlement to public assistance. States now administer programs referred to as Temporary Assistance for Needy Families, which are funded by federal block grants and state revenues. Under a philosophy of welfare to work, TANF imposes strict work registration, employment, training requirements, and time limits. To "strengthen" families, TANF encourages the establishment of paternity and aggressively enforces child support obligations. Benefits to pregnant teens, teen parents, and legal aliens are limited. TANF is a needs-based, means-tested program of cash assistance operated by state departments of health and human services, territories, and tribes. When applicants apply for TANF, they also usually apply for Medicaid and food stamps (Food Stamp Act, 1974; P.L. 93-86; current reauthorization under Farm Bill of 2002).

According to the Child Welfare League of America (CWLA) Fact Sheet of 2004, 2 million families were receiving TANF, a decline of 3.6% from the previous year. Between 1996 (welfare reform enacted) and 2001, the number of families receiving welfare assistance decreased by 52%.

Approximately 5 million people (half of them children) are removed annually from poverty as a result of the earned income tax credit (Revenue Act of 1978; P.L. 95-600). The earned income tax credit is a refundable tax credit designed to support the working poor. The EITC has been expanded three times since the early 1980s. Working families with two or more children can receive an EITC of up to $3,888 (Sweeny et al., 2000). The EITC is received through the federal income tax system. One does not have to owe federal taxes to apply. It assures minimum-wage workers who work full time an income above the poverty level without the need to obtain food stamps (Wilson, 1996). Eleven states have developed state earned income tax credits to complement the federal EITC (Sweeny et al., 2000). Many nonprofit agencies offer tax services to the working poor to assist them in claiming their EITC. This is perhaps the most effective income enhancement strategy for low-wage workers.

Major Food Programs

In 1999, nearly 1 of every 25 children and 1 of 9 poor children (11.8%) lived in households where adults had difficulty securing food and where at least one adult and sometimes children experienced moderate or severe hunger. In 2001, 2.3 million Americans received emergency hunger relief. From 2002 to 2003, requests for food assistance for families with children increased 18% in 25 major U.S. cities. One-fourth of these requests went unmet. In 2003, the national school lunch program provided lunches to more than 28 million children (CWLA National Fact Sheet, 2004).

Social welfare policies provide the following programs to combat hunger: (1) food stamp provisions, (2) school breakfast programs, (3) summer food service, (4) supplemental nutrition program for women, infants, and children, (5) special milk program for children, (6) national school lunch program, and (7) homeless children's nutrition program.

Need for Housing

According to the CWLA Fact Sheet (2004), an estimated 2.3 million people experience homelessness at some point each year, including more than 1 million children. Children comprise 25% of the overall homeless population. Sixty percent of homeless children are between birth and age 8. In 2003, families with children accounted for 40% of the overall homeless population in 25 major U.S. cities. Requests for emergency shelter for homeless families with children increased 15% in these same cities in 2003. More than one-third of the requests went unmet. Almost 75% of poor households spend more than 30% of their income on rent and utilities. The number of affordable housing units (defined as housing where families pay less than 30% of their income) has been declining since 1991.

Evidence: Is Work the Solution to Poverty? Evaluating TANF Outcomes

PRWORA is a policy-based (legislated) program (TANF) administered by social workers on state (DHS) and local (agency) levels. It is implemented through face-to-face direct contact by social work practitioners on the frontline. Policy makers, program administrators, and frontline practitioners all play a role in TANF programs.

Is TANF a program that reduces poverty? To answer this question, Anderson and Gryzlak (2002) did a secondary data analysis (N = 12 studies) of TANF-leaver studies from 12 states with large caseloads. To be included, studies had to have used random sampling techniques. Anderson and Gryzlak (2002) report that state studies typically found employment levels among TANF leavers in the 55–65% range but average earnings fell below the poverty level. Those who did remain employed could expect earnings growth, however, job instability proved to be a significant barrier and contributed to a return to TANF at a rate of 21–35% within the first year. The study found that available support services (Medicaid, food stamps, and childcare subsidies) were underutilized primarily because TANF leavers did not understand that they were eligible for such services. These findings are consistent with earlier findings by Loprest (1999), cross-state findings (Acs & Loprest, 2001; Brauner & Loprest, 1999; Parrott, 1998; Tweedie, Reichert, & O'Connor, 1999; U.S. General Accounting Office, 1999), and findings reported by the National Survey of America's Families. Anderson and Gryzlak suggest that the PRWORA was more effective in reducing welfare caseloads than it was in reducing poverty.

■ What Is the Nature of the Worker-Client Relationship in Family Welfare?

The desired end goal of the redistribution of resources through social policies and programs is a just and humane society. As distributors of social resources, social workers meet humanitarian needs. In doing so, they also regulate access to benefits and ensure regulatory compliance (social control). When working with impoverished individuals and families, the nature of the worker-client relationship is one of alliance to match needs with resources and one of social control (regulation of family functions and access to resources).

■ Family Violence

Scope

Individuals are more likely to be killed, physically assaulted, sexually victimized, hit, beat up, slapped, or spanked in their own homes by other family members than by anyone else in our society. Roberts and Roberts (2005) estimate that 1,400 women are abused every day in the United States. Between 3 million and 10 million children witness some form of violence in the home each year. In 2001, an estimated 903,000 children were victims of abuse and neglect (National Family Preservation Network, 2003).

Definition: Child Maltreatment

Child maltreatment is defined as a heterogeneous group of acts (of commission and omission) that place children at risk. There are four main types of child maltreatment: (1) physical abuse, (2) child neglect, (3) sexual abuse, and (4) emotional abuse. *Physical abuse* is the infliction of physical injury by various methods, even if the perpetrator does not intend harm. *Child neglect* is the failure to provide for the child's basic physical, educational, medical, or emotional needs. *Sexual abuse* is the involvement of a child in any kind of sexual action, including incest, sexual molestation by a family member, prostitution, or pornography. *Emotional abuse* is an act or omission that has caused or could cause serious behavioral, cognitive, emotional, or mental disorders. Current definitions of emotional abuse include exposure to domestic violence.

From Personal Problem to Public Issue

The federal government established the Children's Bureau in 1912. It was concerned with a broad range of child welfare issues that included child labor, delinquency, and orphaned children. Under the Social Security Act of 1935, Title V directed the bureau to cooperate with states to develop child welfare services. The enactment of the Social Security Act included limited funds for child welfare services under Title V.

Battered child syndrome emerged as a public issue in the 1960s. John Caffey, a pediatric radiologist, was the first to identify child abuse as a social problem. Between 1962 and 1965, every state passed legislation prohibiting child abuse. In 1967, child welfare funding under Title V became Title IVB, Child Welfare Services. The Child Abuse Prevention and Treatment Act (CAPTA) was enacted in 1974. It is the only federal legislation exclusively dedicated to the prevention, assessment, identification, and treatment of child abuse and neglect. It was reauthorized in 2003 as the Keeping Children and Families Safe Act, P.L. 108-36. Laws mandating reports of suspected child abuse were enacted in every state during the 1970s. This led to an enormous increase in the number of children in foster care.

To counter foster care drift, the Adoption Assistance and Child Welfare Amendments of 1980, P.L. 96-272, mandated permanency planning within a reasonable time. States were charged with monitoring cases, including reviewing them every 6 months. In 1985, Title IVE was amended to include a new independent living program to assist youth who age out of the foster care system (CWLA, Timeline of Major Child Welfare Legislation, retrieved 2005).

Service Delivery

Three major pieces of legislation have guided child welfare services delivery at the turn of the 21st century (CWLA, 2004). These are (1) Title IVB, amended to create a new Family Preservation and Family Support Program, 1993; (2) the Multiethnic

Placement Act of 1994, amended 1996; and (3) the Adoption and Safe Family Act, 1997. Contemporary child protective services reflect competing demands: protection of the child and family preservation (Reed & Kirk, 1998; Schuerman, Rzepnicki, & Littell, 1994). Passage of Title IVB, in 1993, created the Family Preservation and Family Support Program. Since then, child welfare practices have been guided by three principles: (1) permanency planning (in 1997, the Adoption and Safe Family Act created timelines for moving children to permanency), (2) reasonable efforts (Adoption Assistance and Child Welfare Act of 1980, P.L. 96-272, which requires states to show that reasonable alternatives to placement have been tried or considered and which requires a judicial certification of reasonable efforts to accompany a court order for substitute care), and (3) the least restrictive alternative (usually tied to family reunification on the premise that government interference should occur only insofar as necessary to ensure safety). Critics of Title IVB charge that the policy contains conflicting premises at the operational level: family preservation and the child's best interest.

Concerns for the preservation of racial and ethnic identity led to the passage of the 1994 Multiethnic Placement Act (MEPA). This act required consideration of race and ethnicity in placement decisions. The act supported efforts to recruit and expand the racial and ethnic diversity of the foster parent and adoptive parent pool. In 1996, MEPA was amended by the Interethnic Adoption Provisions, and language specifically permitting the consideration of race in placement decisions was deleted.

Mandatory Reporting

Scope

Knoke and Trocme (2005) note that the inclusion of exposure to domestic violence as a category of child emotional abuse contributed to an enormous increase in reports of child abuse and neglect. Between 1981 and 1991, the number of reported cases increased 133% in Canada. Following mandatory reporting of child abuse in the 1970s, the number of children in foster care homes and institutions increased. According to the Urban Institute, the cost of out-of-home care was estimated to be at least $9.1 billion in fiscal year (FY) 2000.

During the early 1970s (1970–1974), there were approximately 250,000 child abuse reports annually. In fiscal year 2000, there were 2 million reports of suspected child abuse and neglect, representing 2.7 million children. Of this number, 879,000 were found to be victims of maltreatment. There were 1,200 child fatalities that year (CWLA Fact Sheet, 2004). Increased caseloads, increasingly severe cases of abuse and neglect, and insufficient resources placed demands on social work administrators to find ways to manage the services demand and to allocate limited resources effectively (Brown & Bailey-Etta, 1997). Child abuse rates are similar in Canada, England, and Australia (Trocme et al., 2001).

Conceptual Quagmires: Defining Harm

According to Gelles and Straus (1987), although physical force against children is prevalent in the United States, acts (beatings, use of weapons) that have a high probability of resulting in severe physical harm requiring medical treatment occur at much lower frequencies than milder forms of abuse. Severe physical harm occurs in a minority of maltreated children (Zuravin, Orme, & Heger, 1995).

Most cases investigated for child maltreatment involve no physical harm or minimal harm. Knoke and Trocme (2005) define *minimal harm* as a bruise, scratch, or sprain but no need for medical treatment. In a study conducted by Trocme, MacMillan, Fallon, and DeMarco (2003), some form of physical injury occurred in 28% of the total number of reported cases and severe physical harm in 4% of the cases.

Among cases resulting in severe physical harm, shaken baby syndrome accounts for the highest rate of harm. In 75% of the reports for shaken baby syndrome, the baby suffered some harm while 50% suffered severe harm. In contrast, of those cases reported for inappropriate punishment, 63% resulted in no harm and 3% resulted in harm.

Some critics charge that harm is too narrowly defined as physical injury requiring medical attention and does not take into account the psychological harm associated with living in an environment where one is repeatedly physically assaulted even though such assaults do not require medical attention. Nor do such definitions of harm take into account verbal assaults that leave no visible scars.

On the other hand, others observe that many children and families are unnecessarily subjected to investigative intrusions that result in unsubstantiated reports (in FY 2000, approximately 1.8 million reports were unsubstantiated). Where maltreatment has been substantiated, often there is no severe physical harm. Should families be separated under such circumstances?

Assessing Safety and Risk

In protective services, assessment must begin with an assessment of safety (step 1: fiduciary responsibility: duty to protect). If a child is perceived as being in imminent danger, the child will be temporarily removed pending further assessment of the situation. Because not all reported cases of neglect and abuse pose an imminent danger to the child, practitioners may choose to work intensively with the family (family preservation) or work with the family through the provision of traditional casework services (a combination of foster care, family reunification, or adoption). Two principles guide decision making: safety and least restrictive environment. Family preservation holds that intensive services can deescalate a family crisis that has precipitated referral to protective services. Family preservation is designed to prevent out-of-home placements. Traditional child welfare casework service removes the child until the crisis (imminent danger) is resolved.

The literature distinguishes between safety assessments (imminent danger) and risk assessments (potential for reabuse). The kind of information collected in a safety assessment is more narrowly focused than the kind of information gathered in a comprehensive child and family assessment, where broader aspects of child and family well-being are considered. Safety and risk assessments are intended to categorize families on the basis of their likelihood of future maltreatment in order to assist agencies in targeting the most extensive services to children with the highest risk (English & Pecora, 1994). Safety assessments provide an index of the extent to which an acute family crisis places the child at significant risk for harm (imminent danger). In contrast, risk assessments facilitate clinical decision making about the interventions required to avert future crises of neglect and abuse (Knoke & Trocme, 2005). Safety assessments involve decisions in the short term while risk assessments involve decisions in the long term.

According to Knoke and Trocme (2005), accuracy in assessing risk is crucial to ensure that appropriate intervention is provided. Two types of instruments are used as tools in documenting risk and making decisions about the type and intensity of services required. Structured risk assessment tools are actuarial instruments that incorporate client characteristics shown to be statistically predictive of future maltreatment (Rycus & Hughes, 2003). Knoke and Trocme note that each risk factor is weighted in terms of its overall risk rating as determined by a formula designed to maximize the predictive accuracy of the instrument. Such an instrument is FRAAN (the Michigan Structured Decision Making Systems: Family Risk Assessment of Abuse and Neglect).

The other type of instrument is based on consensus. Such instruments use expert clinical judgment to determine which client characteristics are predictive of harm. Both case files and case vignettes have been used with expert panels to arrive at items. Knoke and Trocme observe that many of the consensus-based instruments are "blended" instruments, using items that are both actuarial and consensus based. Consensus instruments are the Washington Risk Assessment Matrix and the California Family Assessment Factor Analysis (CFAFA).

The initial determination of safety and risk, upon which decisions are made to utilize either foster care or family preservation services, is itself fraught with difficulties. Several factors complicate the decision-making process in services provision. In a majority of substantiated cases of neglect and abuse, there is no physical harm or there is only minor (bruise) harm. Yet in 4% of the substantiated cases, the harm is severe. One cannot accurately predict which substantiated cases of child neglect or abuse will result in severe harm or death. In FY 2003, there were 1,500 child fatalities. It is also important to try to understand reentries to protective services. Is a reentry indicative of a new problem/crisis or indicative of chronic/untreated problems? In addition to values preferences and ideological philosophy, treatment decisions are circumscribed by the state of the art.

■   Child Protective Services Programs

Foster Care

Definition

Foster care is defined as 24-hour substitute care for children outside their own homes. Foster care settings include but are not limited to family foster homes, relative foster homes (whether payments are being made or not), group homes, emergency shelters, residential facilities, childcare institutions, and preadoptive homes.

Scope

There were an estimated 542,000 children in foster care in the United States as of September 30, 2001. Of this number, 260,000 were in nonrelative foster care. Children who entered foster care in FY 2001 numbered 290,000. More than 263,000 children exited foster care in that same year. When compared with previous data, foster care entries have remained stable while exits increased slightly and children in care at a given point of time decreased slightly (CWLA, 2004).

Approximately 12% of homeless children are placed in the foster care system (CWLA, 2004). An estimated 57% of the children in foster care in 2001 were reunited with their parents or principal caretakers after an average stay in out-of-home care of 11.7 months. The average length of stay for all children exiting foster care that year was 22.1 months. The average age of a child in foster care was 10 years. The average length of time in foster care for all children was 33 months.

Safety and Stability

Proponents of traditional protective services argue that children are safer in foster homes than they are in their parental homes. Abuse does occur in foster care, for example, in FY 2001, 0.5% of the perpetrators of abuse or neglect were foster parents. This percentage represented 5,133 instances of abuse and neglect in 2001. There were 8 child fatalities in FY 2001 attributed to foster parents. In comparison, studies in FY 2003 found that 10.7% of child fatalities (175 cases) had received family preservation services in the last 5 years, and 2.8% of the children had been reunified with their families in the past 5 years. While studies indicate that family preservation programs reduce the number of out-of-home placements, it is less clear that family preservation programs prevent reabuse. By design, such programs are short term and crisis oriented. Practitioners need to be aware of the short-term (prevention of outplacement) and long-term (reabuse) effects of family preservation programs.

Proponents of traditional service provisions claim that there is little evidence to suggest that children in stable foster care fare worse than those left in their own homes. Critics charge that children in foster care often experience multiple place-ments and lengthy stays. This affects the child's long-term emotional, cognitive, and social development. Critics charge that the quality of foster homes can be poor, average, or good. Foster homes can be approved after inadequate investiga-tion or can be inadequately supervised after they are selected. There is a large lit-erature on foster care drift (Bagdasaryan, 2005).

Adoption

Returning home was not an option for approximately 126,000 children (18% of those) in the foster care system, who were free for adoption in 2001. More than half of these children are children of color. Of those who were adopted, 67% were adopted by strangers and 23% by relatives. Another 10% (26,084 children) went to live with relatives though they were not adopted. For adoption to occur, parents must surrender their rights to the child or have their rights legally terminated.

Family Reunification

The Adoption Assistance and Child Welfare Act of 1980 (P.L. 96-272) requires states to show that reasonable alternatives to placement have been tried or consid-ered. A judicial certification of reasonable efforts must accompany a court order for substitute care. As an offshoot of the family preservation philosophy to keep families together, every state is required to make reasonable efforts to reunify chil-dren with their kin. Data show that about one-quarter of the children who are re-unified with their family return to care after 2 years (Bagdasaryan, 2005).

Family Preservation and Family Support Services

Family preservation services are triggered when a family has a member who is at risk of outplacement due to abuse, neglect, delinquency, or need for in-patient care due to mental illness. Outplacement is viewed as the option of last resort (Everett, Chipungu, & Leashore, 1991).

Enacting Legislation

Evidence that children were "adrift" in foster care with no plans for exiting the system served as the catalyst for the enactment of the Adoption Assistance and Child Welfare Act of 1980 (AACWA, P.L. 96-272). The primary objective of the AACWA was to mandate that families at risk of having their children placed in foster care be kept intact whenever safe and appropriate (without risk of injury to the children). The legislation states that "reasonable efforts" be made by child welfare agencies "to prevent the removal of a child from his or her home and make it possible for a child to return home."

According to the legislation, children are to be kept in their homes whenever it is safe to do so. Social workers are charged with addressing the problems that led to a family's referral to protective services. In the years that followed passage of the AACWA, more than 30 states and numerous counties implemented programs that provided family preservation services. In FY 2000, family preservation programs served 314,766 children. For more on reunification programs, see Leashore, McMurray, and Bailey (1991).

Description of Family Preservation Services

Family preservation services were developed to prevent the unnecessary placement of children in foster care. Family preservation programs were initially modeled after Homebuilders (Kinney, Haapala, & Booth, 1991). Services criteria include (1) acceptance of families who have been referred because they are at imminent risk of having a child removed, (2) services delivery in the families' homes, (3) initial response to request for service within 24 hours, (4) services are intense (5–20 hours per week), (5) caseloads are small (6–8 families), (6) service is short (4–6 weeks), (7) scheduling is flexible (24/7 availability), and (8) a blend of "hard" (auxiliary funds) and "soft" (mental health counseling) services is offered. The primary objectives of the program are to prevent out-of-home placements; to keep the child, family, and worker safe; and to improve the skills of family members so they can handle problems that arise.

Intended to be a model to help families with acute (crisis) problems, family preservation has been altered for use with families with more chronic problems. The length of service in some models extends to several months (3, 6, or 12), and programs provide different types of services. Services provision can include crisis intervention, auxiliary funding, parenting skills training, in-home emergency caretakers, child care, housing, transportation, teaching/demonstrations, worker visits, in-home counseling of individuals and the family, referral for group counseling, substance abuse treatment, and mental health treatment.

Kinship Care

Kinship care (permanent placement with the option to have contact with the biological parents) is a form of foster care with relatives (kinship adoption is not an economic alternative for many). According to the evidence, kinship care results in fewer placement moves for children in foster care and greater retention of children's ties to their families during and following foster care (Usher, Randolph, & Gogan, 1999). Evaluation of kinship care has indicated a reduction in reliance on out-of-home care, fewer placement moves, and lower rates of reentry to care (Usher, Gibbs, Wildfire, & Gogan, 1997). Kinship care accounts for approximately 50% of all foster care placements. Many believe that relative care meets the least restrictive and permanency principles.

Family Collaboratives

Family collaboratives work with protective services but adopt principles that are more in line with the service provisions and philosophy of family preservation. Family collaboratives are usually located within public housing communities. The community context brings to bear principles of community practice. Consistent with postmodernism, the worker is positioned as part of the associational fabric of the community, thereby challenging bureaucratic understandings of the worker as other. The family collaborative becomes the village it takes to raise a child. Collaborative family services are not time limited but may be constrained by funding. Family collaboratives seek and operate on a variety of grants.

■ The Worker-Family Relationship in Protective Services

Services, Not Therapy

Therapy is not the function of child welfare services (Hartmann and Laird, 1983). What, then, guides the direct face-to-face contact between the provider and recipients of protective services? In their capacity as agents of the state, social workers have historically relied on casework or case management in protective services. Now such services are conducted within the context of the principles of family preservation. Both a strengths perspective and a postmodern perspective inform the face-to-face contact between the worker and the family in child protective services. In contrast to earlier perspectives, postmodern philosophy nurtures sensitivity to the marginalization of disempowered and at-risk populations.

Postmodern Principles

Ungar (2004) writes, "[S]ocial workers interested in postmodernism have been provided an abundance of principles but little to guide them in direct practice" (p. 488). Practitioners in protective services, corrections, welfare, and mental health work on the frontlines of services delivery within the mandates of the profession and the employing agency. Such mandates, however, conflict with postmodern philosophy and values which task the worker with the deconstruction of his/her privileged (status) position. For elaboration, see the discussion in chapter 10 on the worker-client relationship in case management.

Strengths-Based Model

Both traditional models and strengths-based perspectives attempt to reduce the problems for which the client seeks or is mandated for help. Critics charge that traditional methods of clinical social work practice have led to a "deficit" literature, which has disproportionately disadvantaged marginalized populations. Individual and family pathology have been overemphasized at the expense of individual and family strengths. To counter this, advocates of the strengths perspective focus on how individuals and families cope in the face of adversity. They seek to identify individual and/or family strengths in order to build on these strengths as a way to reduce problems. Here, the emphasis is on resilience rather than pathology. Advocates of the strengths perspective have two agendas: (1) to develop an empirical literature on resilience and strengths to counter the literature on vulnerability and deficits, and (2) to develop an applied model of practice based on individual and family strengths.

Moore, Chalk, Scarpa, and Vandivere (2002) define *family strengths* as the set of relationships and processes that support and protect families and family members, especially during times of adversity and change." Early and GlenMaye (2000) note that few authors have applied the strengths perspective to practice with families. The practice (applied) literature on family strengths is small (e.g., de Shazar, 1995; Dunst, Trivette, & Deal, 1994; Ronnau & Poertner, 1993; Werrbach, 1996). In contrast, the literature on family preservation is quite large and highly empirical.

Critics charge that a strengths perspective, like other clinical perspectives, sustains the social order and the status quo. It does not address the root causes of family violence. Second, critics charge that a strengths perspective gives formal services a pass when such services are inadequate or fail to meet demand. Individuals and families are encouraged to rely on their own resources. Scarcity is not a myth, as some proponents of this perspective would hold, but rather is an objective reality and is often a root cause of a family's need for help.

Therapy: DSM-IVR

Therapy may be a co-occurring method of choice for children who have been abused and neglected and for the perpetrator of the abuse. The DSM-IVR contains appropriate V Code classifications for such treatment (e.g., V.61.21 for a perpetrator of physical abuse, sexual abuse, or neglect of a child; V.995.5 if the focus is on the victim). Children may benefit from a therapeutic alliance informed by theory-based therapeutic processes designed to address loss and trauma. They may benefit from narrative therapies and strengths-based models that prevent internalization of victimization. They may benefit from ego-supportive techniques that provide psychoeducation and skills training as they grow and develop. Children who are abused and neglected may experience difficulties secondary to the abuse and neglect related to the care system (repeated placements, educational disruption, inconsistencies, etc.).

EXHIBIT 15.1   *Decision Schema: Family Protective Services*

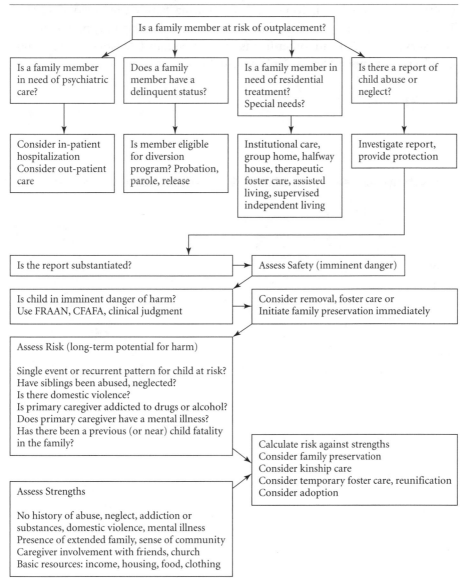

■ Evidence: Is One Program Better Than Another?

Most descriptive reports and other nonexperimental research cite the effectiveness of family preservation services in keeping families together. Prevention rates for out-of-home placements as high as 97% have been reported (Bagdasaryan, 2005). Findings from experimental and quasi-experimental studies, however, are more mixed. Studies by Festinger (1996), Lindsey (1994), and Stovall and Dozier (1998) documented high reentry rates following family preservation services. There is a greater number of child fatalities associated with family preservation as an intervention than with other forms of interventions (statistics from FY 2003, Children's Bureau Fact Sheet, Table 4–7, 2005).

16
Use of Groups in Clinical
Social Work Practice

■ Group Work as a Method

Value-Added Skills

Steps 5, 6, and 7 of the decision tree guide the practitioner in the choice of an appropriate social work method based on the facts of the case at hand. When using group work as a method (step 7) of intervention, whether in clinical practice (this chapter) or in policy, advocacy, community, and management practice (chapter 17), the practitioner must acquire additional (value-added) skills associated with the method itself. In addition, competent group work practice requires learning two distinct skill sets, one for the use of group method in clinical practice and another for its application in policy, advocacy, community, and management practice. The two-chapter format on group methods differentiates and teaches the two skill sets. Several authors (Bion, 1961; Foulkes, 1964; Knopka, 1963; Nitsun, 1996; Gummer, 1990) observe that there is a universal ambivalence toward groups, whether in clinical or nonclinical settings (communities and organizations), because constructive and destructive forces coexist in any form of group life.

The Paradox of Groups

The group as an entity is inherently paradoxical. According to Smith and Berg (1988), it is impossible to have any kind of group without the occurrence of contradictory processes, such as individuality and belonging, attachment and alienation, progress and regression. Certain types of tension are inevitable in groups, e.g., competition, rivalry, envy, dominance, submission, criticism, rejection, group pressure, scapegoating, and hostility. According to Nitsun (1996), the paradox of group life deepens when groups are used as a method of therapy. Though most analytic group therapists perceive groups optimistically for their potential to alleviate problems and to bring about healing (Foulkes, 1964), groups can also become pathological, mobilizing aggressive and destructive forces (Bion, 1961; Nitsun, 1996). According to Bion, neurotic and psychotic conditions are in essence group disruptive. The paradox of group life generally is exaggerated by the psychotherapy group and specifically by the conditions that members bring to the group. In contrast to the hypothesis that disturbed individuals cause group pathology, Knopka and Nitsun hold that groups possess destructive power even when they are composed of healthy, rational, well-meaning individuals. Otherwise good people harm other good people when the destructive forces of group life are not properly managed.

Aggregations, Natural Groups, and Formed Groups

A group differs from an aggregation. An *aggregation* refers to a gathering of people in time and place who have no intent of forming or maintaining an affiliation, e.g., a gathering of individuals waiting at a bus stop or those gathered to attend a movie. A group may be natural or formed. A natural group is referred to as a primary group (Homans, 1950). A *natural group* comes together spontaneously on the basis of naturally occurring events, interpersonal attraction, or the mutually perceived needs of its members. The family is the primary natural group, followed by friendship and neighborhood groups. In contrast, a *formed group* comes together through some outside influence or intervention. A formed group usually has some sponsorship (Boy/Girl Scouts, agency auspice) and is convened for a particular purpose. A formed group implies a professionally trained leader though there are formed self-help groups without professionally trained leaders, such as Alcoholics Anonymous. Social work practitioners work clinically with both formed and naturally occurring groups.

■ History of Clinical Social Work With Groups

Multidisciplinary Roots

Clinical group work has its roots in disciplines such as psychology, sociology, education, and recreation (Greene & Ephross, 1991). Not unlike the history of social work itself, the history of social group work entails commitment to two goals: individual change and social change. When focused on individual change, groups are referred to as clinical groups. *Clinical groups* are used to instill conformity to social norms, to boost resiliency in the face of a harsh or discriminatory social reality, to provide a sense of connectedness and belonging, and to bring healing to those who suffer emotional pain.

Unique Aspects of Group Work

Clinical group work takes from the early settlement house movement the use of programmed activities and skills training. Such programs act as a medium through which group members socialize and improve their lives. Group work takes from recreation the pursuit of leisure activities to encourage the constructive use of time and to create a sense of community. It takes from progressive education the use of small groups to solve shared problems and to foster mutual aid. Group work borrows psychodynamic concepts from the mental hygiene and child guidance movements to promote health (prevention and early intervention) and to bring healing to those who suffer from emotional pain (tertiary intervention). Foulkes, a psychoanalyst, is credited with fathering the group analytic method. Residential-living and treatment facilities (Maier, 1965) have traditionally relied on the use of groups to foster a therapeutic milieu.

Professionalization

Grace Coyle (1948) is credited with establishing group work as a method within the profession of social work. The National Association for the Study of Group Work (NASGW) was formed in 1936 and began publishing the journal *The Group in Education, Recreation, Social Work* in 1939. The NASGW was later transformed into the American Association of Group Workers (AAGW), which merged, along with other specializations, to form the National Association of Social Workers (NASW) in 1955. The Association for the Advancement of Social Work Practice with Groups was formed in 1979 with the goal of revitalizing group work within social work. It is active to the present day.

Encounter Groups

During the 1970s, *encounter groups* promoted intensive interactions to increase self-awareness and to improve interpersonal relations. Members were encouraged to be completely honest and open, reacting to each other with their immediate feelings and exploring a full range of emotions. Those encounter groups that were not professionally led (and some that were) resulted in harmful confrontations and/or emotional commitments. Encounter groups exacerbated the existing general mistrust of groups among the public and caused backlash over their use in clinical practice.

Residential-Living Groups

Agencies that serve highly vulnerable client populations have always relied on groups to deliver services. Managing group life in a residential setting (group home, halfway house, in-patient or residential treatment center, juvenile correctional facility, or jail) is referred to in the literature as creating a *therapeutic milieu*. As part of a therapeutic milieu, a variety of groups are used as mediums of recreation and sport, athletic and health training, psychoeducation, and self-expression (dance, music, bibliotherapy, and art). Such groups are therapeutic but are not considered to be therapy in the group analytic sense.

As part of quality assurance, managed care now monitors the client's right to effective treatment. Therefore, administrators must be able to document that clients are receiving treatment. Because groups are perceived to be a cost-effective method of delivering services, residential facilities often rely on groups. Critics charge that groups in such settings are often neither therapeutic nor therapy but rather aggregations, i.e., individuals gathered together on a particular day in a given facility. Those running such groups often lack training in group method and therefore in managing group dynamics. Because destructive and constructive forces coexist in any form of group life, it is critical that group leaders be trained in group methods.

Merger With the NASW: The Disappearance of Group Work

In her analysis of the history of group work, Andrews (2001) documents the turf war between group work and casework following group work's merger with the NASW. Though group work gained professional status through the merger, its significance as a method was overrun by the sheer number of caseworkers in the profession. Because of group work's tilt toward professionalization as a clinical model, its standing as a significant method of practice in policy, advocacy, community, and management practice was lost. Group work's significance as a method was further eroded with the move toward generalist practice. Though group work has waxed and waned within the profession, social work practice can neither be competent nor lead to best practices without group methods.

■ Group Work

In clinical social work practice, group is one choice among several method options (the others are individual and family). *Clinical group work* is defined as goal-directed activity with small groups aimed at meeting the social and emotional needs of individual members and the group as a whole. Its purpose is to promote, enhance, or restore individual mental health and/or social functioning. The two purposes (mental health and social functioning) are not mutually exclusive. The distinction is important, however, in delineating the theory-based therapeutic process to be followed. Not all clinical group work is group psychotherapy, but all clinical group work serves therapeutic goals.

EXHIBIT 16.1   *Typology: Use of Groups in Social Work Clinical Practice*

Northern	Toseland and Rivas
Reciprocal	Support
Remedial	Education
Rehabilitation	Growth
Social goals*	Socialization
	Therapy

*Social goals "fits" better in the use of groups for policy, advocacy, management, and community practice. It is not a good fit for clinical practice. Early typologies mixed clinical goals and social goals.

Typology of Clinical Groups

Several typologies on the use of groups in social work practice have been proposed. Exhibit 16.1 reflects the two most common typologies found in the social work literature (Northern, 1982; Toseland & Rivas, 2001).

Some typologies (e.g., Northern, 1982) contain mixed goal categories (i.e., clinical and social goals). Others (e.g., Toseland & Rivas, 2001) present separate typologies, one for clinical goals, another for administrative goals, and a third for community goals. Within clinical social work, it is helpful to distinguish psychotherapy groups from therapeutic groups because the theories that inform the interventions differ for the two types of groups.

EXHIBIT 16.2   *Use of Groups in Clinical Practice*

Therapeutic Groups	*Psychotherapy Groups*
Recreation, fun, sports Skill acquisition: budgeting, cooking, car repair, sewing	ANALYTIC GROUPS Psychodrama, sociodrama
Play groups: development of interpersonal skills: taking turns, listening, sharing	Play therapy Psychoeducation Mutual aid Ego supportive
Enhancement of self: dance, poetry, drama, music	SOCIAL MICROCOSM Social identity Socialization to societal norms, law and order
Social milieu, residential	

Optimism and Caution

As the father of the analytic group, Foulkes is optimistic about the group's potential to bring about healing. Like Yalom (1995) and Shulman (1999), Foulkes believes in the curative properties of the group. His often-cited admonition is to
trust the group. Foulkes's belief in wholes is based on a philosophy of integration
and transformation. Foulkes's core psychotherapeutic position relies on the notion of coherence. *Coherence* is the meaningful organization of parts, which leads
to identity, integration, and unification. According to Nitsun, Foulkes emphasizes
the creative properties of groups at the expense of ignoring their destructive
properties.

In contrast to Foulkes's optimism is Nitsun's premise of the *anti-group*. Citing universal ambivalence toward the group, Nitsun identifies the following aspects of group life that cause anti-group sentiments: (1) The group is a collection
of strangers; (2) it is unstructured; (3) it is created by the members; (4) it is a
public arena; (5) it is a plural entity; (6) it is a complex experience; (7) it creates
interpersonal tension; (8) it is unpredictable; (9) it fluctuates in its progress; and
(10) it is an incomplete experience. Both optimism and caution are warranted in
the use of group methods in clinical practice.

Empirical Studies

Social scientists and research practitioners have conducted research (Bales, 1958;
Lippett, Watson, & Westely, 1958; Lewin, 1951; Hare, 1962; Cooley, 1909/1983; Le
Bon, 1895/2002; Whyte, 1943; Pines, 1982; Ephross & Vasil, 1988; Nitsun, 1996)
to determine how groups work. Studies have focused on (1) leaders-followers,
(2) in-group and out-group dynamics, (3) communication and interaction patterns, (4) the power of groups, and (5) the anti-group. The discussion on group
properties that follows elaborates on the findings of these studies.

■ Group Properties

Since groups vary so much in terms of size, form, content, context, duration, and
purpose, there is no single conception of "group" that holds true for all (Hargie
et al., 1991). Nonetheless, all group workers must take into account the following
group properties: (1) purpose, (2) size, (3) composition, (4) open or closed membership, (5) degree of desired cohesion, (6) group stages, (7) structure, (8) inter-
action/communication patterns, (9) curative factors, and (10) the anti-group.

Size

Size refers to the optimum number of members needed to form a group to accomplish purpose-driven goals. The ideal group size for achieving clinical goals is 5 to 10 members. This allows for absences and attrition. Considerable empirical research has been devoted to group size and its effect on goal achievement.

Composition

Group composition affects group dynamics and ultimately the effectiveness of the outcome. The practitioner must weigh the importance of homogeneity and heterogeneity on numerous composition variables. Does homogeneity or heterogeneity best serve the purpose of the group? Should the group be single gender or mixed gender? What ages should be grouped together? Should all members have the same problem to be worked (e.g., addictions), or should there be a mix of problem foci? Are there some problem foci that should not be mixed? What happens when you put 10 hyperactive children together in a group? Should groups contain those in different stages of well-being, or should all members be in the same state? What degree of difference should be introduced to produce the tension for change? How compatible or incompatible will members find each other? If the members perceive each other as too different or too similar, no work is likely to occur. The answers of course vary. Yalom, to use an example, composes his in-patient psychiatric agenda groups using the following criteria: heterogeneous on diagnoses; homogeneous on level of functioning, capacity for insight, attention span (1 hour), not being disruptive, able to talk.

Stranger composition is the sine qua non of the therapy group. Stranger anxiety is intensified in the group. Nitsun notes that the psychological challenges of belonging to a group may be greater than is commonly recognized. Group life often re-evokes and recreates feared interpersonal situations. Because the group is a public arena, members may feel that it lacks the essential requirements of containment and protection. Members fear breach of confidentiality and exposure to a wider community. Sentiments against the group make its composition difficult.

In composing a group, how shall a clinician handle racial, ethnic, religious, gender, or sexual orientation issues? According to Davis and Proctor (1989), individuals may act differently depending on the composition of the group. If the focus of the group is designed to explore sociodemographic differences, a diverse group composition may produce the tension necessary for change but may also produce subgroups that reinforce intolerance and block change. Though the literature differs in its response to these issues, group workers are held accountable in matters of group composition.

Open or Closed Membership

Whether or not group membership should be open (anyone welcome, at any time) or closed (no new members once formed) is related to the purpose of the group and the degree of cohesion sought. Analytic groups tend to be based on closed membership. Trust, which is necessary for self-disclosure, requires time to develop. Members must feel safe in groups and be assured that what is said will be respected and kept confidential. In contrast, a recreational group or a skills training group is likely not to be as affected if membership is open.

Cohesion

Cohesion is a variable that requires assessment. Sometimes, the goal of the group is to break down cohesion. When groups act cohesively to achieve unhealthy ends by excluding or harming others (Ku Klux Klan, Nazis, gangs), the group worker acts to break down the cohesion. On the other hand, where no camaraderie exists, the worker uses the group to foster a sense of group identity and belonging.

Group Stages

Every group and every session within a group passes through identifiable stages. Though naming them differently, several authors have identified common stages through which a group passes (see Exhibit 16.3). It is important that the worker recognize these stages and deal with them in order to facilitate the work of the group. Failure to recognize and work with group stages can lead to therapeutic errors and missteps.

It is widely agreed in the psychotherapy literature that the stage of the group's development strongly influences the dynamic processes in the analytic group. According to Nitsun, the beginning stage of group formation is likely to be characterized by mistrust. Members commonly express the following sentiments: the

EXHIBIT 16.3   *Group Stages*

Tuckman	Bion	Gans	Generic	Northern
Forming	Dependency	Early	Beginnings	Orientation, inclusion
Norming	Independence Fight-flight	Middle	Middles, work	Dissatisfaction, power conflict
Storming	Interdependence Pairing	Mature	Ends	Mutuality, work
Performing	Work	Termination		Intimacy, differentiation
Ending	Termination			Separation, termination

group is not good enough; it is directionless; it doesn't help; other members are liabilities, not assets; it is artificial; it feels unsafe; and there is too little time to work on individual problems. Members fear exclusion, attack, hostility, prejudice, shameful exposure, loss of control, and injury to self-esteem. Anxiety and hostility toward the therapy group is high during the beginning stage of its development.

During the middle stage, issues of dominance, power, and rivalry are uppermost. Members clash with each other during this stage. Hostility, anger, hurt, and defiance characterize this stage. The mature stage implies some resolution or reduction of destructive group tendencies. However, group development is complicated, and destructive forces can be triggered at any stage of group development.

Structure

Consistent with systems theory, group workers must be cognizant of group structure. The group system consists of the individual, the subgroups, and the group as a whole. Subgroups interfere with the development of the group as a therapeutic entity. Subgroups may come in pairs, triads, or foursomes. Subgroups (cliques) have boundaries and act to include or exclude others in the group. Internal leaders vie with each other and the group worker for influence over other members. Internal leaders may act to oppress or to empower other members. They may act to challenge the power of the worker, or they may act as a therapeutic ally of the worker. Leaders and followers are structural targets of therapeutic intervention.

A role structures interaction. Roles may interfere with the work of the group. Therefore, the group worker must be cognizant of and intervene when the roles played by members block the work of the group as a whole and prevent individual change. Shulman (1999, pp. 474–532) has identified and described the dynamics at work in several roles played by members in groups (see Exhibit 16.4). As structures, roles are targets of assessment and intervention.

In addition to working with such structural formations (leaders, subgroups, member roles), the worker also uses physical space, time, and activities to structure member interactions.

Communication/Interaction Patterns: Sociograms

Group cohesion develops as members establish and help each other to accept norms governing their communication and interaction patterns, e.g., is it safe to trust, to take risks, to be angry, to miss a session, to cry? Often, groups begin by using a maypole or round-robin pattern of communication where each member says something directed toward the group worker. As with family methods, group norms are explicit and implicit. *Explicit norms* may govern when (day and time), where (physical location), how frequently (once a week), for how long (1.5 hours), and for how many sessions the group will meet (e.g., 8–12 sessions or open-ended).

EXHIBIT 16.4   *Roles Played by Group Members (Shulman, 1999)*

Gatekeeper	Member acts in a manner to help the group avoid painful or deeper work; humor can be a form of flight
Deviant	Often used to express deeply held feelings; may be expressing authority theme for the group; acts differently from others
Scapegoat	Member who is attacked verbally or physically by other members; usually reflects group need related to fear of being weak
Internal leader	Played by same member or different members at different times; indication that work of group is going well when internal leader takes risks and others follow; indication that work is not going well when internal leader challenges worker's agenda
Quiet member	Member who remains noticeably silent for periods of time; may be listening and not comfortable with speaking; may feel his/her problem is different from that of others in the group
Defensive member/in denial	Member who does not admit existence of a problem or accept responsibility for the problem; uses denial as a way of coping with painful issues
Monopolizer	Member who talks too much, fails to listen to others

Implicit norms are reflected in communication and interaction patterns. Often, a sociogram is used to capture implicit patterns. A *sociogram* depicts who talks to whom, how frequently, and who initiates the exchange. It also captures who sits next to whom. *Implicit norms* determine what is discussed. As with other methods, what is communicated may be expressed verbally or nonverbally. Members communicate through their thoughts, feelings, and behaviors. Groups members may discuss *"near" problems* or bring up problems as the group session is about to end (doorknob). The concept of the *nonproblem* refers to analytic groups, where individual problems are recast as group themes and interpreted on the group level. Norms about interaction and communication can sabotage or support the work of the group. Consistent with systems theory, the worker must attend to the process of the group as well as to its structure. Group workers must attend to the group as a whole, its subgroups, and its individual members.

Curative Factors and Mutual Aid

According to Yalom (1995), 10 curative factors constitute the therapeutic ingredients of group method: hope, universality, imparting of information, altruism, the corrective recapitulation of the primary family group, imitative learning, interpersonal learning, group cohesion, catharsis, and existential factors. Schulman (1999) also identifies 10 different factors, which he categorizes as the dynamics of mutual aid: sharing data, the dialectic process, discussing a taboo area, the all-in-the-same-boat phenomenon, developing a universal perspective, mutual support, mutual demand, individual problem solving, rehearsal, and the strength-in-numbers phenomenon.

The Anti-Group

Traditionally, the literature on group psychotherapy is optimistic. This optimism for group method is countered by the experience of many psychotherapists. Nitsun (1996) was one of the first to write about the destructive forces in therapy groups, referring to such forces as the "anti-group." According to Nitsun, the anti-group is not a monolithic force that inevitably destroys the group, but rather it is a complementary dynamic in relationship with creative group processes. However, because of its destructive potential, the anti-group requires recognition and handling. In the foreword to Nitsun's book, Tuttman writes, "The anti-group is a concept which challenges the conventional optimism of group psychotherapy. The disruptive elements it comprises place a burden on the therapist and threaten the integrity of the group" (Nitsun, 1996, pp. ix–xi). Not only do some groups fail to develop as therapeutic entities, some act pathologically.

For example, Nitsun notes that the flipside of interpersonal learning (Yalom's core curative factor) is interpersonal threat. Nitsun identifies the following as anti-group phenomena: (1) a rise of anger and hostility, (2) a high dropout rate, (3) excessive member absences, (4) a state of tense, negative impasse, and (5) the abrupt ending of the group. Nitsun differentiates these group phenomena from the individual analytic phenomena of negative transference, negative therapeutic reaction, and acting out.

Foulkes believes that reparation and transformation lie in the confrontation of anxiety about destructiveness. Confrontation awakens the urge to repair. Containment, if not resolution, of the destructive forces relieves some anxiety. In contrast, Nitsun remains skeptical about the ability of the group (or the therapist) to control the group's own destructive processes. Brief and short-term models of therapy appear to minimize the likelihood that destructive group forces will be unleashed.

■ Theories: Group Purpose

There is no single theory that explicates the use of groups as a method in clinical social work practice. Two major theories are presented.

Psychodynamic Theory: Recapitulation of the Primary Group

Psychodynamic theory (Freud, 1960) is the dominant explanatory theory in analytic groups. The purpose of analytic groups is to change individual maladaptive patterns of communication and interpersonal interactions. Analytic groups (Slavson, 1964; Foulkes, 1964; Bion, 1961; Whitaker & Lieberman, 1964; Wolf, Schwartz,

McCarty, & Goldberg, 1972; Yalom, 1995) interpret and offer corrective emotional experience related to feelings, cognitions, and behaviors. Depending upon the worker's selected theory of therapy, the group process may be structured or unstructured. In analytic groups, the process is unstructured. Unstructured groups tend to increase member anxiety and to trigger conscious and unconscious coping patterns. According to Nitsun, the unstructured nature of the analytic therapy group opens the door to spontaneous, unpredictable, and irrational group behavior. The absence of structure frustrates dependency needs and arouses fears of aggression. The worker's activity level and use of structure control the level of group anxiety.

According to the theory, an individual's maladaptive personality traits or interpersonal behavior is reenacted and corrected through the medium of the group. It is thought that flawed personality or interpersonal behavior result from the client's family of origin (nurturing) and play out in the individual's current interactions. Group dynamics, through recapitulation of the family, elicit diagnostic hypotheses of what went wrong (there and then) and how it plays out currently (here and now). The individual benefits both from insight (interpretation) and from experiencing self and others correctively in the interactive group moment. Group members and the therapist substitute for the individual's family and those in the client's current interactive environment. Like individual psychoanalysis, group analysis relies on regression, interpretation, and transference. Foulkes adds to these analytic techniques the techniques of mirroring, exchange, free-floating discussion, resonance, and translation. Less intense, ego-supportive groups rely on psychoeducation as a means of improving the coping capacities of those involved in stressful life events. Support groups promote mutual aid and skills acquisition.

Psychodrama (Moreno, 1934) is an offshoot of psychodynamic theory. It is known as the theater of spontaneity. The enactment of problem scenes in the client's life is followed by corrective scenes. Warm-up precedes enactment and sharing concludes enactment. To see the same event from multiple perspectives, the client plays both the protagonist and the antagonist. Other group members may stand in for significant others in the client's life. Other members are thought to recognize their experience in that of the other and to gain insight and healing vicariously.

Gestalt therapy (Perls, 1976) rejects analytic orthodoxy. Perls uses a *hot seat* to have the group focus on one member. The worker follows the participant's experience but does not direct it (as do psychodramatists). The emphasis in Gestalt therapy is on the client's moment-to-moment awareness and feeling state.

The Group as a Social Microcosm

The second treatment rationale is that the group is a social microcosm of an individual's environment of socialization. Group dynamics reflect members' experiential learning about self related to culture, ethnicity, race, religion, sexual orientation, gender, socioeconomic class, and handicapping condition. Issues of poor self-esteem, identity, social status, and stigma arise through group dynamics and become the focus of attention. Groups influence an individual's social definition of self and how that individual thinks, feels, and behaves. The group is a medium through which the individual can challenge the definition of self made by others.

In the first rationale, it is hypothesized that how an individual feels, thinks, and behaves are results of faulty nurturing (psychodynamic theory). In the second rationale, it is hypothesized that how an individual feels, thinks, and behaves are results of socialization to status (structure-functional theory) and reference group membership (symbolic interaction theory).

■ Managing the Destructive Behavior of Groups

Transference and Countertransference

Transferences flourish under unstructured circumstances. Group interactions trigger multiple transferences and countertransferences. This has potentially positive and negative consequences. Group workers who lead analytic therapy groups need additional training. Groups are often co-led. This adds extra resources and complications to group method.

Managing the Anti-Group

While some follow Foulkes's admonition "to trust the group" and its curative factors (creative dynamics), others remain skeptical. Nitsun wonders whether it is possible to control the destructive forces of group life or transform them once they are unleashed. Acknowledging that destructive and constructive forces coexist in group life is a first step.

■ Contraindications

Not all treatment groups are appropriate for all clients. When composing a group, a clinician must be able to predict and balance the needs, vulnerabilities, and strengths of members in a manner that will benefit each member of the group and the group as a whole. A worker should not knowingly compose a group that will lead to group dynamics that s/he is unable to manage. This applies to the use of sensitivity-training groups in the workplace. The most-often cited incidence of negative group experience comes from mandated participation in such groups.

Common contraindications for the use of group psychotherapy include individuals who are nonverbal, individuals who are unable to take into account the viewpoint of another, individuals who may be overwhelmed (secondarily traumatized) by listening to others or by having to retell their own story, individuals possessing a cultural norm against self-disclosure, those unable to distinguish self from other, and those who are highly vulnerable to the aggressiveness of others or who are themselves highly aggressive.

Even when groups are indicated, it is a misstep to allow a member to leave the group in a vulnerable state because of the group's process. Competency requires the practitioner to actively intervene in negative group dynamics. The worker should not leave unchecked the attack of one member or the group on another member. Competency requires that the worker recognize and address group stages, in-group/out-group dynamics, individual acting out or negative reaction to group process, and the presence of anti-group phenomena.

■ Sample Process Recording: Socialization Group

Because foundation-year students are most likely to be involved in therapeutic groups (rather than in analytic groups), a description (Exhibit 16.5) and sample process recording of such a group (Exhibit 16.6) are included for purposes of illustration.

Due to the absence of the coworker, the student intern is leading the group.

EXHIBIT 16.5   *Therapeutic Group Properties of Recreational Groups*

Type of group	Therapeutic
Boys' activity group	Sports
Leadership	Co-led: Experienced male recreational leader and female social work intern
Size	N = 6: J, M, D, R, A, L
Composition	Homogeneous on gender, age, place of residence, school, and type of parental household
Formation variables	Males ages 10–12 living in single-parent households in Plum Tree public housing
Stage	Session 6
Communication	Maypole: member to worker
Planned activity	Basketball, brownies, cocoa
Norms	Group meets regularly once a week. If a member leaves the activity, he may not rejoin the group that session; at end of session, group grades itself

EXHIBIT 16.6   *Process Recording: Therapeutic Group*

Thinking Declarative Knowledge	Dialogue Theory-Driven Therapeutic Process	Worker Self-Awareness Monitoring Skill and Feeling
Activity: Outside basketball	Worker: Do you want to go inside?	Inadequate: I'm not as much fun as the other leader
Testing a norm: A left the activity and should not be allowed to continue the session; testing new leader	Boys: Yeah, it's cold out here. Can A come inside too?	Anxious: I'm not sure how to handle this
Checking with group	Worker: What do you guys think?	I am checking with internal leader
Evidence of group cohesion in that all agree to include A	M: Well, he played almost the whole time so he should be allowed back in.	
	All boys agree.	
	Worker: OK.	
Food is a cohesive activity	Inside, the boys get brownies and muffins and serve themselves.	Feeding others is more comfortable than playing basketball for me
Role	Worker: Who wants to help me make the cocoa?	
	J: I will.	Glad someone volunteered
Shift from activity to talk	As water boils, talk continues.	
Member attendance and absence important	Worker: D, why haven't you been at group?	Aware I want the group to be a talk group more than an activity group
	D shares that he forgot once, was gone once, and was punished once. Discussion of why.	
	[Later]	

(continued)

285

EXHIBIT 16.6   *Process Recording: Therapeutic Group* (*continued*)

Thinking Declarative Knowledge	Dialogue Theory-Driven Therapeutic Process	Worker Self-Awareness Monitoring Skill and Feeling
	M helps worker serve the cocoa.	Happy for the allies
Role acting-out Fight-flight stage of session Abrupt ending of group A in role of deviant	As the group is drinking hot cocoa and talking, A gets up and turns out the lights. Someone hides under the table.	Upset and not in control
Taking charge	Worker turns on the lights.	
Issue of how safe is the group, member anxiety over switch from activity to talk, absence of male leader Following end-of-session ritual	W: I'm not putting up with this. I think it is time to grade the group.	Can I keep the group safe for the members?
Member-worker struggle for leadership	A: I give the group an E and myself an A++.	
	Worker: How can you give the group an E and yourself an A++?	
	A snickers.	Feeling vulnerable
Invokes norm	Worker: Please leave the group now.	Regaining control
	A leaves.	
	R: He always acts like that.	

EXHIBIT 16.7   *Decision Schema: Clinical Group Work*

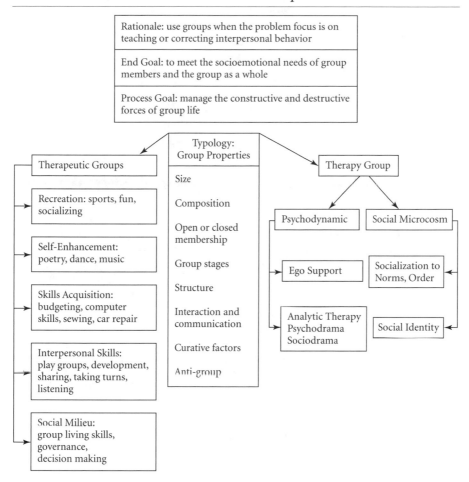

Rationale: use groups when the problem focus is on teaching or correcting interpersonal behavior

End Goal: to meet the socioemotional needs of group members and the group as a whole

Process Goal: manage the constructive and destructive forces of group life

Typology: Group Properties

Therapeutic Groups

Recreation: sports, fun, socializing

Self-Enhancement: poetry, dance, music

Skills Acquisition: budgeting, computer skills, sewing, car repair

Interpersonal Skills: play groups, development, sharing, taking turns, listening

Social Milieu: group living skills, governance, decision making

Size

Composition

Open or closed membership

Group stages

Structure

Interaction and communication

Curative factors

Anti-group

Therapy Group

Psychodynamic

Social Microcosm

Ego Support

Socialization to Norms, Order

Analytic Therapy Psychodrama Sociodrama

Social Identity

■ Commentary

The two co-leaders are not on the same page as to the purpose or medium of the group: constructive use of free time through sports activity versus talk to explore individual feelings and behaviors. The sample illustrates the importance of understanding group method even when the group is intended to be a recreational sports group.

17

The Use of Groups in Policy, Advocacy, Management, and Community Practice

■ Managing Group Dynamics in Nonclinical Practice

The decision tree promotes competency in practice by holding the practitioner accountable for making decisions that will result in the selection of the best intervention possible under a particular set of circumstances. Steps 5, 6, and 7 of the decision tree present the practitioner with method choices. Unlike clinical social work practice, where group method is one choice among several method options (including individual and family), the use of groups is integral to policy, advocacy, community, and management practice. Accountability lies therefore not in the decision to use groups but rather in the practitioner's ability to manage group dynamics consistent with the demands of the practice area. This chapter explores the use of groups in nonclinical areas of practice.

■ History of Group Work in Policy, Advocacy, Community, and Management Practice

Not unlike the history of social work itself, the history of group work is one committed to two goals: individual change (see chapter 16) and social change (this chapter). At its inception, group work was considered a movement, then a field, and subsequently a method. In macro practice, group methods are applied to achieve social goals (reform), accomplish work within agencies, and build healthy communities.

Social Goals

Settlement House Roots

The use of groups to meet social goals began with the settlement house movement. Settlement house workers engaged in activist research and advocacy (reform) to assure that the needs of all members of the community were met. Settlement houses responded to poverty, discrimination, and population shifts (rural to urban, South to North, immigrant waves) by providing basic goods, education in participatory democracy, opportunities for skills acquisition, and leisure pursuits to build a sense of community (Dewey, 1933/2004). Follett (1924) believed in the power of small groups to problem solve social issues at the local level (planning and organizing).

Large Groups and Social Movements

Social workers have been involved in major social reform movements: the civil rights movement, the labor movement, the feminist movement, the welfare rights movement, the human rights movement, and the environmental movement. Social work has close ties to the Peace Corps, VISTA, community action programs, and the War on Poverty. Consistent with participatory democracy and political social work, social workers have been elected to office or have worked on the election campaigns of others. They have engaged in social policy advocacy. Social workers have variously supported and protested against armed conflict here and abroad. They have raised consciousness about issues of social justice.

Community Goals: Intergroup Dynamics

Courses on intergroup dynamics became a dominant part of the social work curriculum targeting racism (and other isms) in the 1980s when the Council on Social Work Education (CSWE) made content on cultural diversity an accreditation standard. Controversy (Jacobs & Bowles, 1988) over the name of such courses exists to date, as does controversy over the use of an experiential approach versus a didactic approach when teaching such a course. How subgroups within a community relate to each other and to the community as a whole is a matter of group dynamics. Community, citizenship, participatory democracy, social reform, and social activism are powerful concepts related to the use of groups in social work community practice.

Management Goals: Cooperative Work Force—The Use of Task Groups

Task groups have always played a role in accomplishing the goal-directed activities of organizations. Groups in the form of committees, project teams, and task groups have been used in administrative practice to facilitate the work of the organization and to manage workplace morale. Administrators use human relations training and sensitivity-training groups to create a cooperative and creative workforce.

■ Typology of Theories Used to Inform Nonclinical Groups

The use of groups in macro social work practice requires knowledge of how groups work, for what purposes, and with what consequences. Exhibit 17.1 identifies some relevant theories from social science, sociopolitical thought, and moral philosophy that are used to inform the use of group methods when applied to policy, advocacy, community, and management practice. Group methods and dynamics differ when applied to social goals (policy and advocacy), community practice (the common good), and organizational work (tasks).

EXHIBIT 17.1   *Theories*

Social Science	
Theory	Purpose
Structure-Functionalism	Socialization to law and order, conformity to rules and norms
Symbolic Interaction	Social and reference group identity Cultural pluralism, tolerance
Power-Conflict Theory	Participatory democracy, empowerment, advocacy, social activism, organizing, disruption of the status quo
Social Exchange Theory	Regulating exchanges between individuals, between individuals and organizations, and between organizations
Organizational Theory	Agency administration
Human Relations	Management of work force

Moral Philosophy
Virtues: Common good versus minority rights, communitarianism versus liberalism
Deontological versus teleological reasoning
Analysis of purposes and consequences (outcomes)
Analysis of goals and means
Social justice: egalitarianism, utilitarianism, libertarianism, contractarianism (Rawls)

Sociopolitical Thought
Forms of rule: totalitarianism, anarchy, kingdom/monarchy, democracy
Political thought: conservative, liberal, socialist, other

■ Nonclinical Groups

Constructive and destructive forces coexist in nonclinical groups. Not to be neglected in the teaching and practice of group work with nonclinical groups, then, is the "disastrous power of group associations and the skilled misuse that could be made of them" (Konopka, 1972, p. 6).

All social workers, regardless of their concentration (clinical or nonclinical) will lead or staff groups throughout their professional careers. A social worker may chair or serve as a member of a board, delegate council, coalition, committee, meeting, task group, or activist group. Despite the frequent use of groups in social work practice, social work curricula usually include little on managing the dynamics of nonclinical groups. Competent social work practice requires that the practitioner be knowledgeable about how (cause and effect) groups work, be able to assess to what ends and by what means the dynamics of groups are used (moral reasoning and ethics), and possess the skills (theory-based techniques) needed to manage the dynamics of such groups specific to each practice area: policy, advocacy, community, and management. As members of nonclinical groups, all social workers share collective responsibility for the group's process and outcome.

■ Management Practice

The following typology applies to the use of groups in management practice.

EXHIBIT 17.2   *Typology of Groups in Management Practice*

Administrative Functions	Division of Labor
Boards, Cabinets	Task Groups
Deliberative Meetings	Project Teams
Organization as a Group	Committees

Boards and Cabinets

Small groups are used in management practice. Social exchange theory informs the creation and use of boards and cabinets. Board and cabinet members are recruited and appointed to serve on the basis of their political or social influence, their ability to make financial contributions and/or engage in fundraising activities, their representation of a constituent group that has a stake in the agency, or their possession of a needed expertise. The goal-directed activity in forming such boards and cabinets is to provide the agency with high-profile support, thereby making the organization attractive to donors and valuable in the exchange of social and political influence. In addition, such boards and cabinets provide administrative oversight to the chief executive officer of the organization or agency. Those who serve on such boards and cabinets may do so for altruistic and philanthropic reasons. In return, they may receive awards and honors. Positive publicity adds to the prestige of board members and agency alike (reciprocity in the exchange).

Deliberative Meetings

Meetings also serve an administrative function. Meetings are the most common form of group used in all areas of social work practice. Every social worker, regardless of specialization, will participate in meetings (as a convener or attendee) throughout his/her career. As common as meetings are within the profession of social work, good meetings are rare. Because meetings are so common, conveners and attendees alike fail to perceive a meeting as a specific type of group with its own unique set of dynamics. Consequently, most meetings range from boring to unsatisfactory to destructive. With good reason, conveners and attendees alike may be suspicious of the process and outcome. Within a business model, meetings may be strictly informational (information and announcements are handed down from the top). However, all organizations call meetings where some members are expected to participate in collective decision making on actionable items as part of legitimized shared governance. Such meetings are referred to as *deliberative*.

Stages

Like other groups, meetings go through group stages. The mechanics of beginning a meeting appear to be straightforward but can be manipulated for personal or political gain. A chair calls the meeting to order. Official meetings require a quorum to do business. Robert's *Rules of Order* (Robert, 1971) govern interactive procedures and provide a mechanism (majority or two-thirds vote) for validating group decisions. New members or guests are introduced. All attendees are provided with an agenda. The number of agenda items should be manageable within the time frame allowed for the meeting. Members are asked to approve the agenda. Minutes of the previous meeting are distributed. The chair asks for corrections or additions to the minutes as written and calls for their approval as amended. The chair makes a brief opening statement about the purpose of the meeting. Though intended to set the stage for the work to come, often the beginning phase of a meeting is used to divert or delay the substantive work of the group. Like other groups, meetings can get stuck in the beginning phase.

The group accomplishes its most difficult work during the middle phase of the meeting. The most important (and often most difficult) agenda item should come second during this phase. If placed first, the item might prevent discussion of other items; if last, it might be avoided by running the clock on previous items. Like other groups, meetings have endings. The chair summarizes the accomplishments of the meeting. Agenda items are identified for the next meeting, and individuals or task groups are designated to follow up on requests or decisions made at the meeting. Decisions made at meetings where procedural tactics disfranchise members are highly likely to be undermined during the implementation phase.

Organizational Problem Solving and Shared Governance

A good meeting depends on one's perspective. Often, meetings become the forum for the enactment of organizational politics. When political strategies govern discourse, discussion is scripted and votes for or against action items are already counted. The meeting is simply a presentation (Goffman, 1959) of decisions reached outside the designated forum for governance. Participants align (consistent with social exchange theory) with power bases seeking a predetermined outcome. Though effective, organizational politics undermine legitimate collective authority and responsibility. Bad process inevitably leads to poor outcomes or sabotaged implementation.

In contrast, meetings can be a forum for collective responsibility. The group entity can choose to conduct a meeting and make decisions based on evidence and open discourse involving value analysis. Groups can decide to use their collective power to advance the common good over personal or subgroup gain. When deliberative meetings are evidence-based, position papers delineating the facts are presented and discussed. Where values are at stake, moral argument is used to advance a higher moral order. Respect for dissent and efforts to reach consensus are benchmarks of rational, accountable, collective decision making and shared governance.

Meeting Context

Because issues of governance and power are present when groups meet, the following group dynamics should be analyzed: (1) physical setting, (2) agenda, (3) procedural rules, and (4) membership. Analysis of the physical setting examines where the meeting is being held. Is it held within the organization, over lunch, after work, over a drink, at a retreat, in someone's office or home? Is the setting of the meeting designed for work, comfort, or pleasure? Who is included and who is excluded? Analysis of the agenda also provides information. Is the agenda confined to safe issues? Are the issues discussed in principle with an absence of details, thereby allowing an administrator freedom to do whatever s/he wishes? In terms of procedures, are procedural rules used to prevent sufficient time to deliberate the issues? Are procedures used to defer decisions to other bodies? When deferred, is committee membership composed to represent one position over another or to ensure a particular outcome? Are procedural rules used to block dissenting viewpoints? The dynamics of leaders and followers are presented in chapter 8, and the virtues of deliberation, nonrepression, and nondiscrimination are discussed later in this chapter in relation to community values. Deliberation is both an aspect of administrative practice and a key virtue of community practice.

Management and the Workforce

Task Groups and Project Teams

Small groups are used within organizations to perform work. Organizations rely on project teams, committees, and task groups to divide the work load. A task arises from the need to do something. A task may be stated as an instruction, a perceived concern, or a perceived opportunity. Task performance requires a tangible product and a process. To be productive, work needs to be structured and to follow a *timeline*. The goal-directed activity of a project or team leader is to *manage* the socioemotional needs of individuals so that group members work cooperatively to produce a quality *product* or service in a timely manner. This is different from the use of groups in clinical practice, where the goal-directed activity of the group leader is to *meet* the socioemotional needs of group members.

Most task groups mirror an organization's top-down bureaucracy or political alliances. Such composition defeats the rationale for the use of groups to produce work. The decision to use task groups is based on the premise that the composition flattens bureaucracy, thereby allowing diverse talent and leadership to emerge. A management consulting model, Coverdale (M. Taylor, 1990; Coverdale, 1990; Smallwood, 1958), uses a systematic approach to structure the work of task groups.

Coverdale

The systematic approach facilitates cooperation and maximizes the use of individual talent within groups. The model holds that each member possesses unique strengths that will benefit the work of the group if members perceive these differences as assets rather than as liabilities. Coverdale begins, therefore, with an exercise that requires members to identify the strength(s) they bring to the work process. Some members are conceptualizers (i.e., the idea or big-picture people). They clarify the task, set goals and objectives, determine standards, and envision the final product. Others are detail people who organize who will do what, when, in what order, within what timeline. Some like to secure needed resources and materials while others are hands-on people who like to do the actual work. Still others like to facilitate the process of the group by encouraging and praising members. Depending on the assigned task, members will vary in terms of who possesses the "star" technical or artistic skill needed for a particular task. A star performer in one task is not likely to possess the star expertise needed in a different task.

If a group lacks diverse talents, the group is likely to rush to action without planning or, alternatively, remain in the planning stage without ever getting to the action or production phase. Potential discord occurs when members are too similar (too many conceptualizers or too many who rush to action without a plan). Potential discord also occurs when members perceive each other as too different. Conceptualizers find planners and organizers to be too detailed, while planners and organizers find conceptualizers to be too abstract. Workers (doers) find conceptualizers, organizers, and planners to be too talkative and prefer to get on with the work at hand. Conceptualizers, organizers, and planners find that workers rush to action without clear goals or means. Emotional caretakers are perceived as caring more about the process than about the product of the group. Members with dissimilar talents tend to view each other as a liability while members with similar talents tend to compete for power. To be competent, a practitioner requires the skills to intervene in the dynamics of task groups so that the diverse work talents of all of its members can be utilized to benefit the work of the group as a whole.

Despite the prevalence of task groups, most individuals are reluctant to work in teams because of the risks it entails. Allowing others to be seen as competent is a risk in the work world, where merit often determines promotion and salary increases. Coverdale exercises help members to take reasonable risks to promote cooperative teamwork (Plionis & Lewis, 1998). When there is a mandate and skills training in managing the dynamics of task groups, risks can be managed and cooperative teamwork made possible.

The Organization as a Group

Like a community, an organization is a large group composed of subgroups. Like communities, organizations must engage in problem-solving deliberations and governance related to the organizational environment. Organizations permit workers to influence the policies and procedures of the organization to varying degrees, ranging from a suggestion box to the incorporation of partners as part of a shared governance structure. In managing the dynamics of organizations, it is critical to have a clear delineation of who has the authority and power to develop or change agency policies. When organizations are constructed as hierarchical bureaucracies, decisions are made at the top with minimal input (if any) from those lower in the chain of command. Those who disagree with management decisions have the option of going along or moving along.

Decision making in organizations with shared governance (e.g., partners, tenured faculty, senior management) is more complex. Without belaboring the point, collective governance obligates the organization and its members to approach organizational problem solving with an open mind (rational deliberation) and a participatory process that is not corrupted by organizational politics. As discussed earlier, deliberative meetings serve as the forum for such governance.

Organizational politics always pose a risk to collective governance. According to Gummer (1990), organizational politics are based on the competing interests of actors within and outside the organization. Irreconcilable differences over positions and prerogatives as well as differences over deeply held values and beliefs related to organizational goals and programs trigger political behavior. Therefore, an organization should be analyzed and understood in terms of how those within it exercise and enhance their own power. Competency in collective governance and organizational problem solving requires leadership (see chapter 8) capable of intervening in the destructive dynamics of organizational politics.

■ Community Practice

The term *community practice* may be narrowly or broadly construed. In its more narrow construction it often refers to the administration and face-to-face delivery of community-based mental health services (Lightburn & Sessions, 2006). See Exhibit 17.4 at the end of the chapter. The section that follows is more broadly focused on community as a sociopolitical concept attuned to moral prescriptions on inclusion/exclusion and shared governance.

Purpose

Groups are the foundation of community practice. Psychologically, it is held that all humans have a basic need for group connectedness and shared values. Sociologically, it is held that communities are necessary for survival. According to Kirst-Ashman and Hull (2000), communities perform five functions: (1) socialization: the transmission of values, culture, beliefs, and norms to members, (2) resource allocation: the distribution of goods and services to members, (3) social control: enforcement of community norms through laws, ordinances, and a police force, (4) support: formal and informal sources of aid, and (5) socializing opportunities: opportunities to participate in activities to enhance the quality of group life. As reflected in Exhibit 17.3, a community is a political entity and a social web of moral values and shared meanings. The exhibit should be read from top to bottom to ascertain within-category differences and across to ascertain comparative conceptualizations of community.

EXHIBIT 17.3   *Typology of Communities: Comparative Conceptualizations*

Geographical	Homogeneous	Idea	Particularistic, tribal	Common Good	Public Square	State
Functional or Identity	Heterogeneous	Crisis	Universalistic, global	Minority Rights	Private	Civil
Reference Group		Memory				

Typology of Communities: Comparative Conceptualizations

Geographical, Functional, and Reference Groups

Communities may be geographical (defined by a specific physical space), or communities may be functional (defined by an auspice independent of geography, e.g., membership in a profession, adherence to a specific religion, or allegiance to a specific political party). In communities of reference, membership is based on sociodemographic criteria, such as class, race, ethnicity, gender, age, education, etc.

Homogeneity and Heterogeneity

For some, the ideal community is based on assimilation where members adhere to similar values and behaviors, e.g., become homogeneous. For others, the ideal community is heterogeneous, composed of members whose differences are in tension (culture wars). According to Tocqueville (2001), the best protection against totalitarianism is a pluralistic society. Homogeneous communities risk turning similarity into conformity, placing individual rights, autonomy, and dissent at risk. Heterogeneous communities risk chaos as competition between different subgroups prevents consensus on the common good and allows conflict to simmer. Some writers (Etzioni, 1995; Falck, 1988) give priority to community rights while others prioritize individual/minority rights (e.g., ACLU; Gutmann, 1995). Still others hold that neither the community nor individuals have ontological or normative primacy.

Communities of Ideas, Crises, and Memory

Fowler (1995) conceptualizes communities in terms of ideas, crises, and memory. He divides communities of ideas into two types: (1) those based on rationality and formalized documents, and (2) those based on inspiration and emotion. He conceptualizes communities of crises as those groups formed to overcome some social or ecological crisis through tribal or global communities of purpose (e.g., Greenpeace, Habitat for Humanity). In contrast, communities of memory consist of those who adhere to traditional beliefs linked to a particular faith in God.

Communities of memory seek renewal through shared virtues. Communities are also conceptualized as local, tribal, and particularistic as well as global (national and international) and universalistic (i.e., the human race).

Social Bonds: The Relationship Between the Individual and the Community

The relationship between the individual and the community differs from the worker-client (one-on-one) relationship in clinical social work practice, which is based on belief bonding and the enactment of a theory-specific therapeutic process. The social bonds of relationship between individual and community are nuanced, both mutually supportive and tensed (Etzioni, 1995). Understanding this relationship requires understanding of the philosophical (moral and ethical reasoning) and social (political-economic) theories that inform it. All communities face problems that they must solve, primary among which are problems related to (1) composition (inclusion-exclusion), and (2) collective governance and decision making.

Hans Falck

In discussing the relationship between the individual and his/her community, Falck (1988) takes social work to task for promoting individual autonomy. He takes issue with the idea that the end goal of client self-determination is independence. He argues that all decisions, self-determined or not, are social in nature. Any individual decision has consequences for everyone. Sleznick (1995) argues that self-determination is the freedom to find one's proper place within a moral order, not outside of it.

Assumptions About Human Nature

There are two basic schools of sociopolitical thought on human nature. Liberals assume that humans are basically good and reasonable. They hold, therefore, that individuals should determine the direction of the collectivity. In contrast, conservatives perceive the individual as impulsive and irrational. Therefore, conservatives subscribe to a rule of law and promote indoctrination of community values among the citizenry.

Community Values: Etzioni and the Common Good

Etzioni (1995) writes about the tension inherent in the quest for community. The tyrannical possibilities of community must be weighed against the anarchical dangers of the desiccation of community (order versus chaos). In his work, Etzioni (1995) focuses on how communities determine their value commitments. As a communitarian, he argues for renewed commitment to public virtues and social institutions. He prioritizes the public good over the private good. He tempers this preference with a call for values scrutiny. Even if a community follows a consensus-building process to arrive at the community's values, says Etzioni, such values must be scrutinized against a universalistic ethic (i.e., core or overarching values). According to Etzioni, traditional, values-based communities may be authoritarian and oppressive, leading to particularistic evils, such as intolerance, group egotism, and atavism. In contrast, Rorty (1991), a postmodernist, argues against a universal ethic, holding that all communities are locally constructed and none privileged. Where there is group consensus, it is argued, the values of the group are appropriately moral. Etzioni takes sharp leave from this position.

Moral Scrutiny

By advancing the idea of core or overarching values, Etzioni holds that community values deserve open, critical, and normative examination. Community values are legitimate, he says, only insofar as they are not in tension with overarching values. Normative values exploration is possible only in democracies. Values exploration is guided by philosophical theories and sociopolitical thought.

The Danger of Majoritarianism and the Role of Democracy

Understanding the role of democracy in values exploration is fundamental to the study of community values. According to Gutmann (1995), community values must not violate the two cardinal principles of democracy: nondiscrimination and nonrepression. *Nondiscrimination* secures the equal moral and political standing of all citizens in the public realm. The principle of *nonrepression* ensures that civil liberties are guaranteed and that the capacity for political deliberation is cultivated among citizens (Hollenbach, 1995; Follett, 1924).

Sociopolitically, conservatives and communitarians hold that the pursuit of the common good is integral to social and moral order. They believe that strains of individualism and privacy in American culture have led to a retreat from the public square (public virtues). In contrast, liberals are concerned about protecting individual and minority rights. Virtue, they say, is not a matter of state rule but rather a matter for civil society, i.e., religious institutions, universities, businesses, nonprofits, the arts, and individuals (Taylor, 1995).

To assure the protection of individual and minority rights, the U.S. government is a constitutional democracy, not a simple democracy. Under a constitutional democracy, some rights (Bill of Rights) are declared out of bounds for the rule of the majority. Some matters are exempt from consensus building. To safeguard against majoritarianism, the tilt in America is toward a civil society rather than state rule. To safeguard against majoritarianism, democracy requires the virtues of deliberation, nonrepression, and nondiscrimination.

Virtues of Deliberation, Nonrepression, Nondiscrimination

Hollenbach (1995) and Gutmann (1995) make a compelling argument for these virtues. According to Hollenbach, communities must engage in discourse to create the common ground needed to solve social problems. To the extent that such discourse is deliberative (leads to action), the standard of reasonableness applies. The pluralistic composition of the United States requires that all citizens be given the means of addressing and deciding public issues even in the face of deep disagreement.

Deliberation, in dialectical fashion, depends on and generates such virtues as honesty, tolerance, and nonviolence. Deliberation is complemented by two other necessary virtues: nonrepression and nondiscrimination. As a positive virtue, nonrepression requires the assurance and cultivation of the capacity for political deliberation among community members (Breyer, 2005). From this perspective, citizens come together in a town meeting based on the expectation that reasonable people will deliberate to reach an agreed-upon course of action. The rights of citizens are balanced by their obligation to responsibly shape and play a role in their public institutions. However, when the powerful thwart honest deliberation, "soft despotism" crowds out alternative opinions and subverts democratic participation in collective governance.

In contrast to the idea of active liberty is ordered liberty (Etzioni, 1995). Communitarians hold that individual rights presume a communitarian foundation. Less optimistic about the capacity of humans to engage in evidence-based and morally reasoned decisions, Etzioni holds that social mores assist emotionally driven, impulsive, and self-interested individuals in making reasoned choices (the rule of law) and moral decisions (social justice). Without social moorings, individuals lose their capacity to reason or act in a morally responsible manner. The unanswered question in Etzioni's writings is the question of source. What is the source of a universalistic ethic or core overarching values? Some suggest that the source lies in the religious prescriptions of Scripture (e.g., the Old and New Testaments, the Koran, the Torah), or in natural law, or in deontological reasoning, or in utilitarian and consequentialist approaches.

Application: Case Example

Because the techniques of working with communities are values-neutral, they require referral to sociopolitical thought and philosophy to determine whether they meet the standard of reasonableness and moral standing. Like other applications of group methods in macro practice, community practice requires skill in managing group dynamics. The difference lies in the number of systems and the system sizes to be managed. In addition to managing internal group dynamics, a community practitioner must be skilled in managing the dynamics between groups, i.e., the dynamics between community subgroups with competing interests and the dynamics between a particular subgroup and the community as a whole.

In heterogeneous (pluralistic) communities, competing interests often result in decisions that benefit one community subgroup at the expense of another community subgroup. Who wins and who loses is an important analytic tool when evaluating intergroup dynamics. Furthermore, moral scrutiny in the decision-making process is essential. The following is a case in point.

A social worker was assigned to work with the local community to build a coalition that would support the establishment of a group home for citizens with mental retardation who are in need of residential care. In an interfaith meeting with local clergy, it was suggested that a rumor be started that the house on the market was being considered for purchase by the Hare Krishnas. The speaker's premise was that community members would be more accepting of those with mental retardation than they would be of those who subscribe to Hare Krishna beliefs.

Though fear is known to be an effective tactic, such a strategy sustains discriminatory practices and fosters community intolerance. The goal-directed activity of social work community practice is to increase tolerance for the rights of *all* subgroups. Following discussion and analysis, the suggestion was retracted. This incident is a potent reminder that social work practitioners are obligated (and possess the skills) to intervene in the harmful dynamics of social groups. Teaching community practice skills requires that these skills be taught within a context of moral scrutiny.

Intergroup Dynamics: Tavistock and Sensitivity-Training Groups

Tavistock (Shaffer & Galinsky, 1974) is a major resource for teaching skills in community practice. As an experiential learning tool, the Tavistock approach allows members to learn about group dynamics by studying their own group process. It teaches members how to manage within- and between-group dynamics. Applied to communities, Tavistock teaches practitioners the skills needed to manage the destructive potential of groups toward each other and toward the community as a whole. It emphasizes the importance of individual conscience within groups to safeguard against the group's potential (group mentality and mob action) to inflict harm on others. Not a clinical model of practice, Tavistock recognizes how individuals and population subgroups suffer as a consequence of harmful group dynamics (e.g., hate crimes). Prevention and intervention target the destructive dynamics of social groups by promoting, within the individual, the retention of individual identity and moral conscience. Experiential exercises teach members how to recognize the harmful potential of groups (through critical observation) and provide the practitioner with the skills needed to hold the group collectivity responsible for its actions by raising moral discourse.

■ Social Goals

Social Planning: Incremental Change

Bobo, Kendall, and Max (1991) state in *Organizing for Social Change: A Manual for Activists in the 1990s* that the purpose of organizing groups is to build a better society and to empower the disfranchised. Organizing seeks to alter the relations of power. This is done by mounting a campaign. A *campaign* refers to a series of organized events, such as photo opportunities, actions, public hearings, accountability hearings, negotiations, and media events. These events are extended over a period of time and are designed to achieve a specific desired outcome.

There are several types of campaigns: An election campaign seeks to elect a candidate to office, an educational campaign to raise consciousness, and a fundraising campaign to raise money for a cause. An issue campaign focuses on a partial solution to a larger problem, e.g., passing rent control laws as part of an affordable housing strategy. An issue campaign seeks to win a specific victory, e.g., local rent control. When exercising power in an issue campaign, citizen groups tend to pressure administrators, bureaucrats, or regulators; to conduct boycotts; and/or to pursue legal and regulatory processes to win.

Social Action

Direct-Action Organizing

Unlike community practice, where groups are used to build tolerance and cohesion, the use of groups in direct-action organizing is to disrupt the equilibrium of the status quo. To achieve social goals (reform), small and large groups are used tactically to create instability and to provoke conflict. Organizing harnesses the power of groups (strength in numbers) to bring about structural changes within an existing social order. America has a history of direct-action organizing for social, economic, and political justice. The labor movement, civil rights movement, feminist movement, welfare rights movement, human rights movement, environmental movement, and consumer rights movement are examples. Direct-action organizing is often linked to radical social work practice (Alinsky, 1946).

Demonizing the Other

Coteaching in the group work curriculum at the university I attended were a Holocaust survivor and a defeated German soldier. Side by side, they taught, through their witness, that the dynamics of social groups can involve an otherwise "good" person in the harm of another "good" person. Demonizing the other was considered neither a valid explanation nor effective intervention (cause and effect). Understanding and controlling group dynamics were, however, considered

EXHIBIT 17.4   *Decision Schema: Use of Groups in Nonclinical Circumstances*

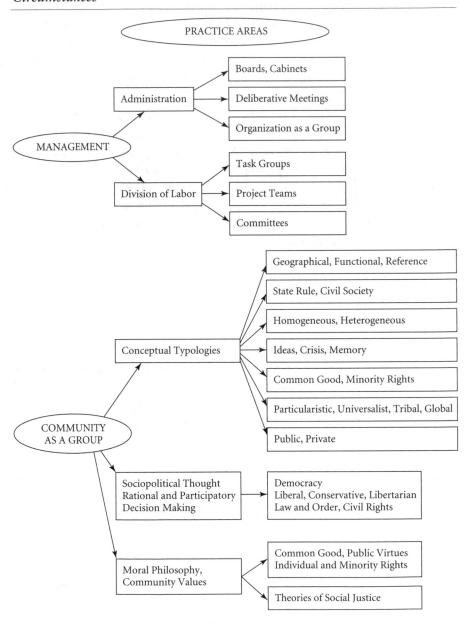

EXHIBIT 17.4   (*continued*)

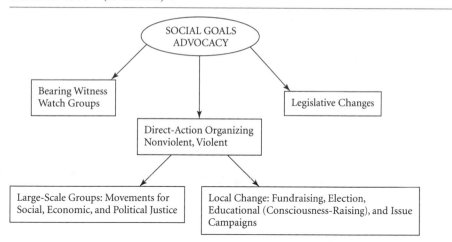

to be critical. The use of groups to achieve social goals requires competency in the tactical use of power (strength in numbers) and moral judgment. Power tactics used to reform an existing social order may lead to a different social order but do not, in and of themselves, lead to a higher moral order.

18

Theory, Research, and Predictions About the Future of Social Work Practice

■ Best Practices: The Role of Evidence

Empirical evidence is needed to support best practices. Evidence-based practice begins with a specific question that emanates from the problem of selecting an effective and appropriate intervention strategy for a specific client or situation. Understanding how to access and weigh the strength of empirical evidence is critical in determining which treatment option is better than another. To this end, evidence-based practice requires an understanding of methodological rigor and the difference between quantitative and qualitative research. Evidence-based practice is a commitment to adhere to empirically supported treatments as a standard in one's own practice. Research plays a key role in determining the efficacy of intervention outcomes.

■ Best Practices: The Role of Theory

Like evidence, theory is critical to best practices (Chaiklin, 2004). Empiricism is necessary but not sufficient to build knowledge. No array of statistical techniques can produce cumulative knowledge. Empirical data become knowledge when referred to theory for understanding. Theory, as knowledge, is a body of interrelated propositions, statements, and concepts that have been subjected to empirical verification. As part of the research process, theories become self-corrective. Scientific knowing differs from knowing based on animal instincts and belief in ideology or magic. The holistic property of theory (cause and effect) moves the practitioner, in an orderly and conceptually consistent manner, from declarative knowledge (what is known) to enactment of a therapeutic process based on that knowledge. According to Polansky (1986), there is nothing as practical as a good theory to guide action.

■ Science as a Way of Knowing

Social work practice has long subscribed to science as a way of knowing. The scientific paradigm is based on trust in reason (rules of discourse), logic, rigorous research methodology, a belief in progress (new knowledge builds on previous knowledge), and academic freedom (the pursuit of truth). Science adheres to standards against which comparative evaluation occurs. Science holds that a large part of reality is measurable and therefore capable of being known. Science produces knowledge. Theory and research work together to develop schools of thought (different theories). Scientific knowledge is stated in such a form as (a) to make it comparative, (b) to prove or disprove it, (c) to integrate it, and (d) to generate and test new knowledge. Knowledge is a set of ideas whose acceptability is determined by the criteria of science. When practice is evidence-based, it asks: what works, with whom, under what circumstances, and at what cost?

■ Case Example: Night Crying

Theory as knowledge is constructed as part of the research process. Empirical observations yield facts. Facts are in turn referred to concepts, thereby raising the level by which the facts can be understood. Concepts are then referred to theory for the formation of hypotheses. Deductive hypotheses are in turn submitted to inquiry for documentation of their veracity. If supported, the evidence contributes to the cumulative knowledge base of the theory used to explain the facts. A fact or concept in and of itself cannot explain anything. Its meaning depends upon the specific theory to which it is referred for understanding. Theory then guides action.

A case example illustrates this process. A mother comes to a social worker for help because her 18-month-old infant has developed a pattern of night crying. The pattern of night crying is an observable fact. This fact may be raised conceptually to what is termed "sleep disturbance." The concept of sleep disturbance for an 18-month-old infant may in turn be referred to different schools of thought, each of which offers a different working hypothesis as to what accounts for the observed pattern of sleep disturbance or night crying. A developmental psychologist might hypothesize that the pattern of night crying is caused by biological development (teething). A behaviorist might hypothesize that the pattern is learned behavior, that is, crying brings a comforting parent, which reinforces the crying pattern. A psychodynamic theorist might hypothesize that night crying is related to emotional development, e.g., separation anxiety. All theories offer plausible hypothetical explanations of night crying. In the specific case at hand, however, only one of the hypotheses will prove to be true. Because explanation leads to prescription, knowing what is the matter in a specific case is critical to selecting the best treatment option from among many available options.

Ambesol (teething pain ointment) would not be an appropriate treatment for separation anxiety.

■ What Makes a Good Theory?

According to Polansky (1986), a good theory is dynamic. A dynamic theory is phrased as sets of predictions. When X is done, Y will follow; or, if this, then that. Dynamic theory deals with regularities among events. Reason says that if the cause of something is known, then one can predict that its effect will follow. Preventing undesired effects requires intervention to break the cause-and-effect chain. In other words, declarative knowledge (knowledge of what is the matter) leads to the enactment of an appropriate therapeutic process designed to alter or change the outcome.

■ Open Assessment and Multiple Theories: Too Much Knowledge

Over time, social work has recognized that no single theory, whether narrow (psychodynamic) or grand (general systems), can guide practice. Generalist practice represents a paradigm shift to open assessment and consideration of multiple theories. The profession has gone from a paucity of theories to a plurality of theories. Compared to the use of a single theory, a plurality of theories creates choice. According to Turner (1996), no single theory can capture all of reality. Therefore, all theories must be taught if practice is to be considered competent and ethical. However, if so many theories can offer plausible explanations of the same phenomenon, then it seems that no one theory is better than another (Lehmann & Coady, 2001). Determining the efficacy of one theory-based treatment option compared to another is the core of evidence-based practice.

■ Ways of Knowing

Faith (knowing based on religious beliefs), rational discourse (knowing based on logic, rational argument, and philosophical proof), and science (knowing based on empirical evidence) are the three basic ways of knowing. Those who subscribe to science as a way of knowing make assumptions of linearity and probability in their analyses. Scientists (positivists) assume that the world is largely measurable and adopt a neutral stance in framing a research question. Neopositivists link empirical data and theory through the use of concepts. Those who adhere to science as a way of knowing maintain that explanation-prediction (cause and effect) makes prevention and intervention possible. Clinical social work relies heavily on science as a way of knowing.

Constructionists contend that an objective world, capable of measurement, does exist (Drisko, 1997). Constructionists hold that socialization (bias) causes individuals to misjudge this world. Claims of scientific knowledge are appraised therefore in light of the effects of socialization on the formation of the research question, the measures employed, the sample selected, the design used, and the theory selected to interpret the findings.

Logic, or rationalistic philosophy, is another way of knowing. Philosophical proof (the equivalent of empirical evidence in science) lies in the logic of argument. As a branch of study within the discipline of philosophy, moral philosophy uses logic and rational discourse to explore values in terms of desired end goals and the means to those goals. Within social work, policy, advocacy, and community practice are largely values-based. Consequently, they rely on moral philosophy as a way of knowing. Theories of social justice inform desired end goals while rational discourse guides discussion of values-based normative means and outcomes. Political acumen, not scientific evidence, directs the implementation of values-based interventions. Science is used within policy, advocacy, community, and management practice to document needs and resources. It is used in program evaluation (formative and summative) to assess process and outcome effectiveness for purposes of funding.

■ Scientific Rigor as a Criterion of Evidence-Based Practice

Determining the relevance of research to evidence is dependent on the methodology used to conduct the research (Roberts & Yeager, 2004). Levels of evidence help practitioners to select treatment options based on the methodological quality of the studies used to generate the empirical evidence. Understanding scientific rigor requires familiarity with the differences between quantitative and qualitative research methodologies. Exhibit 18.1 compares and contrasts these research methodologies on key elements.

Clearly, promoters of evidence-based practice tilt toward quantitative research and research rigor. Quantitative research is a type of research that tests well-specified hypotheses concerning predetermined variables. It gathers information in numeric form, using valid and reliable instruments, and produces findings by statistical procedures or other means of quantification (Roberts & Yeager, 2004, p. 998).

On the other hand, social work finds merit in qualitative research methodology. According to Padgett (1998), there are several good reasons for engaging in qualitative research: (1) It is used in program evaluation (formative research) and in activist research; (2) it is used when little is known about the topic being explored or when the topic is sensitive (taboo) and/or emotional; and (3) it is used when a researcher reaches an impasse in data collection or in interpreting quantitative data. Though such research does not lend itself to causal inference and prediction, it does lend itself to the discovery and understanding of the unique.

Qualitative	Quantitative
Design Rigor	*Design Rigor*
A "family" (over 50) of approaches from numerous disciplines. Major designs are participant observation, case studies, and the focused interview. Qualitative designs are associated with ethnology, grounded theory, narrative analysis, constructivism, phenomenology, cultural studies, feminist studies, sociology, and social work.	Experimental designs, random assignment to treatment and control groups, replicated, in laboratory or field. Systematic reviews of meta-analyses of multiple, well-designed controlled studies. Nonreplicated experimental designs and meta-analyses. Quasi-experimental designs: comparison groups in natural settings. Single subject and single group pre- and post-test.
Sampling	*Sampling*
Nonprobability (nonrandom) sampling recruitment of subjects; cannot claim representativeness or generalizability of findings. Studies cannot be replicated. Techniques of triangulation may be used to claim transferability of findings.	Probability and nonprobability. Probability sampling is more rigorous, assures representativeness, generalizability, and replication.
Measures	*Measures*
Researcher is instrument of data collection; may be overt or covert participant observer	Standardized, reliable, and valid preexisting instruments
Data Gathering	*Data Gathering*
Annual reports, books, newspaper articles, field notes, audio- and videotapes, photographs	May be either primary or secondary. Instruments may be paper-and-pencil surveys (self-administered or researcher-administered), direct observation, interrater reliability, semistructured interviews
Data Type	*Data Type*
Nonnumerical data; can transform some qualitative data into quantitative data; thick description for understanding; some inferential understanding related to emergent hypotheses at associational level	Numerical; statistical analysis leads to cause-and-effect and associational levels of knowledge. It has predictive properties. Numerical data may document prevalence and incidence.
Dynamic reality	Stable reality

(continued)

EXHIBIT 18.1   *Comparison of Quantitative and Qualitative Research Methodologies (continued)*

Qualitative	Quantitative
Categories	*Categories*
Variables result from data analysis	Testable hypotheses, variables precede data analysis
Sample Size	*Sample Size*
Undetermined; as small as N = 1	Predetermined; usually small sample is N = 30
Some "family members" reject science as way of knowing	*Some* adherents reject qualitative methods as science
Reporting of Results	*Reporting of Results*
Usually as a book or monograph, descriptive and narrative	Usually as article in scholarly journal, statistical and critical analysis

■ Predicting the Future of Evidence-Based Practice in Social Work Practice

Clinical Social Work Practice and Evidence

Treatment choice is now a condition of competent practice. Confronted with a myriad of treatment options, practitioners are held accountable for selecting that treatment option which will result in the best outcome for the client at hand. Choice necessitates conscious decision making based on criteria. Evidence-based practice particularly lends itself to this challenge. It relies on scientific rigor to evaluate intervention outcomes. Statistical significance is one indication of whether a given treatment option is better than another. Clinical significance, involving theory choice and practitioner skill, is another indicator. Best practice is composed therefore of both art and science. Given choices among theory-based therapies, evidence-based practice is necessary and inevitable in clinical practice.

Having said this, three major barriers interfere with the widespread acceptance of evidence-based practice among clinicians: (1) difficulty accessing systematic reviews of meta-analyses of multiple, well-designed controlled studies (dissemination), (2) difficulty implementing empirically supported treatments (ESTs) in everyday clinical practice, and (3) concern over the role of relationship (art) in therapy.

Briefly stated, systematic reviews of multiple, rigorous, controlled studies are in their infancy. It is difficult to locate studies appropriate for meta-analysis. This is because methodological rigor is rarely documented when empirical studies are published as journal articles. Search software is not programmed to identify studies by scientific rigor.

According to Noble (2006), meta-analysis is strong in revealing structural flaws and sources of bias in primary research and in posing promising research questions for future study. Meta-analysis cannot exceed, however, the limits of what is reported by the primary researchers. According to Noble, primary researchers tend to err on the side of overreporting positive effects while underreporting significant adverse effects. The dissemination of and access to evidence are also barriers to evidence-based practice. The Campbell Colloquium (2004) has dedicated itself to the dissemination of systematic reviews of rigorous empirical studies and meta-analyses.

Implementing an empirically supported treatment in practice is difficult (see chapter 6 for elaboration). Clinicians argue that the strict protocol of an EST takes the therapist and the art (creativity) out of therapy. Empirically supported treatments, it is said, leave no flexibility for dealing with the unexpected or for dealing with variations in client, setting, problem severity, problem complexity, or the therapist's skill level (novice versus master).

Policy, Advocacy, Community, and Management Practice and Evidence

Evidence-based practice faces a different set of barriers regarding its acceptance in policy, advocacy, community, and management practice. Traditionally, research in macro practice has focused on rigor in documenting needs and resources. Program evaluation, however, has often tilted toward process (formative research) evaluation over outcome (summative) evaluation. Because of its emphasis on process evaluation, the tilt in program evaluation has been toward qualitative research. Recently, "results-oriented" legislation has shifted the emphasis to program outcomes. Is the program effective in doing what it says it does, and at what cost (economic analysis)?

The standard of scientific rigor (multiple, replicated, experimental, controlled studies) becomes less feasible when applied to program evaluation. Furthermore, the desired end goals of most social work programs are values-determined in contrast to the more scientifically determined (cause-and-effect) outcomes of clinical practice. Decision making in policy, advocacy, community, and management practice relies on science (documentation of needs and resources), moral philosophy (values-based, desired end goals), and political strategies to implement policies and programs.

Consider the following. If one wants to know whether a school lunch program improves student educational performance (outcome), one must look for scientific proof. However, should there be no statistical evidence that the lunch program increases educational performance, the decision to cut or maintain the program must look beyond statistical outcome evidence. Values also guide decisions to feed the hungry. Practitioners must weigh political factors when deciding to cut or maintain a program. What stake does the government have in the program? What sentiment for and against the program (public outcry) exists? What are the economic costs (actual cost, cost effectiveness, and cost-benefit analyses) associated with the program?

For public policies and programs to be evidence-based, government must be committed to research and must finance the infrastructure needed to conduct such research. Such a commitment and infrastructure exist in England (Lee, 2004; Campbell Colloquium). While it is more difficult to apply evidence to policy, advocacy, community, and management practice, policy makers and program managers do improve their practice when they use evidence to guide their decisions. Evidence-based policies and programs serve as an antidote to opinion-based policies and programs that rely on ideology, prejudice, or conjecture.

■ Conclusion

Several conclusions may be drawn about social work theory and practice today compared to 10 years ago. As Turner (1996) predicted, social work has accepted a plurality of theories. Earlier speculations of a unitheory, monotheory, or megatheory have not come to pass. So, too, social work has rejected practice devoid of theory, whether based on relationship-empathy only or empiricism only. Contrary to Turner's expectations, similar theories from the same school of thought (ego psychology, psychoanalytic, psychosocial) have remained distinct. Since he wrote the 4th edition of his book *Social Work Treatment* (1996), the role of generalist practice has become clearer. Like theory, the profession has avoided adopting generalist practice as a unimethod, monomethod, or megamethod. Generalist practice has remained a conceptual framework that is both multitheory and multimethod. It works with client systems of different sizes.

As predicted, the profession has realized that neither theories nor methods can be so comprehensive as to be of little use for day-to-day purposes nor so one-tracked as to leave most of the real world out of account. As predicted by Turner, polarizing debates over the importance of one theory or method over another (either/or positions) have been replaced by discussions of the appropriateness or lack of appropriateness of a theory or method for the situation at hand. Divisiveness over theory focus (pathology/deficit versus resiliency/strength) has also diminished. Previous attempts to deny or exclude have been replaced by the recognition that all theories and all methods have equal value in themselves and differential value in their proper or improper application (Turner, 1996, p. 9). Method and theory diversity are more aligned with the multicultural and complex world within which social workers practice. Though differences remain over the methodological merit of quantitative versus qualitative research designs in determining the efficacy of an intervention outcome, the evidence-based movement has strengthened the link between theory, research, and practice.

What has been missing is a means by which practitioners can take responsibility for what they know and what they do given so many intervention options. This need is met through the decision tree. The decision tree is a very pragmatic tool that adds precision and proof of process when applying theory and evidence to practice. Its use provides some assurance of competency commensurate with the decision-making responsibilities of the social work practitioner. Skill sets consistent with a sufficient range of system sizes, whether individuals, dyads, families, groups, or communities, support the steps of the decision tree. How well do we do (tacit knowing) what we know (declarative knowledge) is linked to education. The text maintains that progress from novice to master practitioner requires didactic learning (classroom) and mentoring (apprenticeship under field supervision). The text is based on the premise of best practice (e.g., that clients benefit when practitioners are aware of the availability of theoretically sound and empirically verified diverse treatments). Finally, the text shows how practitioners can apply more than one theory and more than one method to complex data in the same case through case-specific model building and the use of the decision tree. The decision tree is intended to promote competency in generalist practice.

Glossary

Absolute Efficacy. An outcome of meta-analysis. Refers to the difference in outcome for people receiving psychotherapy compared with those who have not received psychotherapy.

Abuse of Power. The excessive use of psychological and/or physical coercion to achieve a desired end by those in power.

Allostatic Overload. Refers to an individual's continuing exposure to stress resulting in continuous autonomic arousal

Auspice. A term used to describe the patronage and guidance offered by a profession or an agency to its members.

Authority. Power that accompanies an assigned or acquired position; "legitimate" power. Leadership based on authority is considered rational-legal. Followers believe in the right of the person in a position of authority to direct their behavior.

Belief Bonding. Refers to the social work relationship as bonding. Both worker and client believe in the worker's competency and the client's capacity to change. The term implies that there is an affective component in the clinical relationship.

Bureaucracy. A form of social organization whose distinctive characteristics include a task-specific division of labor. A vertical hierarchy with power centered at the top, clearly defined rules, and formalized channels of communication.

Case Management. Coordination and monitoring of fragmented services to highly vulnerable client groups in need of multiple services from diverse disciplines. Social work has neither full ownership nor control over the term "case management." In this text, it refers to a model of practice that provides concrete services to meet urgent client needs in a timely manner.

Charismatic or Inspirational Leadership. Refers to an emotional transaction between leader and led. The inspirational leader captures hearts, minds, and souls based on a leader's passionate, uncompromising strength of conviction, or particular world view. Charismatic leadership can be used to pursue good or bad ends.

317

Client Rights.   Clients possess all civil rights which include the right to privacy, the right to treatment that works, the right to the least restrictive environment, and the right to withdraw from or refuse treatment.

Clinical Crisis Intervention.   A practice model designed to intervene in an acute, life threatening event (basic crisis intervention) and in its aftermath (advanced crisis intervention).

Clinical Practice.   General term use to refer to methods of therapy (individual, couple, family, group) as well as different theory-guided therapies (psychodynamic, cognitive-behavioral, solution-focused, empowerment, narrative, etc.).

Clinical Social Work.   The term is used to denote licensed social work practice. Clinical social workers perform two functions as licensed clinical social workers: the delivery of concrete services and therapy. Practitioners earn a degree as a master of social work (M.S.W.).

Collaboration.   Interdependency, rather than client autonomy or worker expertise, is central to the worker-client relationship. Each has power and is expected to use it to solve the problem collaboratively. Extends beyond worker-client to include professional collaborative teaming at other levels. Holds that power is generated through a number of collaborative alliance. Sometimes referred to as a relationship of partnership.

Compassion Fatigue.   Sometimes, the result of caring for traumatized individuals over a period of time.

Confidentiality.   Confidentiality broadly refers to a practice principle that protects a client from unauthorized disclosure or misuse of information provided in the context of a professional relationship. Confidentiality is governed by ethics.

Constructivism.   Refers to how individuals make meaning in their lives through their perceptions, the operation of cognitive and affective processes, and the mechanics of memory storage and retrieval.

Consumer-Driven Case Management.   A model of case management based on a strengths perspective, principles of postmodernism, and empowerment.

Context of Practice.   A set of goal directed parameters within which a clinician conducts practice. It includes a field of practice, regulatory policies and procedures, an agency structure or setting, a client population, a method and theory of practice, and a problem to be addressed as defined by the agency's mission statement.

Contract.   A contract clearly stipulates what is to be exchanged between parties. In social work there are four levels of contracts. (1) between the profession and society, (2) between the profession and the individual professional, (3) between the individual professional and the employing agency, and (4) between the practitioner and the client or the client's representative.

Countertransference.   A concept from psychodynamic theory that refers to unconscious feelings, wishes, fears, and defenses assigned to the client by the therapist. These unconscious elements are related to the therapist's relationships with past significant others. It causes strains and ruptures in therapeutic alliance.

Crisis.   A sudden, shocking, intense, often catastrophic event that overwhelms the coping capacity and resources of individuals, populations, and communities.

Critical Incident.   An event to which emergency personnel and mental health professionals respond. It is a term linked to debriefing.

Cross-Cultural Social Work.   A worker-client relationship where the worker and the client are native to other countries and each speaks a native tongue that is foreign to the other. The term is also used to connote worker-client differences based on race, ethnicity, gender, and class though both worker and client are native to the same country and share the same language.

Culture.   Signifies commonalities of ethnicity, race, religion, values, norms, and patterns of behavior developed by groups of people within a larger society.

Declarative Knowledge.   A form of knowledge that consists of facts, theories, principles, and rules about a knowledge domain; knowledge that is taught, learned, stored, and retrieved during assessment and intervention. Also referred to as procedural knowing.

Delirium.   An acute brain disorder marked by confusion and disorientation; often accompanied by visual and auditory hallucinations.

Dementia.   A significant loss of mental abilities that result from a variety of conditions and involves impairment of the central nervous system.

Direct Practice.   Realm of practice where licensed clinical social workers deliver either concrete services or therapy or both.

Disaster.   Denotes complex interactions between nature, the human-built environment, and social processes that lead to significant harm to people and their sustainable environment.

Duty to Protect.   Professional obligation to report and take action to prevent serious, foreseeable, and imminent danger to a person's self or to others.

Duty to Report.   Legal obligation to report all incidents of suspected child or elder neglect and physical or sexual abuse. The duty to report includes the duty to warn law enforcement officials and the intended victim of a crime when a threat is serious, foreseeable and imminent. Administrators of facilities are required to report communicable diseases so preventive action can be taken.

Effect Size.   In meta-analysis, a fair statistical comparison obtained by combining the results of many studies across different measures with differing numerical scores to obtain a measure of outcome success.

Empowerment.   Refers to a social work practice model where the central issue is one of power: ownership of power, inequalities of power, the acquisition of and redistribution of power.

Enculturation.   An anthropological term referring to ideas, customs, and patterns of behavior communicated within the same culture or subculture.

Ethnic.   A sociological distinction regarding a social group or category that differs in its values, world view, and traditions from the other social groups in a complex society.

Ethnic Minority.   Denotes ethnic groups whose members are numerically fewer in the overall population of a country and who are unequal in status and power relative to the larger majority group.

Ethnocentrism.   Unquestioning assumption of the superiority of the ideology of one's own culture or ethnicity. Ethnocentrism imposes one's own beliefs and values on others.

Ethnographic Interviewing.   Refers to a technique that focus on the linguistic features, casual words, and phrases that are familiar to a client but unfamiliar to the worker. The worker uses the client as a guide to acquire a terminology reflective of the cultural and personal language habits of the client.

Expectancy.   Refers to a ritualized format (such as therapy) that brings about positive client change due to the instillation of hope that the individual's circumstances will improve.

Fiduciary Responsibility.   The legal obligations accepted by those who enter a profession. Specific legal obligations vary according to the profession. By accepting membership in a profession, a member agrees to abide by the profession's knowledge base and practice parameters.

Field of Practice.   A particular practice domain characterized by the need for specialized knowledge e.g., medical social work, school social work.

Generalist Practice.   Refers to a social work practice model based on multiple theories and multiple methods. The generalist practitioner is required to engage in open assessment to obtain all of the facts relevant to the case/situation at hand before selecting one or more interventions. Generalist practice encompasses direct and indirect social work practice.

Grief, Normal.   Denotes time-limited symptoms of bereavement. The individual is able to resume normal social, physical, or emotional functioning following this period.

Highly Vulnerable Client Populations.   Characterized by the need for continuous, long-term, and community-based help. The primary focus of intervention is maintenance (or enhancement or optimization of client self-sufficiency) in the community. Multiple helpers from a variety of disciplines offer a variety of services to meet the multiple needs of such clients. The model is marked by care over cure and breadth of services. Case managers usually coordinate and monitor fragmented services.

Indirect Social Work Practice.   Refers to the use of policy, advocacy, community, and management methods of practice to bring about an equitable allocation of resources through social policies and programs to benefit populations. Reform and social change are goals of indirect practice. It is an area of practice that requires nonclinical social work skills.

Ineffective Leadership.   Refers to a leader's use of tactics and strategies that are not up to the task at hand. In other words, either the means that are employed or the failure to deploy correct means result in failure. Goals are not accomplished.

Influence.   Influence is based on the use of noncoercive tactics. Influence relies on persuasion, inspiration, and charisma to motivate others to follow. When linked to unethical means, *undue influence* consists of psychological threats, bribes, or promises of personal gain.

Informed Consent.   Clients have the right to access their records and to participate in all decisions related to their care. Informed consent covers disclosure of student status and methods to be used in treatment.

Integrated Crisis Intervention.   A practice model designed for domain-specific areas of practice. Clients living with an ongoing condition/situation experience a periodic eruption or flare-up resulting in a life-threatening crisis episode. Specializations in domain-specific crisis intervention include such fields as mental health and domestic violence.

Involuntary Clients.   Those clients who interact with social workers because they wish to avoid the consequences of not doing so, i.e., they are required by courts, hospitals, and other institutions to get treatment. Involuntary clients are mandated or engage in treatment because of pressure from agencies or other people (spouse, parent, teacher).

Leadership.   The exercise of authority, power, and influence to accomplish tasks for which there is some degree of consensus (between leaders and followers) as to the desired outcome of organized, structured activities.

Managed Care.   Managed care (health) and behavioral managed care (mental health and substance abuse) are systems of providing services that are paid for, all or in part, by a third party. Refers to managed health and behavioral health care insurance coverage

Management.   Oversight of day-to-day operations (functions) of an enterprise. A manager possesses technical expertise and/or expertise in managing human resources.

Mandated Clients.   Clients who have been court ordered into treatment as a condition of legal proceedings. Such clients are considered involuntary clients but the source lies in legal mandate or court order.

Meta-analysis.   An empirical approach to summarizing the results of multiple studies around a focal problem.

Method of Practice.   A method refers to the specific manner in which practice is conducted. Examples of social work methods in direct practice are (1) one worker to one client, (2) one worker to a dyad (parent-child or husband-wife), (3) one worker to a single family, or (4) one worker to a group composed for clinical treatment. In both family work and clinical group work, there are variations that allow for two clinicians to work as cotherapists or as individual clinicians doing conjoint therapy. Each method possesses assets and liabilities and therefore its indication or counterindication for a specific client or family must be assessed.

Macro Practice.   Indirect social work practice; refers to policy, advocacy, community, and management practice. Sometimes referred to as nonclinical practitioners, these social workers earn a degree as a master of social work (M.S.W.). They serve populations through policies, programs, and social change (reform) efforts.

Micro Practice.   Direct social work practice; clinical social work practice; or the delivery of concrete services and therapy. It refers to the methods of individual, family, or group treatment.

Mission Statement.   These are informed by values and articulate the purpose of an agency. The values contained in agency mission statements get institutionalized through policy in the form of public laws.

Moral Leadership.   Refers to ethical leadership. It consists of working for the common good, putting the needs of others before the needs of the leader, and using ethical means to achieve goals in a manner that raises the level of humanity. It differs from charismatic leadership, which may or may not be moral or ethical.

Partnership Model.   Refers to a case management model of practice based on empowerment and client strengths. Also known as consumer-driven case management.

Placebo Effect.   Refers to positive client change brought about by the client's and therapist belief that the intervention will work.

Planned Change Processes.   This consists of (1) the establishment of rapport (relationship beginnings, middles, and endings), (2) assessment, (3) contracting and goal setting, (4) intervention, and (5) evaluation.

Point of Entry.   The intersection of the help-seeking and help-giving people (client and social worker).

Political Leadership.   Term used by Kellerman to denote effective leadership used to pursue unethical ends by unethical means.

Political Social Work.   Refers to a model of practice whereby the social worker connects a client's personal issue with organizational and political policies and actions.

Posttraumatic Stress Disorder.   A DSM-IVR classification of symptoms resulting from an event experienced as traumatic. Symptoms include uncontrollable intrusive imagery, generalized fears, sleep disturbances, changed world views, and affective arousal.

Power.   A necessary condition of authority and leadership. Power is the basic energy to initiate and sustain action translating intention into reality. Without it, leaders cannot lead.

Privileged Communication.   A form of confidentiality. It is based upon a legal statute granting licensed certified social workers the "privilege" of protected communication. Not all states grant such a privilege. Where such statutes exist, the privilege is often limited.

Procedural Knowing.   Refers to stored declarative (learned) knowledge as cognitive map; reflection on action; denotes the novice clinician.

Procedures.   The specific written directions to professional staff for implementing a particular policy-based program. They are usually contained in an agency manual.

Profession.   An applied science possessing a unique body of knowledge, core values, and skills in the application of its science.

Psychotherapy.   Interventions based on a therapeutic alliance within which a theory-guided enactment of a therapeutic process occurs.

Rational Leadership.   Refers to that leadership which is effective. It may or may not be ethical.

Relationship.   The emotional interaction between people. It refers to the connecting bond of feeling between interviewer and interviewee which gives a sense of alliance.

Relative Efficacy.   Used in meta-analysis; refers to differences in outcome between different types of psychotherapy.

Right to Privacy.   Information obtained in the course of treatment cannot be shared with others without the explicit, written consent of the client.

Secondary Trauma Response.   The effects of loving or feeling responsible for someone who is directly traumatized and consequently experiencing their symptoms.

Social Casework.   Refers to an early conceptualization of social work (Mary Richmond and friendly visitors). Social casework tied receipt of resources to the receipt of therapy based on the assumption that the failure to secure basic necessities reflected personal flaws rather than flawed markets or social forces.

Social Constructivism.   A concept that focuses on the social and cultural milieu of a client to understand the client's circumstance as rooted in language, cultural beliefs, social interaction, and institutional behavior; used as part of narrative therapy, critical theory, and postmodern principles.

Socialization.   Sociological term referring to the experiences one has that shapes one's life.

Social Policy.   A set of principles (values), usually expressed in law and governmental regulations, that guides the delivery of specific services. Policies assign specific benefits and opportunities to people.

Social Program.   The means by which an agency delivers policy-based benefits to a client population.

Sociopolitical Empowerment.   Skills in organizational development, political activism, and action research that effect changes in resource allocation at the agency, state, and national policy levels.

Stored Information.   Knowledge acquired through a course of study in a school of social work as well as that knowledge acquired through practice experience. The practitioner retrieves this information when engaged in assessment and intervention.

Street-Level Bureaucracy.   Refers to social workers engaged in case management with highly vulnerable client populations. Case managers on the frontlines of service delivery have substantial discretion over their work.

Strengths Orientation.   A practice perspective that focuses on client resiliency rather than client deficits or psychopathology.

Stress.   Continuing exposure to work or life events that keep an individual's autonomic nervous system in arousal.

System-Driven Case Management (Broker Model).   Case management services that are bureaucratically driven with an aim of efficiency. Services are predetermined and client eligibility must be established to acquire goods and services. The model is criticized because concrete services are often delivered under conditions of inadequate resources and large caseloads.

Tacit Knowing.   Reflection in action; automatic use of self denotes the master clinician in action; spontaneity and creativity in the moment.

Technique.   A clear formulation of what a practitioner should do in a given situation to offer service effectively and efficiently. Technical skill is not antithetical to spontaneity. It permits a higher form of spontaneity.

Therapeutic Alliance.   The type of worker-client relationship needed to deliver therapy based on a theory-driven therapeutic processes.

Therapeutic Interview.   Refers to the use of psychological principles and procedures in an effort to exercise a deliberate, controlled influence on the psychic functioning of the interviewee, with his/her consent and on his/her behalf. The purpose of such an interview is helping and healing through communication in a therapeutic relationship.

Therapy.   As a process, the transformation of declarative knowledge of human behavior, pathology, and change into tacit knowing; the art of healing. As defined in this text, therapy denotes a generic term. It refers to the necessity of a therapeutic alliance and therapeutic process in order to being about individual change. Any theory-specific model of practice can inform the therapeutic process.

Traditional Client/Voluntary Client.   Refers to those clients who feel subjective discomfort and voluntarily seek out help. Compared to highly vulnerable clients, the emphasis with a traditional client is cure over care. Therapy is time limited and characterized by depth over breadth of service.

Transactional Leadership.   In contrast to transformative leadership, transactional leadership is based in power and is task focused. Transactional leadership forms power bases that shift over time.

Transcrisis or Transcrisis Points.   The increased risk of serious reactions to a new crisis in those individuals who have unresolved, dormant symptoms from a previous crisis.

Transference.   Unconscious feelings, wishes, fears, and defenses assigned to the therapist from the client. Transference content is related to the client's relationships with past significant others.

Transformative Leadership.   In MacGregor's definition, refers to the type of leadership where one or more persons engage with others in such a way that leaders and followers raise one another to higher levels of motivation and morality

Trauma Response.   Autonomic hyperarousal related to an event that involves actual or threatened death or serious harm to self or others. The individual experiences fear, helplessness, or horror at the time of the event. Uncontrollable memories and images of the event (flashbacks) recur after the event is over.

Triage.   The sorting of and allocation of treatment in a disaster according to a system of priorities designed to maximize the number of survivors.

Unethical Leadership.   Fails to distinguish between right and wrong. Common codes of decency and good conduct are violated, thereby derailing ethical leadership. The following acts constitute unethical leadership: (1) the leader puts self-interest above the needs of others; (2) the leader lacks private virtues such as courage and temperance; (3) the leader does not act in the interest of the common good.

Values.   What one considers to be good or desirable (i.e., values reflect desired end goals). Values underlie judgments or decisions about relative worth (i.e., what is more or less valuable). Values are derived from philosophical thought or are derived from theological belief.

Vicarious Traumatization Response.   The transformation of a worker's inner self as a result of empathic engagement with a traumatized client.

Voluntary Clients.   Those who voluntarily seek help.

Working Relationship.   The observable ability of the worker and the client to work together in a realistic, collaborative manner based on a mutually committed belief in the helping relationship

References

Acs, G., & Loprest, P. (2001). *Initial synthesis report of the findings from ASPE's "leavers" grants.* Washington, DC: U.S. Department of Health and Human Services.

Administration for Children and Families—Children's Bureau (2003). Factsheets/publications. *Fatalities by prior contact with CPS 2003.* Retrieved from www.acfihhs.gov.

Adoption and Safe Family Act. (1997).

Adoption Assistance and Child Welfare Act. (1980). P.L. 96–272.

Ahn, H., & Wampold, B. (2001). Where oh where are the specific ingredients? A meta-analysis of component studies in counseling and psychotherapy. *Journal of Counseling Psychology, 48*(3), 251–257.

Albert, R. (2000). *Law and social work practice.* New York: Springer.

Alinsky, S. (1946). *Reveille for radicals.* New York: Vintage.

American Association of Social Workers. (1929). *Social case work generic and specific: A report of the Milford conference.* New York: Author.

American Psychiatric Association. (1994). *Diagnostic and Statistical Manual of Disorders* (4th ed.). Washington, DC: American Psychiatric Association.

American Psychiatric Association. (2000). *Diagnostic and Statistical Manual of Disorders* (4th ed., rev.). Washington, DC: American Psychiatric Association.

Anderson, L. A., Sundet, P. A., & Harrington, I. (2000). *The social welfare system in the United States: A social worker's guide to public benefits programs.* Boston: Allyn and Bacon.

Anderson, S. G., & Gryzlak, B. M. (2002). Social work advocacy in the post-TANF environment: Lessons from early TANF research studies. *Social Work, 27*(3), 301–314.

Andrews, J. (2001). Group work's place in social work: A historical analysis. *Journal of Sociology and Social Welfare, 28*(4), 45–65.

Association of Social Work Boards. (2006a). *Licensing requirements.* Retrieved January 22, 2006, from www.aswb.org/lic-req.shtml.

Association of Social Work Boards. (2006b). *Social work laws and regulations online comparison guide.* Retrieved January 22, 2006, from www.aswbdata .powerlynxhosting.net.

Atkinson, D. R. (1983). Ethnic similarity in counseling psychology: A review of the research. *Counseling Psychologist, 11,* 79–92.

Austrian, S. G. (1998). Clinical social work in the 21st century: Behavioral managed care is here to stay. In R. Dorfman (Ed.), *Paradigms of clinical social work* (Vol. 2, pp. 315–336). New York: Brunner/Mazel.

Bagdasaryan, S. (2005). Evaluating family preservation services: Reframing the question of effectiveness. *Children and Youth Services Review, 27*(6), 615–635.

Balanced Budget Act. (1997).

Bales, R. (1958). Task roles and social roles in problem-solving groups. In E. E. Maccoby et al. (Eds.), *Readings in social psychology* (pp. 437–447). New York: Holt, Rinehart, and Winston.

Bandura, A. (1977). *Social learning theory.* Englewood Cliffs, NJ: Prentice-Hall.

Bandura, A. (1997). *Self-efficacy: The exercise of control.* New York: Freeman.

Barbre, E. S. (2006, January). Communications to social workers as privileged. 50 A.L.R. 3d 563. Sent by westlaw@westlaw.com.

Barker, R. (2003). *Social work dictionary.* Silver Spring, MD: National Association of Social Workers.

Barlow, D. (Ed.). (2001). *Clinical handbook of psychological disorders: A step by step treatment manual.* New York: Guilford.

Bateman, N. (1995). *Advocacy skills: A handbook for humans service professionals.* Aldershot, England: Arena.

Beck, A. T. (1976). *Cognitive therapy and the emotional disorders.* New York: International Universities Press.

Beck, D., & Jones, M. A. (1973). *Progress on family problems: A nationwide study of clients' and counselors' views on family agency services.* New York: Family Service Association of America.

Beck, J. S. (1995). *Cognitive therapy: Basics and beyond.* New York: Guilford.

Becker, H. (Ed.). (1967). *The other side: Perspectives on deviance.* New York: Free Press.

Bennis, W., & Nanus, B. (1997). *Leaders: The strategies for taking charge.* New York: Harper Business.

Bennis, W. G., & Thomas, R. J. (2002). *Geeks and geezers: How era, values, and defining moments shape leaders.* Boston: Harvard Business School Press.

Bergin, A. E., & Garfield, S. L. (Eds.). (1994). *Handbook of psychotherapy and behavior change.* 4th ed. New York: Wiley and Sons.

Bertanlaffy, L. (1968). *General systems theory: Foundations, development, application.* New York: Brazilier.

Berzoff, J., Flanagan, M. L., & Hertz, P. (1996). *Inside out and outside in: Psychodynamic clinical theory and practice in contemporary multicultural contexts.* Northvale, NJ: Aronson.

Beutler, L., Machado, P., & Neufeldt, S. (1994). Therapist variables. In A. Bergin &

S. Garfield (Eds.), *Handbook of psychotherapy and behavior change* (4th ed., pp. 259–269). New York: Wiley.

Biddle, B., & Thomas, E. J. (Eds.). (1966). *Role theory: Concepts and research.* New York: Wiley.

Biestek, F. (1957). *The casework relationship.* Chicago: Loyola University Press.

Binder, J. L. (2004). *Key competencies in brief dynamic psychotherapy.* New York: Guilford.

Bion, W. R. (1961). *Experiences in groups.* New York: Basic.

Bisman, C. (1994). *Social work practice: Cases and principles.* Pacific Grove, CA: Brooks/Cole.

Bloom, S. L. (1998). *Bearing witness: Violence and collective responsibility.* New York: Haworth Maltreatment and Trauma Press.

Bobo, K., Kendall, J., & Max, S. (1991). *Organizing for social change: A manual for activists in the 1990s.* Santa Ana, CA: Seven Locks.

Borden, W. (2000). The relational paradigm in contemporary psychoanalysis: Toward a psychodynamically informed social work perspective. *Social Service Review, 74*(3), 352–377.

Bowen, M. (1978). *Family therapy in clinical practice.* New York: Aronson.

Brace, C. (1973). *The dangerous classes of New York and twenty years among them.* New York: NASW Reprint.

Braeger, G., & Specht, H. (1973). *Community organizing.* New York: Columbia University Press.

Brauner, S., & Loprest, P. (1999). *Where are they now? What states' studies of welfare leavers tell us: Assessing the new federalism.* Washington, DC: Urban Institute.

Brower, A. (1998). The construction of small groups. In C. Franklin & P. S. Nurius (Eds.), *Constructivism in practice: Methods and challenges* (pp. 203–214). Milwaukee, WI: Families International.

Brown, A. W., & Bailey-Etta, B. (1997). An out-of-home care system in crisis: Implications for African-American children in the child welfare system. *Child Welfare, 76*(1), 65–84.

Bruyn, S. T., & Rayman, P. (1979). *Nonviolent action and social change.* New York: Irvington.

Breyer, S. (2005). *Active liberty: Interpreting our democratic constitution.* New York: Knopf.

Campbell, A. (1975, May). The American way of mating: Marriage si, children only maybe. *Psychology Today, 8,* 37–43.

Campbell Collaboration Colloquium. (2004). 4th Annual Conference. A first look at the evidence. February 17–20, Washington, DC.

Canadian Association of Social Workers. (2005). *Social work code of ethics.* Ottawa: Author.

Caplan, G. (1964). *Principles of preventive psychiatry.* New York: Basic.

Carter, B., & McGoldrick, M. (1989). *The changing family life cycle: a framework for family therapy* (2nd ed.). Boston: Allyn & Bacon.

Carter, B., & McGoldrick, M. (2004). *The expanded family life cycle: Individual, family and social perspectives* (3rd ed.). Needham Heights, MA: Allyn and Bacon.

Casey, R. J., & Berman, J. S. (1985). The outcome of psychotherapy with children. *Psychological Bulletin, 98,* 388–400.

Castonguay, L., Goldfried, M., Wiser, S., Raue, P., & Hayes, A. M. (1996). Predicting the effect of cognitive therapy for depression: A study of unique and common factors. *Journal of Consulting and Clinical Psychology, 64,* 497–504.

Chaiklin, H. (2004). Problem formulation, conceptualization, and theory development. In A. R. Roberts and K. Yeager (Eds.), *Evidence-based practice manual* (pp. 95–101). New York: Oxford University Press.

Chamberlain R., & Rapp, C. A. (1991). A decade of case management: A methodological review of outcome research. *Community Mental Health Journal, 27,* 171–188.

Chambers, D. (2000). *Social policy and social programs: A method for the practical public policy analyst* (3rd ed.). Boston: Allyn and Bacon.

Chestang, L. (1976). Environmental influences on social functioning: The black experience. In P. S. J. Cafferty & L. Chestang (Eds.), *The diverse society: Implications for social policy* (pp. 59–74). Washington, DC: National Association of Social Workers.

Child Abuse Prevention and Treatment Act (CAPTA). (1974). Reauthorized June 25, 2003, as the Keeping Children and Families Safe Act, P.L. 108–36.

Child Welfare League of America (CWLA). (2004). *National Fact Sheet 2004.* Retrieved July 2005 from www.cwla.org.

Christopherson, E. R., & Mortweet, S. L. (2001). *Treatments that work with children: Empirically supported strategies for managing childhood problems.* Washington, DC: American Psychological Association.

Ciarlariello v. Schacter. (1993). S C R 119 at 135.

Cloward, R., & Ohlin, L. (1960). *Delinquency and opportunity.* Glencoe, IL: Free Press.

Cohen, J. (1997). *Statistical power analysis for the behavioral sciences* (Rev. ed.). New York: Academic.

Comas-Diaz, L., & Greene, R. (1995). *Mental health and women of color.* New York: Guilford.

Comas-Diaz, L., & Griffiths, E. W. (Eds.). (1988). *Clinical guidelines in cross-cultural mental health.* New York: Wiley.

Commission on Social Work Practice. (1958). Working definition of social work practice. *Social Work, 3,* 5–8.

Community Mental Health Centers Act. (1963, October). P.L. 88–164.

Compton, B. R., & Galaway, B. (2004). *Social work processes* (7th ed.). Pacific Grove, CA: Wadsworth.

Cooley, D. (1983). *Social organization: A study of the larger mind.* New Brunswick, NJ: Transaction. (Original work published 1909)

Cowger, C. D. (1994). Assessing client strengths: Clinical assessment for client empowerment. *Social Work, 39*(3), 262–269.

Cox, F. M., Erlich J. L., Rothman, J., & Tropman, J. E. (Eds.). (1984). *Tactics and techniques of community practice.* Itasca, IL: Peacock.

Coyle, G. (1935). Group work and social change. In *Proceedings of the National Conference of Social Work* (p. 393). Chicago: University of Chicago Press.

Coyle, G. (1948). *Group work with American youth.* New York: Harper.

Daft, R. L., & Marcic, D. (2001). *Understanding management* (3rd ed.). Orlando, FL: Harcourt Brace.

Davanloo, H. B. (1980). *Short-term dynamic psychotherapy.* New York: Aronson.

Davis, L., & Proctor, E. (1989). *Race, gender and class: Guidelines for practice with individuals, families and groups.* Englewood Cliffs, NJ: Prentice-Hall.

Davis, S. R., & Meier, S. T. (2001). *The elements of managed care.* Belmont, CA: Wadsworth Thomson Learning.

Day, P. J. (2000). *A new history of social welfare* (3rd ed.). Boston: Allyn and Bacon.

DeJong, P., & Miller, S. D. (1995). How to interview for client strengths. *Social Work, 40,* 729–736.

DePoy, E., Hartman, A., & Haslett, D. (1999). Critical action research: A model for social work knowing. *Social Work, 44,* 560–569.

DeRubeis, R. J., Hollon, S. D., Amsterdam, J. D., Shelton, R. C., Young, P. R., Salomon, R. M., et al. (2005). Cognitive therapy vs. medications in the treatment of moderate to severe depression. *Archives of General Psychiatry, 62*(4), 409–416.

de Shazar, S. (1985). *Keys to solutions in brief therapy.* New York: Norton.

Devore, W., & Schlesinger, E. (1998). *Ethnic-sensitive social work practice* (5th ed.). Columbus, OH: Merrill.

Dewey, J. (2004). *Democracy and education.* Mineola, NY: Dover. (Original work published 1933)

DiNitto, D. (1991). *Social welfare politics and public policy* (3rd ed.). Englewood Cliffs, NJ: Prentice-Hall.

Dionne, E. J., Jr. (2005, August 12). The unconscionable: Bush's plan for the welfare state. *Commonweal, 132*(14), 7.

Dorfman, R. A. (Ed.). (1988). *Paradigms of clinical social work.* New York: Brunner/Mazel.

Dorfman, R. A. (Ed.). (1998). *Paradigms of clinical social work* (Vol. 2). New York: Brunner/Mazel.

Drisko, J. W. (1997). Strengthening qualitative studies and reports: Standards to promote academic integrity. *Journal of Social Work Education, 33*(1), 185–197.

Drisko, J. W. (2004). Common factors in psychotherapy outcome: Meta-analytic findings and their implications for practice and research. *Families in Society: The Journal of Contemporary Social Services, 85*(1), 81–90.

Dryegrov, A. (2003). *Psychological debriefing: A leader's guide for small group crisis intervention.* Ellicott City, MD: Chevron.

Dunst, C. J., Trivette, C. M., & Deal, A. G. (Eds.). (1994). *Supporting and strengthening families: Vol. I. Methods, strategies, and practices.* Cambridge, MA: Brookline.

Early, T. J., & GlenMaye, L. F. (2000). Valuing families: Social work practice with families from a strengths perspective. *Social Work, 45*(2), 118–130.

Earned Income Tax Credit (Revenue Act). (1978). P.L. 95–600.

Eitzen, D. S., & Zinn, M. B. (2003). *Social problems* (9th ed.). Boston: Allyn and Bacon.

Eitzen, D. S., & Zinn, M. B. (2004). *In conflict and order.* Boston: Pearson.

Elkin, I., Gibbons, R. D., Shea, M. T., Sotsky, S. M., Watkins, J. T., Pilkonis, P. A., et al. (1995). National Institute of Mental Health Treatment of Depression Collaborative Research Program: Initial severity and differential treatment outcome. *Journal of Consulting Clinical Psychology, 63*(5), 841–847.

English, D. J., & Pecora, P. J. (1994). Risk assessment as a practice in child protective services. *Child Welfare, 73,* 451–473.

Ephross, P. H., & Vasil, T. V. (1988). *Groups that work.* New York: Columbia University Press.

Epstein, L. (1992). *Brief treatment and a new look at the task-centered approach.* New York: Macmillan.

Erikson, E. (1963). *Childhood and society.* New York: Norton.

Eron, J. B., & Lund, T. W. (1996). *Narrative solutions in brief therapy.* New York: Guilford.

Etzioni, A. (1968). *The active society: A theory of societal and political processes.* New York: Free Press.

Etzioni, A. (1993). *The spirit of community: The reinvention of American society.* New York: Touchstone/Simon and Schuster.

Etzioni, A. (Ed.). (1995). *New communitarian thinking: Persons, institutions, and communities.* Charlottesville: University of Virginia Press.

Everett, J., Chipungu, S., & Leashore, B. (1991) *Child welfare: An Africentric perspective.* New Brunswick, NJ: Rutgers University Press.

Everly, G. S., Jr. (Ed.). (1995). *Innovations in disaster and trauma psychology: Applications in emergency services and disaster response.* Ellicott City, MD: Chevron.

Eyerdam, R. (2003). Hurricane Andrew. In M. Lattanzi-Licht & K. Doka (Eds.), *Coping with public tragedy* (pp. 27–40). New York: Brunner-Routledge Hospice Foundation of America.

Eysenck, H. J. (1952). The effects of psychotherapy: An evaluation. *Journal of Consulting Psychology, 16,* 319–324.

Fairbairn, W. R. D. (1952). *An objects theory of personality.* New York: Basic.

Falck, H. (1988). *Social work: The membership perspective.* New York: Springer.

Family and Medical Leave Act. (1993).

Federal Privacy Act. (1974). P.L. 93–579.

Festinger, T. (1996). Going home and returning to foster care. *Children and Youth Services Review, 18,* 383–402.

Figley, C. (1995). *Compassion fatigue: Coping with secondary traumatic stress in those who treat the traumatized.* New York: Brunner/Mazel

Fisher, R. (1995). Political social work. *Journal of Social Work Education, 31*(2), 194–203.

Follett, M. P. (1924). *Creative experience.* New York: Longmans Green.

Food Stamp Act. (1974). P.L. 930–86.

Forbes, D., Phelps, A. J., McHugh, A. F., Debenham, P., Hopwood, M., & Creamer, M. (2003). Imagery rehearsal in the treatment of posttraumatic nightmares in Australian veterans with chronic combat-related PTSD: 12-month follow-up data. *Journal of Traumatic Stress, 16*(5), 509–513.

Foster-Fishman, P. G., Salem, D. A., Chibnall, S., Legler, R., & Yapchai, C. (1998). Empirical support for the critical assumptions of empowerment theory. *American Journal of Community Psychology, 26*(4), 507–536.

Foulkes, S. F. (1964). *Therapeutic group analysis.* New York: International Universities Press.

Fowler, R. B. (1995). Community: Reflections on definition. In A. Etzioni (Ed.), *New communitarian thinking: Persons, institutions, and communities* (pp. 88–98). Charlottesville: University of Virginia Press.

Fraiberg, S. (1959). *The magic years.* New York: Scribner's.

Frank, J. D., & Frank, J. B. (1991). *Persuasion and healing: A comparative study of psychotherapy* (3rd ed.). Baltimore: Johns Hopkins University Press.

Freire, P. (1970). *Pedagogy of the oppressed.* New York: Herder and Herder.

Freire, P. (1973). *Education for critical consciousness.* New York: Seabury.

Freire, P. (1990). A critical understanding of social work. *Journal of Progressive Human Services, 1*(1), 3–9.

French, J. R. P., Jr., & Raven, B. (1959). The bases of social power. In D. Cartwright, (Ed.), *Studies in social power* (pp. 150–167). Ann Arbor, MI: Institute for Social Research.

Freud, S. (1960). *Group psychology and the analysis of the ego.* New York: Bantam. (Original work published 1921)

Freud, S. (1969). *The complete psychological works of Sigmund Freud* (J. Strachey, Ed.). London: Hogarth. (Original work published 1908)

Friedman, M. J. (2001). *Post-traumatic stress disorder: The latest assessment and treatment strategies.* Kansas City, MO: Compact Clinicals.

Galper, J. (1980). *Social work practice: A radical perspective.* Englewood Cliffs, NJ: Prentice-Hall.

Gambrill, E. (1997). *Social work practice: A critical thinker's guide.* New York: Oxford University Press.

Gambrill, E. (2005). *Critical thinking in clinical practice: Improving the quality of judgments and decisions* (2nd ed.). New York: Wiley.

Gans, J. S. (1989). Hostility in group psychotherapy. *International Journal of Group Psychotherapy, 39*(4), 499–516.

Garfield, S. (1994). Research on client variables in psychotherapy. In A. Bergin & S. Garfield (Eds.), *Handbook of psychotherapy and behavior change* (4th ed., pp. 190–228). New York: Wiley.

Garvin, C. D., & Seabury, B. A. (1997). *Interpersonal practice in social work* (2nd ed.). Boston: Allyn and Bacon.

Geismar, L. L. (1980). *Family and community functioning* (2nd ed.). Metuchen, NJ: Scarecrow.

Gelles, R. J., & Straus, M. A. (1987). Is violence toward children increasing? A comparison of 1975 and 1985 survey rates. *Journal of Interpersonal Violence, 2,* 212–222.

Gergen, K. J. (1999). *An invitation to social construction.* Thousand Oaks, CA: Sage.

Germain, C. B., & Gitterman, A. (1980). *The life model of social work practice.* New York: Columbia University Press.

Gil, D. G. (1998). *Confronting injustice and oppression.* New York: Columbia University Press.

Gil, D. G. (2000). Challenging injustice and oppression. In M. O'Melia & K. Miley (Eds.), *Pathways to power: Readings in contextual social work practice* (pp. 35–54). Boston: Allyn and Bacon.

Gilbert, N., & Specht, H. (1987). Social planning and community organization. In A. Minahan, *Encyclopedia of social work* (18th ed., Vol. 11, pp. 602–619). Silver Spring, MD: National Association of Social Workers.

Gilbert, N., & Terrell, P. (1998). *Dimensions of social welfare policy* (4th ed.). Boston: Allyn and Bacon.

Gilligan, C. (1982/1993). *In a different voice.* Cambridge, MA: Harvard University Press.

Ginsberg, L., & Keys, P. R. (Eds.). (1995). *New management in human services* (2nd ed.). Silver Spring, MD: NASW.

Glass, G., McGaw, E., & Smith, M. L. (1981). *Meta-analysis in social research.* Beverly Hills, CA: Sage.

Goffee, R., & Jones, G. (2000). Why should anyone be led by you? *Harvard Business Review, 78*(5), 62–70.

Goffman, E. (1959). *The presentation of self in everyday life.* Garden City, NY: Doubleday/Anchor.

Goffman, E. (1961). *Asylums: Essays on the social situation of mentally ill and other inmates.* Chicago: Aldine.

Goldstein, E. (1996). Ego psychology theory. In F. Turner (Ed.), *Social work treatment* (4th ed., pp. 191–217). New York: Free Press.

Gordon, W., & Trafton, J. (2003). *Best practices in the behavioral management of chronic disease.* Los Altos, CA: Institute for Management.

Gould, R. (1972). The phases of adult life: A study in developmental psychology. *American Journal of Psychiatry, 129,* 33–43.

Green, J. (1995). *Cultural awareness in the human services* (2nd ed.). Englewood Cliffs, NJ: Prentice-Hall.

Greene, R. R., & Ephross, P. H. (1991). *Human behavior theory and social work practice.* New York: Aldine de Gruyter.

Greene, G. J., Lee, M. Y., Trask, R., & Rheinscheld, J. (2000). How to work with clients' strengths in crisis intervention: A solution-focused approach. In A. R. Roberts (Ed.), *Crisis intervention handbook* (2nd ed., pp 31–55). New York: Oxford University Press.

Gummer, B. (1990). *The politics of social administration: Managing organizational politics in social agencies.* Englewood Cliffs, NJ: Prentice-Hall.

Guthrie, E. (2000). Psychotherapy for patients with complex disorders and chronic symptoms: The need for a new research paradigm. *British Journal of Psychiatry, 177,* 131–137.

Gutierrez, L. M., Parsons, R. J., & Cox, E. O. (1998). *Empowerment in social work practice: A sourcebook.* Pacific Grove, CA: Brooks Cole.

Gutmann, A. (1995). The virtues of democratic self-constraint. In A. Etzioni (Ed.), *New communitarian thinking: Persons, institutions, and communities* (pp. 154–169). Charlottesville: University of Virginia Press.

Haley, J. (Ed.). (1971). *Changing families: A family therapy reader.* New York: Grune and Stratton.

Hare, P. A. (1962). *Handbook of small group research.* New York: Free Press.

Hargie, O., Saunders, C., & Dickson, D. (1991). *Social skills in interpersonal communication.* London. Rutledge.

Harris, M., & Bergman, H. C. (1993). *Case management for mentally ill patients: Theory and practice.* Langhorn, PA: Harwood Academic.

Harry, J. (1976). Evolving sources of happiness for men over the life cycle: A structural analysis. *Journal of Marriage and the Family, 2,* 289–296.

Hartman, A. (1981). The family: A central focus for practice. *Social Work, 26,* 7–13.

Hartman, A., & Laird, J. (1983). *Family centered social work practice.* New York: Free Press.

Hasenfeld, Y. (1987). Power in social work practice. *Social Service Review, 61,* 469–483.

Haynes, K. S., & Mickelson, J. S. (2000). *Affecting change: Social workers in the political arena* (4th ed.). Boston: Allyn and Bacon.

Health Insurance Portability and Accountability Act. (1996). P.L. 104–191. http://www.cms.hhs.gov/HIPAAGenInfo.

Hepworth, D. H., Rooney, R. H., & Larsen, J. A. (2002). *Direct social work practice: Theory and skills* (6th ed.). Pacific Grove, CA: Brooks/Cole.

Hobbes, T. (2006). *Leviathan.* Minolo, NY: Dover. (Original work published 1660)

Hobfoll, S. E. (1989). Conservation of resources: A new attempt of conceptualizing stress. *American Psychologist, 44*(3), 513–524.

Hodgetts, R. M. (2001). *Modern human relations at work* (8th ed.). Mason, OH: South-Western.

Hoffer, E. (1951). *The true believer.* New York: Harper and Row.

Hollenbach, S. J. D. (1995). Virtue, the common good and democracy. In A. Etzioni (Ed.), *Communitarian thinking: Persons, institutions, and communities* (pp. 143–153). Charlottesville: University of Virginia Press.

Hollis, F. (1964). *Casework: A psychosocial therapy.* New York: McGraw-Hill.

Hollis, F., & Woods, M. (1981). *Casework: A psychosocial therapy* (3rd ed.). New York: McGraw-Hill.

Homans, G. (1950). *The human group.* New York: Harcourt Brace Jovanovich.

Hubble, M., Duncan, B., & Miller, S. (1999). *The heart and soul of change: What works in therapy.* Washington, DC: American Psychological Association.

Hudson, W. W. (1982). *The clinical measurement package: A field manual.* Homewood, IL: Dorsey.

Hunter, J., & Schmidt, F. (1990). *Methods of meta-analysis: Correcting error bias in research findings.* Thousand Oaks, CA: Sage.

Interethnic Adoption Provisions. (1996). Amendment to Multiethnic Placement Act.

Ivey, A. E. (1994). *Intentional interviewing and counseling* (3rd ed.). Pacific Grove, CA: Brooks/Cole.

Jacobs, C., & Bowles, D. (Eds.). (1988). *Ethnicity and race: Critical concepts in social work.* Silver Spring, MD: NASW.

James, R. K., & Gilliland, B. E. (2004). *Crisis intervention strategies* (5th ed.). Pacific Grove, CA: Brooks/Cole.

Janoff-Bulman, R. (1992). *Shattered assumptions: Towards a new psychology of trauma.* New York: Free Press.

Janson, B. S. (1999). *Becoming an effective policy advocate: From policy practice to social justice* (3rd ed.). Pacific Grove, CA: Brooks/Cole.

Jessop, B. (2004). Hollowing out the "nation-state" and multi-level governance. In P. Kennett (Ed.), *Handbook of comparative social policy* (pp. 11–22). Northampton, VT: Elgar.

Jones, E. E., & Pulos, S. M. (1993). Comparing the process in psychodynamic and cognitive-behavioral therapies. *Journal of Consulting and Clinical Psychology, 61*(2), 306–316.

Jones, M., Neuman, R., & Shyne, A. W. (1976). *A second chance for families: Evaluation of a program to reduce foster care.* New York: Child Welfare League of America.

Jones, S. L. (1980). *Family therapy: A comparison of approaches.* Bowie, MD: Brady.

Kadushin, A. (1990). *The social work interview* (3rd ed.). New York: Columbia University Press.

Karger, H. J., & Stoesz, D. (1998). *American social welfare policy: A pluralist approach* (3rd ed.). New York: Longman.

Karls, J., & Wandrei, K. (Eds.). (1994). *Person-in-environment: A PIE classification system for social functioning problems.* Washington DC: National Association of Social Workers.

Kazdin, A. (2001). Progression of therapy research and clinical application of treatment require better understanding of the change process. *Clinical Psychology: Science and Practice, 8,* 143–151.

Kazdin, A. E., & Weisz, J. R. (Eds.). (2003). *Evidence-based psychotherapies for children and adolescents.* New York: Guilford.

Kellerman, B. (2005). *Bad leadership: What it is, why it happens and why it matters.* Cambridge, MA: Harvard Business School Press.

Kennett, P. (Ed.). (2004). *Handbook of comparative social policy.* Northampton, VT: Elgar.

Kernberg, O. (1984). *Severe personality disorders: Psychotherapeutic strategies.* New Haven, CT: Yale University Press.

Kinney, J., Haapala, D., & Booth, C. (1991). *Keeping families together: The homebuilder model.* New York: Aldine de Gruyter.

Kirk, S. A., & Kutchins, H. (1992). *The selling of DSM: The rhetoric of science in psychiatry.* Hawthorne, NY: Aldine de Gruyter.

Kirst-Ashman, K. K., & Hull, G. H. (2000). *Generalist practice with organizations and communities.* Chicago: Nelson-Hall.

Kirst-Ashman, K. K., & Hull, G. H., Jr. (2004). *Understanding generalist practice* (3rd ed.). Pacific Grove, CA: Brooks/Cole.

Knoke, D., & Trocme, N. (2005). Reviewing the evidence on assessing risk for child abuse and neglect. *Brief Treatment and Crisis Intervention: A Journal of Evidence-based Practice, 5*(3), 310–327.

Konopka, G. (1972). *Social group work: A helping process* (2nd ed.). Englewood Cliffs, NJ: Prentice-Hall.

Koestler, A. (1967). *The ghost in the machine.* New York: Macmillan.

Kohut, H. (1977). *The restoration of the self.* New York: International University Press.

Korr, W. S., & Cloninger, L. (1991). Assessing models of case management: An empirical approach. *Journal of Social Service Research, 14,* 129–147.

Kotlowitz, A. (1991). *There are no children here.* New York: Anchor.

Kubler-Ross, E. (1969). *On death and dying.* New York: Macmillan.

Kutchins, H. (1991). The fiduciary relationship: The legal basis for social workers' responsibilities to clients. *Social Work, 36,* 106–113.

Kutchins, H., & Kirk, S. A. (1997). *Making us crazy: DSM—the psychiatric bible and the creation of mental disorders.* New York: Free Press.

Lakey, G. (1987). *Powerful peacemaking: A strategy for a living revolution.* Philadelphia: New Society.

Lambert, M., & Asay, T. (1984). Patient characteristics and their relationship to psychotherapy outcome. In M. Herson, L. Michelson, & A. Bellack (Eds.), *Issues in psychotherapy research* (pp. 313–359). New York: Plenum.

Lambert M., & Bergin, S. (1994). Assessing psychotherapy outcomes and processes. In A. Bergin & S. Garfield (Eds.), *Handbook of psychotherapy and behavior change* (4th ed., pp. 143–189). New York: Wiley.

Lambert, M., & Hill, C. (1994). Assessing psychotherapy outcomes and processes. In A. Bergin & S. Garfield (Eds.), *Handbook of psychotherapy and behavior change* (4th ed., pp. 72–113). New York: Wiley.

Lantz, J. (1996). Cognitive theory and social work treatment. In F. Turner (Ed.), *Social work treatment* (4th ed., pp. 94–115). New York: Free Press.

Lattanzi-Licht, M., & Doka, K. (Eds.). (2003). *Coping with public tragedy.* New York: Brunner-Routledge Hospice Foundation of America.

Lazarus, R., & Folkman, S. (1984). *Stress, appraisal and coping.* Toronto: McGraw-Hill.

Leashore, B. R., McMurray, H. L., & Bailey, B. C. (1991). Reuniting and preserving African American families. In J. E. Everett, S. S. Chipungu, and B. R. Leashore (Eds.), *Child welfare: An Africentric perspective* (pp. 247–265). New Brunswick, NJ: Rutgers University Press.

Le Bon, G. (2001). *The crowd: A study of the popular mind.* Mineola, NY: Dover. (Original work published 1895)

Lee, J. (2004). Speaker, 4th annual Campbell Collaboration Colloquium. A first look at the evidence. February 17–20. Washington DC.

Lee, J. A. B. (2001). *The empowerment approach to social work practice* (2nd ed.). New York: Columbia University Press.

Lehmann, R., & Coady, N. (2001). *Theoretical perspectives for direct social work practice: A generalist-eclectic approach.* New York: Springer.

Leong, F. T. (1986). Counseling and psychotherapy with Asian Americans: Review of the literature. *Counseling Psychology, 32*(4), 196–206.

Levinson, D. (1978). *The seasons of a man's life.* New York: Knopf.

Levitt, E. E. (1963). The results of therapy with children: A further evaluation. *Behavior Research and Therapy, 60,* 326–329.

Lewin, K. (1951). *Field theory in social science.* New York: Harper and Brothers.

Liebow, E. (1993). *Tell them who I am: The lives of homeless women.* New York: Free Press.

Lightburn, A., & Sessions, P. (Eds.). (2006). *Community-based clinical practice.* New York: Oxford University Press.

Lilienfeld, S. O., Lynn, S. J., & Lohr, J. M. (2003). *Science and pseudoscience in clinical psychology.* New York: Guilford.

Lindemann, E. (1944). Symptomatology and management of acute grief. *American Journal of Psychiatry, 101,* 141–148.

Lindsey, D. (1994). *The welfare of children.* New York: Oxford University Press.

Linley, P. A. (2003). Positive adaptation to trauma: Wisdom as both process and outcome. *Journal of Traumatic Stress, 19*(6), 601–610.

Linz, M. H., McAnally, P., & Wieck, C. (1989). *Case management: Historical, current and future perspectives.* Cambridge, MA: Brookline.

Lippit, R., Watson, J., & Westely, B. (1958). *The dynamics of planned change.* New York: Harcourt.

Lipsey, M., & Wilson, D. (2001). *Practical meta-analysis.* Thousand Oaks, CA: Sage.

Locke, J. (1995). *An essay concerning human understanding.* Amherst, NY: Prometheus. (Original work published 1690)

Loprest, P. (1999). *Families who left welfare: Who are they and how are they doing?* Discussion Paper No. 99–02. Washington, DC: Urban Institute.

Luborsky, L., McClellan, A. T., Diguer, L., Woody, G., & Seligman, D. A. (1997). The psychotherapist matters: Comparison of outcomes across twenty-two therapists and seven patient samples. *Clinical Psychology: Science and Practice, 4,* 53–65.

Luborsky, L., Rosenthal, R., Diguer, L., Andrusyna, T. P., Berman, J., Levitt, J., et al. (2002). The dodo bird verdict is alive and well-mostly. *Clinical Psychology: Science and Practice, 9,* 2–12.

Luborsky, L., & Singer, B. (1975). Comparative studies of psychotherapies: Is it true that "everyone has won and all must have prizes"? *Archives of General Psychology, 42,* 602–611.

MacDonald v. Clinger. (1982). N.Y.S. 2d. 801 (App. Div.).

Machiavelli, N. (1975). *Machiavelli's* The Prince: *Text and commentary* (Jean-Pierre Barricelli, ed.). Woodbury, NY: Barron's. (Original work published 1513)

Mahler, M. S., Pine, F., & Bergman, A. (1975). *The psychological birth of the human infant.* New York: Basic.

Maier, H. W. (Ed). (1965). *Group work as part of residential treatment.* New York: NASW.

Maione, E. V., & Chenail, R. J. (1999). Qualitative inquiry in psychotherapy: Research on common factors. In M. Hubble, B. Duncan, & S. Miller (Eds.), *The heart and soul of change: The role of common factors in psychotherapy* (pp. 57–88). Washington, DC: American Psychological Association.

Maluccio, A. N. (1979). *Learning from clients: Interpersonal helping as viewed by clients and social workers.* New York: Free Press.

Mayo, E. (1977). *The human problems of an industrial civilization: Work, its rewards and discontents.* New York: Arno.

McEwen, B. S. (2000). The neurobiology of stress: From serendipity to clinical relevance. *Brain Research, 886*(1–2), 172–189.

McGoldrick, M., Giordano, J., & Pearce, J. K. (1996). *Ethnicity and family therapy* (2nd ed.). New York: Guilford.

McGregor, D. (1960). *The human side of enterprise.* New York: McGraw-Hill.

McInery v. MacDonald (1992).

McKay, A. E., Goldberg, M., & Fruin, D. J. (1973). Consumers and a social service department. *Social Work Today, 4*(16), 486–491.

McPheeters, H. L. (1984). Statewide mental health outcome evaluation: A perspective of two southern states. *Community Mental Health Journal, 20,* 44–55.

Merton, K. (1975). *Social theory and social structure.* New York: Free Press.

Messer, S., & Warren, S. (1995). *Models of brief psychodynamic therapy.* New York: Guilford.

Milgram, S. (1974). *Obedience to authority: An experimental view.* New York: Harper and Row.

Miller, S. D., Hubble, M. A., & Duncan, B. L. (Eds.). (1996). *Handbook of solution-focused brief therapy.* San Francisco: Jossey-Bass.

Ministry of Health and Long-Term Care. (2000). Brian's law. Mental Health Legislative Reform, Canada.

Minuchin, S. (1974). *Families and family therapy.* Cambridge, MA: Harvard University Press.

Mitchell, J., Reithoffer, A., & Blythe, B. (2000). *Outcome studies in social work research: The state of the art.* Paper presented at the Fourth Annual Conference of the Society for Social Work Research, January, Charleston, SC.

Moore, K. A., Chalk, R., Scarpa, J., & Vandivere, S. (2002). *Family strengths: Often overlooked, but real.* Washington, DC: Child Trends.

Moreno, T. (1934). *Personality and social change.* New York: Dryden.

Moxley, D. P. (1989). *The practice of case management.* Newbury Park, CA: Sage.

Multiethnic Placement Act (MEPA). (1994).

Munson, C. (2002). *Handbook of clinical social work supervision.* New York: Haworth.

Nadelson, C. C., & Polonsky, D. C. (Eds.) (1984). *Marriage and divorce: A contemporary perspective.* New York: Guilford.

Nathan, P., & Gorman, J. (2002). Efficacy, effectiveness and the clinical utility of psy-
    chotherapy research. In P. Nathan & J. Gorman (Eds.), *A guide to treatments that
    work* (pp. 643–654). New York: Oxford University Press.

National Association of Social Workers. (1999). *Code of ethics.* Washington DC:
    Author.

National Association of Social Workers, New York Chapter. (2000). *How to lobby:
    Developing an advocacy agenda.* Retrieved July 9, 2000, from http//www
    .presentelderabuse.org/frame/online/techniquesleg.htm.

National Association of Social Workers. (2001). *Standards of cultural competence in
    social work.* Washington, DC: Author.

National Clearing House on Child Abuse and Neglect. (2003). Information. Foster
    care national statistics 2003. Retrieved January 2006 from www://acf.hhs.gov.

National Family Preservation Network. (2003). *News notes.* Retrieved August 2005
    from www.casanet.org/library/family-preservation.

National Institute of Mental Health. (1989). *Guidelines for planning and implement-
    ing case management systems: P.L. 99–660, Title V.* Washington DC: U.S. Gov-
    ernment Printing Office.

Netting, F. E., Kettner, P. M., & McMurtry, S. L. (1997). *Social work macro practice.*
    New York: Longman.

Nitsun, M. (1996). *The anti-group: Destructive forces in the group and their creative
    potential.* London and New York: Routledge.

Noble, J. H., Jr. (2006). Meta-analysis: Methods, strengths, weaknesses, and political
    uses. *Journal of Laboratory and Clinical Medicine, 147*(1), 7–20.

Norcross, J. C. (Ed.). (2002). *Psychotherapy relationships that work: Therapists' con-
    tributions and responsiveness to patients.* New York: Oxford University Press.

Northern, H. (1982). *Social work with groups* (2nd ed.). New York: Columbia Uni-
    versity Press.

O'Hanlon, W., & Weiner-Davis, M. (1989). *In search of solutions.* New York: Norton.

O'Keefe, D. J. (2001). Persuasion. In T. O. Sloane (Ed.), *Encyclopedia of rhetoric* (pp.
    575–583). New York: Oxford University Press.

Older Americans Act. (1992).

Olsson, D. E. (1968). *Management by objectives.* Palo Alto, CA: Pacific.

O'Melia, M., & Miley, K. K. (Eds.). (2000). *Pathways to power: Readings in contextual
    social work practice.* Boston: Allyn and Bacon.

O'Neill, J. (1999, June). Profession dominates in mental health. *NASW News, 44,* 1.

Orlinsky D., Grawe, K., & Parks, D. (1994). Process and outcome in psychotherapy.
    In A. Bergin & S. Garfield (Eds.), *Handbook of psychotherapy and behavior
    change* (4th ed., pp. 72–113). New York: Wiley.

Orlinsky, D. E., & Howard, K. I. (1986). Process and outcome in psychotherapy. In
    S. L. Garfield & A. E. Bergin (Eds.), *Handbook of psychotherapy and behavior
    change* (pp. 331–381). New York: Wiley.

Ouchi, W. G. (1981). *Theory Z: How American business can meet the Japanese chal-
    lenge.* Reading, MA: Addison-Wesley.

P. (L. M.) v. F (D) (1994). 22 C.C.L.T. (2d) 312 (Ontario, Gen div).

Padgett, D. (1998). *Qualitative methods in social work research: Challenges and rewards.* Thousand Oaks, CA: Sage.

Parad, H. J. (1965). *Crisis intervention: Selected readings.* New York: Family Service Association of America.

Parrott, S. (1998). *Welfare recipients who find jobs: What do we know about their employment and earnings?* Washington DC: Center on Budget and Policy Priorities.

Parsons, T. (1970). *Social structure and personality.* New York: Free Press.

Parsons, T. (1977). *Social systems and the evolution of action theory.* New York: Free Press.

Patterson, C. H. (1984). Empathy, warmth, and genuineness: A review of reviews. *Psychotherapy: Theory, Research and Practice, 21*(4), 431–438.

Patti, R. J. (1983). *Social welfare administration: Managing social programs in a developmental context.* Englewood Cliffs, NJ: Prentice-Hall.

Paul, H. (2004). Issues and controversies surrounding recent texts on empirically based psychotherapy: A meta-review. *Brief Treatment and Crisis Intervention 4*(4), 389–399.

Pearlin, L. I., Meaghan, E. G., Lieberman, M. A., & Mullin, J. T. (1981). The stress process. *Journal of Health and Social Behavior, 22,* 347–348.

Pennell, J., & Buford, G. (1997). *Family group decision making project: Outcome report, summary.* St. John's, Newfoundland: Memorial University, School of Social Work.

Perlman, H. H. (1957). *Social casework: A problem solving process.* Chicago: University of Chicago Press.

Perlman, H. H. (1979). *Relationship: The heart of helping people.* Chicago: University of Chicago Press.

Perls, F. (1976). *Gestalt therapy verbatim.* New York: Bantam.

Personal Information Protection and Electronic Documents Act. (2000). www.laws.justice.gc.ca/en/p-8.6/93196.html.

Personal Responsibility and Work Opportunity Reconciliation Act. (1996). P.L. 104–193.110 Stat. 2105.

Peters, T. J., & Waterman, R. H., Jr. (1982). *In search of excellence: Lessons learned from America's best-run companies.* New York: Warner.

Piaget, J. (1950). *The psychology of intelligence.* New York: Harcourt Brace Jovanovich.

Pincus, A., & Minahan, A. (1973). *Social work practice: Model and methods.* Itasca, IL: Peacock.

Pinderhughes, E. (1983). Empowerment for our clients and for ourselves. *Social Casework, 31,* 214–219.

Pines, M. (1983). *The evolution of group analysis.* London: Routledge and Kegan Paul.

Plionis, E. M. (2004). Decision tree: A conceptual tool for best practices. *Brief Treatment and Crisis Intervention, 4*(1), 37–47.

Plionis, E. M., Bailey-Etta, B., & Manning, M. (2002). Implementing the generalist model in practice: Implications for curriculum and best practices. *Journal of Teaching in Social Work, 22*(3–4), 103–120.

Plionis, E. M., & Lewis, H. J. (1998). Teaching cultural diversity and oppression: Preparation for risk: The Coverdale model. *Journal of Teaching in Social Work, 12*(1–2), 175–192.

Polansky, N. (1986). There is nothing so practical as a good theory. *Child Welfare, 65*(1), 3–15.

Poloma, J. (Ed). (1979). *Contemporary sociological theory.* New York: Macmillan.

Popple, P. R., & Leighninger, L. (1998). *Social work, social welfare, and American society* (4th ed.). Boston: Allyn and Bacon.

Poulin, J. (Ed.). (2000). *Collaborative social work: Strengths-based generalist practice.* Itasca, IL: Peacock.

Poulin, J. (Ed.). (2005). *Strengths-based generalist practice: A collaborative approach* (2nd ed.). Belmont, CA: Brooks/Cole.

Privacy Act. (1985). www.laws.justice.gc.ca/en/P-21.

Prochaska, J. O. (1999). How do people change and how can we change to help many more people? In M. A. Hubble, B. L. Duncan, & S. D. Miller (Eds.), *The heart and soul of change* (pp. 227–258). Washington, DC: American Psychological Association Press.

Psychiatric Survivor Action Association of Ontario. (2006). In C. Regehr and K. Kanani (Eds.), *Law for social work practice in Canada* (p. 82). Ontario, Canada: Oxford University Press.

Punamaki-Gitai, R. L. (1990). *Political violence and psychological responses: A study of Palestinian women, children and ex-prisoners.* Tampere, Finland: Tampere Peace Research Institute.

Rapp, C. (1998). *The strengths model: Case management with people suffering from severe and persistent mental illness.* New York: Oxford University Press.

Rapp, C., & Chamberlain, R. (1985). Case management services to the chronically mentally ill. *Social Work, 30*(5), 417–422.

Reamer, F. G. (1987). Informed consent in social work. *Social Work, 32,* 425–429.

Reamer, F. G. (1995). *Social work values and ethics.* New York: Columbia University Press.

Reed, K., & Kirk, R. (1998). Intensive family preservation services: A short history but a long past. *Family Preservation Journal, 3*(1), 47–57.

Regehr, C., & Bober, T. (2005). *In the line of fire: Trauma in the emergency services.* New York: Oxford University Press.

Regehr, C., & Kanani, K. (2006). *Law for social work practice in Canada.* Ontario, Canada: Oxford University Press.

Regehr, C., & Sussman, T. (2004). Intersections between grief and trauma: Toward an empirically based model for treating traumatic grief. *Brief Treatment and Crisis Intervention, 4*(3), 289–308.

Reibl v. Hughes. (1980). 114 D.L. R. (3d) I (S.C.C.).

Reid, W. (1997). Evaluating the dodo's verdict: Do all interventions have equivalent outcomes? *Social Work Research, 21*(7), 5–15.

Reid, W., & Epstein, L. (1972). *Task-centered casework.* New York: Columbia University Press.

Reid, W., & Shyne, A. (1969). *Brief and extended casework.* New York: Columbia University Press.

Reisch, M. (1997). The political context of social work. In M. Reisch & E. Gambrill (Eds.), *Social work in the 21st century* (pp. 80–92). Thousand Oaks, CA: Pine Forge.

Reitsman-Street, M., & Brown, L. (2003). Community action research. In M. O'Melia & K. K. Miley (Eds.), *Readings in contextual social work practice* (pp. 74–94). Boston: Allyn & Bacon.

Reynolds, B. C. (1951). *Social work and social living.* New York: Citadel.

Reza, A., Mercy, J. A., & Krug, E. (2001). Epidemiology of violent deaths in the world. *Injury Prevention, 7,* 104–111.

Richmond, M. (1899). *Friendly visiting among the poor: A handbook for charity workers.* New York: Macmillan.

Richmond, M. (1917). *Social diagnosis.* New York: Russell Sage Foundation.

Richmond, M. (1922). *What is social casework?* New York: Sage.

Rivas, R. F., & Hull, G. H., Jr. (Eds.) (1999). *Case studies in generalist practice* (2nd ed.). Belmont, CA: Brooks/Cole.

Robert, H. M. (1971). *Robert's rules of order revised.* New York: Morrow.

Roberts, A. R. (Ed.). (1990). *Crisis intervention handbook: Assessment, treatment, and research.* Belmont, CA: Wadsworth.

Roberts, A. R. (1991). *Contemporary perspectives on crisis intervention and prevention.* Englewood Cliffs, NJ: Prentice-Hall.

Roberts, A. R. (Ed.). (1997). *Crisis management and brief treatment: Theory, technique and applications.* Chicago: Nelson-Hall.

Roberts, A. R. (Ed.). (2005). *Crisis intervention handbook: Assessment, treatment, and research* (3rd ed.). New York: Oxford University Press.

Roberts, A. R., & Everly, G. S. (2006). A meta-analysis of 36 crisis intervention studies. *Brief Treatment and Crisis Intervention, 6*(1), 10–21.

Roberts, A. R., & Roberts, B. S. (2005). *Ending intimate abuse.* New York: Oxford University Press.

Roberts, A. R., & Yeager, K. (2004). *Evidence-based practice manual: Research and outcome measures in health and human services.* New York: Oxford University Press.

Robinson, C. (1993). Managing life with a chronic condition: The story of normalization. *Qualitative Health Research, 3*(1), 6–28.

Robinson, L., Berman, J., & Neimeyer, R. (1990). Psychotherapy for the treatment of depression: A comprehensive review of controlled outcome research. *Psychological Bulletin, 108,* 30–39.

Robinson, V. (1930). *A changing psychology in social casework.* Chapel Hill, NC: University of North Carolina Press.

Rogers, C. R. (1957). The necessary and sufficient conditions of therapeutic personality change. *Journal of Counseling Psychology, 121,* 95–103.

Rokeach, M. (1973). *The nature of human values.* New York: Free Press.

Ronnau, J., & Poertner, J. (1993). Identification and use of strengths: A family system approach. *Children Today, 22,* 20–23.

Rorty, R. (1991). *Objectivity, relativism, and truth.* New York: Cambridge University Press.

Rosenthal, R. (1984). *Meta-analytic procedures for social research.* Beverly, CA: Sage.

Roth, A., & Fonagy, P. (1996). *What works for whom? A critical review of psychotherapy.* New York: Guilford.

Rothman, J. (1994). *Practice with highly vulnerable clients: Case management and community based services.* Englewood Cliffs, NJ: Prentice-Hall.

Rousseau, J. J. (1987). *Basic political writings* (D. A. Cress, ed. and trans.). Indianapolis: Hackett. (Original work published 1750, 1754, 1755, 1762)

Rubin, A. (1992). Is case management effective for people with serious mental illness? A research review. *Health and Social Work, 17,* 138–150.

Rycus, J. S., & Hughes, R. C. (2003). *Issues in risk assessment in child protective services: Policy white paper.* Retrieved August 31, 2005, from http://www.ihs-trainet.com/CCWP/publications.htm.

Sackett, D., Richardson, W., Rosenberg, W., & Haynes, R. (1997). *Evidence-based medicine.* New York: Churchill Livingston.

Saleebey, D. (2001). The diagnostic strengths manual? *Social Work, 46*(2), 183–187.

Saleebey, D. (Ed.). (1997). *The strengths perspective in social work practice* (2nd ed.). Boston: Allyn and Bacon.

Saleebey, D. (Ed.). (2002). *The strengths perspective in social work practice* (3rd ed.). Boston: Allyn and Bacon.

Sansbury, E. (1975). *Social work with families.* London: Routledge and Kegan Paul.

Satir, V. (1964). *Conjoint family therapy.* Palo Alto CA: Science and Behavior.

Schiller, B. R. (2001). *The economics of poverty and discrimination* (6th ed.). Englewood Cliffs, NJ: Prentice-Hall.

Schloendorff v. Society of New York Hospital. (1914). 105 N.E. 92.

Schneider, R. L., & Netting, F. E. (1999). Influencing social policy in a time of devolution: Upholding social work's great tradition. *Social Work, 44*(4), 349–357.

Schram, R. W. (1979). Marital satisfaction over the family life cycle: A critique and proposal. *Journal of Marriage and the family, 41*(1), 7–12.

Schuerman, J., Rzepnicki, T. L., & Littell, J. H. (1994). *Putting families first: An experiment in family preservation.* New York: Aldine de Gruyter.

Segal, E. A., & Brzuzy, S. (1998). *Social welfare: Policy, programs, and practice.* Itasca, IL: Peacock.

Seligman, M. E. P. (1995). The effectiveness of psychotherapy: The *Consumer Reports* study. *American Psychologist, 51*(12), 965–974.

Selye, H. (1936). A syndrome produced by diverse nocuous agents. *Nature, 138,* 32.

Shaffer, J. B. P., & Galinsky, M. D. (1974). The Tavistock approach to groups. In J. Shaffer & M. Galinsky (Eds.), *Models of group therapy and sensitivity training* (pp. 164–188). Englewood Cliffs, NJ: Prentice-Hall.

Sharp, G. (1973). *The politics of nonviolent action.* Boston: Porter Sargent.

Sharp, G. (1979). *Gandhi as a political strategist.* Boston: Porter Sargent.

Sheehy, G. (1977). *Passages.* New York: Bantam.

Shera, W. (2001). Managed care and the severely mentally ill: Current issues and future challenges. In N. Veeder & W. Peebles-Wilkins (Eds.), *Managed care services: Policies, programs, and research* (pp. 230–242). New York: Oxford University Press.

Shera, W. (2002). Empowering mental health consumers: Assessing the efficacy of a partnership model of case management. In M. O'Melia & K. K. Miley (Eds.), *Pathways to power: Readings in contextual social work practice* (pp. 214–229). Boston: Allyn and Bacon.

Shulmen, L. (1999). *The skills of helping individuals, families, groups, and communities* (4th ed.). Itasca, IL: Peacock.

Slavson, S. R. (1964). *A textbook of analytic group psychotherapy.* New York: International Universities Press.

Sleznick, P. (1995). Personhood and moral obligation. In A. Etzioni (Ed.), *New communitarian thinking: Persons, institutions, and communities* (pp. 110–125). Charlottesville: University of Virginia Press.

Smalley, R. E. (1967). *Theory for social work practice.* New York: Columbia University Press.

Smallwood, A. J. (1958). *Coverdale: The philosophy of achievement.* Arlington, VA: Coverdale.

Smith, K. K., & Berg, D. N. (1988). *Paradoxes of group life.* London: Jossey-Bass.

Smith, M., & Glass, G. (1977). Meta-analysis of psychotherapy outcome studies. *American Psychologist, 32,* 752–760.

Smith, M., Glass, G., & Miller, T. (1980). *The benefits of psychotherapy.* Baltimore: Johns Hopkins University Press.

Smith v. Jones. (1999). 1 S.C.R. 455 Can L11 674 (S.C.C.).

Social Security Act. (1935).

Solomon, M. (1990). *Working with difficult people.* Englewood Cliffs, NJ: Prentice-Hall.

Specht, H., & Courtney, M. E. (1994). *Unfaithful angels: How social work has abandoned its mission.* New York: Free Press.

Steadman, H., Davidson, S. E., & Brown, C. (2001). Mental health courts: Their promise and unanswered questions. *Psychiatric Services, 52*(4), 457–458.

Sterling, P., & Eyer, J. (1988). Allostasis: A new paradigm to explain arousal pathology. In S. Fisher & J. Reason (Eds.), *Handbook of life stress, condition, and health* (pp. 629–649). New York: Wiley.

Stevens, S., Hynan, M., & Allen, M. (2000). A meta-analysis of common factors and specific treatment effects across the outcome domains of the phase model of psychotherapy. *Clinical Psychology: Science and Practice, 7,* 273–290.

Stovall, K. C., & Dozier, M. (1998). Infants in foster care: An attachment theory perspective. *Adoption Quarterly, 2,* 55–88.

Strean, H. S. (1978). *Clinical social work theory and practice.* New York: Free Press.

Strean, H. (1985). *Therapeutic principles in practice: A manual for clinicians.* Beverly Hills, CA: Sage.

Sue, D. W., & Sue, D. (2003). *Counseling the culturally different: Theory and practice* (3rd ed.). New York: Wiley.

Sue, S., Zane, N., & Young, L. (1994). Research in psychotherapy with culturally diverse populations. In A. Bergin & S. Garfield (Eds.), *Handbook of psychotherapy and behavior change* (pp. 738–820). New York: Wiley.

Sullivan, H. S. (1954). *The psychiatric interview.* New York: Norton.

Sullivan, P. W. (2000). Generalist practice with persons with serious and persistent mental illness. In J. Poulin (Ed.), *Collaborative social work: Strengths-based generalist practice* (pp. 235–261). Itasca, IL: Peacock.

Sundel, M., & Sundel, S. (1982). *Behavior modification in the human services.* Englewood Cliffs, NJ: Prentice-Hall.

Supplemental Security Income Amendments. (1972). P.L. 92–603.

Sweeny, E., Schott, L., Fremstad, S., Goldberg, H., Guyer, J., Super, D., et al. (2000). *Windows of opportunity: Strategies to support families receiving welfare and other low-income families in the next stage of welfare reform.* Washington, DC: Center on Budget and Policy Priorities.

Szasz, T. (1963). *Law, liberty, and psychiatry.* New York: Macmillan.

Tallman, K., & Bohart, A. (1999). The client as a common factor: Clients as self-healers. In M. Hubble, B. Duncan, & S. Miller (Eds.), *The heart and soul of change: What works in therapy* (pp. 91–133). Washington, DC: American Psychological Association.

Tarasoff v. Regents of the University of California. (1976). 13Cal. 3d. 177 (Sup. Ct.).

Taylor, C. (1995). Liberal politics and the public sphere. In A. Etzioni (Ed.), *New communitarian thinking: Persons, institutions, and communities* (pp. 183–217). Charlottesville: University of Virginia Press.

Taylor, M. (1990). *Coverdale on management.* Oxford: Butterworth-Heinemann.

Temporary Assistance to Needy Families. (1996). P.L. 104–193.

Thomlinson, B., & Thomlinson, R. (1996). Behavior theory and social work treatment. In F. Turner (Ed.), *Social work treatment* (4th ed., pp. 39–68). New York: Free Press.

Thurz, D. (1976). Social action as a professional responsibility. *Social Work, 21,* 42–52.

Timberlake, E. M., & Cutler, M. M. (2000). *Developmental play therapy in clinical social work.* Boston: Allyn and Bacon.

Tipton, R. M., & Worthington, E. L. (1985). The measurement of generalized self efficacy: A study of construct validity. *Journal of Personality Assessment, 48,* 345–348.

Tocqueville, A. de. (2001). *Democracy in America.* New York: Penguin Putnam. (Original work published 1835, 1840)

Toseland, R. W., & Rivas, R. F. (2001). *An introduction to group work practice.* Needham Heights, MA: Allyn and Bacon.

Trafficking Victims Protection Act. (2000).

Trocme, N., MacLaurin, B., Fallon, B., Daciuk, J., Billingsley, D., Tourigny, M., et al. (2001). *Canadian incidence study of reported child abuse and neglect: Final report.* Ottawa: Minister of Public Works and Government Services, Canada.

Trocme, N., MacMillan, H., Fallon, B., & DeMarco, R. (2003). Nature and severity of physical harm caused by child abuse and neglect: Results from the Canadian incidence study. *Canadian Medical Association Journal, 169,* 911–915.

Truax, C., & Carkhuff, R. (1967). *Toward effective counseling and psychotherapy.* Chicago: Aldine de Gruyter.

Tuckman, B. (1966). Developmental sequences in small groups. *Psychological Bulletin, 63,* 384–399.

Turner, F. (1978). *Psychosocial therapy.* New York: Free Press.

Turner, F. (1983). *Differential diagnosis and treatment in social work* (3rd ed.). New York: Free Press.

Turner, F. (Ed.). (1996). *Social work treatment* (4th ed.). New York: Free Press.

Tuttman, S. (1995). Foreword in Morris Nitsun, *The anti-group* (pp. ix–xi). London: Routledge.

Tweedie, J., Reichart, D., & O'Connor, M. (1999). *Tracking recipients after they leave welfare.* Washington, DC: National Conference of State Legislators.

Ungar, M. (2004). Surviving as a postmodern social worker: Two P's and three R's of direct practice. *Social Work, 49*(3), 488–496.

Usher, C. L., Randolph, K. A., & Gogan, H. C. (1999). Placement patterns in foster care. *Social Service Review, 73*(1), 22–36.

Usher, C. L., Gibbs, D. A., Wildfire, J.B., & Gogan, H. C. (1997). *Evaluation of family to family.* Chapel Hill: University of North Carolina, Jordan Institute for Families.

U.S. General Accounting Office, Health, Education, and Human Services Division. (1999). *Welfare reform: Information on former recipients' status.* GAO/HEHS 99–48. Washington, DC: Author.

Vacco v. Quill. (1997). 521 U.S. 793, 117 S CT 2293.

VandenBerg, J., & Grealish, M. (1996). Individualized services and supports through the wraparound process: Philosophy and procedures. *Journal of Child and Family Studies, 5,* 7–21.

Van der Kolk, B. A., McFarlane, A. C., & Weisaeth, L. (1996). *Traumatic stress: The effects of overwhelming experience on mind, body, and society.* New York: Guilford.

Van der Kolk, B. A., McFarlane, A. C., & Weisaeth, L. (1997). *Traumatic stress.* New York: Guilford.

Vargas, L. A., & Koss-Chionio, J. D. (Eds.). (1992). *Working with culture: Psychotherapeutic interventions with ethnic minority children and adolescents.* San Francisco: Jossey-Bass.

Vourlekis, B. S., & Greene, R. R. (Eds.). (1992). *Social work case management.* New York: Aldine de Gruyter.

Wampold, B. (2001). *The great psychotherapy debate: Models, methods, and findings.* Mahwah, NJ: Erlbaum.

Wampold, B., Mondin, G., Moody, M., Stich, F., Benson, K., & Ahn, H. (1997). A meta-analysis of outcome studies comparing bona fide psychotherapies: Empirically, "all must have prizes." *Psychological Bulletin, 122,* 203–215.

Weber, M. (1958). *Essays in sociology.* New York: Oxford University Press.

Webster's New Collegiate Dictionary. (1977). Springfield, MA: Merriam.

Weisz, J. R., Donenberg, G., Han, S., & Kauneckis, D. (1995). Child and adolescent psychotherapy outcomes in experiments versus clinics: Why the disparity? *Journal of Abnormal Child Psychology, 23,* 83–106.

Wells, K., & Biegel, D. E. (Eds.). (1991). *Family preservation services: Research and evaluation.* Newbury Park, CA: Sage.

Werrbach, G. B. (1996). Intensive family preservation services research: Current status and future agenda. *Social Work Research and Abstracts, 28*(1), 21–27.

Whitaker, D. S., & Lieberman, M. A. (1964). *Psychotherapy through the group process.* New York: Atherton.

White, M. (2000). *Reflections on narrative practice: Essays and interviews.* Adelaide, South Australia: Dulwich Centre.

Whyte, W. F. (1943). *Street corner society.* Chicago: University of Chicago Press.

Wilson, W. J. (1996). *When work disappears: The world of the new urban poor.* New York: Knopf.

Wolf, A., Schwartz, E. K., McCarty, G. J., & Goldberg, I. A. (1972). Psychoanalysis in groups: Contrasts with other group therapies. In C. J. Sager (Ed.), *Progress in group and family therapy* (pp. 47–53). New York: Brunner/Mazel.

Yalom, I. (1995). *The theory and practice of group psychotherapy* (4th ed.). New York: Basic.

Zuravin, S., Orme, J. G., & Heger, R. L. (1995). Disposition of child physical abuse reports: Review of the literature and test of a predictive model. *Children and Youth Services Review, 17,* 547–566.

Index

Page numbers in bold indicate exhibits.

349